William H. Chafe is professor emeritus of history and Alice Mary Baldwin Professor of History emeritus at Duke University's Sanford School of Public Policy. He is the author of more than ten books. **Raymond Gavins**, a professor of history at Duke University and project director of Behind the Veil, is the author of *The Perils and Prospects of Southern Black Leadership*. **Robert Korstad**, project director of Behind the Veil, is the Kevin D. Gorter Professor of Public Policy and History at Duke University.

REMEMBERING JIM CROW

AFRICAN AMERICANS TELL ABOUT
LIFE IN THE SEGREGATED SOUTH

SENIOR EDITORS

William H. Chafe,

Raymond Gavins, Robert Korstad

ASSOCIATE EDITORS

Paul Ortiz, Robert Parrish,

Jennifer Ritterhouse, Keisha Roberts,

Nicole Waligora-Davis

THE NEW PRESS

NEW YORK
LONDON

In Association with Lyndhurst Books of the Center for
Documentary Studies of Duke University

In memory of Joe Wood,
whose vision helped make this book possible

Major funding for the Behind the Veil Project at the Center for
Documentary Studies at Duke University was provided by
the National Endowment for the Humanities and the Lyndhurst
Foundation with additional support from the Rockefeller Foundation,
the Devonwood Foundation, and the Graduate Schools at
Duke University and the University of North Carolina at Chapel Hill.

Requests for permission to reproduce selections from this book should be mailed to:
Permissions Department, The New Press,
120 Wall Street, 31st floor, New York, NY 10005.

First published in the United States by The New Press, New York, 2001
This paperback edition published in the United States by The New Press, New York, 2014
Distributed by Perseus Distribution

ISBN 978-1-62097-027-0 (pbk.)
ISBN 978-1-62097-043-0 (e-book with audio)
CIP data available

The New Press publishes books that promote and enrich public discussion and understanding
of the issues vital to ur democracy and to a more equitable world. These books are made possible
by the enthusiasm of our readers; the support of a committed group of donors, large and small;
the collaboration of our many partners in the independent media and the not-for-profit sector;
booksellers, who often hand-sell New Press books; librarians; and above all by our authors.

www.thenewpress.com

Composition by dix!

Printed in the United States of America

2   4   6   8   10   9   7   5   3   1

CONTENTS

ILLUSTRATIONS

Then it dawned upon me with a certain suddenness that I was different from the others; or like, mayhap, in heart and life and longing, but shut out from their world by a vast veil. I had thereafter no desire to tear down that veil, to creep through; I held all beyond it in common contempt, and lived above it in a region of blue sky and great wandering shadows. (p. 38)

Within the Veil was he born, said I; and there within shall he live,— a Negro and a Negro's son. Holding in that little head—ah, bitterly!— the unbowed pride of a hunted race, clinging with that tiny dimpled hand—ah, wearily!—to a hope not hopeless but unhopeful, and seeing with those bright wondering eyes that peer into my soul a land whose freedom is to us a mockery and whose liberty a lie. I saw the shadow of the Veil as it passed over my baby, I saw the cold city towering above the blood-red land. I held my face beside his little cheek, showed him the star-children and the twinkling lights as they began to flash, and stilled with an even-song the unvoiced terror of my life. (p. 160)

—FROM *THE SOULS OF BLACK FOLK* BY W.E.B. DU BOIS

ACKNOWLEDGMENTS

Oral history is a collaborative enterprise. From the beginning, the Behind the Veil Project has relied on a national network of community and institutional contacts, academics, undergraduate work-study students, independent scholars, transcribers, elders, and other individuals and groups who share a passion for collecting, preserving, and presenting African American history. Above all, we are profoundly indebted to the scores of African American elders who gave so much of their precious time and energy in the course of being interviewed. African Americans who came of age during the period of legal segregation deserve a much broader audience than they have received. Black elders who survived Jim Crow can teach us—if only we will listen—vital lessons about equal citizenship, spiritual striving, and community-building.

This book had its origins in conversations among the senior editors in the late 1980s. We were struck by the paucity of sources reflecting the experiences of African Americans during the era of segregation and feared that, as generations passed away, the first-person testimony of that critical period in our nation's history would be lost. These conversations coincided with the creation of the Center for Documentary Studies at Duke University, which eventually became the home for the Behind the Veil Project. During our initial planning, Vicki Crawford, John Frey, Jacquelyn Hall, Robin D. G. Kelley, and Julius Scott shared their knowledge of African American history and oral history with us as we began conceptualizing the project. We also benefited from early discussions with colleagues at Jackson State University.

From the very beginning, Iris Tillman Hill, the Center's founding executive director, has been our most steadfast supporter. She has helped plan and coordinate every aspect of the project, including the preparation of this volume. The Behind the Veil Project owes her an enormous debt.

Three other individuals deserve special mention. First, the Behind the Veil Project could never have succeeded without the energy and intelligence of Leslie Brown and Annie Valk. As history graduate students at Duke University, they played many roles on the project between 1990 and 1996, organizing the National Endowment for the Humanities (NEH) Summer Institute and coordinating the curriculum development project. Most important, they served as the research coordinators of Behind the Veil during its fieldwork phase. They conducted site visits, organized conferences, created and nurtured relationships with community contacts, coordinated meetings, facilitated the summer orientations, and performed the administrative work that kept the Behind the Veil Project running between 1990 and 1996. Leslie and Annie ensured that graduate researchers had housing and transportation as well as the historical background necessary to conduct successful interviews. In addition, Leslie and Annie first proposed the idea of a documents-collection book that would highlight Behind the Veil materials. Paul Ortiz joined the project as a graduate student assistant in 1993, and he was part of the interview teams in 1994 and 1995. In 1996, he became the graduate research coordinator and oversaw much of the archival preparation of the oral history materials. He has played a major coordinating role in the preparation of *Remembering Jim Crow.* His passion for recovering the history of African Americans has been critical for the success of the project and this book.

In undertaking a major oral history research project, our first task was to survey the scholarly literature and to get scholars to help us frame our research questions. With guidance from the staff of the NEH, we convened a national research conference at North Carolina Central University on March 15–17, 1991, where Beverly Jones, Freddie Parker, and other members of the history department provided valuable support. Over 75 scholars participated in the conference and heard presentations by Helen G. Edmonds, John Hope Franklin, Leon Litwack, Elsa Barkely Brown, Robin D. G. Kelley, Nan Woodruff, Gavin Wright, Joe William Trotter, Evelyn Brooks Higginbotham, Trudier Harris, and Richard Powell. Vicki Crawford, Mary Ellen Curtin, and CDS staff members Darnell Arnoult and Kira Dirlik made valuable contributions to the conference.

From the very beginning, we conceived of Behind the Veil as a multifaceted, collaborative effort that included the participation of scholars at historically black colleges and universities in the South. An important part of that collaboration was a curriculum development project designed to prepare course materials to teach students about African American life in the Jim Crow South. The advisory committee for the curriculum development project included Carolyn Denard, Alfredteen Harrison, Beverly Jones, Mary Coleman, Tenita Philyaw, and Alma Williams. Toward that end, CDS sponsored an NEH Summer Institute that brought together scholars of African American history and faculty from 18 Historically Black Colleges and Universities (HBCUs) and four African American studies programs at predominantly white institutions. The presenters at the institute included Alex Harris, Lynn Marshall-Linnemeier, Tom Whiteside, R. Kelly Bryant Jr., Ginny Daley, Beverly Jones, Pete Daniel, Tera Hunter, Evelyn Brooks Higginbotham, Bob Hall, James Anderson, Alfred Reid, Gavin Wright, Robert Byrd, Robin D. G. Kelly, Valeria Lee, Charles Reagan Wilson, Christina Greene, Richard Powell, Richard Dozier, Larry Adelman, Alex Albright, Glenn Hinson, Charles Frye, Karen Fields, Thomas Adams, Jacqueline Rouse, John Hope Franklin, Margaret Walker Alexander, Trudier Harris, Richard Long, Dorothy Spruill Redford, Sharon Harley, and Thadious Davis.

The advisory board for the research project included Beverly Jones, Jessie Dent, Mary Coleman, Alfredteen Harrison, Charles Frye, as well as William Chafe, Raymond Gavins, Iris Tillman Hill, and Robert Korstad.

Twenty-five graduate students from research universities and HBCUs conducted the oral histories that form the basis of this volume. The full archive of Behind the Veil, including nearly 1,300 oral histories, is housed in the John Hope Franklin Collection of African and African-American Documentation, Special Collections Library, at Duke

University. Individuals who served as community and institutional contacts provided initial interview lists, arranged housing for graduate researchers, served as mentors, and assumed an ever-growing range of responsibilities as each summer's fieldwork progressed. Without the expertise provided by these individuals and community organizations, the Behind the Veil Project could not have succeeded.

The interviewers during the summer of 1993 were Chris Stewart, Sonya Ramsey, Kara Miles, Rhonda Mawhood, Karen Ferguson, and William Crumpton.

Primary community and institutional contacts during the summer of 1993 were Gary R. Grant and Dorothy White Cannon, Concerned Citizens of Tillery, Tillery Community Center, Tillery, North Carolina; Tillery Open Minded Seniors; Vivian Wynn, Franklinton Center at Bricks, Inc.; Mrs. Wills, Bricks School Club; Willie Powell, Rocky Mt. Opportunities Industrialization Center; Vermelle Ely, Second Ward High School Alumni Association, Charlotte, North Carolina; Jesse Dent, Johnson C. Smith University; Mary White, Grace George, and Ben A. Watford, James City Historical Society, New Bern, North Carolina; Marea K. Foster and Joseph Patterson, Memories of New Bern, New Bern, North Carolina; Joanne Gwaltney, New Bern Historical Society; Thelma Chadwick, United Senior Services, Inc., New Bern, North Carolina; David Cecelski, Institute for Southern Studies, Durham, North Carolina; Dorothy Phelps Jones and Doris Terry Williams, St. Joseph's Historical Foundation, Durham, North Carolina; R. Kelly Bryant Jr.; Gwen Rountree, Little River Community Center; Andre Vann, Alex Rivera, and Howard Fitts, North Carolina Central University.

The interviewers during the summer of 1994 were Mausiki Stacey Scales, Paul Ortiz, Tywanna Whorley, Charles H. Houston Jr., Gregory Hunter, Sally Graham, Tunga White, Felix Armfield, Katherine Ellis, and Michelle Mitchell.

Primary community and institutional contacts during the summer of 1994 were Horace Huntley, University of Alabama–Birmingham and the Birmingham Civil Rights Institute; Carolyn Ray, Miles College; Larry Henderson, Birmingham, Alabama; Willie Fluker and Frank J. Toland, Department of History, Tuskegee University; Daniel T. Williams, Hollis Baker Frissell Library, Tuskegee University; James Eaton, Black Archives

Research Center, Florida A & M University; Shirley and Charles Sherrod, Federation of Southern Cooperatives, Albany, Georgia; Barbara A. Woods and Willie Legette, Department of Political Science and History, South Carolina State University; Lesley Williams, McKissick Museum, University of South Carolina, Columbia; Frank Solomon, African American Culture Center, Allendale, South Carolina; Alice Doctor Waring and John K. Adams, Scott's Branch "76" Foundation, Inc., Summerton, South Carolina; Emory Campbell, Penn Center, St. Helena Island, South Carolina; Vennie Deas Moore, independent researcher; Veronica Gerald, Coastal Carolina College; Florence Borders and Charles Frye, Center for African and African American Studies, Southern University at New Orleans; Shereen Minvielle, Shadows-on-the-Teche, New Iberia, Louisiana; Capt. Nathaniel Mitchell, Iberia Parish and Corrections; and Toby Dopsit.

The interviewers during the summer of 1995 were Mausiki Stacey Scales, Doris Dixon, Paul Ortiz, Laurie Green, Blair Murphy, Kisha Turner, and Mary Herbert.

Primary community and institutional contacts during the summer of 1995 were Geraldine Davidson, Fargo Agricultural School Museum, Brinkley, Arkansas; Calvin King and Marvin Schwartz, Arkansas Land and Farm Development Corporation, Brinkley, Arkansas; Paula Hickey, Delta Cultural Center, Helena, Arkansas; Freeman McKindra, Winthrop Rockefeller Foundation, Little Rock, Arkansas; Willard B. Gatewood, University of Arkansas; Rev. Willie C. Tims, Magnolia, Arkansas; Forrest City Senior Care, Forrest City, Arkansas; Rev. Randolph Meade Walker and Barbara S. Frankle, Le Moyne Owen College, Memphis, Tennessee; Steven J. Ross, Allison Graham, and Charles Crawford, University of Memphis; Michael Honey, University of Washington–Tacoma; Judy Peiser, Center for Southern Folklore, Memphis, Tennessee; Andrew Ewing, Arthur Kinnard, and Robert Moore, Mississippi Valley State University; Chiquita Willis, University of Mississippi; Pete Daniel, National Museum of American History, Smithsonian Institution, Washington, D.C.; Charles Payne, Northwestern University; Tommy Lee Bogger, Norfolk State University; Essie Dozier, Virginia Historical and Genealogical Society, Tidewater Chapter; Clarice Sharp; and Rev. A. M. Lawson.

Additional interviews were done by Alex Byrd in Muhlenberg County, Kentucky, with assistance from Bethel Baptist Church in

Drakesboro; Wesley Chapel AME Zion Church in Greenville; Raymond and Erletta Robinson; Maggie Dulin; James and Elcie Eaves; and Aldrich Horton.

Several thousand family photographs were copied by the graduate student researchers over the three summers of fieldwork, and these photographs form an important component of the Behind the Veil archive. We thank the many families who shared their precious albums with us, and are especially grateful to Larry Henderson of Birmingham, Alabama, for sharing hundreds of photographs from his collection. From these photographs Susan Page and Keisha Roberts selected the photographs that are included in this book.

From the outset, a small army of graduate and undergraduate research assistants did the invisible work of oral history including site research, editing transcripts, duplicating materials, copying photographs, and compiling research databases. The individuals who served as research and administrative assistants were Greta Ai-Yu-Niu, Chris Ross, Arthur Smith, Alex Byrd, Paul Ortiz, Blair Murphy, Aminah Pilgrim, Keisha Roberts, Luba V. Zakharov, Josh Levinson, Keith Townshend, David Wu, John Hayes, Homer D. Hill, Mendi Drayton, Latasha Davidson, Jason Ward, Serena Rhodie, Kimberly Parker, and Carson Harkraden. Combing through interview tapes and transcripts, Arthur Smith and Chris Ross made important editorial suggestions in the early stages of the development of this book. Carolyn Wiggleton and Darnell Arnoult provided important administrative support to the research assistants at every step of the process.

Cathy Mann, Frances Copeland, and Technitype Transcripts collectively transcribed close to 300 oral history interviews from the Behind the Veil collection. Their work speaks for itself. Students of Sarah Wilkerson-Freeman at Arkansas State University transcribed portions of several interviews done in their state.

Ginney Daley, Bob Byrd, Karen L. Jefferson, Sharon Knapp, and Lisa Stark of Duke's Special Collections Library provided critical expertise in the processing and archiving of Behind the Veil materials.

Charles Frye, Alma Williams, and Gregory Hunter, who contributed richly to this project, have tragically passed away. We cherish the memory of their colleagueship.

excerpt adheres as closely as possible to the original spoken version with two important exceptions: First, interview questions are, by and large, omitted from the texts, but at times these questions reappear within brackets, rephrased at the beginning of an excerpt, to provide the context for the speaker's response. Informants are indentified in the Appendix. Second, editors have on occasion altered the sequences of some of the interview passages and deleted unnecessary or repetitive sentences and extraneous paragraphs. All of these revisions were intended to clarify and strengthen the narrative and fit the excerpt into the thematic focus of each chapter.

EDITORIAL METHOD

The oral histories and most of the photographs in this volume are drawn exclusively from the Behind the Veil: Documenting African American Life in the Jim Crow South Collection housed at Duke University's Special Collections Library. The editors shaped these published excerpts by listening to the original audiotaped interviews and comparing them with professional transcriptions. The editorial team of *Remembering Jim Crow* convened on a regular basis to critique each other's excerpts for accuracy and clarity as well as to review chapter introductions and headnotes. In formulating an editorial method, *Remembering Jim Crow* borrowed from the editorial methodology presented in *Remembering Slavery: African Americans Talk about Their Personal Experiences of Slavery and Emancipation,* as well as other published works in oral history.

Our methodology is framed by the need to present the material in a clear form. We chose to omit certain spoken idiosyncrasies such as "uh," "mmm" and "you know" as well as other repetitive conversational forms of speech that would be distracting to most readers. Any words or phrases added by editors, or any conjectural renderings of semi-intelligible words, appear in brackets. If there is doubt about the conjecture, a question mark follows the word.

Chapters were assigned to members of the editorial team, and all selections and decisions were reviewed and edited collectively. Every

In the spring of 1998, Joe Wood Jr. came to Durham, North Carolina, on a mission to convince a skeptical Behind the Veil Project team that it had the wherewithal to complete a documents-collection book. Joe worked closely with Behind the Veil staff to lay out the initial ideas and guiding principles of the manuscript. This brilliant man, who touched so many lives with his kind and giving spirit, set *Remembering Jim Crow* in motion.

INTRODUCTION

L ooking back from the perspective of the 1990s, the black North Carolinian Charles Jones recalled delivering clothes and toys to sharecroppers at Christmastime during the height of the Jim Crow era. The gifts had been sent by northern churches to be distributed by Jones's father, a minister, to their less fortunate southern brethren. In order to get access to the sharecroppers, Jones remembered, his father had to secure the permission of the white landlord to enter his plantation. He would shuffle and defer to the white landlord, Jones noted, but "I remember when we left, him looking at me and kind of winking [as if to say] 'that's the only way we can get back here.' "

The son later chose a different tack, joining civil rights demonstrators and becoming a leader in the worldwide youth movement. But he also understood the world his father inhabited and how much his father had achieved "by being wise enough to know what to say, how to say it, how to position your body in a submissive position so as not to [alienate the owner]." Reflecting on this experience later, Jones developed a new appreciation for what his father had accomplished. "I began to understand my father's restraint, my father's wisdom—because it was more important to accomplish a common object with dignity than to challenge at every stage everything . . . that white males were confronting us with. So we assumed the higher ground, took all the rhetoric that the Christian white church and the Constitution had taught us, and beat the devil out of them with it."

This vignette, taken from one of the 1,265 interviews compiled by the Behind the Veil Project at the Center for Documentary Studies at Duke University, speaks in myriad ways to the rich, complicated, heroic, and ultimately ambiguous texture of African American lives during the era of segregation. By dint of circumstance and necessity, there had to be role-playing—holding one's hat, acting the part of servant to the white master. But there was, in addition, transcendence and purposefulness—defining a goal, reaching out to achieve it, using whatever means were available to secure the victory at hand. And there was also a community—churched people in the North ready to stand in solidarity and support, congregants in the South prepared to use the primary institution they controlled and shaped, to deliver on a promise and keep intact a dream. The edited interviews that appear in this volume represent the rich diversity of those experiences.

The paradoxical truths of the Charles Jones story reflect the insights of the original architect of the "Behind the Veil" concept, W.E.B. Du Bois. Writing in *The Souls of Black Folk*, his 1903 classic, Du Bois described what it was like growing up as an elementary school student in Great Barrington, Massachusetts. He was engaged in a youthful ritual, that of exchanging calling cards with his classmates. But suddenly, Du Bois discovered, the world he inhabited was not a shared community. While he gave his card to his white peers, they had no intention of giving their card to him. And at that moment the "veil descended," separating the two worlds of white and black. Behind the veil, African Americans developed their own life, hidden and estranged from the lives of white people. This, in turn, created the remarkable "two-ness" or "double-consciousness" of African Americans—an American and a Negro, "two warring souls in one dark body," seeking to "merge his double self into a better and truer self."

Yet in Du Bois's brilliant metaphor, the "veil" had multiple meanings. It not only created the separation that produced the suffering, inequality, and oppression of Jim Crow; it also, as in the West African tradition of a child born with a veil-like membrane covering its head, created special spiritual powers and strengths. "Behind the Veil" thus conveys its own dual message—a separate existence suffused with coping with racism and its consequences, and a community of hope and struggle, replenished by the strength of its distinctive values and institutions, striving to find a "better and truer self."

The Behind the Veil research project at Duke University sought to explore that paradox. It began at the end of the 1980s as an intensive collaborative effort to recover the history of African American life in the segregated South. The idea behind the project emerged from the lessons that many of us had learned as a result of doing research on civil rights and labor history. There, we discovered that however much written sources such as newspapers, government documents, or manuscript collections of individual leaders might tell us, those sources most often reflected the perspective of powerful, rich, and primarily white male historical participants. Far less present in those written sources were the perspectives of black, working-class, or women citizens. Yet civil rights and labor history can only be understood by listening to the voices of those who generated, shaped, and carried forward those movements.

There was only one way to discover those voices: using interviews and oral history to gain access to the experiences and perspectives of ordinary men and women who otherwise would not be represented in the historical record. Clearly, one could not write the history of the southern sit-in movement or the direct-action student movement without talking to the individuals who brought those movements to life. Police reports or government documents represented only one side of the story. As a result, oral history became the pivotal research instrument for recovering and giving visibility to the historical actors who occupied center stage in the story being told.

Largely because oral history proved so indispensable to recent civil rights and labor history scholarship, the question inevitably arose: Why did we not use this valuable tool to recover the historical experience of others whose voices have long been muted or ignored? Nowhere was that need more clear than in seeking to understand the experience of African Americans who lived during the age of Jim Crow. And in no instance was there greater urgency to move forward immediately to recover that experience, lest death take from future historians the vital sources necessary to understand better this critical and neglected period in America's recent past.

This need was made all the more urgent by the relatively "flat" nature of existing historiography on the age of segregation. Virtually every student of American history understood, from Rayford Logan and others, that this was the "nadir" of recent African American history, a time of severe legal, economic, political, and social oppression, all reinforced by the pervasive threat of extralegal violence, especially lynching. C. Vann Woodward had earlier traced the inauguration of this era with the infamous Compromise of 1877, when Republican politicians sold out the civil and political rights of black Americans by agreeing to remove federal troops stationed in the South to enforce Reconstruction in return for electoral commission votes for the Republican, Rutherford B. Hayes, in the disputed Tilden-Hayes presidential election of 1876. From that point on, the "equal protection" supposedly guaranteed to black citizens under the Fourteenth Amendment disappeared in practice, helping to usher in and legitimize an era of systematic disenfranchisement that flourished starting in the 1890s with the imposition of Jim Crow segregation statutes that were ultimately sanctioned by the U.S. Supreme Court in the *Plessy v. Ferguson* case in 1896.

The so-called Jim Crow era was, in fact, a combination of the de facto second-class citizenship and racial separation that emerged in 1877 at the end of Reconstruction, and the de jure arsenal of laws and official regulations that came to fruition in the 1890s. Although to all intents and purposes, blacks in the South during the late 1870s and 1880s had little but white goodwill to protect them, there remained during these years a tacit recognition that blacks might still benefit from federal (Republican) patronage and exercise certain rights, including the franchise, as long as in local and state politics they accepted the domination of white Democrats and the white upper class.

By the end of the 1880s, however, economic and political insurgency began to rear its head in the South. The Southern Farmers' Alliance inaugurated a vigorous campaign designed to end the economic exploitation of sharecroppers and tenant farmers by the elite of white plantation owners. The Farmers' Alliance, soon to become allied on a national level with the Populist Party, promoted the development of farmers' cooperatives to put an end to the crop lien system where small farmers mortgaged their crops in return for supplies and household goods from merchants (usually the plantation owners) who charged exorbitant sums; the Farmers' Alliance also urged creation of federally funded agricultural warehouses where farmers could store their crops awaiting an ideal market while receiving government loans, using their crops as collateral; and the same insurgents pushed for a new political system, directly challenging the monopoly of railroads and banks.

More threatening than anything else, however, was the prospect that white farmers and black farmers might ally on the basis of their common class interests and overthrow the political and economic hegemony of the rich white farmers. Tentatively, and then with growing vigor, a movement toward a biracial Populist coalition developed.

It was at this point that the ruling Democrats raised the "bloody flag" of Southern victimization during the Civil War and insisted that all whites band together in the name of racial solidarity to turn back the "mongrelizing" threat of a biracial political movement from the left. In the name of political "reform," blacks must be denied the vote. To prevent any further danger of race-mixing, segregation must be enforced. Using the race issue as a means of permanently dividing and conquering any possibility of biracial organizing, the Democrats succeeded in putting into place the system of official Jim Crow statutes that defined southern politics from the end of the nineteenth century all the way through into the 1950s and 1960s. Economically and politically, dominance by a narrow band of well-off white Democrats was guaranteed. Indeed, since almost as many poor whites as poor blacks lost the vote with the new disenfranchisement statutes, there was almost no threat of a challenge to rich white rule.

Despite the excellent work of historians in documenting the emergence of this citadel of oppression, little has been written about the actual experience of black Americans during the age of segregation. One learned about the crusade of W.E.B. Du Bois to fight Jim Crow, about the great migration of the World War I period and the terrorizing race riots that followed the armistice in 1918, about the Harlem Renaissance of the 1920s and the achievements of black writers and artists. But there was no larger sense of what occurred in the everyday lives of blacks from the 1890s through the onset of World War II. Instead of being understood as a time of complexity and struggle, the Jim Crow era appeared as a barren wasteland of oppression. It was almost as though the Stanley Elkins model of a "closed system," with no outlets, that had once been applied to slavery, now had become the prism through which we understood the era of Jim Crow. Oversimplified, static, and without nuance, the historiography of Jim Crow became a tale of total oppression, on the one hand, and passive submission, on the other.

This portrayal was all the more anomalous given the degree to which slavery and Reconstruction historiography had undergone a sea change in the 1970s and 1980s, with a new focus on black agency and institutional development. From John Blassingame's *The Slave Community* (1971) to Eugene Genovese's *Roll Jordan Roll* (1974) and Herbert Gutman's *The Black Family in Slavery and Freedom* (1976), a generation of historians had dismantled simple stereotypes and described far more complex patterns of slave life on plantations and as freedmen and women after emancipation. Variety, not uniformity, emerged as the watchword, as historians wrote about the multiple ways African Americans created family lives; practiced religion; made their living; and found the means to preserve pride and maintain some forms of self-determination, even in the face of pervasive structures of oppression. The new historiography of slavery and emancipation brought to light the traditions African Americans had preserved from their cultures of origin. New studies explored African American creativity in adapting to the restrictions and regulations that black people were forced to live under. Despite severe obstacles, blacks managed to develop their own instruments of resistance and self-affirmation. What had once been a stark portrait in black and white became, as a result of this scholarship, a tapestry woven of multiple colors, with diverse themes and subthemes, all highlighting the multiple dimensions of the African American experience.

A similar richness of scholarly endeavor emerged in the scholarly rendering of the civil rights era. Initially, historians focused on the heroic national struggle that culminated in the *Brown v. Board of Education* (1954) repudiation of *Plessy*, and the charismatic leadership of individuals such as Martin Luther King Jr. But soon there developed a new appreciation of the insurgencies that shaped the civil rights movement on a local level, with a focus on the "organizing tradition" in Mississippi, the precedents for resistance that blossomed into activism in Greensboro, St. Augustine,

Tuskegee, and Jackson, and the pivotal—and previously unsung—role of women in shaping movement events, from Ella Baker to Hazel Palmer to Septima Clark to Fannie Lou Hamer.

Above all, what came out of this scholarship was a new appreciation for the importance of understanding the roots of the civil rights era. As one group of graduate students at Duke discovered when they started to study the civil rights movement in North Carolina using the tools of oral history, the beginning date of the movement kept changing. One group came back from a series of interviews with local citizens saying it was 1954 and 1955, with *Brown* and Montgomery; but soon other groups came back talking about the Freedom Rides of 1947, the emergence of student protest at an all-black high school in the early 1950s, or the founding of the local NAACP branch at a Baptist church in the 1930s. Suddenly the age-old historiographical question of continuity versus change assumed a new and powerful relevance, only this time not regarding such perennial questions as whether the New Deal was a departure or a continuation of Progressivism; now, the question was whether the sit-in movement represented a revolutionary departure from black acquiescence and passivity, or simply a new way of expressing an ongoing tradition of resistance.

This set of inquiries provided a point of entry into re-interrogating the era of Jim Crow and challenging those untreated notions of black acquiescence and passivity. Why not "unpack" the ordinary lived experiences of African Americans in that period in the same way historians had rethought stereotypes of slave life and developed new sources and fresh ways to analyze the diversity of life on the plantation or the complicated origins of civil rights protests?

The Behind the Veil Project thus began with two frames of reference: first, the belief that, as with the civil rights era, recovering the voices of average citizens provided the best means of exploring the commonalities and differences of the black experience during the Jim Crow period; and second, the conviction that behind the two-dimensional story of oppression and submission there existed a richer, deeper, and more compelling reality that an investigation of the institutions, family and community patterns, spiritual life, and daily living experiences of black Americans in diverse southern communities would reveal. Based on these departure points, the Behind the Veil Project succeeded in raising funds from foundations and from the National Endowment for the Humanities to conduct up to 1,300 interviews with African Americans who lived during the era of Jim Crow. Selecting communities based on different economic, social, and cultural lifestyles (urban/rural, industrial/agricultural, Piedmont/Delta, rice/cotton), the project chose to do in-depth research in 25 communities in 10 different states.

Each summer for three years, 10 graduate students from history programs throughout the country came to Durham for training, then journeyed to three or four different communities where they took up residence for two weeks. Using research lists compiled by project coordinators—lists cultivated through churches, senior citizen centers, and various black voluntary associations—the graduate students immersed themselves in the histories of their selected communities, using the initial lists of sources to generate more names, digging into personal papers, photographic files, and local archives to flesh out information about critical events and people in a community's history. By the end of each local visit, the researchers had gained some sense of the dynamics of a local community, had ranked the quality of the interviews for transcribing purposes, and had developed a set of insights and scholarly queries that would facilitate the larger, overall team coming to grips with the rich array of sources that had been developed.

Simultaneous with this process, a new generation of historians was producing scholarly studies of the Jim Crow era that paralleled those earlier done for the eras of slavery and civil rights. Books by Leon Litwack, Evelyn Brooks Higginbotham, Glenda Gilmore, John Dittmer, Deborah Gray White, Neil McMillen, Earl Lewis, and Tera Hunter created a richer framework within which to understand the interview data that the Behind the Veil Project had accumulated. Indeed, the oral history materials developed by the Behind the Veil Project ideally complemented and deepened the findings of this new scholarship. What remains most exciting, however, is the way that the voices of these ordinary people illuminate, as if viewing something afresh and for the first time, the compelling story of accommodation and resistance, love and fear, pride and humiliation that constituted the everyday working lives of black Americans who lived during this era.

What are the lessons that these stories teach us? They are as multiple as the colors of a rainbow perceived at different angles in the sunlight after a storm.

First is an understanding of the dailiness of the terror blacks experienced at the hands of capricious whites—the man who told of his brother being killed in the middle of the night because he had not sufficiently deferred in the presence of a white man, another story of an African American being dragged to his death behind a horse-drawn wagon, or a pregnant wife having her womb slit, with both mother and child killed, because her husband allegedly had offended a white woman. From lynching to being denied the right to be called "Mr." or "Mrs.," to having cars or school buses intentionally hit puddles of water to splash black people walking, there was neither escape from, nor redress for, the ubiquitous, arbitrary, and cruel reality of senseless white power.

What makes the stories in this book so revelatory, however, is not the constant reminder of white terror, but the extraordinary resilience of black citizens, who, individually and collectively, found ways to endure, fight back, and occasionally define their own destinies.

The second lesson, therefore, is the capacity of the black community to come to each other's aid and invent means of sustaining the collective will to survive and perhaps even inch forward. As Booker Federick told one of our interviewers, "we had much more a [a sense of community] then than we do now. [If] you had 15 acres and you wasn't quite through, we'd just take our hoe and go over there without any questions." Sometimes community self-help came through pooling resources to build a new office for a health worker or farm agent; at other times in enforcing standards of community behavior when a teacher or principal acted in ways that were harmful. But always, there was the sense that no matter how bad off people might be in their own right, they would come together to help others, as Reverend Jones did on behalf of his own congregation and their northern partners, in the vignette that opened this introduction.

The third lesson is the enduring capacity of families to nurture each other, and especially their children, in the face of a system so dangerous and capricious that there were no rules one could count on for protection. One of the Behind the Veil informants recalled how his father taught him to watch out for whites. "He told us what to expect, how to act, how to stay away from them . . . so we . . . kind of knew what we were supposed to do." But even as parents sought to protect their children, they also conveyed a sense of right and wrong, strength and assurance. "When some things really got out of hand," another woman told us, "[my parents] would sit down and talk to you and tell you, 'Now this is wrong. But the situation is that your father can't do anything about this [right now].' " At the same time, parents instilled pride wherever possible. Notwithstanding Jim Crow rules, one woman recalled, her mother "always told us . . . that we were as good as anybody else," while another man's parents insisted on the importance of "stand[ing] up for what you believe. Don't try to take advantage of anybody, but don't let anybody take advantage of you." There was always a tightrope to be walked—cautions that would create hypersensitivity to situations of potential danger, but also a sense of being somebody. As one person's mother told him, "You are my children. You look like you do because of your father and me, and you can do anything you want to do. . . . Don't ever be ashamed of how you look because of your color."

The fourth lesson from these interviews is the way that same tightrope pervaded the world of work. On the one hand, a job could be a source of pride, whether it consisted of planting and harvesting a crop on shares, teaching in a Jim Crow school, laying bricks, being a domestic servant or a seamstress, or, on rare occasions, working in a mine or a mill where there was a union. On the other hand, the same job often carried with it daily reminders of the humiliating power that whites held over their black employees. Sharecroppers annually confronted the stinginess of many white landlords. "Those people were watching . . . [to] make sure [we] didn't get no top price for that cotton," Booker Federick noted. Teachers held the highest status jobs in the black community, but that did not prevent them from experiencing the cruelty of whites, such as when a woman teacher tried to have a prescription filled, only to have the pharmacist slap her because she had not said "sir" when she thanked him. Women who worked in the homes of whites ran the constant threat of sexual harassment from men in the house, and even skilled bricklayers confronted the desire of some whites to belittle or undermine their achievements. Thus the workplace was a perennially contested ground, potentially a source of pride and accomplishment, but just as often, a site of threat, danger, and unpredictable cruelty.

In such a world, where did African Americans look for hope and a sense of possibility? Education—the fifth lesson from these interviews—offered one answer. If local planters insisted that schools remain open only four to five months so that youngsters could work in the fields, blacks in the community pooled resources and contributed meat, vegetables, and eggs so that the work of a teacher could continue for an extra month. Teachers, in turn, encouraged students to have higher aspirations. "We were leading the children to be the best persons they could be," one North Carolina teacher declared, while a Mississippi instructor sought to inspire her students by saying that one of them might be president of the United States within 100 years. In a world where there seemed no safe and predictable outlet for progress, education held out a glimmer of hope that a better day might emerge.

Sustaining that hope were a series of black institutions that provided pivotal support and affirmation within the African American community. The powerful role of these black institutions or "sanctuaries" represents the sixth lesson from the Behind the Veil interviews. The church stood at the center of the community, the place where people shared their pain, their hope, the news of the community, and the life of the spirit. After Charles Jones's father distributed the clothes and toys he had brought to North Carolina sharecroppers, they gathered together in their church to sing, and, Jones noted, "after the songs, and the spirit and the holding of hands, and the hugging," people had such hope in their faces. Not only did the church provide a place of worship; it also served as a shelter where political discussions could freely occur, and where a local NAACP might even be organized.

Other institutions also nourished a sense of pride. In a city like Durham, companies like the North Carolina Mutual Insurance Company or the Mechanics and Farmers Bank suggested the achievements possible for black Americans once they were given a chance to succeed. Black schools and colleges did the same, even in the face of poor governmental financing. Women's and men's voluntary associations provided the networks for developing social welfare activities and sharing political information. The black Masonic hall in Birmingham, for example, served as the foundation for a unionization effort in that city in the 1930s, while a pinochle club in Tallahassee provided an organizing base for black political campaigns in that city. Creatively, and with ingenious methods of communication and mobilization, the multiple "sanctuaries" of Jim Crow America served as the home bases from which efforts were launched to undermine and eventually topple the structures of segregation.

Which, in turn, leads to the final lesson of these interviews—the extraordinary and multiple ways in which resistance to Jim Crow occurred and was nourished even in the face of brutal, arbitrary, and systemic discrimination. Much of this resistance necessarily took the form of pushing back within the constraints of existing mores. African Americans daily faced the challenge of adapting the rules and regulations of Jim Crow to their own purposes, sustaining a delicate balance between appearing to comply with prescribed norms, on the one hand, and finding ways to subvert those norms on the other. Clearly, this was a task fraught with difficulty. It would be a mistake to understate the degree to which, in the circumstances, many African Americans complied with the roles prescribed for them, and if for no other reason than preserving their own and their family's personal safety, failed to resist or challenge the system of Jim Crow. Yet the remarkable reality was the degree to which some black citizens managed to walk the tightrope and engage in subversion even as they appeared to be accepting the racial system of white dominance.

Nothing better illustrates that dynamic than the story told by Henry Hooten of Tuskegee, Alabama, about an annual fishing trip that he and his neighbors took to the Gulf near Mobile. The group had purchased an old bus for the yearly foray, which of course posed the dilemma of where to stop for food and fuel. One year Hooten went to a place where he hoped to get both needs met. "We were always taught never to talk back to the white man, but to tell him what he would like to hear," Hooten remarked, so as he was in the midst of filling the huge gas tank on the bus, Hooten politely asked the station owner if all the hungry children he had with him could get fed at the station restaurant. "The white man thought you knew less about psychology [than him]. He didn't think you had enough sense to [get your way]." But Hooten also understood economic realities. And so when the station owner said that feeding the children was not allowed, Hooten politely demurred, responding that, in the circumstances, he would have to stop filling his tank and move on. "Suddenly," Hooten said, "he's ready to feed the kids. And put the white customers to work feeding the kids"—an arrangement that continued every year thereafter.

As suggested in Hooten's story, there often existed an economic dimension to the ability of blacks to push back. When a young female student was treated rudely by a postmaster when she went to pick up the mail for Boggs Academy in Keysville, Georgia, the headmaster indicated that he would take his business elsewhere until the postal official mended his ways. An apology was soon forthcoming. Similarly, when a white insurance man came into the house of Ralph Thompson's mother to collect a monthly payment and called her "Auntie," she exploded, declaring, "I'm not your 'Auntie,' " and telling him if he wanted her business, he could call her "Mrs. Thompson."

There were no clashes more volatile or emotion-packed than those involving sexual harassment. One person interviewed by the Behind the Veil Project proudly recounted how his mother, ironing clothes in the house of her employer, pressed her burning iron into the back of a white salesman when he grabbed her in a sexual advance. Another person remembered an episode when her mother's employer approached her sexually. In response, her mother declared, "If a black man done that to a white woman, you'd be the first to . . . find a limb to hang him to. So if you would hang the black man about doing it, you think I'm going to let you do it to me?"—a retort that evidently deterred similar advances from that point forward.

Occasionally, the protest also took a physical form, or was expressed in terms of forceful retaliation. When one sharecropper was threatened with a whipping by his white employer while working in the fields, he replied, "No sir, somebody'll die . . . and it's got to be more than me." On another job site, a black bricklayer struck a white coworker when the white man knocked off a brick he had just put in place and simultaneously insulted the black man's wife. In Tuskegee, a local minister, who also worked in a barbershop serving whites, used his position to gather and convey intelligence about the local Klan to his neighbors. When the Klan found out, they descended on the man's home garbed in their white sheets and called him out. The minister responded by taking out his long gun, shooting out the porch light, and sending the Klan members scurrying to their cars.

Oftentimes, of course, such responses created dire peril for the individuals involved, evoking the community solidarity that provided the ongoing foundation for black resistance and protest. The sharecropper who said "more than one's going to die" was sheltered by friends until he could escape by dead of night. In Georgia, a black man who struck back when a white assaulted him for allegedly insulting the man's wife was harbored at the all-black Boggs Academy and taken out of the county under armed guard later on. Such episodes became legendary. "We had a few black men [here]," Booker Federick noted about his experience in rural Alabama, "known as the men that didn't take anything [from whites]. The white folks would put on like they wasn't afraid of them, but they were."

Naturally, with these interviews as with those collected from former slaves during the 1930s WPA project, exaggeration and selective memory may occur. Veterans of the Jim Crow experience understandably point to instances where they or their friends engaged in heroic resistance. Tales of deception and of hoodwinking whites logically shape the narrative of how African Americans dealt with their oppressors. And humor abounds, as in the episode, proudly described by a mother, of how her young children would play "drink and run" when they were in a department store, using the "white" fountain rather than the "black." Such stories punctuate the lore of Jim Crow, like variations on a theme, highlighting and dramatizing, with vivid detail, the larger saga being transmitted.

Still, these stories convey a compelling body of evidence that fleshes out, in colorful specificity, the ultimate product of the Behind the Veil venture: the incredible variety, richness, and ingenuity of black Americans' responses to one of the cruelest, least yielding social and economic systems ever created. With these 1,265 interviews available to future scholars—more than one-quarter of them transcribed—no longer will it be possible for historians to see the Jim Crow era as only a "nadir" of African American history. The "flatness" of a previous historical landscape has given way to hills and valleys full of countless scenes, some of them a tragic confirmation of how little power and space black Americans had during the age of segregation, but others a riveting reminder that blacks still sought control of their destiny, retained agency in their own lives, and helped build—inch by inch—the foundation for a final assault on the fortress of Jim Crow.

Charles Jones learned from his father the importance of keeping one's "eyes on the prize" and doing what was necessary to carry on to another day. Charles Jones and his father embody the continuity of the struggle that links the era of Jim Crow with the era of the Freedom Movement. That is why Charles Jones and his father—together—were the first blacks to integrate the Rexall Drugstore in downtown Charlotte in 1960, and why these stories, in this book, will help future American students to understand how one generation makes possible the hopes of the next generation.

REMEMBERING JIM CROW

ONE

BITTER TRUTHS

Jim Crow was not merely about the physical separation of blacks and whites. Nor was segregation strictly about laws, despite historians' tendency to fix upon such legal landmarks as *Plessy v. Ferguson* (1896), *Brown v. Board of Education* (1954), and the Civil Rights Act of 1964. In order to maintain dominance, whites needed more than the statutes and signs that specified "whites" and "blacks" only; they had to assert and reiterate black inferiority with every word and gesture, in every aspect of both public and private life. Noted theologian Howard Thurman dissected the "anatomy" of segregation with chilling precision in his classic 1965 book, *The Luminous Darkness*. A white supremacist society must not only "array all the forces of legislation and law enforcement," he wrote; "it must falsify the facts of history, tamper with the insights of religion and religious doctrine, editorialize and slant news and the printed word. On top of that it must keep separate schools, separate churches, separate graveyards, and separate public accommodations—all this in order to freeze the place of the Negro in society and guarantee his basic immobility." Yet this was "but a partial indication of the high estimate" that the white South placed upon African Americans. "Once again, to state it categorically," Thurman concludes, "the measure of a man's estimate of your strength is the kind of weapons he feels that he must use in order to hold you fast in a prescribed place."

As the interviews in this chapter—and indeed most of the interviews in this volume—suggest, the arsenal of weapons white southerners felt it necessary to use against black southerners was truly prodigious. In firsthand recollections stretching back to the early twentieth century, Behind the Veil informants tell stories of rapes and beatings, of houses burned to the ground and land stolen, of harrowing escapes in the middle of the night to evade lynch mobs or to avoid the slower, grinding death of perpetual poverty and indebtedness on southern tenant farms. Even informant Arthur Searles's offhand comment about needing a pass to travel in Baker County, Georgia, is revealing. Passes had been common in the slave South and were used extensively in South Africa during apartheid, but the idea that an American citizen might need one to travel in his own home state in the post–World War II era seems outrageous, and in fact passes were not typical after slavery ended. Yet, Searles had been given one. He had seen the mutilated body of a Baker County lynching victim, and he knew how desperately white southerners wanted not only to keep blacks in a fixed position socially, but also to control their movements. Above all, he, like others of his generation, knew at some level that white control over black bodies and therefore black labor was key to southern agriculture and to the region's slowly industrializing economy. Thus, whites rarely hesitated to use force against African Americans who threatened to destabilize labor arrangements or who tried to "steal away," escaping from debt and abuse on tenant farms in much the same way that slaves had escaped from bondage a generation or two earlier. The legacy of whites' drive for social stability and control includes both the broken bodies of lynching victims and the grim wariness of men and women like Arthur Searles.

While a number of the stories in this chapter are about lynching and other forms of racial violence, informants also tell of moments that were less dramatic but nonetheless humiliating. "You could shop," Theresa Lyons of Durham, North Carolina, suggests, "but if you walked up and a white person walked up later, they waited on the white person first. I mean, it was just a known that you weren't going to get waited on. Even when I knew that [something] was *it*, no matter how bad I wanted it, I wouldn't buy it. I would leave."

For African Americans such as Lyons and Searles, life in the Jim Crow South was a process of navigating treacherous waters. Just as any stretch of ocean might offer smooth sailing on any given day, individual white southerners might be friendly and even helpful at times. However, they might also be unaccountably hostile and prejudiced. Thus, blacks had to remain ever vigilant in case storms of white fury should suddenly begin to blow.

Because they had to fight racist *people* as well as institutions the struggle of blacks against racial oppression was never so impersonal as a seaman's struggle against the elements. Instead, living Jim Crow meant confronting bitter truths about human nature, including the arbitrary unpredictability of alleged white "friends" suddenly becoming mortal enemies. Among the most poignant of these realities emerged when African American children came to understand that blacks and whites were different in the eyes of their society. Often, the circumstances that led up to this realization were mundane, but the realization itself could be devastating. Walking to school, going to the store, playing on rural farms and city sidewalks, black children confronted racial differences in the taunts of white children, in the degrading treatment of black adults, and in their own observations of who was better off than whom. Under such circumstances, "you just automatically grow up inferior," as Charles Gratton of Birmingham, Alabama, laments, "and you had the feeling that white people were better than you." Yet, parents and other black adults worked hard to counteract such lessons. Employing a variety of child-rearing strategies, they encouraged black youths to maintain their self-respect regardless of white attitudes.

Children's experiences also varied. Those who lived in or near cities often remember the physical signs of segregation—placards above water fountains, separate platforms at the train station, the often-shifting terrain of racial separation on the street car or bus. In the rural South, children's memories of learning about racial difference are sometimes more subtle (rural children played together) and sometimes brutally stark (in the countryside, white violence tended to be even less restrained). The stories of boys and girls also differ. Ferdie Walker's memory of white policemen exposing themselves to her at a Fort Worth bus stop is but one case in point.

Woman opening oysters in St. Helena, South Carolina, sometime after World War I.
(Courtesy of Earnestine Atkins, Lula Holmes, and Louise Nesbit, St. Helena, South Carolina)

Even after age and experience had taught them the roles Jim Crow
required them to perform, adult blacks regularly encountered new limita-
tions on their freedom. Every visit to the doctor, every effort to get a job
or buy land, much less register to vote, could result in a further restric-
tion, an additional humiliation arbitrarily imposed. African Americans'
efforts to meet even basic needs such as health care could take them into
minefields of white recalcitrance, as the testimonies of Milton Quigless
and G. K. Butterfield suggest. Henry Hooten found that white southerners' prejudices went with them even across the Atlantic during World
War II. And, in 1958, Walter Cavers uncovered the bitter truth that a
seemingly straightforward car accident, for which he was not at fault,
could result in terrible consequences.

For many Behind the Veil informants, a deep personal knowledge of
American race relations at their worst has resulted in a sense of obligation
to pass on an understanding of Jim Crow's bitter truths to subsequent
generations.

Chapter 1 ends with long narratives by Willie Harrell and Ann
Pointer, both of whom describe African American life in the plantation
South in the pre–World War II era and both of whom clearly feel they

have important stories to tell. As these final two excerpts suggest, the history that Behind the Veil informants self-consciously narrate is a history with a purpose. "I'm telling you," Ann Pointer insists to the young man conducting her 1994 interview, "it sound funny to you because you never have been subject to nothing like this, but that's what I want to tell you: how horrible it is when everything you do, the [white] man's got to approve it."

RALPH THOMPSON

Young children in every era interrogate the world around them as they come of age. During the years of segregation, African American children, encountering the puzzling realities of Jim Crow, looked to their parents and elders for answers to questions such as: "Why can't I drink out of the water fountain?" "Why can't we try on clothes at this store?" Or: "Why do we have to move out of the way when white folks come walking down the street?"

Explaining the laws of segregation and the practices of racial "etiquette" was a constant and extraordinarily difficult task for African American parents. How could they teach children the rules they had to follow in order to survive without damaging their self-esteem? Ralph Thompson, who grew up on a tenant farm in the Memphis area in the late 1930s and early 1940s, describes his parents' efforts to explain segregation and racism to him and his siblings.

They talked to us a little bit about that, but as [things] happened. They might *respond* to things. I can remember the insurance man coming over there one day and called my mother "Auntie." And she looked at him and said, "Don't you call me 'Auntie.' I'm not your 'Auntie.' " I can remember that. His name was Mr. Watson, and this was back in the forties. You could just see little things like that and how they responded, how they would respond to embarrassing things. They tried to keep you away from things that would be embarrassing when they couldn't fight back. For instance, going in a grocery store or something like that. If we went downtown and they had the colored drinking fountain and white drinking fountain—in looking back, my sister [and I] talk about it now—my mother would always tell us to drink water before we left home. So we didn't get caught into drinking water out. Little things like that. Things like going in a store and you can't try the clothes on. When I got up to about 12, 14, 15 years old, and I'd go to Thom McAn to buy shoes, if I had a $20 bill, they would check that $20 bill like it was counterfeit. I couldn't walk in a Thom McAn shoe store and buy a pair of shoes because they didn't want to take my money. They would treat me like this is counterfeit, and they'd look at it. I'm serious. You don't know how that hurt to do that. You go to a store, and you're standing there and a white person walks up, and they'll wait on that white person and just make you stand. So my parents kind of kept us away from that and they wouldn't let us do certain things.

When you look back at it, you can tell why—because they couldn't defend [us]. So they tried to shield us from it by sending us or taking us in a different direction, and whatever was going on, they tried to keep it away from us, so to speak. My daddy, if it was a white person around talking to him in some kind of business format, he would move away from us or tell us to go play or something. I guess that was to protect us from something that might be said to him that he wasn't able to defend. If they were talking about planting or settling up or something like that. He very seldom would do anything like that around us. He would go outside or somewhere else.

But just being called a "nigger," I can't remember no adult person calling him one. I remember kids did it, but I don't remember any adults doing us like that. I can remember at the drugstore, some evenings we would stop in there and get ice cream, and the pharmacist was real nice to us. He could scoop the ice cream up. He'd scoop it up and he could throw it up in the air and catch it with the cone, and that was kind of entertaining. We'd come through there in the afternoon. If we bought ice cream, he'd do that for us. In this particular drugstore he didn't put any stools at his counter. When you look back I guess he said I'll treat you as fair as I can and if I don't put the stools here, I don't have to worry about nobody sitting down. You get your ice cream. You have to move on. And looking back at it now that's what it seemed like. I can remember that guy.

LILLIAN SMITH

A few years older than Ralph Thompson, Lillian Smith grew up in a predominantly black neighborhood in Wilmington, North Carolina, in the 1930s. She, too, describes how her elders approached the task of instructing children in the laws and practices of Jim Crow.

The main thing, the theme throughout, was that we're living in a segregated society. I didn't understand segregation until I was maybe nine or ten years old, when I was reading and I could see the signs saying "colored" and "white." You couldn't drink at a water fountain even though you were shopping in the same store that people of any other nationality were shopping in. We would ask questions about that and [my parents and grandparents] said: "You would get arrested." So, when that word was used, any time you saw "white" and "colored," unless you wanted to be arrested and be in jail, you didn't dare. So that was the dividing line, and that lesson was really laid down solidly when we were, I would say, between seven and nine.

Naturally, you would ask, "Why?" The question would always come back that we were living in a country that had segregated laws, and [we were] called "colored" people at that time. See, the signs said "colored." You were not looked upon as having full rights that all other citizens should have. We should be treated differently. That was what the sign was. And then, of course, they started talking about slavery. So from about age seven on, they started giving us information about slavery— before I even read about it in a book. Because in our culture, [which] was our racial group, what most of us knew about slavery was handed down from word of mouth, from family members or friends or neighbors or whatever, and maybe a lot of it never was written. Most of that was black storytelling, but with a message to let you know what to avoid and how to respond and behave. Because, see, the working word there was "behavior." You have to watch your behavior.

CHARLES GRATTON

*Charles Gratton was born in 1932 and grew up in the Norwood
neighborhood of Birmingham, Alabama. Asked when he first became
aware of segregation, he describes how he was "programmed" in the bitter
truths of Jim Crow.*

Actually, when I got old enough to know myself, to really know I existed.
I mean, I was born into this thing and raised in it. I can remember very
close in my mind [times] when my mother would send me to this grocery
store that was approximately a mile away, which was the only grocery
store in Norwood. She would give me instructions before I'd leave home
and tell me, "Son, now you go on up to this store and get this or that for
me. If you pass any white people on your way, you get off the sidewalk.
Give them the sidewalk. You move over. Don't challenge white people."
So I was just brought up in that environment.

They also had a park. It was about a block from where I was born and
raised and where I lived, and it was known as the white people's park.
They had a tennis court there and nice park trees, and blacks wasn't allowed in that park. I mean we just couldn't go there. You know, it's just
one of those things.

Some days I would be sick, and I could hear the schoolchildren
playing during their lunch hour down at Norwood Elementary School,
which was all white, and that's what really stuck in my mind. I'd say, "It's
a shame that I have to walk so far to school every day." When I'd hear
those schoolchildren playing, I'd say, "Here I am a block and a half from
the elementary school, and I've got to walk six or seven miles to school
every day."

Even now, I can almost hear those kids, those white kids down at this
elementary school playing, and the noise and laughing and playing, and
I'm at home sick basically from the exposure of walking those six and
seven miles to school every day. Whether it was raining or not, I had to
go. So those are some of the memories that I have of my childhood growing up over at Norwood.

I don't know if I ever just specifically came out and asked that question [of why things were the way they were], but it was one of those

Street crossing in Wilson, North Carolina, in the early 1960s.
(Courtesy of G. K. Butterfield, Wilson, North Carolina)

things where you had been programmed all along, ever since you got old enough to know right from wrong. To challenge white people just was the wrong thing to do. You just automatically grow up inferior, and you had the feeling that white people were better than you. It just really wasn't any question asked then about why. I mean, that was white people things. That was a white people school, and I just didn't feel that I had any right to go there. It basically never entered my mind.

Most blacks in the South felt that way, until the late fifties and sixties, when Dr. [Martin Luther] King [Jr.] come along with his philosophy, and it started giving black people some hope that the way we were being treated wasn't right and this thing can change. Just some hope that we were waiting on. Whenever I would hear Dr. King talk, it seemed like he was touching me from the inside. He could touch your feeling from the inside, things that you would want to say but you just didn't know how, things that were right and wrong but you kept it inside of you because you didn't know how to express it. So he was really a great leader and a great man, and I think he done a wonderful job in what he done for our people as a whole.

FERDIE   WALKER

Ferdie Walker was born in 1928 and grew up in Fort Worth, Texas. She describes a stage in African American children's growing awareness of Jim Crow, when children encountered racist stereotypes about black men and women's sexuality. From the days of slavery on, whites justified the sexual exploitation of black women by describing them as lustful "Jezebels" who supposedly wanted the sexual attentions white men forced upon them. Meanwhile, black men's efforts to advance politically and economically after the Civil War encouraged white southerners to create a new black male character-type to go along with the "Uncle Tom" and "Sambo" of the old plantation: that of the black beast rapist. The rape or attempted rape of a white woman became the standard explanation for why thousands of black men were lynched in the South in the late nineteenth and early twentieth centuries, despite the fact that rape was not even a charge in the vast majority of cases.

Just as lynching persisted into the post–World War II era, degrading sexual stereotypes continued to affect individual black men and women's lives in myriad ways. In Ferdie Walker's case, two white police officers clearly felt they could get away with sexually harassing an 11-year-old child simply because she was black. As Walker explains, her terrifying childhood experiences resulted in a lifelong distrust of the police, shaping her own child-rearing practices and her work as a public health nurse in the 1950s.

I tell you this one thing that really sticks in my mind, one really harassing kind of thing that I went through at that time. I was 11 years old, and I will never forget it. I used to go back and forth to church on Sunday afternoons to the United Methodist youth group, and I always rode the bus. You had to stand on the corner, which was about two blocks from my house, to catch the bus. In those days, all police people were white, and all bus drivers were white, and these policemen would harass me as I was standing on this corner waiting for the bus to come. Sometimes the two of them would drive up. The bus stop was up high and the street was down low. They'd drive up under there and then they'd expose themselves while I was standing there, and it just really scared me to

Colored and white water fountains in a tobacco warehouse, Lumberton, North Carolina,
around 1940. (North Carolina Department of Archives and History, Raleigh, North Carolina)

death. And the only reason I did not go home at that time was because if I had gone home, my mother would have made me stay. So I just stepped back from the corner, and because I rode that way all the time, the bus driver didn't [have to] see me standing there at the corner. He'd always stop and I'd get on the bus.

But it was these *same cops*. So I had a morbid fear of policemen all of my life and it has not completely gone away. This was in the broad open daylight with the sun shining. But I will *never forget* it, and it always comes back to me every time I get into a really tight experience. That was really bad and it was bad for *all black girls*, you know.

It was really hard for me to tell my children that [policemen] were helping people. It was really hard. I really prayed a lot over that, and I said, "Well, this is something that you got to do." I had a job as public health nurse at Topeka, Kansas, and we had a lot of child abuse even then and that was in the fifties. My supervisor gave me a situation. She said, "Now when you go to a house and a man is beating his wife, what are you going to do?" I said, "Call the minister." And she said, "Ferdie, you're an intelligent person. You know that's not right." I told her. She's a wonderful person. I said, "Alice Jensen, I know that's not the right answer. I should call the police, but I don't believe in the police." And that was after my third child was born. So it has taken a long time for me to have any kind of trust in policemen as a group even when I tried to say to myself, "It's one person and everybody is not like everybody else." But it's really very difficult for me. That has stayed with me.

STINE GEORGE

When blacks in the Jim Crow South aspired to economic and social equality with whites, their white neighbors often met them with disapproval or even violence. Such was the case when Stine George's father William bought a piece of coveted real estate at the urging of his white boss, Jesse Morgan, who also helped him negotiate a loan from the Federal Housing Authority (FHA). Morgan believed that William George had earned the right to the land since he had always been a "good nigger." Morgan's sons disagreed, and the George family soon saw their house burned to the ground. Stine George's younger brother and sister died in the flames.

[Mr. Morgan] said [to my father], "You've been a good nigger, so I'll tell you what I'm going to do. I'm going to sell you this farm." Dad said, "Sell me a farm, Mr. Morgan? I can't buy no farm." He said, "The government will buy it for you. In fact, we already started buying it. You just go over there and talk with Brown"—that was the FHA man—"and he'll let you sign the papers. I've already got them made up. We're the government." [Laughter.] That was it. Talk to my daddy, he'll tell you the same. "We're the government," [Morgan] said. "Just go over there and sign the papers."

That's what happened. [Morgan] didn't tell his sons about what he had done. He didn't want to tell [them] until after my dad signed the papers. [That farm was] on the main road at that time, see, and nothing but white folks [there], and good land on a hill, too. See, black folks would always get in the bottom, but this was on a hill, nice hill land, because that was one of his choice farms. But anyway, them sons had a fit. It was two of them. Boy, they had a fit, and they went over there and they were going to stop it because they said [their] daddy was senile, he didn't know what he was doing. The people at the FHA office said, "Well, he's done signed the papers. We can't withdraw it now."

So then they came out to the house mad. See, [one of Morgan's sons] had a fence put all the way around the farm. In fact, my dad did all the work, but he bought the fence and the posts and everything. It was new wire. It had just been up about a year. So they came out there and told my dad, "That's our wire." Said, "You've got to take all that wire down and roll it up and give it back to us." Around that whole farm, see, take up the posts. That's what they wanted.

My dad said, "Yes sir, I'll do that." So my dad went back over there to this Brown man's place and asked the FHA office. [He] said, "Mr. Morgan's son came out here and told me I had to take all that wire down from out there and give it to him because it belonged to him." The man told him, "You don't have to do that. The wire belongs to you because you done bought the farm." Said, "But now if you want to get along with them, you might want to take it down." So that's what my dad did. He had to take up all that wire up. To get along with him.

See, that's when black folks were going north because they said the white folks would either come back and lynch you or do anything, burn your house down. That's another thing. I don't talk about this too much. They built us this government house to live in. All government houses looked alike. You could always tell a government house because all of them were white, and they all looked alike. All over the South [if] you saw one, you saw more.

Anyway, that was a part of the deal in buying this farm. They put a house out there and that was part of the deal in the farm operation. So we had this house out there, but the white folks resented the fact that we were out there and had this frame house out there. We're not so sure what happened, but one night, probably about two o'clock in the morning, my oldest sister started running through the house [yelling], "Hey, Daddy,

Daddy, the house is on fire!" And so the house started burning on the front porch and went all the way around, and when she hollered, we all were asleep. [It was] two o'clock in the morning, and then, of course, my dad ran out and she ran out and my dad thought he could put the fire out.

So then I came out. My baby sister and my baby brother didn't ever wake up and got burnt up in that fire. That has hurt so much [that] I've never been able to talk about that much. I've never told but one or two persons in my whole life. We ran out there, and we took water and throwed it in the fire all the way around the house. It was said the white folks gassed our house and caused it to burn down and burn up two children.

[My brother and sister were] about three and four. My sister never waked up; she was still in bed, but the boy got up and got as far as the door and just didn't make it out. It was very painful. It was very painful that this happened.

And of course, white folks came over. In fact, my daddy didn't sleep with his pants on. [Laughter.] Well, a lot of people don't sleep with clothes on, but that's why I sleep with clothes on now because he didn't have any pants on, and he was out there trying to put the fire out because we were in a hurry. My sister, when she came out her hair got burned almost all off. And so a white man that lived across the hill, he brought them some clothes.

They never did anything about it. Nobody ever did anything about it, never tried to find out who did it or anything, but we surmised that the white folks done it. My sister had been ironing that day before. If it had caught from the iron, it would have caught inside the house, not outside. But they said, "Yeah, when did you iron over at that house?" My sister said, "Well, we ironed yesterday, ironed something yesterday afternoon." "Well, that was what it was, [it] was the clothes! That's where it caught." But it didn't catch inside the house. It caught on the front porch, went around the house, and burned the house up. It went around fast, too, burned the house down.

That's why we couldn't go back in and get the others out. But you see, a seven- or eight-year-old child, you couldn't expect him to go back and get nobody. Well, you know, I'm scared, I'm a nervous wreck. See, we had a bucket trying to draw the water out of the well, and my oldest sister was running, throwing the water on there. Shucks, in a little while that fire was all the way around the house, so that ended that little bit. Like I said, white folks came around and they were talkative, but nobody ever tried to apprehend anybody who committed the crime.

I had to walk 12 miles a day [to and from school], and there's a wood bridge, and I was kind of afraid to go across that bridge. Of course, my daddy always told me, "Now if you come up that bridge and somebody's on it, you just go back in the woods and stay in the woods until they leave, and then you come on home or go on to school." I'll never forget there were at least two nights that I had to stay in those woods all night long because white folks were fishing up and down the bridge. They never would go back anywhere so I laid over in the woods till they left. I thought they would throw me in the water, you know, throw me in the river, so I just stayed back off the road in the woods, and I slept in the woods at least two nights.

[My daddy] knew, probably, what it was. He loved me. He knew something had happened, but there was no way of getting in touch with me, so instead of going on home, I'd get up and walk on back to school the next morning. I had no other way to work it. [Laughter.] I got up and went on back to school, and the next evening I'd be able to get home, and they knew what transpired.

It was just some white guys on the bridge messing around at night, but they was there until late. I fell asleep in those woods, and so after twelve o'clock, it wasn't no point in going home. [Laughter.] So I just stayed in the woods.

I shall never forget this, and this is something nobody ever knew because we don't tell it. I wouldn't tell it now because it's painful, it will be painful to even tell it, but with what you are doing, I'll tell it. Some Sunday mornings we would get a mule and five or six of us would get the wagon. All of us [were] under ten years old. We'd get the wagon and go up about six miles away to see some of our first cousins. So one Sunday morning, it wasn't but three of us in the wagon, my sister, my brother and myself, and we were going up to see my uncle Chilton. Like I said, my sister was but nine or ten. Of course, I was driving, and she was sitting in the wagon. So we went by this house where these white guys were out there playing ball. I guess it was eight guys, young white boys probably about 18, 19, 20, something like that.

One of those white guys ran and jumped on the wagon. He said, "I'm going to ride with you, I'm going to ride." We were going by this house, you see; we knew him, see, and he got on the back of the wagon, and he was riding with us. When we got to the house, he took the mule from me and stopped the mule at the house, took the wagon from me and tied the mule to a tree in the yard. Then he made my sister get out and go in the house with him. He raped my sister. Like I said, she was about nine at that time.

When he took her in the house, my brother and I jumped out the wagon and ran through the woods. We were scared. We didn't know where to go, and we were scared because, really, we hadn't been anywhere before. He was about six or seven then. No, he was about four or five years old, and I'm seven or eight. Anyway, he followed me down through them woods and went on down through the woods and briars. We were scared for somebody to see us, and so we finally went on through the woods and tried to get back where we thought our daddy was. See, that house where this guy was, we wouldn't dare go by there and be seen, so that meant we had to go way around through the woods and then come back around. My dad was within seeing distance from where this guy got on the wagon.

So about the time we got halfway back to Gum Branch, almost back where we could see the house, we heard the wagon going back down that road, running. See, what he had done, after he raped my sister, he told her to get in the wagon and go home. So she was driving the wagon and she went on home. She went by the house where my dad was, and all them got out, and they couldn't understand where I was and what happened. They were alarmed. They didn't know we were down in the woods. We heard that wagon running but the corn was tall. We knew it was her with that wagon, but the corn was tall, and so I was scared and naturally my brother would be [too]. So finally they had her, but they didn't know where we were. They finally called the sheriff, and of course, he didn't do nothing. He did arrest this guy. We finally came out of the woods, and then we went back down to the house, and we didn't have any more trouble out of them, but they never didn't, never do nothing to that guy for what he did.

CORNELIUS SPEED

Like Stine George's family, Cornelius Speed's family found their white neighbors in Florida unwilling to see blacks get ahead economically through landownership. After Speed's grandfather died, his father tried to reclaim land that had been in the family since the 1880s but that was currently mortgaged to white businessman T. S. Green. Green made sure Speed could not pay off the mortgage and instead sold the land to a white plantation owner. Legal cheating was by no means the only method whites used to dispossess African Americans of their land and agricultural produce.

I knew my grandfather. When I was a little boy, I would go and stay with him. He was a minister. He [also] had a large area of about seven hundred acres. He cut the timbers and built the first church at Rock Hill. The first church he built was a log church. Following that, when they outgrew that church, he then cut timber and hauled it to the mill and had it cut in lumber and built a larger church. He pastored that church until his death. Now, after my grandfather's death, most of his children, all except two daughters and a son, had given up the farm and moved to either Washington, D.C., or Philadelphia, Pennsylvania. They had moved, and of course their attitude was, "We're through with the farm. We're through with the farm."

Of course, my granddaddy had some indebtedness. He had borrowed some money trying to buy cars and things, like most Negroes did at that time. They had a little and the white people took advantage of you. I can tell you who the mortgager was: T. S. Green.

So my daddy tried to pay off [my grandfather's] mortgage. T. S. Green told him he couldn't pay it off. So, my daddy then mortgaged what he had to get money to try to pay it off. And he always told me this story. He said, "Son, I had gone to Mr. Green's office to talk to him about trying to pay the property off and he had given me an appointment." My father finished [only] fourth grade, incidentally, but he could read and write and figure as well as anybody. He was sitting in Mr. Green's office waiting because [Green] was talking with another person. He was sitting there by the door waiting, and Mr. Green said "That nigger, Cornelius,

[is] out there waiting to worry me. He thinks he's going to get his daddy's property, but hell, he'll *never* get it as long as I'm alive. He'll *never* be able to redeem it as long as I'm alive." So my daddy was fighting about it, and the news got back to his brothers and sisters who were in Washington that [Green] was trying to *take* his daddy's property. I don't know who spread the propaganda. He had one brother who came home, and if it had not been for one of the people in the community, he probably would have gotten hurt because this brother had come home and told some community people that he was going to kill T. S. Green because he was trying to take all of his daddy's property. This person, who was a deacon in the church along with my father, came to my father and told him [what his brother was saying].

But it ended up that they didn't want [Daddy] to have the property; they were going to sell it. They sold seven hundred and fifty acres of property for $25 per acre in Leon County, and my daddy didn't get enough of his portion even to pay off the mortgage he had on his own property. They wouldn't let *him* have it, and it was sold for $25 per acre to a white plantation owner.

[There were also] many black people in that community who lost their property through taxes. They didn't take [news]papers, [where property foreclosures were announced]. I could name 25 or 30 people who lost property for nonpayment of taxes, and they didn't know it. I don't know if [the government] advertised it [the impending foreclosure], but they had no way of knowing [even if] they advertised. They didn't have television. They didn't have radios. Radios were just beginning, the old phonograph, you know, where you wound it up. They didn't know. When they knew anything, they were being moved out because of nonpayment. There was a person who bought my aunt's property, bought 40 acres of her 80, a man whom I'd known all of my life. He bought it, and he was trying to farm it, and he bought, I believe, a 1941 Ford tractor, $750. He borrowed money from T. S. Green to buy the tractor, and he didn't make enough money to pay it as he should. Before he knew anything, the sheriff had come there to set all of his things out for a $750 tractor. There were people who would have bought the property [from him], but he was too embarrassed to tell and denied that he owed anything when his things were sitting on the ground [for auction]. That's the honest to goodness truth.

There was another gentleman named Tom Atkinson who used to run a market on West Gaines Street that sold a little of everything. And this is a fact: Tom Atkinson would go out and pick up some black street walkers [day laborers], you know just hanging around the street. They used to hang out down in that area, and he would get in his truck and ride through the rural community. He did black people a terrible disfavor. He would ride through and the Negroes would be planting watermelons and things, and he would [say], "Oh, I know, this is old John Brown's field here. I bought them watermelons. Go out there and let's put a load on the truck." He'd just go out there and get your watermelons. I understand he used to get people's cows and butcher them the same way. "I got this cow from old Jim Brown, load him, let's go." And he'd go out there and *get them* and people were afraid to do anything about it.

MERLIN JONES

Merlin Jones spent the first 22 years of his life in Canton, Mississippi, before leaving home to serve in the armed forces during World War II. He describes a flourishing black community life in the Canton of his youth, but also makes it clear that African Americans had to be always on their guard because of the ever-present threat of racial terror. According to Mr. Jones, even disputes over family pets could escalate into fatal confrontations. Meanwhile, Jones's story of how a neighbor boy escaped Canton after being falsely accused of theft suggests how little had changed since Virginia bondman Henry "Box" Brown gained fame for escaping from slavery by shipping himself north in a packing box almost a hundred years before.

I remember one incident. I was small. There was a widow who lived down the street from me. I told you where the white property ended and the black property started? The lady who lived in the first black house was a widow, Mrs. Cage. She had at home a daughter and three sons. Her oldest son worked for some Jewish people. Someone broke into that house and stole some silverware and jewelry. They accused him of doing it, and I remember seeing the only mob crowd I'd ever seen in my life. They passed and my parents told me. We could peek out of the windows. Everybody had the lights off; everybody was quiet. There were these people in their cars, and some were walking, and they were using profanity—what they were going to do to him, and this and that. And they went there, and Mrs. Cage was much older than my mother because her oldest daughter was perhaps as old as my mother, so she was a pretty elderly lady. They went through her house and turned the beds over looking for him under the beds, and they tore the doors off the closets. They slammed her against the wall, and one of the boys wanted to react, and they beat him up. It wasn't the son they were looking for, this was the next oldest son.

But what had happened, the son of the man that was accusing him had told him, "Get out of town because my father's having a mob crowd come after you because he said that you were the one that broke into our house." They were about the same age. He worked for them as a butler, chauffeur, and this son—I guess the two young men [were] near the same age, and they had a close relationship. No matter what society says, people are just going to be people. He told him, "Get out of town," and he had left the day before. He didn't leave by train because they had been watching, even though he didn't know [it]. They had been watching the railroad stations, the bus stations there, and in Jackson, they were watching the airport. And what had happened, Mr. Mackey, I believe it was, owned a little freight truck. He hauled stuff for people, and hauled stuff from nearby towns, and he had crates on his truck. They carried him to one of the towns 40 or 50 miles away and put him on a train. He was left there in a box just like he was being shipped out, just like he was being shipped to another town by truck, and that's how he got away.

But, seeing those people, I was too small to understand why my parents were so afraid. I couldn't have been over seven or eight years old at the time, and all of these cars—I had never seen so many people. They were talking and walking, and cars were bumper to bumper. They were lined up, they were stopped, they were far beyond our house, and I lived about seven houses from [Mrs. Cage's house], and these cars were bumper to bumper on beyond where I lived. I had never seen anything like that.

I do remember hearing about a lot of that. There was a Mr. Fields that was killed by a lynch mob. You will never guess why he was killed. One of his dogs jumped on this white man's dog and beat him up. They killed him because he should have been able to control his dogs. They killed him because "my dog beat your dog."

There was another case in which a [black] man was killed because this [white] woman says that he had tried to have sex with her. But later on I learned that she was the aggressor and he wasn't. Some of the men who had had sex with her said that if you didn't, she'd have you killed. One man said he did. He was afraid, but he said if he was going to die, he was going to be guilty. He said it didn't happen one time, had to happen several times, and he eventually left town because he got scared. And so, it was strange how those people worked, how they lived.

I had an aunt who was the only black person who owned any downtown property. She owned three downtown buildings. [Whites] tried to get her to sell it, she said, a couple of times. They dynamited the front of some of her property, but she still stayed there. She held on to it.

MILTON QUIGLESS

African Americans who needed medical treatment often encountered some of the bitterest of Jim Crow's truths. There were too few black doctors, and whites often gave health care grudgingly, if at all. Hospitals and other medical facilities were inadequate and far from the farming communities where most blacks lived prior to World War II. They were also segregated, adding humiliation to patients' distress. Apart from these concerns, few blacks had the means to pay for even the most necessary procedures, especially if they worked as sharecroppers or tenant farmers.

Dr. Milton Quigless was born in 1904 and grew up in Port Gibson, Mississippi. He left Port Gibson as a young man and worked his way through school as a sleeping car porter, eventually serving on trains that ran between St. Louis, the Dakota Badlands, and Seattle. A graduate of Meharry Medical College, Nashville, Tennessee, Dr. Quigless came to Tarboro, North Carolina, in 1936 to begin a medical career that eventually spanned six decades. In this excerpt, he describes the woeful state of medical care for African Americans in rural North Carolina. As he struggled to collect payments from reluctant plantation owners, Dr. Quig-less also caught glimpses of the grim exploitation that sustained southern agriculture.

If you got sick out there in the country, if the boss man didn't agree to pay for your medical care, then you're on your butt. That's all. People were having babies and having an infection from it and dying. After I had been there about a month, I went out to see this lady in the country, and she had a baby and the placenta, the afterbirth, didn't come down. Two weeks of that. That damn thing got infected, and she had septicemia. She had it so bad she had abscesses in her eyes. I got it out, but it was too late because she died.

Of course, all the landowners around here had sharecroppers. Very few blacks owned their own home farms. One man who had several farms in this area, he had overseers to watch over, you know, manage the farms. One of the overseers called me in the middle of the night and said, "Doc, got a lady out here. One of the tenant's wives is having a baby, and she's in trouble. She's bleeding like everything. Will you go see about her? I'll see that you get your money." I went out there, and I saved her. Everybody was enthused about it. So the landowner called me and said, "Just go out and see my tenants and come back at the end of the year. I'll pay you just the one time every year. In October." I saw these patients out there, coming in here, out in the woods and everything until October. I had a bill of over $900. I took it to the landowner. He said, "Well, Doc, my son looks after these things. Just take it over there and see him. He'll take care of you." But, in the meantime, another white man in town knew I was coming along. In fact, I had bought a house from him. He said, "Doc, I want to tell you something about some of these folks here. I like you, and I'm trying to help you, but everybody's not in your corner. See, now certain people around here, they'll have you work on their tenants, and then when you take the bill, they want to try to Jew you down." He said, "Don't you let them do it. Don't you let them intimidate you like that. It's all right to give them 10 percent but don't let them go any more than that." So sure enough, when I took this bill over to this guy, he said, "My son takes care of that." [I] took it to his son. He said, "Well, Doc, you got a big bill here. It's over $900." He said, "Well,

Segregated movie theater in Leland, Mississippi, in 1939.
(American History Slide Collection, National Museum of American History, Smithsonian Institution)

you know, we're giving it in one piece so listen, can't we sort of knock this down to about $700?" Then it came back to me about what this other man had said. I said, "Look, there it is. Give me any damn thing you want. I don't give a damn. Just whatever you want to do. If you don't want to give me nothing, just tell me. I'll get out of here and won't bother you anymore." "Oh no, Doc. It isn't anything like that." So he paid me my money less 10 percent.

That's the way they got everything. They charged the tenants 25 percent for lending them money, and [when they made someone wait for payment for services rendered to tenants] they charged them 10 percent. That'd be 35 percent on every dollar they loaned a tenant. See what I mean? That's the way they got all these damn farms.

Ten days after I opened this hospital here, I had 25 beds, 20 of them were filled. Most people didn't have any damn money. They were all sharecroppers and whatnot. I remember this lady. She was in labor and her husband ran in one day. Said, "Doc, come out right quick and see about my wife." She lived about 10 miles out in the country. So I went out there. The lady had had a precipitous labor. That baby just burst out every damn thing. Lacerated the vagina, lower part of the intestines, the uterus. Every damn thing. Blood was just shooting out. Put a sheet up there. Told my receptionist to come out with some ether. She poured the damn ether, and I had to sew on that lady about an hour and a half. Well, she healed all right except for one little place. We got along very well. No blood transfusion. Hell, wasn't no blood bank or nothing in those days. The Lord just wasn't ready for her to go. Anyway, she healed all right except for one little place, and I knew about Duke [Hospital], and I heard about the OB/GYN men over there, Obstetrics/Gynecology men. So I wrote this Dr. David R. Carter, the Chief, and told him about what had happened. He said, "Send the patient over here." So I sent the lady over there. He read the letter again, and he looked at her. He called me and said, "How in the hell did you ever do this in the country? How were you able to do that?" I said, "Nobody else was able to do it. I was here. I had to do it. Or she would die." So then he said, "Send her on over here, and if you get any cases like that, just send them on over because we'll manage it." He gave me encouragement and he helped me out all the way along. So I just got started from that, and it went on and on.

GEORGE   KENNETH   BUTTERFIELD   JR.

A lawyer and judge, G. K. Butterfield Jr. describes his hometown of Wilson, North Carolina, as a city that did not begin to integrate its public schools until the mid-1960s, despite the Supreme Court's ruling in Brown v. Board of Education *in 1954. Perhaps it is not surprising, then, that Wilson's health care facilities for African Americans were racist and backward as well.*

We had basically two local black physicians. Each was in a solo practice. Their medical resources were limited. If they need[ed] lab work done or an X-ray done, they would have to send you to another location to get it done, but they were good men. They worked hard, and they served their patients as best they could. As far as institutional care, there was, up until 1965, a black hospital referred to as Mercy Hospital which was understaffed and underfunded and was just a second-rate hospital. Nevertheless, that was the hospital for black citizens and the only hospital for black citizens. There was no rescue squad. Back then, if you needed to be transported to a hospital in an emergency situation, you would call the funeral home. This applied to both black and white. You would call the local funeral home, and they would send out an ambulance, which also doubled up as their hearse. Of course, black funeral homes would transport black patients, and white funeral homes, white patients. I saw a case one time where a white funeral [home] was called, and [they] got to the scene and found it was a black patient and turned around and went back. [They] did not render assistance. I remember that quite well. That was in '63. I was driving for an elderly minister at the time as a chauffeur. I would take [his wife] out daily to the bank and places, and she got out one day and fell, broke her hip. The white funeral home was two blocks away. Someone called the funeral home. The ambulance came down. [They] saw that she was black and turned around and went back.

In '64 we had a public hospital constructed, and at that hospital, blacks were segregated by room. Blacks in one room. Whites in another. I found this out doing my research for the voting rights case. HEW, [the Federal Department of] Health, Education, and Welfare, came down and inspected the hospital and found out that it was segregated by race. [They] wrote a letter to the hospital—this is a public record—telling them that they were violating federal law, and if they didn't correct the problem and admit patients to rooms regardless of race, federal funds would be withdrawn. The hospital called an emergency meeting [of] the board of trustees. There was a colored man on the board of trustees. I don't even give him the credit as being a "Negro" or "black." I mean, he was just a person of color who did not represent any of the interests of the black community whatsoever. Hines was his name, William Hines. Mr. Hines was on the board, and at the conclusion of the meeting, the minutes reflect that Mr. Hines made a motion that a telegram be sent to the Department of Health, Education, and Welfare informing them that "[w]e did not segregate on the basis of race, and that if blacks and whites were in separate rooms, it was because they wanted to be there." The letter went off. Another letter came back from HEW saying, "We received your letter. That's insufficient. That's inadequate. You're still segregated, and we will be cutting off your federal funds in very short order." [The trustees] called another meeting, voted on it, and finally they were forced to integrate the rooms at the hospital, but the feds had to make a grand stand before that happened. So as a result of that, blacks and whites ended up in the same rooms together in the hospital.

Nash General Hospital over in Nash County got around the problem by building a new hospital with all private rooms. There are no semi-private rooms in Rocky Mount. All rooms are private. People have forgotten it now, but the reason was to get around integration. So health care was terrible.

There were two clinics staffed by white physicians—Carolina General Clinic and Wilson Clinic—and blacks could go to those clinics to see white doctors, but the rules were different. You had to sit in a very, very, very small room bunched up together with very poor ventilation. You couldn't see out of the room very much. It was maybe a 18″ by 18″ hole that the nurse, the receptionist, would talk to you through. You were called by your first name. "John, James, come on. Dr. So and So will see you now." Whereas whites had this spacious, beautiful waiting room with plants and windows and the light.

Black patients would always be the last. The same uncle that was active in voter registration with my father, my mother's brother, was involved in a tragic car accident in 1949. He was on a bicycle, and a motorist struck him. He was taken to the black hospital, and my family called a white doctor to come down to see him. The white doctor said, "I will be there." This was like eleven or twelve o'clock in the morning. The white doctor said, "I'll come." Didn't show up. Several hours later, they called the black doctor, and the black doctor said, "Well, you have called the white doctor first, and I don't want to offend him." The black doctor and the patient were fraternity brothers. They were friends. Of course, he may have been upset because he wasn't called first, you know, but he refused to go and see his friend because the white doctor had been consulted first and [he] didn't want to hurt his feelings. He refused to see my uncle. So they kept waiting on the white doctor, and several hours later, I mean like eight or ten hours past the accident, he came in and checked him and left. A couple of hours later, he died.

I don't know if the reason for it was because he had been an agitator in the community for voter registration, and they just didn't want to give him medical attention. Regardless of whether that was the motive or not, he didn't receive proper attention, and he died, from internal bleeding, something which today would be very routine. But he died, right in Mercy Hospital, back in '49. So medical care was not really available at the same level that it was to white patients. Most blacks consulted black doctors, and they could not pay black doctors what white doctors were making. So black doctors ended up being providers of free medical care. Most of the patients had high blood pressure and problems that poor people generally have. So black doctors really couldn't prosper. Even though they were perceived as being rich men, they couldn't prosper. They made house calls. It was nothing for Dr. [Joseph F.] Cowan, who was one of the doctors, to go around at night from house to house with his little bag and see elderly patients. Couldn't get paid for it.

HENRY HOOTEN

World War II brought new opportunities for African Americans as they advanced through the military ranks or moved to northern and western cities to work in wartime industrial jobs. Nevertheless, Jim Crow persisted in the military throughout the war years, and racist attitudes accompanied white soldiers as they fought on European, Asian, and African shores. In this excerpt, Henry Hooten of Tuskegee, Alabama, recalls a clash between black troops and a white officer over the issue of black men dancing with white women at a party in Birmingham, England.

When I first was inducted into service, I was up in Michigan. In fact, I was on steamboats when I was called. My cousin was called to go in December. My aunt and uncle wanted me to go along with him so that he'd be comfortable. So I did. I volunteered to go in service with him. We went in at Detroit, and they sent us to Fort Custer, Michigan. When we got to Fort Custer we stayed there for about three weeks and then we parted. He went to the South Pacific, and I went to Europe. I went to England.

Well, I worked up through the ranks. I went in as a private, and soon I became corporal, and then staff sergeant and first sergeant. It was very rewarding. I had been taught to do what you are told to do and never question it. [They] said if you want to be successful in service, that's the way you would have to do.

It was well segregated. We went one way and the whites went another. Each outfit was equipped with the same equipment and whatnot. After I went overseas, we could see the segregated part. As a black soldier, you had truck drivers and laborers. If you had any education at all you could maybe be a company clerk, or you'd go up in the ranks. But I found that it was much easier to follow orders and stay out of trouble because they would court-martial you if you didn't.

The first trouble I really had was in London. We were getting ready. The English people had invited us to a party one night, and we knew that we were going overseas. We were getting ready for [the] invasion of North Africa at the time, and so the people in London was trying to show their appreciation toward us black servicemen.

So they made up the passes to go to the dance that night, and I put them on [the commanding officer's] desk. He had signed four or five of them before he read the first one. So he looked and he asked the first sergeant of the outfit, "What are these passes for?

Sergeant Johnson said, "They are passes for the men to go to a party in Birmingham, England."

He says, "Birmingham, England?"

He said, "Yes."

My company commander was from Mississippi, and he didn't want his black boys fraternizing with the white girls in that area. He said, "Well, there ain't no black girls in Birmingham, England. None of my black boys are going to dance with no white girls." And so he began to tear the passes up. He tore all of them up.

When he tore them up, the first sergeant tore his stripes off.

He said, "Well sir, I've been in this man's army 27 years, but we're going to the dance tonight if I have to go to the guardhouse tomorrow."

We had about 12 trucks. [We] loaded up the whole outfit and we went to the party. While we was at the party, the company commander sent the military police to arrest all of us. Well, the little guardhouse wouldn't hold but say 50 or 60 men. You couldn't put [the whole outfit] in the guardhouse. So they arrested us in our quarters. You couldn't go out of your quarters. You had to stay. [Word of this incident was sent to

Washington, D.C. The general sent a brigadier general to investigate the matter. The brigadier general reprimanded the company commander and sent him to Leavenworth federal prison for his role in the incident.]

THERESA LYONS

Rationing during World War II sometimes meant new restrictions on African Americans' everyday lives, as Theresa Lyons of Durham, North Carolina, explains.

I remember the principal of the Little River School, because you couldn't buy meat, and I remember he got beat up real bad by some people, some white people at a store on Roxboro Road. Being a principal, he thought he was somebody, and he stopped in there and asked them if they had any meat. It was just something like fatback or a strip of lean or something like that. They beat him real bad because they said he was out of his place, that they didn't sell meat to niggers.

And I remember when they wouldn't sell you a Coke. You could only buy Pepsi. You could buy a Pepsi, but you could not buy Coke. If you'd go in a store and ask for Coke, they would reach in there and give you Pepsi. They only sold Cokes to white folks.

ARTHUR SEARLES

Arthur Searles was born in 1915 in Albany, Georgia, the son of a schoolteacher and a railroad man. His parents were the only home owners in their neighborhood, which was commonly known as "CME" because it centered on a Colored Methodist Episcopal church. Remembering how neighborhood boys guarded their turf and their "little CME girls" when he was a teenager, Searles is reminded of a much grimmer story: the lynching of a black man by the sheriff of Baker County, Georgia, in the mid-1940s.

Because of my mama and papa, we were sort of the upper echelon [and] the young men over in CME chose me as their leader. If you wanted to

Lynchings, which were epidemic in the South between 1890 and 1910, often became public spectacles, with entire communities watching and often actively participating.
(American History Slide Collection, National Museum of American History, Smithsonian Institution)

come into CME, especially to see our little CME girls, you had to get a pass from me. We issued passes like the sheriff of Baker County does now. You didn't know that, did you? The sheriff of Baker County still has to issue you a pass if you want to go and travel freely in Baker County. If he doesn't issue you one and any of the white folks beat you up, you're just a beat-up nigger. Even today. Just one step from hell. That's what Congressman Oscar DePriest said about Baker County. Said he was born in Newton, Georgia, which is just one step from hell. [Laughter.]

They had me come down there on one occasion to take some pictures and to do an article on a ham-and-egg show. Now that's normally agricultural agents' big to-do throughout the South, in Georgia and Florida, Alabama and all that. As a matter of fact, the ag agent told me, "Searles, we want you to come down here and take some pictures. We don't have any money we can pay you but we'll give you a ham." I said, "All right. I don't mind." I said, "But now, I've got to have a letter of introduction or promotion so that when these folks stop me, I can present this letter to them." And so the sheriff wrote me a letter that I could pass through and walk around in Baker County. I was under the protection of his office, the sheriff. Of course, I went on down there, but I was scared to death all the while I was there.

One of my personal experiences with them was that a young man named Bobby Hall was lynched by the sheriff of Baker County, Screws, Sheriff Screws. See, there was a whole lot of inbreeding or mixing, and the Hall family looked just like white folks because there was some white people in there. That's the heritage. So [the] daddy, him and his son, had a beautiful pearl-handled pistol. And this has been validated so I don't mind putting it on tape. The son [Bobby Hall] would carry the pistol around in his glove compartment, which is legal as long as you're not exposing it or that sort of thing. You don't have to have a license. Well, Sheriff Screws told [Bobby Hall], "Let me see what you've got in your glove compartment." He let him see, and [Sheriff Screws] said, "Oh, this is a pretty pearl-handled pistol. I know you must have stole it." So he said, "No, sir. My daddy gave it to me." He said, "Well, I'm going to take it on in and look over my list of stolen pistols and see if it has been stolen." So he took it on away from him. He carried it on away from down there up to the sheriff's office.

About two months later, [Bobby Hall] came down there and asked him for his pistol. [The sheriff] told him, "You get on away from around here." He ran on away. So about four months after that, he saw him again and he said, "Sheriff, you know you've had plenty of time to see whether that pistol was stolen or not." Sheriff said to him, "Well, you come on down to the courthouse and we'll see about it. Don't come all that early because I'm going to be in and out. But you come down here about six o'clock in the evening, and if I haven't found anything about it . . . I even forgot about looking it up." [Bobby Hall] came around there that evening, and that man shot him in the head two times, beat him, [beat] his face bloody, as I put it in my paper, as a ripe tomato, and tied his body to the back of his truck and drug him around the square.

And they called the funeral home up here. This is how I got into it.

O.T. Funeral Home. They called them to come get the body. I went over and took pictures of the body and marked the various places on it and everything. The sheriff had killed him, and we reported it to the Georgia Bureau of Investigation and the FBI, and the sheriff brought his car and siren and parked it in front of my place out here. My place was across the street then. [He] turned the siren on and let it go on all evening. I was in there and knew I better not come out there. And, of course, I didn't go out there, to be honest with you. I don't want to be a dead brave man. I want to live so I can write again, keep writing.

So I wrote the article about the man, Bobby Hall. I knew his father real well, and Bobby Hall was a nice little fellow. Whole family are. And all the sons and the girls' husbands all work together, and they had one man, the big Hall, Mr. Hall, to get all the cotton together and take it to the cotton gin. Things like that. They were very prosperous, very prosperous. Nobody believed the sheriff would kill them. They were white-looking black folks.

Oh, they freed that man. He was doing his official business, and the uppity Negro came in, and they claim he tried to attack the sheriff, which you know is a lie. No black man is going to attack the sheriff when he's got pistols and everything. Ain't too many white folks that would even do that, let alone black folks. So, incidentally, I told you I ain't no coward, but I ain't no hero either. I was scared to go down there when they had the funeral. So I sat at my desk over there and I felt like I'd been to many black funerals. So I knew exactly how that black funeral was going to go. I talked with some other people who were there and they told me how it went. How people came in cars, wagons, motorcycles, any way you could get there. The name of the church was Thankful Baptist Church in Baker County, Newton, Georgia. And everybody seemed to be in sympathy with this boy. Most of the people had tears in their eyes and all. It was a sorrowful day.

But as a result of this and the other publicity that I gave out about it, the Ku Klux Klan marched around my house on several occasions. They threw a brick up there with a note on it. It said, "Tend to your own race and tend to your own business or else you're going to have yourself killed." Of course, I didn't print that because I didn't want anybody to know that they had gone quite that far with it.

WILLIE ANN LUCAS

Born in 1921, Willie Ann Lucas worked as a midwife in rural Arkansas from the 1940s to the early 1970s. Here she responds to the question, "What were race relations like during those days in Phillips County?"

Well, they were all right as long as you didn't try to attend any of [the whites'] functions or their schools or anything else. You were supposed to be considered a good person if you just tend to your own business and you "Yes, sir" and "No, sir." But if you tried to attend any of their functions or socialize with them or anything, you might come up killed or anything, whipped, caught and whipped, and this, that, and the other.

I never will forget, my mother farmed on Mr. Clapworthy's farm down at Marvell. They never gave anybody any trouble, and he would always come down and he'd talk to my mother and grandmama and granddaddy and all. When he died, he left it as, "I want you all to make a room—they had his funeral at his house—for all my black neighbors so they can come to my funeral." And they did. They had a special little old room there for them to sit, but you had to sit off to yourself. You couldn't sit in the crowd. You sat off to yourself in that little room, but you could go because he thought a lot of them and he thought they were good people and he wanted them there, and so therefore they could go. But other than that, you just didn't go.

When we moved here [to Brinkley, Arkansas], it wasn't integration here. We had two kids, and we had to send [them] clear across town to school, when we had a school right here. You could stand on your porch and talk to [the students] over there on the steps. My son graduated in '69. He went over there the last two years of high school, to Brinkley High School. We had all kinds of threats that, if we sent our children over there to school, we might as well dig our grave and stuff like that. We had [that] years before they made them integrate. Then they did it two grades at a time, so by the time they got around to my son, he only had two years. He was in eleventh grade. My daughters had already graduated from high school, and they didn't know anything about integration because they went over here to [a] school which was all black. Now everything seems to be going smoothly.

[But] it was hard at that time because of segregation. Take my husband. [He] went in World War II, and he was a mail clerk. When he got out of service, he came here and he took the exam. They had [an] open exam at the post office. He went down and he took the exam. Veterans [were] supposed to have had first preference. He made the highest mark of anybody who took the exam, and they didn't hire him because he was black. The man right across the street worked at the post office, and he spoke up for him, and they got on him, so he lost his mind. Lost his mind. They sent him down [to] Florida somewhere. Staggs, his name was, lived right across the street in the brick house. He's the one came over here and he wanted to know what did they tell [my husband] about the job because he made the highest score of anybody. Because, see, he did that when he was in the service, and he was a college graduate. So he just knew all about it, but they didn't give him the job carrying mail.

WALTER M. CAVERS

Born in 1910, twenty miles outside of Selma, Alabama, Walter Cavers felt compelled to leave his family in the late 1930s and "hobo" to Charlotte, North Carolina. When he finally returned some 20 years later, neither his eight siblings nor his father recognized him. The conditions that Cavers was trying to escape were common among rural African Americans in the Jim Crow era: poverty, maltreatment, brutal and often unpaid labor, a lack of educational opportunities, and the constant threat of white violence. Such conditions underlie both Cavers's account and the two long narratives that conclude this chapter: Willie Harrell's story of escaping from Mississippi and Ann Pointer's rich description of growing up poor in rural, Depression-era Alabama. As Cavers suggests, even well-intentioned New Deal programs such as the Works Progress Administration (WPA) did relatively little to alter the bitter truths of many black sharecroppers' lives.

We lived out in Autauga County [Alabama]. [My parents] were farmers. We had three rooms. There were nine of us. Our house was partly built with slabs. I don't know whether you know what a slab is. That's the outside of a log wood. [We were] just dusty farmers, and we lived on a plantation where, when the crops matured, we'd take the grain or cotton up to the boss's house. So many times I can remember that he'd sell the cotton and give us the cotton seeds. Back then everything was cheap. One of my ambitions, the biggest one, was to go to college. See, we didn't have no public schools back then. I attended school three months in a year. Then that's all we got until the next year. The white [children] would be going to school up to May or June. But we only had our school open in November and it closed in March or the last of February.

[One day] we were picking velvet beans. It was the kind of bean that would eat you up, scratch and sting you. I told my boss that I wanted to go to school. He asked me where I wanted to go. I told him Tuskegee. He turned around and hit me in the mouth and told me George Washington Carver should have been killed a long time ago.

I used to work for the gentleman [whose] place we stayed at. He asked me to turn a big log, and I couldn't turn it, and I walked off and came home. I told [my mother] what happened. She said, "Well, you better move on somewhere else and not let them find you here tonight." Sure enough they came. Just because I said I couldn't turn the log. Part of it did dawn on me before I left, that I wasn't a man, and I wasn't respected [by] the other race. I soon found that out. The whites, we lived on their place. We'd go possum hunting together, all that sort of thing. They never would bother you if they had a gripe against you until that night. Your best friend in the white race would come for you at night. They'd laugh and smile and everything until that night. You couldn't trust them. Then night come and they come for you and give you a good thrashing. Who were you going to complain to about it? Nobody. You just got a good whipping.

[In Alabama] I used to work on the WPA. I couldn't get nothing to eat. There wasn't no jobs. When [you] worked for the WPA, you saw no money. They gave you a slip, a little piece of blue paper, and you could take it up there where you buy your coal; they specify how much coal to give you. Then you got your meal. They put it in there and you put it in a croaker sack and throw it over your shoulder and come on home. We cleaned out ditches. You didn't get no money. You only got food. I was scheduled to work two days a week. That's all I could work. Say if you go in on Monday, you'd work Monday and Tuesday. Tuesday [at] three o'clock the truck would bring you back by the canteen. No, before we went to the canteen, they came around to all the employees and give them a green slip. That was to buy coal, food, and then they would give you a supplement which was dried beans, hog jaws, hog head, butter, meal, and I think it was five pounds of flour, five pounds of loose sugar. It depended on how many you had in the family.

I worked for 10 cents an hour in Alabama. If I was picking cotton— I never was a good picker—I would get 50 cents for that day's work. On a Sunday when they got ready to go, [my sisters] would wrap their hair in plaits out of a cotton stocking. My shoes, brogans, I'd take lard and soot and make up the shoe polish. A car was out of the question. I had worked all year and didn't get anything, didn't have anything, and I couldn't see where I was getting no more. So a gentleman came down. I saw him coming down across the field on his horse. He said to me, "Walter, let the mules cool off a little bit." I said, "Okay." I let them cool off and I got to thinking while I was out there and I just kept walking. Just kept walking. They looked for me and I was gone. What prompted me to leave there, it was spring and we were breaking land. I didn't even get a pair of shoes for the winter. I didn't get nothing. [The landlord] gave us an acre. My brothers and sisters, we worked hard on it and [made] a bale and a half of cotton. He took the cotton and gave us the seed. It wasn't nothing my father could do about it. So that was in the back of my mind. I said, "Well, I'm going to leave here. Don't know where I'm going, but I'm going to leave here." I had nothing to look forward to. He had taken everything I'd made. So I'm going to go through another year and come up with the same thing, not even shoes. Uh uh, [I] couldn't do that. So I just wandered off.

I didn't go back there no more. That was back in the thirties. I just had to get out from down there and I walked until I got to Calera. Then from Calera I went on to Saginaw, and I'd go around to the back door of some white residence and ask for some food. They'd always hand me something. I kept on trying to make it. Finally, I managed to reach Anniston, Alabama. That's where I got the train to come here. I remember, shortly after I was here [in Charlotte], sleeping outdoors for three or four nights in February. I took pneumonia and fell uptown on [the]

Howard University students picket the National Crime Conference in December 1934,
where they protested the refusal of conference leaders to discuss lynching as a national crime.
(American History Slide Collection, National Museum of American History, Smithsonian Institution)

street. Some people came by, and I told them I was sick, and they took me to a widow lady's house on Palmer's Street. That's where I stayed until I felt better and recuperated. They told the lady to take care of me, some of the church members from one of the large churches here. So she did. From there I managed to get a better place to stay.

I remember in my traveling: I was very tired. I'd been walking all day and it was hot. I decided to go out and lay down beside the road. I went off, I reckon about 15 feet. It was dark, and [I] laid down and went to sleep. I was awakened by a wagon. That was about one or two o'clock. It was a two-horse wagon. Whoever was driving it had a lantern, a light down in the bottom. So I said, "Guess, you're somebody going to town." So I went to sleep. I woke up a little after daylight. I didn't think of it no more. So then I noticed where I went to sleep. There wasn't no way in the world that a wagon or mule could come up through that cemetery because brush was all in the old slavery-time road. There were no tracks of no kind, no nothing. I said, "Let me get out of here. I laid down in the wrong place." I don't know what that was. I don't believe in ghosts, but people say there are ghosts. I've never been able to figure that out.

So I went on to Saginaw, later made my way to Anniston and the train. [It was a] steam engine, and they had what you called the mail car. I got between there and stood there until we got in Atlanta. When I got in Atlanta, the sheriff discovered me. I mean the conductor or somebody discovered I was on there. I ran through the yard, and finally they turned around and left. I was talking with a colored person who worked there in the yard, and he said Number 67 and 66 were going to pull out at 6:15. He said, "Now they've got to stop up here to get water." See, you pull that thing down and water the train. He said, "If you get in it, I'll show you where to stand." So I went with him up there. After a while, two locomotives came up with a string of cars. He pulled that thing down and put the water in there, and after he put it up, everybody went back in the train, [and] I climbed up between the mail car and the engine. That's where I stood all night long. So when I got in Charlotte somebody said to the conductor, "We got company back there." He came around there looking for me, and I went out on the right side and jumped off and went up Trade Street and then turned and went to Swatts Junkyard. Went over in there where they couldn't find me, and I stayed over there until the train left. Then I said, "Let me go and see if I can find something to eat and a place to stay." I never did that day, never did. So I slept at Martin's Shop up here on Statesville Avenue that night. The next night I didn't find anything. I was walking with no money and nowhere to live, and I was just sick. Those two Christian gentlemen, [Bailey Young and Dr. Moore, found me]. It was all I could do to make it to [Miss] Butler's. They put me to bed, and I had pneumonia. [Miss Butler] put tar, what they get out of pine, and covered my chest with that tar. I don't know what was in that stuff, but anyway, it made me well. I didn't have no doctor.

The gentlemen told her they would pay her. I had nothing to pay her with. She was an elderly lady, and she liked the home remedies. She used one of her home remedies. The next morning, I believe it was on a Friday, the Sunday school department [of] First Baptist Church, that I am now a member of, sent me thirteen dollars. The pastor there saw to it that I got food. I didn't know nobody, and I've been here ever since. Up and down. I just didn't know all of this could happen to a person in their lifetime.

I have had an uphill battle. I've been in jail. I've been accused of things I wasn't guilty of. But I got by. I got by. I had to go to jail for something I did not do. I spent a year in jail. A gentleman ran into me, a white gentleman, and they condemned me of driving too big a car. They didn't like that I had a new Lincoln. They couldn't give me a [proper] lawyer because you couldn't get a lawyer in [York, South Carolina]. The lawyer that I did get was a neighbor of the deceased. They played chess together. So I went to jail for that. I had a lot of aid. I had people from all over the country helping, trying to declare me [the victim] of a false charge. But it didn't do any good.

I saw a car coming. I was going south. When I got to the intersection where the light was green, I was sure the car meeting me would stop. He didn't. He tried to cross in front of me, and I hit his right fender. He was 84 years old, and he passed away. They say he had a heart attack. I don't know about that. But it wasn't any damage [to the car]. You couldn't hardly tell it was hit. I heard my attorney say, "Blow that picture up and make it as bad as you can." [And] I'm paying him! The [old man] was the one made the turn. He wasn't supposed to make a left-hand turn with ongoing traffic against the light, but he did it. Now it would have been something if I had hit him in the side or back, but it was on his left fender and I had to spend a year [in jail] for that.

A gentleman 10 miles from where the accident occurred said he heard my car speeding at 75 miles an hour. I had a lot of support because nobody didn't believe it. I still keep the brief. Everybody wanted to read it. But it was just a shame. I got no justice. If I had not admitted that I was a member of the NAACP, it probably wouldn't have been so hard. But you know how most people feel about the NAACP. If it had been here, tried in [North Carolina], I don't believe I would have got anything. The gentleman was 84 years old and blind, but he was white. So it cost me my freedom for some time. I had to stay away from my home for more than five years.

I was in jail only 12 months. The judge gave me probation, and they wanted me to come to South Carolina to live. You see, if you are on probation, unless you can get the probation officer in [another] state or country to supervise you [you cannot leave the state], and I wasn't lucky enough to do that. Finally, a gentleman in New York, a minister, gave me a job [and] then I got out. But I thought it was wrong [for them] to railroad me. It wouldn't happen this time of day, but it did happen back then. That was back in 1958, in York, South Carolina.

After [we moved back to Charlotte], we had a lot of threats, but they never identified themselves. We'd been here about a week. We had stayed in New York for most of the time. I remember one night shortly after we came back somebody called here and called me an SOB and said, "You're not going to live here and you'd better get out of town." So I hung up the telephone because I didn't think much of it. I thought it was just some-body playing a prank. In a few minutes the hospital called and said my wife was receiving the same threats. So then they brought her home and kind of looked out, patrolled this area. Nothing ever did happen about it. They thought I had hit that gentleman. It was just some white gentle-man would call. If I had known who [was threatening us], I would have had them arrested, but I didn't know who did it. Every afternoon we'd see cars parked. The lady on the corner called me and asked why this gentleman was up there, coming in to park every evening. So I called the police. The police came out and didn't find anybody. Possibly whoever it was had a [police] scanner. For years after I got back here, I had it pretty rough. I still held on. I got a church soon after, and I didn't have to apply for no job. I stayed there until the end of my probation.

I had a gentleman call me up, the richest person we have here in Charlotte. I knew him very well. I came home for dinner and while I was at dinner the phone rang. I answered it. He told me who he was. "Was that your car you were driving this morning?" I said, "Yes." He said, "Sell it. I don't want to see it on the street no more." That was before I had the accident. That was way back in the fifties. Then he called me again [after the accident] and said, "I could help you but I'm not. I told you to sell that damn car." So I said, "Well, whatever a person wants to drive, if they've got the money, [they] can drive it." Alonzo Mackey, a friend of mine, had to go to Pennsylvania and get a car. It was the biggest Chrysler they were making back then. They wouldn't sell him one here. I got [my Lincoln] through a person in another state. When I built this house, wouldn't a bank in town loan me one dime. I had to build it from scratch.

I got in trouble because I reached for something too big and it wasn't time for me to get it. I've had [church] members say that you can't, you don't drive a car [unless it] was just a secondhand car. When I first got one of those cars, I was living in Fairview Homes [public housing]. The supervisor over there told me she wanted my car. I told her, "No." I wasn't going to trade my new car to her. She wanted to swap. Because I didn't do it, I got outdoors. They told me to move. They told me [I had] a certain length of time. I said, "What are you doing?" I said, "I have a wife and a baby, and I can't move." So it hasn't been an easy road. A few bumps.

WILLIE HARRELL

Leaving Mississippi for Memphis, Tennessee, seems to have been the central fact in Willie Harrell's life. Harrell was born in 1927 and grew up sharecropping on a plantation owned by two brothers—two "old white honkies" whose cowboy hats defined them as much in his mind as their brutality to the men and women who worked for them. As a young man, Harrell decided to leave. He could not pay off his debts as his grandparents had done a short time before, but he managed to save enough money for a train ticket and began to watch for an opportunity to steal away.

Harrell offers suggestive glimpses of a mid-twentieth-century planta-tion life that was only a hairbreadth removed from nineteenth-century slavery. Adhering to racial "etiquette," whites denied blacks the courtesy titles of "Mr." and "Mrs." and forced them to enter white homes through the back door. They employed corporal punishment freely and kept their tenants' children out of school to work in the fields. And, just as slavehold-ers handed out rations, Harrell's landlords controlled "furnishing," the practice of providing clothing and other supplies to farmers on credit in anticipation of the harvest. Although they sometimes took tenants to town to buy supplies, Harrell's landlords more often drove a busload of groceries and other items from house to house, encouraging their workers to buy from them on credit and go ever further into debt.

Harrell's recollections of sharecropping are followed by an escape narrative reminiscent of runaway slaves' struggles to gain their freedom a century earlier. But then, as Harrell explained, it was "just like old slavery time" for him as a young man. "That's the way it was when I come up in the country."

Everything you had to do was outside of the door. It wasn't inside the house, like a bathroom. We had to take a bath in a bathtub in front of the fireplace. They didn't have it like it is [now], when I was coming up. Uh uh. It was in the country. Didn't nothing have it but the white people. Colored didn't have nothing like that.

You couldn't go in a front door down there. You had to go in the back. During that time, if you was allowed to go into white folks' house, you had to go around to the back. They used to feed you outside of the door. Outdoors. You wasn't allowed to go in there.

Didn't nobody have a car but white folks. Them big white people [who] own[ed] them plantations. Naw, we colored didn't know what a car was. Didn't know nothing but mules and tractors. That's all we knowed about. All we ever did [was] farmed. Cotton and corn and everything you could name, we raised it. That's all [we] ever knowed was to do it. Cotton and corn. Beans. Peas. Peanuts and potatoes and everything. They give us so much [farmland] a year, and if we cleared anything, like on the sale of cotton, they would give it. If we didn't, we had to go over another year if we was going to stay on that plantation, but if we were going to move on another plantation, well, that boss man come to pay for what we owe and move us on their plantation. That's the way they did. If you didn't want to stay with them, if you owed them some, this honkie would come over here and buy you from this man, and you go and live with him and work the crop there a year. Sometimes I get to thinking about that, and then when the *Roots* come on [television], that time when they have it on, I cut it off. I couldn't stand to look at it, because I went through some of it. I just flipped it off because it put me in a memory of what I used to go through when I was coming up. I couldn't stand to see it.

They used to come to our house down them dirt roads in the country once a month. That's when we'd get our groceries. They hauled it on a school bus. Wasn't no stores like it is now. They brings it to your house, see, and they allow you so much a month. You get it off of that bus. That's just like a grocery store. You couldn't go to no grocery store. They didn't have that many in town. Your food come out on a bus like that. You couldn't get but one pair of shoes a year off of the bus. You wore boots along there, [and] them overalls. My granddaddy wore a pair of boots until he couldn't get a string in them, but he tore them and just

Colored drinking fountain, county courthouse lawn, Halifax County, North Carolina, April 1938. (Photograph by John Vachon, Library of Congress, Prints and Photographs Division FSA-OWI Collection)

kept putting strings in them, you know, to walk on. Couldn't get no shoes or nothing like that till the end of the year.

You could [also] go to town, and shop there at them stores, and then, like you staying on a plantation, the white people loads coloreds up on the back of their pickup and take them to town and let them buy what they wanted, and they pay for it. Overalls and jumpers and shoes, like that, they would pay for it. They wouldn't give you the money to go and shop. They'd take you to shop. They would furnish you that for the year.

They always called me "Son" or "Harrell." That's all they ever knowed of my name. That's all they ever called me. [They] called [the older people] "Whitman" or something like that or "Uncle." Them old white folks call[ed] the older people "Uncle" or "Auntie." Wasn't nothing [older blacks] could do [about it]. They had to [just] feel good over it, because there's nothing they could do about it, but take it. That's right. That's all.

We couldn't go to no school. You take me. I didn't go to school but once or twice out of the year. That's right. I was in the first grade. I can't read and write now, because I didn't have the chance to go to school like children got now. Back there then, there wasn't no school like it is now. You had to walk seven or eight miles to the school. When it rained and you couldn't do nothing in the field or you couldn't do no other kind of work, that's when you had a chance to go to school, but as soon as the sun comes out and dry off, you in the field. [I] never did have no chance to go to no school in them days. You always doing something, cutting wood or [cutting] cross ties or [working in a] sawmill or doing something, [even] in the winter. I bet you I didn't go two days out of a month or a year or something to school.

Like Fourth of July we might go to a picnic; [the white plantation owners would] allow them to have, a big picnic out in the woods. That's once a year. That's all we would go. That's the only where to go. When they laid by the crops in July, you got something else still to do. You still working. You don't never have no [time] off. When they lay the crop by in July, you still cutting wood or doing something, the whole year.

Shit, you couldn't even look at a white woman hard back then when I come up. You would get hung. Yeah. Sure would. Back then was just all slavery times. Fasten you up and whip you just like you a dog or mule, animal or something. Yeah, they would tie you up or hem you up in a barn or something. [It would] be brothers on the plantation, two or three brothers, old white honkies, you know, wear them old hats. You see them old hats they got on, look like old Texas hats. Old honkies, I call them. Might beat you to death. [You] couldn't try to fight back then in them days. They would kill you. There wouldn't be nothing did about it. Yeah. Back then you couldn't fight back.

Blacks couldn't look at no white. But whites could look at blacks all they wanted. Ain't going to be nothing did about it. Yes sir, that happened right down there where I used to live on the plantation in the country.

If they'd catch you trying to leave, they'd take you back there and whip you, fasten you up in the barn and whip you. It's just like old slavery time. They hemmed me up in the barn like [where] they feed mules, and they whipped me. It was two brothers. Two old white honkies. There wasn't nothing I could do. They had a whip. Shit yeah, they whipped me. Sure. Wasn't nothing you could do, but take it. You try to resist [and] they would kill you.

[It was] just like I'm in prison or something. [They were] watching you. [You] couldn't go nowhere, had to stay there and get them cows and mules up and feed them. Five hundred and some cows and mules every day out of the week. You didn't have a chance to go nowhere. You couldn't go and visit nobody, your friends or nothing. You had to stay right there. I got tired. I made up my mind to get on away from there and I got away. That's what I did. [I] couldn't handle it no more. [If] I'd a stayed on there, [I'd have] probably been dead by now.

When I got here [to Memphis], I had to go out there to Gaston Hospital. They like to killed me down there. I had to slip off at night. When I left Mississippi, I left at night when they was in the bed asleep, around two and three o'clock at night. I got by their house. On a plantation, you can tell when they go to sleep, because the lights go out. When they put them lights out, you know they gone to bed then.

They had a gate. If you cross[ed] there in a car, [the noise] could wake [them] up, just like you crossing an old bridge. But see, I didn't have no car. I just stepped across there. They had the fences up, and the stuff on there would electrocute you, but see, I was smart enough [that] I got across there and hit that dirt road and got in the woods. I bet you I walked about five or six miles in the woods. Onliest way I could see [was] these little lightning bugs at night [that] light up. That's the onliest way I could see at night, and [my] clothes was tore off where I was going through the woods and trees and couldn't see, [and] it was tearing my clothes off until I got from there where I could catch this train. Man, I was as raggedy as a pan of kraut when I got here in them. [I] didn't have nothing but what I had [on], and they was tore all off. Old pair of shoes. Bare, with no socks or nothing on.

I left there around about two or three o'clock that night and caught the train and come into Memphis. Shit, I laid across the railroad track. Train woke me up, hitting the rail. The train was about six or seven miles [away], and they hit that rail and was blowing. It woke me up. I woked up and got up to see, and I just stepped back and took that handkerchief and did three flags like that, and they blowed and flashed that light twice. When they pulled on up beside me, the man, the conductor, whatever you call him, he let the gate down and I walked on in there and come on to Memphis. I had a ticket. I had worked until I made enough money.

I was by myself, because my granddaddy and grandma had done left from there. They left from there and come to Drew, and I was in the hills. See, when they settled up at the end of the year, they paid off, but I just stayed on. I was going to stay on till another year, but they got so bad I had to leave there. I had to run away from there.

I was scared until I got here, and it took me about—shit, it was a year or two before I got back like I should [be], normal. I didn't know nothing about Memphis then, and my auntie was taking me around trying to find a job when I come here. She was up here way before I left from Mississippi. She was working down[town], and I come here, and she was taking me before she [would] go to work [to] try to find a job. That's when I found a job working at Crosstown Storage. That was moving people, furnish[ing]s and stuff.

When I got a little older, I felt [I had become] a man from my boyhood. When I got to where I could manage and take care of myself. That's [after] I got here, but it took me about a couple of years before I could get myself together to see, realize, [that] I was a man instead of a boy. When I was down there [in Mississippi], it was just like the penitentiary or something. [I] couldn't go nowhere. Certain time to go somewhere. Certain time to come in. [I] didn't have the freedom as I got now.

I ain't been back there but once since I left from there and I'm 68 years old. I went down there [last year] because my sister was sick. I was scared then. I spent the night. I didn't sleep the whole night I was down there because I was scared. It was still in me. See? [I was in the] same place I was when they did all that they did to me, you know. But they all dead now. All them people's dead. Shoot, I didn't even know the town, it'd been so long since I had been down there.

I left by myself. I left some of my people down there. But self and God for us all; I was looking out for myself. They had to take care of their self. There's plenty of them [who] left and [live] right here in Memphis since I left from around there. Only thing, my sister [is] still down there, and you couldn't get a bulldozer to push her away from down there. She likes that. She worked for them [same] people, I don't know how long. Now she works in the hospital down there, and she got her own house now. She married and have a man. They got their own home, automobiles and everything. But shit, when I was coming up, there was no such thing. Colored had no automobile and [were] buying no homes down there. Nothing but white. If she wanted to stay down there and take it, that was her business, but I couldn't take no more of it. [I] got tired of it. I got to git, and I got, too.

I say the Lord has really been good to me, has blessed [me]. I'm telling you the truth. I've really been blessed by him. I was lucky they didn't kill me when I come from Mississippi. They tried to, but I got away from down there. [If] I'd have stayed on down there, they would have killed me.

I been misused and everything. I think of that. Sometime it gets next to me. You know how it'll come up, but the Lord blessed me. I'm blessed to be 68 years old for the time when I come up. I come up the hard way, mister. People got it made now. You see me sitting on this porch, but I have worked in my day. I'm telling you. I have worked in my day and that's when I said God blessed me to retire. I'm going to sit here and serve him and enjoy.

ANN POINTER

Ann Pointer grew up during the Great Depression, the youngest of six children of tenant farmers in Macon County, Alabama. She recalls the many ways that her family, particularly her mother, struggled to improve their situation through ingenuity and an emphasis on education. She also describes community life, suggesting that neighbors came together to face the hardships of the 1930s, then grew apart as they experienced greater prosperity during and after World War II.

I went to Chehaw elementary. It was [a] two-room school. One teacher taught one through three, the other taught four through six, and we could not go to school until October. It would have to be after Columbus

Day. And you know why? Because Mr. Childer's cotton had to be picked and gathered before the black children went to school. We started the school in the middle of October. Well, you know, we were the janitors, the maids. The first two weeks of school we had to clean the school, clean around the school, and get the school in shape. So we really didn't start our classes up until November. We went to school November, December, January, February, March, April, and the first of May school closed. That's all of the school that we got. My mother said *they* only went three or four months. I started school in 1934, and I was the youngest in my family. I had four brothers and one sister, and they were all older than me. Well, see, they started school back then, but they went less months than I did.

The house we were living in only had two rooms. One room and a kitchen. They were big rooms, and you did everything you wanted to do in those two rooms. Mama had six children, and her and Papa made eight. There was no walls in this house. It was just the boards on the outside, you see what I'm talking about? There was no ceiling. You could look up and see the tin [roof], because it was just the joist and the tin through there. When it rained, it leaked. It was a stacked chimney, [where] the fireplace was in both rooms. You had a flue, where you could put your stove flue through that chimney. Then you had a fireplace in this kitchen also. The way Mama had her house fixed: the big bedroom was a great big room. She had [a] bed here and a bed there and a small bed here. She had a dresser and a table and chairs, and I can remember a rocking chair she had in that room. She had one or two beds in the kitchen, over against the wall. Over in one section of this kitchen was her kitchen, she had a stove, her table and safe. They called it a safe, but she kept her dishes in there, and down in the bottom was some of her groceries. Just one part of the kitchen was for kitchen use, and she had wooden barrels where she kept her flour. They bought flour by the hundred pounds, and cornmeal. She had big barrels with tops on them where she kept this cornmeal. We didn't have a refrigerator or nothing like that. We didn't have a well in the yard. We had to go to a spring for water. [The landlord] would not dig a well. He did not make it pleasant for his tenants. You lived in that house, and Mama would take cardboard and put up where the wind was blowing in, because when you [were] laying in the bed in the wintertime, the air would be blowing up the sheets on the bed.

And the floor, there were cracks in the boards. Mama stop[ped] up them cracks as best she could with what she had to keep [out] anything that wanted to come in there, any small animal, a possum or anything else. Mama would always [fill] the cracks and try to bolt up the doors. In the wintertime, she would take the ironing board and put it down to the foot of the bed and tuck the covers down to keep the wind from blowing the covers up to keep you cold in the bed.

And in the wintertime, you couldn't open the window. You'd be sitting to an open fireplace like this, and they'd have the door wide open. Everybody would be sitting near the fireplace here, and you sit as close as you could, and your legs in front would be [blistered] from being burnt from sitting too close to that fire. And couldn't nobody laugh at your legs because theirs was burnt up too. [Laughter.] It [the heat-damaged skin?] would soon come off. They would take tallow and rub your legs and get it off. But that's the way you had to live, and, taking a bath, there was not much privacy. [In] the summertime, my brother would bathe in the barn. Mama would heat water in a wash pot. My mother was very strict about baths.

[Mama] was a very proud woman, and she was small in stature, and [had a] nice figure and everything. Even after having those children, she had a beautiful figure. When she would dress up and go downtown [to Tuskegee], she'd buy a big jar of blue-seal Vaseline [and] Octagon soap. Do you know what Octagon soap is? It's like a lye soap. It's made out of red devil lye. They sell it now in the store, and I use it extensively myself because if you had a rash or insect bites or anything on you, [Mama] would lather you with that Octagon soap real good, and it would really take care of insect bites or any rash, anything that you had, and chiggers and all that. This was [Mama's] cosmetics. Nowadays people got a dresser full of everything. She'd buy that Octagon soap. She washed her clothes with it, she washed her dishes with it, you bathed with it, and she bought that blue-seal Vaseline and one can of Cashmere Bouquet talcum powder. That was her cosmetics. It lasted indefinitely.

This was in the thirties, and I didn't have a dress, and Mama had to go into her trunk and get a sheet she could sew, and [she] cut a white sheet and made me a little sundress. When she made it, she washed it out and made starch out of plain flour boiling on the stove and ironed [it.

She] made me a little dress for me, and then made me some panties out of the same material. [I] went to town barefoot as a yard dog. I was a little girl, but I enjoyed it. She would sit up and make her boys' clothes. We didn't have clothes to wear, really and truly.

[My mother] had brothers that was living in New York. They had never seen me and my brother, because they were away from here before we were born, but they [did] know Mama had us. They'd go around and get used clothing by the trunkful. I got one of the trunks up under the house right there. They would get clothes of all description and send them here, and Mama would renovate those clothes, and my mother was so scornful she would take the armpits of those clothes, cut the armpits out and make them over. I realize now why she did it. The only coat I had until 1940 was the coats that came from up there, because there was no way for [my family] to buy nothing. Wasn't no money. [People] were making 50 cents a day, if they worked for a wage hand. You worked as a wage hand, and that mean[t] you worked your little farm and when you caught up with yours, somebody would hire you who had the money, to work for 50 cents. And now don't think you worked eight hours. You went out there at six o'clock in the morning, and you worked until you couldn't see in the evening for that 50 cents. Picking cotton, chopping cotton, pulling corn, pulling fodder, or whatever they had for you to do. You worked as a wage hand for 40 and 50 cents a day. And you know just what kind of living that was. My mother would iron white shirts for those doctors at the veterans' hospital. I have seen her iron 35 white shirts in one day, and they were only paying her five and 10 cents a shirt. But any kind of money beat no money at all. That's what was going on, and everybody was bootlegging, just about, who could.

My mother was a strong person, too. I couldn't have stood what she stood. I don't believe I could have stood it. I would've left, and her brothers tried to get her to come north and bring us out of this hectic situation. But Mama didn't want to go. She said, "I couldn't control my children in the North." Mama wanted us to go to school, she wanted us to be good, and she thought the North would swallow us up. Maybe it would have, you know. I can't tell. But I wanted to go anywhere, but here. I had a nervous breakdown at school. I had a slight heart attack. The teacher didn't know it, either, because we didn't talk about nothing. I couldn't hear, I couldn't talk, but I could see. I was just sitting and staring, and when I sit there so long, when my hearing came back to me, it looked like the children were way off. I could hear them talking. But I'm going to tell you, if you [are] a child, and you get up in the morning time, and there is no food in the house—no kind of food nowhere, I mean nothing, just the cupboard is bare—and you've got to get up and go on to school and act like nothing's happened, [and] you cannot say a word or let anybody know that you haven't had anything to eat, and [you] didn't know when you were ever going to get anything else, that is a horrible experience for a small child. A child seven or eight years old and you don't have food to give them, that child carries a heavy burden. My mother was proud. We could not tell people that we didn't have anything. You had to act like you didn't want anything, just go on. You just could not say nothing.

But I tell you what, even though we were poor as church mice, God still blessed us with a brain. Other children had fine clothes, they had fine homes, they had fathers and mothers who had money, but they were dumb as the devil. God blessed us all with a good brain, therefore the teachers had to take notice because [laughter] everybody excelled. God knows what to do for you. My sister was an excellent mathematician. My brothers were all smart, they had gifts, talents. I don't care how poor you are or how bad you look, if you know and nobody else don't know, that's going to make you out to be out front. That's what kept us out front. I may not be able to repeat this ever again, but I hope you are taking notice of this. That's the only thing that we were able to do, is stay out front at school and at church and everywhere else because of our abilities. All six children had abilities other children couldn't touch. My brothers were great athletes. They were very good in sports. That kept them out front, and [they were] smart in books as well. So the teachers all took a shine because we didn't have nothing, you know. People used to look down on you when you didn't have nothing, you were just a nobody. But if you had a brain, you still was out there. That's what kept us out front. And Mama being the type person she was, she didn't drop her head even though she didn't have nothing. She worked hard, working in people's houses. Seven days a week she had to get there and cook breakfast for them, wash all the clothes, iron all the clothes, clean up the house, and everything for four dollars a week, seven days a week.

I worked at that hospital for $100 a month, $25 a week, but I made it out of there. You see, wages was low, but I told my mother—and I'm glad I got a chance to tell her before she died—I said, "Mama, I went to many extremes working here and working there, but I finally made my living, retired off of what you gave to me." My mother gave me a business course when I was going to high school. I said, "I made my living and retired off of what you gave me." That made her feel proud. So we had a very, very hard life, but we weren't the only ones. There were people that was worse off than we were.

It was a farming community, and most everybody was planting. Cotton was your chief money source. If [they] didn't have but one acre of cotton, most people [still] had their little cotton. They did that to buy their winter shoes and clothes for the children. Everybody had their little flower yard, they had their garden, they had their cows, chickens, and hogs. Everybody was living good. Well, really and truly, in the thirties, it was a kind of a rough go. Everybody was having a tough [time] after that Depression and the banks closed on the people's little money. My grandmother had a little money in the bank when the bank shut down. They didn't give her nothing but a piece of property over in Tuskegee. I think it was a half an acre or something or other. But my grandmother, that was my mother's mother, she raised turkeys and chickens and things, and she said, "I don't want to live in town." She was able to sell that little piece of property to somebody for $35, and that's all she got. My other aunt, my father's sister, she started working at the veterans' hospital when it first opened, in the laundry, and she saved up good money, and they took hers. The bank shut down, didn't give them tootie-squootie. My brother often said that [the] times we went through would make a hog eat onion, make a monkey suck a lemon, and God knows that was the truth.

People were eating what they could get. You never heard about no mud in the water, have you? My father would go and stop off a place, and they would get in the water and roll the[ir] pants legs up. We'd go down there and stand with bags, and they'd dig the bottom, and muddy that hole, and when the water get muddy, the fish come to the top. More fish come to the top, you see. Then they put the cocoa bags down and scoop them fish up, and they'd muddy the water every year like that and get the fish. Everybody would come and get them a big bucket of fish, all kinds, but my mother never appealed all that. She'd say, "Don't come near the house with them." We'd have to cook them outdoors because she didn't allow them to bring just anything in her house. And my father would hunt. He was a great sportsman and would go hunting. They'd kill rabbits, squirrels, possums, birds and anything they could find in the woods to kill, small animals. They cooked it and we ate it. That's why I don't like wild game right now, because I say I've had too much rabbit, squirrel, possum, and everything that crept or crawled. My father killed it and brought it there, and Mama cooked it. He had plenty [of] chickens, and he'd do breeding [of] these fighting roosters. You ever heard of fighting roosters? He raised them game roosters and things, people'd come there for that.

When World War II came along, people was loving in the community. All in the thirties through all of this trouble, from wall to wall, everybody had [been neighborly]. If you had sickness, it was everybody's sickness, and they could ring that church bell down here [in Chehaw]. It was a bell in that church, and they had a sexton. [People] could listen because there wasn't no cars and things running like there are now. I could listen and hear that bell ring and tell you what was the matter. They had a [certain] way to ring it. My grandmother and I were right across up here in a cotton field one day, and she heard the bell, and she say, "You know, [there] is something the matter. Somebody [is] mighty sick down there in Chehaw." She said, "Baby, I'm going to the house, and let's go and see [why] the bell ring." She said, "Put a fire in the stove and heat some water where we can bathe off and go down there." Before we could get to the house, a guy named Sam Kelly came across there. See, they'd get somebody and run them through and tell the news. Wasn't no telephone or anything. [Sam Kelly] said, "Miss Clare, Miss Bees just died a while ago. She stuck a nail on her foot and [it] give her lockjaw." [My grandmother] said, "Well, I heard the bell. We should come right on and down there." If you got sick, they'd come and sit at your house all night long and help you, wait on you and everything. All of that was loving. You'd walk miles. I would be so sleepy, and Mama would stay up with those people and help, take a fan and fan them [because] they'd be so sick. We'd sit down on the floor, and we'd spend the night with them, and everybody did like that.

But when World War II came, the people became indifferent. They began to drift apart, and you know what did it? They were hanging on [to] a little more money. When they didn't have nothing, there was a lot of love existed. But [then] they began to get a little more money, and they went up a little bit on the wages, and they were building these airports and places like that, and men that was making 50 and 75 cents went up to $4 [or] $5 a day. And the people began to become indifferent and get apart. They stopped going to church as much, and they start[ed] their waywardness. I noticed a great change [in] every child, what they began to do. They could get clothes. They had food, and something they weren't used to.

You can't appreciate the sunshine if you ain't never been in the rain. Every time I go in the house, if I go in the bathroom, I [say], "Lord, I thank you," because there are many times I've had to go I-don't-know-where to the bathroom. When I light my heaters, I say, "Thank you Jesus," because I had to cut wood and saw down trees like a man, you understand me? [After] toting water to fill up the buckets and things for bathing [and] washing clothes, I consider thanking Jesus for everything. When I get in that car, I say, "Thank you Jesus," because I used to have to walk to town. Now I can drive, ride.

It was so many things happening back then, when these white people [would] get mad with someone on their farm and kill them and throw them in the creek. When the rain [fell] back here last month [laughter], a party of us [was] sitting out there on the porch, and I said, "Somebody must be in the creek, because God knows in heaven when it used to rain like that, it would rain until it would wash them out." I know one incident [where] they killed a man and threw him in [the] creek down there, and the water washed him up. They said the sheriff killed him. I ain't never found out why, but it was so many things happening around here. It isn't a lynching, just a killing. Now, Walter Gunn, I knew him. Walter Gunn, that was his name. He was messing with some woman, they say. I don't know because I was a girl, but that was in the forties, and they had a deputy here named Fawcett. They said Fawcett was messing with the same woman or something, but Walter Gunn was caught in this man's house, [or] this woman's house, or something. Fawcett [went there and] ran [along] the road outside the house and blowed [Walter Gunn's] brains out right in his own yard. Ain't nothing been done about it. I often think about it.

And do you know, just like you and I sitting here right now, that was a time [when] we [might have] had a sheriff come and knock on the door [knocks]. I might have said, "Who is it?" "The law." Well, you go to the door to see, and he [would] just bust on past you and come on in there and tumble your house up from here to hell, you understand me? Wasn't nothing, no search warrant or nothing. Anything he felt like doing, he just walk in on you and tumble your house up, and don't tell you why or how.

It was a family lived right down the street there. They had a bunch of children, maybe eight or ten, and they were sharecropping with the man at Notasulga. They could not settle up. The crops didn't do well, and so [the landowner] was going to take their possessions. They owned that little house they were in, but they knew that he was going to take it. They had a son that was grown, and at the time, he was in prison, but he broke out [when] he heard about the situation, because they had a lot of tiny tots over there. I don't know where he got a car from, but he got a car and he got word to his mother to sell somebody their little lot and to get ready [because] he was going to come through. [They had] to be ready because he had to pick them up because they were after him. [His family] did just like he told them, secretly. We didn't know about it, living right here, [because] they were so quiet with it. Those people couldn't read nor write, but they had good sense. They went to [a man] and told him they wanted to sell that little place they had [and] he bought it. They got ready, left everything there, except for the clothes they had and a little thing they were going to carry. [The son] came here [about] midnight, and they went to Boston, Massachusetts. That's where they lived and that's where they died, and some of the children are still up there now. They did much better to leave here, and that man [the landowner] didn't know hell nor how they went because [the son] told them not to tell nobody where they were going, and they didn't tell nobody. I went to Boston in 1972, and I called this lady on the phone, and we talked, you know, because she had never come back. Her husband came back through here once and came by to see my mother, and he told her how good it was for him in Boston, how he had found work, and he found health for the children.

He was dressed real nice, and we had never seen him dressed up. I remember the last thing he told my mother, he said, "If I don't see you no more, we'll meet over there." He meant in the promised land, and we never saw him again. Those people went away. They got away from here because that man was going to take everything they had and no doubt come here shooting, but they sure fixed him. And that's what you call one of those things because they were going to have a reprisal and a killing, too, if they hadn't left here.

All of this took place in Macon Country, but this was in the Notasulga area. This man would go and talk to people when they were getting ready to pitch a farm, where[ever he] saw a bunch of children and a husband and wife who was field hand[s]. He'd sit down and offer them a big proposition, "Come on and live in my place. I do this for you and I do that for you." Make a lot of promises, and he went to [another] country and got a man and a wife and his children and moved them up there on his place. He was making a good crop because he had good wage hands. When the cotton was fixing to open, he went there and started a big mess with those people and ran them off away from there, where he wouldn't have to settle up with them. Once this man get his crowd—they call it a mob crowd—and come to your house at night, then you going to leave there as fast as you can. Because you don't know what's going to be the next visit, whether there'd be a killing or not. He ran those people off, and they left. I don't know where they went, whether they went up north or anything. They didn't get nothing. Fixed a whole crop, didn't get a dime.

You know what happened? My husband said he knew this man had been doing that for years, and people never knew how he could do it. He didn't never have to pay nobody because he was running them off when he gathered his crops. [The man] came over and told [my husband] and his [first] wife, "Come on. The people slipped off from me, and they wouldn't gather the crop, so I'm going to need somebody to gather and I['ll] pay you so much a week." [My husband] said he already knew what had happened. He went on and moved into the house and put his furniture and everything in there. [The man] had him cutting stove wood for his stove, keeping the yard up, and gathering the crop, and my husband's [first] wife was cooking for them and washing and doing

all that. So [my husband] told him, "Mr. Hatcher, you're going to have
to pay me by the week." "All right, I don't mind that." He knew how it
was, and said [that] every Friday he would come and pay him. He told
him, "When you get through gathering those potatoes and things, I'm
going to give you so many of them. I'm going to give you so much corn
and so much of peanuts, and I'm going to give you the remnant bale of
cotton for gathering it." [My husband] said he knew he wasn't going to
do it.

So, after he started gathering everything, this man start acting funny.
When you [are] around a person, you can tell. [If] they come up and
don't speak, you know they got hell on them. [My husband] said he told
his wife, "Now I tell you what I want you to do. You just get the baby
and every time you go to your mother's, carry some dishes and glasses
and whatnot, and when you get through carrying the cook things out
of here, I will get the mattresses and things by night and move them
someplace." He said that they moved by night, but he [and his wife]
would go there every day just like they were living there and do the work
[and] act like nothing weren't happening. So, one day, his wife was over
at her mother's, and he went there. He was out there that morning when
Hatcher got up. He was cutting wood, [and] then Hatcher got into it
with him. "You did so and so and so and so and so and so, and I tell
you right now I want you to move out of my house." [My husband] said,
"All right." He dropped the axe and walked on away. Hatcher went and
kicked the door open of the house. Snap! He had already moved. See,
he had planned to do that. He fixed him and got on away from him.
And those type things, child, that happened all of the time. All of the
time.

Everywhere the [white] man has got, maybe from eight to fifteen tenants,
on his place, there is a woman there that he is messing with. Then you
going to see the flowers start to blooming, the children start to popping.
A white woman told me one time—we were talking about a situation—
she say, "What if your husband built a house right adjacent in the back of
your house, and he slept with another woman and was having children
by her right in your yard? What would you do?" I said, "I wouldn't stay

there. I would leave." She said, "Well, I didn't go anywhere because, when he asked for my hand in marriage, he asked my father could I be controlled. My father told him 'Yes' because my father was guilty of the same thing." She said, "I stayed there and while this woman worked in the field, I had to tend to the children." Now that happened right here in Macon County, and his wife had to take that. I told her, "I wouldn't have taken that because I would've been gone, and I wouldn't [have] went back to my father, neither. He wouldn't know where I went. My husband get brazen enough to bring a woman in my house and he going to stay there and have children by her—uh-uh, it ain't going to happen with me. I wouldn't put up with it." But a lot of these white women have had to put up with it and helped raise the children. Now, I know what I'm talking about. They all have been pushed about like that because this man is going to do what he want to. You don't know what he's doing until the flowers start to blooming, that's what they say. When you see these mixed-up children come out [snap] from there, you know that he's stirring about. This woman that's got these children, she's going to dress better than anybody in the community, and she got money all the time, and her children [are] well taken care of. He does it undercover, but everybody know what's going on. But they ain't going to say nothing. They talk about it, but they can't do nothing about it because the man own them. It's like I say, what is slavery? Yes, they abolished the chains, they abolished this here, abolished that, but you still a slave—you understand me?—in so many words because that greenback dollar can make you a slave. When you don't have anything and you trying to make it, you're still a slave. Most people look down on that word, but they'll find out that they are.

You don't have to wonder about these flowers blooming. You can just look at the population and tell. Haven't you paid attention to that? Different people mixed up. You don't know what they are. They got some everything in them, and you can see that there's been visitation by someone just [by] looking at the group, this bouquet. That's what I'm saying. And the Klan [is] talking about they want a pure race. Now who mixed up this race, you understand me? The bouquets have been made now. In the classroom, if you look at a class of 32 children, you see some of everything. You know what I'm saying. It's been like that all of the time, and it

Lillian Hooten with her doll, Pensacola, Florida, early 1920s. Psychologist Kenneth Clark's 1953 doll test asserted that many black children preferred white, not black, dolls. In Brown v. Board of Education, *the NAACP cited this evidence in arguing that school segregation contributed to the psychological damage of African American children.*

(Photograph courtesy of Henry and Lillian Hooten, Tuskegee, Alabama)

brought about a lot of dissension among the blacks as well as whites. If a black man's got a wife, and she have a white baby, he on the man's place [and] he can't say nothing. You see what I'm talking about. Do you see the injustice in that? Even though he doesn't like it. Now you know what he's going to do? He's going to mistreat his wife under the cover and give her a very, very bad time, and this child will be knocked about, which is wrong. Going back to the [white] man, he done stood it all up and he gone on about his business, left it like that.

My brother left early, left school. He said, "I'm going so I can get Mama off of the man's place." And he came back and built the house right there so we wouldn't have to stay on the man's place. My brother paid for it to get us off. It's always somebody in the family to get you off the man's place, and if you ain't got nobody to get you off the man's place, you going to take his foolishness until you slip away from there. You ain't got no money, [but if] you got a relative or friend, they would slip and send you the money. They couldn't send it to his mailbox, because see your mail came to the man's box if you lived on his place, and they censored all your mail. So [your relative or friend had to] send the mail to the minister. See, the church played an important part in this. [Your relative or friend] would send that money to the minister and tell him what it was for, and that minister would [get it to you]. You couldn't catch the train over here at Chehaw. You'd have to go where nobody would see you leave because they [white landowners] would try to stop you. They act like you were their own.

[One time] a man came here. He thought he was talking to a friend, but he was talking to a staunch enemy. He told me, "I ain't got nobody to work. Those damn yo-yos went off up yonder and sent their money back here and slipped all of them away from here." That's what he called them, "the yo-yos." [Laughter.] I said, "Oh yeah?" I knew all about it, but I just pretend I didn't. Shoot, "slipped them all away from here." Once you get one relative or a good friend that go up north and make it pretty good [they could help you]. And then, if they tell [the people they are working for] what's the trouble, they would give them the money, them people up north. [Laughter.] I was working up there and a lady said, "How come you going back to Macon County? You up here, you doing well." I said, "Well now, look, I don't live on the man's place." I said, "We live on our own place, and I'm going to school." She said, "Well I thought the man owned all the places down there." She really had never been south. She said, "I was just saying you ought to be glad to be away from down there." I said, "Oh no, we own our own places. We don't live on the man's place." They call him "the man," you know.

I'm telling you the truth. It was real funny but, you know, one thing: if you got a child and the man want him to work, he go and tell the teacher that "this boy can't come to school right now because he['s] working for me." He'd go there and get him out of school and [laughter] make him go to the field. I'm telling you. It sound funny to you because you never have been subject to nothing like this, but that's what I want to tell you: how horrible it is when, everything you do, the man's got to approve it. Either you [are] his concubine or—many women, you know, fell prey to their [white men's] sexual desires and all that kind of stuff. It's still prevalent, but see they can't do like they used to do. They can't run over these women like they used to.

So, that's the plight of the Jim Crow days. It was something.

HERITAGE AND MEMORY

During the Jim Crow era, African Americans passed down memories of slavery, the Civil War, and Reconstruction as well as lessons about family genealogies, spiritual striving, and the experience of emancipation. These memories formed the bedrock of African American identity in the midst of a social order that sought to deny African Americans a legitimate heritage or place in society. The efforts of black elders to preserve community history and family heritage became powerful tools for maintaining dignity and hope in the grim presence of racial segregation. By talking about the past, African Americans used oral traditions to convey knowledge to the younger generation, much as their slave forebears did.

Elders invoked their experiences of slavery to strengthen African American resolve in the difficult environment of Jim Crow. They also told stories of the adversities slaves faced in order to encourage and cajole younger blacks to excel. Asked why former slaves stressed education to such a great extent, Mary Bodie of Enfield, North Carolina, replied: "The slave parents, they knew they'd had a hard way in life, and they were determined their children [would] have a better life." Ann Pointer recalled that former slaves in Macon County, Alabama, were equally insistent: "They kept saying, 'Make something of yourself, be my dream. I can't read or write, but I want you to make something.' "

Over time, the oral histories of slavery and segregation began to merge into a powerful stream of popular knowledge used to teach young people to be constantly on guard lest they fall prey to the capricious actions of white folks. Jessie Lee Chassion's family in New Iberia, Louisiana, grew up knowing that a young white boy had chopped off the finger of her grandmother during slavery times. Chassion's grandmother, in common with many of her contemporaries, carried the physical scars of slavery for the rest of her life: "She had marks across her back where they had whipped her." Black youths who came of age in early-twentieth-century Wilmington, North Carolina, listened to hushed accounts of the Wilmington Race Riot of 1898, when bands of white men shot down African Americans in the streets. Lillian Quick Smith's grandfather told her: "There were a lot of colored people just falling in the river down there. Killing them. Like flies." Edgar Allen Hunt, whose family had to flee Arkansas in the wake of a racial clash when he was very young, remembered his father's teaching: "He told us what to expect, how to act, how to stay away from them [white people]. Don't trust them. I mean he gave us the whole ball of wax having been in the race riot seeing some things. So, coming up, we kind of knew what we were supposed to do." These memories served as powerful teaching tools for black survival.

Yet, even the most painful recollections also contained stirring memories of religious faith, striving, and resistance. Blanche Davis, born in 1900, recalled, "This old lady, she would tell us about how they would whip the people in slavery times, and, of course, my great-grandma told me a lot about how they would tie them down and beat them. But they didn't ever whip her. She said she [resisted] them when they come up to her and she [would] just knock them out. That was my great-grandma." While working for an abusive employer during the Jim Crow years, Davis invoked the memory of her grandmother's clandestine prayers in slavery times to call on the Lord for a better job: "After serving lunch for them that day—they had a bridge party—I decided I'd go in there and ask God to give me another job. And I did. I went in the kitchen and I said, 'Now, my grandmother, she had to pray with her head in a bucket, but I'm asking you today for another job.' And I got that job, worked on it thirteen years and eight months without any trouble. So I do know the Lord will answer prayers."

Oral traditions played a major role in African American survival during Jim Crow. Without the aid of instructional manuals, African American mothers taught their daughters the skills of midwifery, much the way their own mothers had taught them how to deliver babies. This experiential knowledge was especially vital, given the fact that blacks were excluded from most hospitals in the Jim Crow South. Drawing upon their historical memories, African American midwives and others also handed down the secrets of herbal remedies and medicinal cures to treat ailments ranging from pneumonia to snakebites.

Attempts to piece together a coherent family heritage were gravely burdened by the genealogical wreckage of the domestic slave trade. Historians estimate that nearly one million African Americans from the Upper South were sold into the Cotton Kingdom of the Deep South in slavery's final decades. This destruction of family and kinship ties echoes in the haunting narrative of Ann Pointer who meets a man on a Virginia passenger train who may—or may not—be her relative.

The politics of white supremacy, which decreed by legislation and custom that African Americans should remain in a subordinate place in American society, meant that history itself was transformed into a terrain of cultural and social struggle. Black and white southerners dueled over the meanings and memories of slavery, including the rape of black women and the separation of slaves' families; the Civil War; Reconstruction; and even the Thirteenth, Fourteenth, and Fifteenth Amendments to the U.S. Constitution as surely as they dueled over the everyday workings of segregation in their lives. While many white southerners—and academic historians—viewed slavery as a "benevolent" or "civilizing" institution, African American memories of slavery that were preserved in black communities emphasized its cruelty.

African Americans could expect little if any acknowledgment of their history in America as they had experienced it. For this reason, family and community efforts to preserve and pass down oral traditions were crucial to the survival of African American identity and heritage. Georgia Sutton, a black schoolteacher in North Carolina, recalled, "The only way you would [teach black history] you'd have to sneak that in. It was just never included in textbooks. They followed the white book and we were taught the principles of government. We were taught the Constitution. Most of them, naturally, [omitted] certain amendments especially for the black children. But curriculum-wide, we learned about white America and the white American government, because there were very, very few of us in it then, practically none."

Black and white communities at times observed opposing holidays because their interpretation of the past differed radically. For example, African American communities organized Decoration Day ceremonies that honored black soldiers and sailors who had fought in the Union Army during the Civil War. On these days of remembrance, African Americans' service to the Union cause, and by extension, their struggle for liberation, was celebrated and honored as proof that black people had earned their freedom and citizenship. In a similar manner, Emancipation Day celebrations honored the survivors of slavery. Mr. Otto Gainey of Gainesville, Florida, who was 104 years old when he was interviewed, recalled that during his early youth, Emancipation Day was the most important holiday in his community. In the late nineteenth century, African American communities also celebrated the birthdays of Frederick Douglass and Abraham Lincoln. In contrast, southern white communities commemorated their own days: the birthday of Robert E. Lee; veterans' days that honored Confederate veterans; and ritual observances of the deaths of Confederate icons such as Jefferson Davis.

As the last generation of former slaves and black Civil War veterans aged and passed away, African American elders lamented what seemed to be a tendency of younger people to forget the sacrifices of earlier generations. In addition, memories of slavery were often too painful to share with skeptical youths and those who had not experienced the institution firsthand. Still, African Americans tried to preserve their history by means of oral traditions that most Americans are only now beginning to understand. This was the complex world of heritage and memory into which the people in this chapter were born.

CATHERINE SHAW

Catherine Shaw was born in December 1909 in Chapel Hill, North Carolina. When asked about the stories that her elders passed down to her

Unidentified family portrait, taken at the end of the nineteenth century.
(Courtesy of George Ferrell, Tuskegee, Alabama)

mother, Mrs. Shaw recalled that the slave experiences were paramount:
"I think that's about the biggest thing they talked about was how [slave
owners] treated the folks in the slavery times, what her mother had told
her about the way they did them." In common with other ex-slaves,
Mrs. Shaw's great-grandmother carried the physical scars of slavery for the
rest of her life.

My grandmother said she was a slave. She was my great-grandmother,
my mother's grandmother. And [the slave owners] treated them so bad,
she would run away. I said: "Well Granny, where was you going?" She
said she don't know, she just getting out of there, she'd run away. But
they would catch her, and they would whip her. Then they would stand
her upside the fireplace and let her blister. And then they would take a
paddle and paddle every one of them blisters that was on her and put
salt and pepper in them. And you can't treat anybody any crueler than
that. She said they used to shackle her feet together [to] keep her from
running away. And you'd have to walk from the kitchen to the big house.
Course the kitchen was set off from the big house and in order to walk,

you couldn't walk straight so her feet were like that where she'd have to walk with that chain shackled around her ankles, so she couldn't run away.

ILA JACUTH BLUE

Ila Blue's story about her grandfather's experiences during the Civil War in North Carolina reveals the survival strategies that African Americans employed during and after slavery. Blue's family continues to tell about her grandfather's dramatic encounter with Confederate and Yankee soldiers because it demonstrates the ways that African Americans often masked their true aspirations behind a veil of acquiescence designed to fool powerful white men.

My paternal grandfather . . . Let me tell you about him. Mama told us this. He told Mama, of course, because he was, I think, 17 when the war was over. He lived in Hoke Country [North Carolina] between Laurinburg and Raeford and Fayetteville and Red Springs and Aberdeen. He said that the Yankees came through and just swept anything they wanted to, because they had won. He said that they [the slave owners] called him and said, "Dave, I want you to keep the horses." It's a place we call Lumber River; it's not a river, but there's water and a bridge there and everything. Said, "I want you to keep them down here." And all the white people in there, the white men, brought their best horses—because the Yankees, as you know, were riding through, just taking them—and gave them to Dave. Said, "Dave, you keep them quiet now." He had them down at Lumber River, this place you can go to, you wouldn't see the horses. It's sand all around. It could have been a beach if you had somebody to do it, you know. Because we look at it now when we go to Laurinburg, say, "Dave was down there with the horses." He had a gang of horses, all the best that these people had, because the Yankees would ride through and just take them.

[My grandfather] was listening. He could hear them coming, hear the Yankees coming, because they was making a lot of noise. They had won and they were taking things. He said he just waited. He had on a white shirt. So he took it off and he was down there with the horses. He heard them hit the bridge, a long bridge over Lumber River. He took off, took his white shirt, and he stopped them right there. He said, "Come over here and get all these horses." They went down there, and every man took one, and he rode off with them. He knew he had to go or [the Confederates] would have killed him.

He went on with the Yankees, because he knew he had to go now. He stayed off for years, he said, he rode on, and finally went to New York. He stayed off until he was grown. He gave all the horses away. [Laughter.] Said he took off his shirt. "Come on!" Then he jumped bareback, didn't even have a saddle, like a wild man, rode on off with them. [Later] he came back, and I guess all the masters were dead when he came back.

ANN POINTER

Scholars estimate that approximately one million African American slaves were torn from families and kin groups in the border states and sold into slavery farther south to feed the Cotton Kingdom's expanding frontier in slavery's final decades. Ann Pointer, born in Macon County, Alabama, often wondered about her lost relatives in the Upper South, one of whom she believes she may have met quite by accident on a train in an incident related here. Interestingly, Pointer's grandfather, Jesse Harris, passed down his memory of the Leonid meteor shower of 1833, indicating the power of oral traditions to preserve historical knowledge.

My [paternal] grandmother was in Hurtsboro [Alabama]. Her mother and father were married during slavery, and they only had one child, which was her. That was Carrie Lee, my father's mother. She never knew her real mother because they sold her mother [and] somebody carried her on somewhere else. [Her father], Grandpa Simon, was brought to Macon County. They sold him up here, but he remembered that he had a child down there. After freedom was declared, he married another woman, but he went back to Hurtsboro and found his little girl and brought her up here and she was raised by his other wife. They had many children, but

Louise Fuller's mother, a former slave, when she was more than 100 years old.
(Courtesy of Laura Blount, Albany, Georgia)

my grandmother was the oldest child he had. She was born a slave, and being in Macon County, she met my grandfather, Jesse Harris, down at the Chehaw train station. it was a café and hotel down there, and she was working as a maid or something, cooking and cleaning up down there. [My grandfather] was just a drifter, and they met and they got married and they had many children. Father was the youngest of the bunch that she had.

[My grandparents] moved from Tallapoosa County back to Macon County, sharecropping. [They] had a son, [Charlie Harris,] that was lynched in Tallapoosa County. When I say lynched, he was shot, and the house was [still] there when I grew up. They left it there to show the holes in the door; [it] looked like a sifter. I saw this myself. My father carried me and showed it to me. [My uncle, Charlie Harris,] was a tight man, and he shot some of his aggressors. It was all because of some woman he was married to. She was messing around with these white guys, and they got drunk and come to the house, and he knew nothing about this. When she saw them out there on their horses, she ran out the back door and ran on down through the woods. They got out there with the cussing, raising so much sound, and [Charlie Harris] walked out and he said, "Gentlemen, what's the matter?" He said, "I don't think that you need to carry on like this in front of my house." At that time, you just didn't talk like that to whites, you know what I'm saying? You didn't say anything to them. They did as they please.

They start[ed] cursing at him, and one word led to another, and they fired a shot, and he ran back into the house, and he start[ed] shooting, too, out the door because he didn't know what they was about. They exchanged fire until he was shot in the hip. A bullet hit him in the hip, but he had shot several of them, because he was shooting a high-powered rifle too. He crawled a long way to his parents' house in Tallapoosa County and when he got there and told them what had happened, they said, "Where's your wife?" He said, "I don't know. She ran out of the house long before this happened." They had heard what she was doing. My grandfather got out and walked to Tallassee and got a doctor. [Uncle Charlie] was only wounded in his hip. This doctor came there riding. They didn't know who he had been shooting at or who had been shooting at him, but when this doctor came in, he started probing for this bullet in his hip. My uncle told him, said, "Mama, stop him. He's killing me!" And Grandma says, "Well, Doctor, if he doesn't want you to wait on him, please sir, don't wait on him no more." He picked up his attaché case and say, "You'll never shoot another white man." He put poison into his hip and killed him.

My grandfather being a slave, he was afraid of white people, and he was until he died. But somebody told him to go to Dadeville, Alabama, which was the county seat, and issue a warrant about his son being killed on funny terms. He issued a warrant. They had to serve it. He didn't hardly know what to say, but [they] gave him a court date. He knew some of these men and he called their names, and [the Harris family] had to leave out of their house in Tallapoosa County and come over here to Macon County to [live with] relatives, some of my grandmother's friends and whatnot. Because if ever a mob crowd get after you, I don't care if you are my third cousin, they are going to pick at everybody who's blood kin, if you've killed [a white person] or wounded one. They knew that, and so they ran and left all of their belongings [to] flee to Macon County away from over there. They came that night, and they were going to go back the next day in the daytime and get some of their belongings. But when they got there, those mob crowds had got in there, in the house, and tore up all of their groceries and poured it in the middle of the floor. All the meal, all the flour, all the coffee, all the sugar and poured it all together and stirred it with a hoe. Just tore up everything in that house. So they had to leave bare-handed, and nobody did nothing about it. My grandfather came over here and in about a year's time when the court came, he got up to walk to Dadeville, Alabama. These people knew him, and he didn't know them, and he was walking the road, and they met him and asked him, "Where are you going?" He said, "I'm going to Dadeville, Alabama, to court where they murdered my son." He had the paper in his hand. They took the paper and tore it into a million pieces and said, "You turn around right here and don't you be caught in Tallapoosa no more." He turned. That case is still pending. My son say he going to open the case up. I say, "You better let it alone because them same devils is still there." My grandfather never went back up there. He was a slave, and he was afraid to pursue it.

My father being a man raised by slave parents, he was ruled and raised like they would raise a slave child. When he had children, those same fears were passed down to us, thus giving many of us inferiority complexes. You would be surprised how that can affect a person. I mean, things that I could have spoken about, my father [would say], "No, easy way is the safest way home. Just walk around it. Don't get in their way." See, that's how we were raised in that same fear. It is really sad, but it is true. And every word I'm telling you is true.

My grandmother [Carrie Lee Harris], when her mother was sold away from her, you know how she felt as a child. She never knew where she went or nothing of the kind, so she had no relatives, but just her father. She had sisters and brothers around in the county, but as far as on her mother's people, she never knew [them]. And right now, I can have relatives anywhere [whom] I don't know.

[It's] the same way with my mother. Her grandmother was a slave, and her grandfather was a slave, but her mother and father were not. Her mother's mother was a slave, and her mother's father. Joe Pinkard came from Virginia. That was my great-grandfather. His wife [Caroline], who was my great-grandmother, was a slave here in Macon County, but Joe Pinkard somehow was sold from up there to down here, and that's how they met. Well, she also married in slavery time, my [great-]grandmother did, and had four children born in slavery time. They didn't know much about what happened to those children because I think they sold them. You know, it's a thing that you can think about now and wonder who was kin to you. You don't know who your kinfolk are.

When they took [my great-grandmother Caroline] away, she was a nursemaid for her slave-owner. She was a "missy girl." When you say a "missy girl," maybe she was 12 or 13 years old. This is the story that they tell us. She found a big bundle of money, and she took it and put it in her bosom. She found it on the street. The [master's wife] saw her pick up something and said, "Caroline, what is that you got?" She said, "Nothing." And [the master's wife] just went there and just ripped her dress open and got it. She say, "I knew it" and took it. [My great-grandmother said,] "I want to give this money to my mama and maybe my mama can buy me a dress." "You don't know nothing about no money." [The master's wife] took the money away from her. They often talked about that.

I don't know why, but my father sat down and told us about everything that [he] could think of that happened that [my parents'] parents told them. He would sit down at night and tell us these things. I remember Grandpa [Jesse Harris]. I was seven years old when he died. And Grandma [Carrie Lee?], she died when I was almost three. But my great-grandmother [Caroline], the one I told you about [who] live[d] here in Macon County and her father came from Virginia, she died in '34 also. My grandfather, Jesse Harris, from what I can sit down and figure out now, he was more than 100 years old [when he died]. You know the meteorites fell in 1833? Do you know anything about that? They called it "the stars falling in 1833." Grandpa say he was a lad of a young man in 1833. He didn't know his age, but he said, "Oh, I was a lad of a young man when the stars fell." That meant he might have been approaching 18 years old. You see what I'm talking about? He died in '34. The stars fell in '33. So you know he was far more than 100 years old, far more than 100, but there is no record of his birth.

And my grandmother [Carrie Lee] was well over 100, a hundred and some years old, when she died, my father's mother. Her oldest child, Amanda, was a white child. She was forced to have sex with these landowners and this child was born to her, down there, and when her father went and got her [after Emancipation], she had this child. Good Lord, Amanda just died here in '50-something. She was an old woman then. [So my grandmother was] very, very old [when she died]. She was a very strange-looking woman. I can remember her. She was a tall woman with high cheekbones and she had straight black hair. And when she died, [there] wasn't a gray strand of hair on her head. Mama say she was an Indian woman, mixed and all. She had straight [hair], and I had a brother had hair just like her, jet black straight hair. She had high cheekbones, and she had all of them markings [physical traits], you know, just a mixture like that. Looking at some of her children, you can see that and I just really wonder sometime. I sit down and wonder about this.

[My paternal grandfather Jesse Harris] knew some of his people because he told Mama to name my sister after his mother. Her name is Sarah. But he never talked about his people down in Marengo County. I went down in that area when I was quite a girl, and I was standing there and this lady said, "What is your name?" I told her. She said, "Do you have any relatives in Demopolis?" I said, "No, Ma'am." She called another woman in and said, "I want you to come in and look at this girl." She looked at me and said, "Oh my Lord, that's so and so's daughter." She said, "Oh no, this girl's from Tuskegee. She doesn't even know them." Well, the woman stood there, and she didn't believe her. She thought I was somebody's child from down there, and I said, "There's some relatives we just don't know."

[Another time] I met a man on a train. I was leaving Roanoke, Virginia, [and] going to Cincinnati. I was sitting on the train. I was a grown woman. I was 22 years old. When [this man] walked in that train, he just started staring at me so [that] it made me nervous. I just start reading. When the train start to moving, he came up to me and said, "How do you do?" I said, "Just fine." He said, "Can you forgive me for staring at you like that?" He said, "I just almost fell because I thought you were my niece. Where you from?" I told him where I was from. He asked me if I'd ever been to Demopolis, Alabama. I told him, "No, I had not." He said,

"I'm going to give you some money." [Slap.] Just put it in my hand like that and went on back and sat down. All of that has worried me. You'd be surprised when you wonder about people and when you meet folk. I was courting a man once. We'd met at Tuskegee University. He was going to school, and I was going to school, but he was attracted to me for some reason, and it seemed like we just hit it off real good. In later years, I met his mother, and when I saw her, good Lord I like to fell because she was so much like my grandmother. I told him, "You know we are some kin." He said, "You know, I believe that too." He said, "Along the way you don't know where these people stopped or who they dealt with." I just believe that they were in that Pinkard family on my other grandmother's side. You see people all the time. You just don't know who is who.

Yes, [slavery was] all they talked about. That's all they talked about. Like on Sunday evenings, we'd be out playing, they would all come to visiting and all that. They would sit down and talk about the old times and the work that they did and the hard times that they had. Tell you all about it and tell you to make something of yourself. They kept saying, "Make something of yourself, be my dream. I can't read or write, but I want you to make something." They didn't give but a nickel. You'd take this nickel or anything that they could give you, and [they would] tell you to go on to school. "I don't ever want you to go on those hard times." They was talking about back there. That's all they talked about. At church, they would shout—shout, cry, all that stuff.

My grandmother, my mother's mother, [and] my grandfather was working over here by the Moden field. It was a big farm, and they were tenants on this farm. My grandfather was a handyman around the big boss's house. He milked his cows. He went there in the morning time. He had a key, and he'd go in there and make the fire in the stove so when they get up, they don't have to do it. [They] just walk out in a nice warm house. He'd get up before day and feed his stock. He'd been doing that for years. Then he'd leave and work his farm and everything. Well, he was so humble until this man thought he could do him any kind of way, you know, [like what happens] after you lick around people and act like no matter what they say, you just, "Yes, Boss," and you go on about your business. He didn't know my grandfather at all. So, [one time] they were going to sand the creek. It was his creek [and] when they wanted bass, he could sand. He had company. He had invited all his big-wheel friends out there and [was] going to sand and have a fish fry. So he had my grandfather to come there and help with the sanding and clean the fish and everything. That's all he was, just a flunky.

They was hitting those bottles and cussing and going on, and my grandfather passed by and [the white man] said, "John, pick up that rope down there." He said, "Yes sir." When he stooped down, [the white man] kicked him, before his company. You know, he [was] going to show them that he got somebody he can even kick. He just should not have done it because my grandfather turn around, [and the] first lick he hit him, he popped him on side of the head and knocked him down. He hit him so hard until he knocked the skin off. I mean he bust the hell out of him and kicked him, too. Then, you know, [snap] he had to take to the woods. My mother say [the white man] came by her house and sit down on the steps and went to crying. He said, "Carrie Lee, I didn't know John was like that. John jumped on me down there." She said, "What did you do to him?" "I was just playing with him." She say, "You can't play with him, not if you put your hands on him. Did you hit him?" "I just kicked at him." "Uh-uh, you must have kicked him, because if you kicked him, he's going to kill you." That's what Mama told him.

[The white man] went on up there [to Notasulga], and all his crowd got together, and they was in the middle of the crop. They was cool until the crops [were] almost [in], and [then] he went to Notasulga and got his mob crowd and got two men. [He] paid two men to kill [my grandfather]. And Mama said her baby was young [and] she wasn't in the field. She was sitting out on the porch and she could look down across the field, way down across there. [Her father] was plowing, and she saw him. See, she was living in a house with her husband, and my grandmother was living up further. But [Mama] said she could look down there and saw those two white men. She saw them when they got out and they went 'round the edge of the swamp there. [Her father] was plowing, and when he went in there to make his turn at the edge of the swamp to turn back, they were going to grab him and kill him and leave him in the woods. Mama say she start to calling him, calling him, and I don't know whether he heard her or not, but when he made that round and got to that swamp, those two men grabbed him and tried to cut his throat, but he was very strong. He was very strong, and buddy, he was knocking them so fast. He was worse than that Karate Kid. He beat the hell out of them down there, both of them. But he ran when he [snap] knocked them down and got away from them, although they raked him [across] the head with the knife. He had to take to the woods and keep going, you understand me.

So they couldn't do anything. [The white man] came there and told my grandmother, "Y'all have got to get off my place." [My grandmother] said, "What's the matter? What's the matter?" "Because I said so." She said, "Well, all right." My grandmother [said] she started to argue and say, "Well, you got to give me time. My crop is out here and everything." [The white man said], "I'm going to get half of everything you've got." She said, "I don't see how you can get nothing. I'm renting from you." My grandmother stood up to him and said, "Now what happened between you and John, you took it out on me, but anyway, I'm going." He went and took part of her cows. She had a lot of cows, [and] he [was] going to take half of them. So he got the same man that tried to kill my grandfather. When they went there to get the cows, my grandmother had [one of the cows] by [a] rope. This man came up and hit her. That's right, that man that he had hired, and she had children under age. It was a sad thing, but [my uncle] told me, "I wanted to kill that man about hitting Mama, but Mama told me not to do nothing. I had an axe. I was going to kill him with the axe, and Mama told me not to. She said, 'Uh uh uh uh uh. No, no, no.'" She took that lick because her boys was big enough to kill him, and [my uncle] had an axe [and] he was ready to kill him. [After that, my uncle] said, "I'm going to leave here," and he left. He said, "I'm never living in Macon County again. I couldn't defend my own mother." He left and he did not come back here. He came back to visit but he never stayed. He said, "Babe, I don't care how good it get in Macon County, it don't get good enough for me to stay here." He said, "I saw something I couldn't take. That man hit my mother for nothing, and I had the axe to kill him, and Mama was afraid for my life. They knew I would've been a fugitive because they would've been after me until the day I died if I had cut him with the axe. I was intending to give him a lick where he wouldn't do it [to] somebody else." He was going to get him dead as hell. He left on away from here a very young man and he lived in New York until he died. Just like me: if anybody had hit my mama, they would've had to kill me, you know what I mean? I was just that type. It's good I didn't come along in that day because I would [have] really fought back.

A crust of bread, a corner to lie in, that's what they had, which was nothing. My uncle said [that] when he left here, he had a dollar and 50 cents and one pair of pants. He had to hobo the trains and could [have] got killed, but he said he met some other hobos. He didn't know where he was going. He say, "Babe, I got on that train, and I didn't know where in the world [I was going or] how to get nowhere. The man, like a conductor, asked me, 'Where are you going?' [I] said, 'I want to go to Cleveland, Ohio.' " And that fella helped him to change from this freight train to that freight train until he got there. He said he didn't know nobody, had never been out of Macon County in his life. When he got to Cleveland, Ohio, it was in the summertime. He said he looked like hell. He was smutty and nasty. A man was unloading a truck. This was back in the teens. And [my uncle] was just standing there, looking. The man said, "Come here, boy." "Yes, sir." He went there, and the man said, "You want to help? You want to make some money?" "Yes sir." "Help me unload this truck." You talk about working. He unload[ed] that truck in a little while, and the man saw he wanted to work. He said, "Now I'm going to pay you five dollars. Now you go find your room and get cleaned up, and tomorrow you help me to load to get away from here."

[My uncle] started helping that man, got on his feet up there in Cleveland. He started sending money back here to get my grandmother off that place, off of these white people's places. She bought a little place down on this hill here, [a place] of her own. See, he sent money back when he went off. He didn't forget about them. He wanted her off the man's place altogether, and she bought her own little place because her son saw to it that she had her own little place.

CORA ELIZA RANDLE FLEMMING

Cora Eliza Randle Flemming was raised with a painful story about her family's interracial heritage. Flemming's grandmother was raped by a white man in Oktibbeha County, Mississippi, in 1905. Since for a white man to rape a black woman was not considered a crime in Jim Crow's courts, Flemming's grandmother's rapist suffered no consequences.

They told us my grandmother was raped. Well, in those days you didn't "rape." You just took what you wanted from the women. They always told us that she was cold. It was so cold ice shoots came up from the ground. He raped her in those woods. . . . One child was born to that woman. Her name was Eliza, I believe. [She was a] very pretty woman, they say. Her hair was so long she could sit on her hair, braid it up. She was a very nice person. She gave birth to, I believe, 11 children. That made all of us come in from that rape.

When I was a child growing up, one old white man lived down the road from us, way down the road. I thought he was the one did it. He'd pass by and I'd throw bricks at him and hide behind the tree. I thought he was the one that did it. But it wasn't him. It was somebody else had did it.

HARRIETTA HILL JEFFERSON

During the early twentieth century, Emancipation Day celebrations were an important part of the fabric of African American culture. African American communities in northern Florida commemorated May 20 as Emancipation Day, the day that the Union Army liberated Tallahassee, the state capital. Over time, black Floridians transformed May 20 into an important cultural event that combined the telling of black history, recreation, and pageantry. Music, good food, and speeches by elders, especially those who had survived slavery, were all part of the celebration. Harriet Jefferson grew up in rural Leon County, Florida in the 1920s. Here, she recalls the importance that May 20 held for her family and talks about why she continues to observe May 20 as Emancipation Day.

We didn't go anywhere but to church and back home. And then we always had a picnic on the 20th of May. Twentieth of May. Emancipation. There was Mama and another lady that always ever since I was little girl they used to have this big picnic on the 20th of May and my daddy and all the community would get together and they'd make this great big barrel of lemonade. And they set it up to say speeches. We would all say speeches. We would march and dance behind the drummer. Daddy had some drums and I reckon all my brothers grew up beating the drums. They could really beat them drums. I had two brothers, Carter and Henry. They would beat the drums and they would just start that morning at the sunrise. We'd have this 20th of May Day and my mama would have the May pole. She'd have a May pole wrapping with all red, white, and blue strings on the pole. And we'd practice, but we'd start practicing about April, about the first of April, the last of March, first of April. We'd start practicing how to wrap this May pole and all the children out of the community would come from miles. Would come from all up here about the church and every which a way and she would practice like twice a week. Every Monday night and Friday night. And we'd learn how to wrap this pole. She'd start the small children them to wrap it about like that and then the middle set would wrap the pole. They would always wrap the pole after we wrapped it.

They'd be singing and beating the drums and patting their hand and they'd have a partner and here we'd go and we'd be, you know. Sling their partners and go back and come get another one and swing that one. They just had a big time. So we practice this up until the 20th of May. Then the 20th of May we had to really do that thing and my daddy would [make] a special place down there. There's a place down there aside the road where you'll see a picnic ground at now, and [Daddy] would always whitewash his trees. All the trees in this picnic place in the picnic ground where we'd have the picnic on the 20th of May. They'd lime and whitewash the trees. And then we would all gather there for Emancipation. And then my brothers would always say the Emancipation and why we having the 20th of May we was always taught that from a kid. That is from the day that people was freed. Black people was freed. When we had Emancipation. And we still do that. We do that in remembrance of my mother. Every 20th of May we have a big picnic down there and the grandchildren tell the reason, you know. We had the great-grand. They mostly, you know, they grow up now and they remember it better than I do. And we still have the

Matthew Polk and his grandmother in 1912. (Courtesy of Edith Polk, New Iberia, Louisiana)

wrapping of the May pole. Get all the little children and we wrap the May pole, but people won't, you know, participate. The neighbors and things won't send the children now. They teach children better than that. "That's old folks." Don't teach them to remember it, but we always remembered.

JOHN HARRISON VOLTER

Raised in New Iberia, Louisiana, in the midst of the Great Depression, John Volter inherited a strong sense of self-determination from his elders. Here, he discusses how his grandfather and his brothers saved the family farm from being stolen by whites during Reconstruction. The story reveals that African Americans understood the larger historical forces at work in the segregating South.

My views on a lot of things may be contrary to what other people believe. The Ku Klux Klan was not set up by the lower class of Caucasians. The lower class of Caucasians were recruited into the Ku Klux Klan by former rich plantation owners who saw a way to gain some of their property back. And they used prejudiced ideas, class ideas on these ignorant low-class Caucasians. The act of giving each free slave so many acres of land and then the Ku Klux Klan scared them off it, you know. These poor whites that was the body of the Klan didn't gain nothing. The land went back to the rich owner, you know, it didn't go to *them*. It's just showing you how [they] manipulated their own people.

During that Reconstruction era my grandfather spoke of regulators, they called them, or night riders, and things like that. My grandfather was a farmer and he was nobody's pushover, my mother's father. He was the type that would resort to violence to protect what was his. They tried once without success, and so they ended up leaving him alone. There's a cliché, if they cannot handle you then they label you. You know, "he was a crazy nigger." (Laughter.) So they left him alone. But my mother's father was a man's man. He was kind, gentle. He would give anything to his neighbors, white or black, but you did not push him around period. I think that's where my mother gets it, you know, my mama was nobody's pushover.

You have to realize that the financial backbone of the family was my grandfather, my mother's father who was a sugarcane farmer. You see they [the Ku Klux Klan] were going to frighten my grandfather. Then somebody could buy his farm for a little something and so the word got back to him what night they were coming.

So he sent my grandmother and all of them away and in the meantime his brothers lived like five or six miles away and so they came on horseback. He had three brothers. I don't care what people say about secrets. These guys planned it, but still the word got back to my grandfather when they were coming. So he sent his family away and his brothers came over. They loaded their shotguns with bird shot. They hid their horses in the barn and when they came in the yard all hell broke loose. But they did not load the shotguns with buckshot, just bird shot, something that would pepper you, you know. And that was the end of that. They peppered them.

[The white men] thought that this was going to be an easy thing and remember they had to come across the bridge and they couldn't go out the back way because there was a barbed wire fence. They were just going to ride into the back and get off their horse and everything, but before they could do that they got cross fire and fire from four different directions. And I can just about imagine, you know, horses raring up and everything and they're just trying to get away from there. Because they did not expect that type of reception. They expected a little meek man and there was nothing meek about my grandfather nor his brothers, in spite of [the fact that] one of them was a minister.

TOLBERT CHISM

Like many black southerners, Tolbert Chism, from Fargo, Arkansas, was born into an ethnically diverse family. In this excerpt, Chism traces his heritage back to the Choctaw Indians and the Trail of Tears Indian removal march in the 1830s. In this tragic episode, Native Americans from the East were forced to relocate to the Oklahoma Territory. One leg of this march passed through the area that eventually became the state of Arkansas. While thousands of American Indians died on the Trail of Tears, a few escaped and mixed with African American communities in Arkansas, Missouri, and other areas west of the Mississippi. Tolbert Chism credits his family's Native American ancestry with helping to create a strong sense of independence. Chism also credits the Fargo Agricultural School, founded by Floyd Brown, a graduate of Tuskegee Institute, with teaching black history to its students, thus enhancing black pride.

My grandfather and my father's uncle, the one that I was telling you about who was the molasses maker, they all migrated about at the same time from, I think that was Bolivar, Tennessee, over into the state of Arkansas. This uncle of mine, he was mostly Choctaw Indian. His hair was as straight as yours, but yet he was dark. They say that what had something to do with that—they told us this kind of under the cover— that when they started that great march of the Indians, to move the Indians out of the Delta into Oklahoma, well, the whites made certain agreements with certain Indians that they would settle down on a certain lot of land and become farmers and all of that. They wouldn't have to participate in the migration. And that was the situation that confronted my father's father and his uncle, which was my great-uncle, the molasses maker.

Many people aren't aware of that, and many people aren't aware that all of that long death march that they performed on the Indians, moving them out of the Delta, where the best land was, out to some other rough land and what have you, years after they said that it backfired. You know how, don't you? It was during the time when we were fighting Japan and Bataan fell, and they had that death march of our United States troops from one place to another. That was a retaliation of what happened to the Indians here in the United States. Many people aren't aware of that, never did even give that a thought. Something greater than ourselves intervened and kind of gave those who were in power kind of payback for what they had done in the past.

They would enforce the law for the whites, but they didn't do too much enforcing the law for the blacks, because I can remember one time the story was told there's a fellow that was supposed to have been a deputy that lived in our community. His name was Clem Simmons. There was some whites had it in for some of the blacks that lived up in our community, and in particular this was an uncle of mine that was named Forrest Chism, and Forrest Chism was about half what they call Choctaw Indian and half black, but he was really a marksman with a Winchester or any kind of gun. And so they had gathered up a posse and had the sheriff with them, going to go and get Forrest Chism about something or whatever it was. But I think everybody had been alerted in the community, because everybody had Winchesters. Every black house in the community at one time had a Winchester in it. And the reason why they did that, a lot of those blacks that came in there—and the Indians, like we were talking [about]—from over in Tennessee, they [whites] could just come in there and run them out, take their crops, house, and everything. But the people that were sponsoring them were the ones that put a Winchester in every house in the community so that that wouldn't happen. And so this fellow, Clem Simmons, was at the head of the posse, the story goes, and said he held up his hand when they got to a certain point and said, "Now, I tell you, all of those houses in the community that we're going to destroy, they have a Winchester in them, and Forrest Chism is the captain and he really knows how to shoot those guns. I'm afraid that if we go over there interfering with them that all of us aren't going to come back. It's left entirely up to you, now. If you want to go on with it, we'll go on with it. But if you don't want to, and we all stay alive, it will be best for us to turn around and go on back and leave those people alone." They all decided that it would be the best thing to turn around and go back and leave all of those black folks alone and not attempt to run them out of the community. I mean, these aren't just no wives' tales. These are things that really happened. That was over in Jericho, Arkansas.

And to tell you the whole truth about it, [my interest in black history] comes through the Fargo Agricultural School. You see, every Sunday evening everybody had to go to what was known as vespers service. That was just about the same as the Sunday evening sermon, and this is where the head of the school, who was Floyd Brown, that was well up on that history about blacks, their background, their origin, and what have you, would talk and tell us about our past and our ancestors. Yeah, this was very much known among us. Of course, you couldn't talk too much about it [in front of whites] because it would cause some kind of disturbance or misunderstanding.

At the time when General Benjamin Davis became a general in the United States Army, he was the only black general there was in the U.S. Army. They said to us, the black troops, that he was the first black general in the army, and I told them that is the biggest lie that's ever been told. I mean, that's what I told my army buddies and all that were in the same outfit I was in. And so they asked me who or where was other generals in the army that were black? I told them I was taught in black history that Napoleon Bonaparte, Alexander the Great, and all of the great conquerors of the Far East armies had black generals in them. It looked like they just didn't want that to get through to the black troops. I found that to be rather amazing. You see, our education as black people had been limited to only what the whites wanted us to know about ourselves, but nothing about our background as to what our origin was and where we had come from. I found that out.

MONEY   ALIAN   KIRBY

"My mother was part Indian and part Chinese and her father was
full-blooded Indian. So we are a grand mixture of that makeup," recalls
Money Kirby of Magnolia, Arkansas. Kirby's mother refused to allow race
to define her life. In a notable instance, she adopted some needy white
children whose parents could not support them. This attempt to test the
fabric of racial segregation in her southwestern Arkansas community
forced Kirby's mother to draw upon her prowess with a Winchester rifle.

My name is Money Alian Kirby, born August 8, 1914, Biscoe, Arkansas, on our family's farm. We had owned that in the family since back
through our grandparents. They inherited it as a part of a reservation
because they were Indians and the Indians were in some cases forcibly
integrated with blacks. That's how our heritage began. And one thing
about the philosophy of our family is that they tolerated but never did
accept Jim Crowism, segregation, or subhumanism or any of those type
of things, those stereotypes that were thrown at blacks and encouraged
that they accept it and all that sort of thing. We never did accept it. But
we tolerated it.

There were instances in which, when I first started to school, we had
to walk about a mile. In fact, our farm was approximately a mile from the
little town of Biscoe, Arkansas. And of course we had to walk to town to
school. Just before getting into town they had built a school specifically
for whites. And it so happened that we had some whites to come and live
on our farm.

He was a logger, he and his family, and he put a tent out there. He
had a boy and a girl. Somehow this white fellow and his wife—he ran
off and left the woman and the two children. My mother, being the
good Samaritan that she always was, took the children in. The lady
came and signed a letter asking her to take care of those children for
her until she could go and get with her parents and then come back and
get her children. Of course, Mama took them in and kept them in our
home.

And of course school started. That created a problem because we had
to go right by the white school going to the school designated for blacks,

Bernice Caldwell and her uncle Henry Phifer, Cemetery Street, Charlotte,
North Carolina, 1914. (Courtesy of Bernice Caldwell, Charlotte, North Carolina)

or "coloreds." And Mama simply kind of rode shotgun and carried those
kids on down to the school where we were. She said, "They're in my
house. I have a letter here signed by their mother saying that they are in
my custody." And that old Indian lady marched them right on in school
with us.

And of course the black principal he was excited because he thought
maybe the folks were going to create a mob or something of that type.
But she stood her ground and carried them on to school with us. That
was back there around 1920. Jim was really crowing at that time.
[Laughter.]

Well, as you very well know, our group has always been integrated
against their will, and there were just as many of them kids in there [in
the black school that were] kind of half white looking as was those [white
children who stayed with us]. They didn't stand out too much.

Oh [the local whites], they turned red and had a whole lot of mouth but they dared not come out there.

Incidentally, my mother was the expert with a thirty-eight forty Winchester. A block away from the house sitting up in a big oak tree was a big black bird sitting up on top. And the sheriff had come out there to talk with Mama about all the rumors about she's got these white kids in the house and all that sort of thing. . . . My mother just happened to have this thirty-eight forty standing out there on the porch.

She said, "I'll tell you what, Sheriff. Here's a letter. You read it. These are the kids' mother and it's signed by her and I'm going to take care of them. They will be under my custody until she comes back and gets them. I don't want to cause any trouble, but if anybody messes with me—you see that bird sitting up there on top of that tree down yonder?"

He said, "Yes."

And she just raised that thirty-eight forty up to her shoulder and squeezed it off and that bird disappeared. We went down there and picked up a part of his beak and a few feathers and the sheriff says, "Case closed." He left there and never did come back out there. I think he passed the word around that that lady has a sixteen-shooter out there and don't go out there and mess with her. The Indians were pretty tough folks and she was loaded with it. My mother was part Indian and part Chinese and her father was full-blooded Indian. So we are a grand mixture of that makeup.

You know what? Our people have had a unique technique of diversion here. They learned to brush off [racist] statements and go on. For some reason or other they brought with them one of the highest forms of cultural intellect from Africa. When they thought those people, see what they did they brought them from the cradle of universal intelligence and they didn't realize what they had. They thought they was ignorant because they couldn't speak their language.

In the death march from Tennessee, moving the Indians over to Oklahoma, [my family] came through Arkansas and down here at Monticello that was a part of a little reservation. My grandpa and his folks put up such a fight that they decided they'd leave them alone and went on around and kept on going. Now that's how that part of the family ended up having little property rights there.

It so happened that my grandfather told me, "You're going to be a writer." I went and told my mother. She said, "If Grandpa said it's going to happen it's going to happen." A couple or three days later off in the distance, the sun was shining just like it is now; he said, "Come here." I went to him. He said, "Tell Catherine to get the children in the house." I thought he was being delirious. "Tell her to get the children in, bring them in the house, get them from outside and let's have prayer, it's a twister coming." I asked Mama, "What's a 'twister'?" She said, "That's a tornado." I said, "Grandpa said it's a twister." She said, "I don't care, if he says it's a twister there's going to be a twister." Inside of 15 minutes it was almost jet black with clouds and everything coming up and you could see that tornado coming up out of the west. That fast and he heard it that far off when it was still sun shining everywhere.

His name was Moses. I'm assuming that he was an adopted son of the God of Moses because he was some leader. What happened, the tornado came up and was heading straight toward the house, changes direction, went down this side of the road to the next fellow's house and just as a dog was leaping off the porch they used to have these chickens, they'd put them up in a coop to fatten them or clean them out or whatever, the tornado picked the coop up and the dog leaped off the porch and landed straddle of the chicken coop and there went the dog and the chicken coop, feathers flying everywhere. Picked it up, turned right around and went down the next side of the road and twisted up. An old German had a gas station down there, twisted that gas station up by the roots and a lady went out to grab her clothes off of the clothesline because it started the wind blowing rain and the gas station struck her and broke her back just as she was getting back on the porch. Went on down the country heading out of Cotton Plant back over this way and took the whole top off, left the foundation of a house, a man and his whole family there. One person out of that 10 got killed and it was a little baby and they put out search all over the area right down this flat, down here, and late in the afternoon somebody saw a little piece of gingham cloth sticking up out of the mud and they dug down and it was the baby dead about 10 feet away from the house. So that was 1927.

EDGAR ALLEN HUNT

African Americans used a wide range of herbal remedies and med-icines, many of which had been learned during slavery times. Because African Americans were denied even rudimentary medical care by white-controlled hospitals and doctors, the knowledge that black herbalists and midwives possessed was critical to the health of African American communities. A potentially fatal wagon trip for young Edgar Hunt in Blytheville, Arkansas, during the 1930s instead became an important childhood memory about the importance of medicinal traditions and respect for the wisdom of his elders.

You might not figure that I could go back that far, but I remember when I was three and four years old. I can remember some things that hap-pened, not everything, but there are some things that did happen that I can remember. Well, my earliest recollection is me riding on the back of a wagon with my grandfather. He'd go to the woods and cut down trees, and me and my brother would ride with him on the seat. And I remem-ber that a storm came up one day, and we had to turn around and come back from the woods because that was the only way that you could get any heat. Everything was—no heat, gas, or nothing like that, see. You had to have wood heat and then you had to get it a certain time of year and pile it up so you would have it to last throughout the winter.

And I remember riding on a wagon with him during that time and I remember playing with a snake, getting my finger bit. Nail still hasn't come back. But he was pretty, and every time he tried to crawl off, I catch him and pull him back. Finally, about the third time, he finally got tired of that and he turned around and he popped me. But my daddy, see old folks couldn't go to the doctor then. Didn't have no money to go no way, but old people knew how to do things the young people just don't know how to do. So what my daddy did, he took his pocketknife and split that finger and dug a hole and buried that hand in the ground and made me sit there with my hand buried about three hours. And that ground drew all the poison out of there. And when I got my hand out of the ground, it wasn't even sore. You know, it never swelled up or anything.

But that's the way we had to do things. Old people knew things that we'll probably never know. And when we got sick, we didn't go to the doctor. My mother used to pick certain leaves out of the backyard and off trees and make teas and give us and cut that fever right on out. We had something like pneumonia; we never went to the doctor. She would take a rag and cook some meal on it and put turpentine in that and then wrap our sides and chest up with it. Day or two, we'd be all right. So we never had to go. I don't ever remember going to the doctor until I got to Memphis.

DORA CORDELIA ANDERSON

By the mid-1890s, Thomas A. Harris, the grandfather of Dora Anderson, had been studying law for several years and had successfully passed the Alabama state bar exam. In 1895, Mr. Harris tried to set up a law practice in Tuskegee, Alabama. He was warned by members of the Ku Klux Klan that if he tried to practice law in the town that he would suffer dire consequences. Thomas Harris's confrontation with the KKK in 1895 carried enormous meaning for his children, who passed the story down to Dora Anderson.

My grandfather was attacked by the Ku Klux Klan. He was a lawyer. He had worked *very* hard going to Atlanta and Nashville and Birmingham working with lawyers trying to get ready to pass this bar [exam] because they did not have law schools as such then, especially not for black people. So he passed the bar and they told him then *not* to hang out his shingle, but he hung the shingle out at any rate in Tuskegee. He was the first black lawyer there. He set it up because he had all these nine children and his wife and that was his home. He was not trying to spite anybody.

They [the KKK] gave him so much time to get out of town and told him that if he didn't get out, that they would have him strung up to a tree at the lower part of the town. So my daddy said he had a cousin that was a very good sharpshooter and he put *him* there with Grandpa and Grandma and the children to see after them because my grandfather and my daddy together had a meat market there right on the square there.

And he left this young man there to take care of them while he was at the shop.

So instead of them coming before night, they said they would have him strung up by the time the sun was down. So after it was dark, Grandpa went across the street to Mr. John Alexander's house, and he was the justice of the peace. So he said: "Well now, they have not come and it is night. Do you think they are going to burn me down tonight, burn me and the children and the family up tonight?" Mr. Alexander said he didn't know what they planned to do. About that time, they looked down the street and all of these torches were coming. So he started to wrestling with Mr. Alexander to go through his yard and on out to another street instead of going back home. But Mr. Alexander told him no, he did not want him to go through his yard. They were in the yard out there and he said he didn't want him to go through the yard because he had his daughters in the house there and he didn't want them disturbed.

About that time the mob was there. So they saw that they were wrestling and they started shooting and the first bullet went through Mr. Alexander's neck. And so they planned then to go down lower and they shot my granddaddy's left kneecap off and they left him there to die. But Grandma and her daughters came out and they were teenagers. Well anyhow, she carried them in the house and this young man that was there with them went through the back way downtown to the meat market to tell my daddy. He was the oldest son. He told his cousin to hook up his horse to the buggy and he did and he said it was in July and it was raining. And so he came and put tourniquets over Grandpa's knee. They wrapped him in quilts and he put him in his buggy. But he put up his rain curtain. He put that up to the front and you have a little place for it. And he said he drove right through the mob, right through, you know, where they were. But they had five white doctors there and they did not let any of them take care of Grandpa. So he decided to go to Montgomery, said he had a cousin down there, and he drove all of that night—it's just 35 miles—in and out of places that he didn't even know. But he said that the sun was up good when he arrived in Montgomery. And he got him to this cousin's house and the cousin got him medical help.

My grandfather used to write me long letters. I guess being a lawyer, he would type. I took business [classes]. And I think as I grew up, I decided that that was the reason [I went into business]. Because Grandpa would come to visit my daddy from time to time, and he would have this old big typewriter. You know, the typewriter's under his arm because all the weekend he would be writing, so my mother would always tell us not to ever touch the typewriter. And I guess I wanted to see what the typewriter was all about. But I did business and I graduated but I still stayed in business.

[This has always] hung over our heads the whole time we came along. I have decided that is why my parents were as protective of me. I had two brothers older than I was and two brothers younger than I was, but they always seemed to be very protective of me and I thought it was because of this incident, because Grandpa never came back there to live. He came back when Grandma died and I was about five or six years old then. He was there in Birmingham. He practiced [law] in Birmingham.

And I can remember very well, I guess I was in high school about then, my daddy said, "Well, the last one of those blankety-blanks that were in that mob was buried today." I can remember that *very* well.

RUTHIE LEE JACKSON

Ruthie Lee Jackson grew up in Crystal Springs, Mississippi, in the early 1920s. In these four brief excerpts, she describes aspects of her heritage, including her religious upbringing, community burial practices, the use of folk remedies, and her admiration for her great-aunt, a former slave. Mammy Sue lived long enough to hold Jackson's baby daughter in the early 1920s, a fact that Jackson reports with pride. She also expresses gratitude "that our foreparents prayed that we wouldn't have to go through what they went through."

We been going to church all our days. Mama raised us up in church. Just me and my sister. Ain't never been but the two of us and Mama carried us to Sunday school until we were big enough. We got a little catechism and she carried us as long as we were little small children and then soon as we got [older], [if] she didn't feel like going, we went by ourselves. I was converted at a Baptist church. Called it Good Hope Baptist and my pastor was Reverend Simon Minor and then when I come here—whatever town I went to I joined the church. I was born in 1909 and I was baptized in 1918 when I was converted.

They had a pool, but now most people baptized in these lakes and rivers. When I joined the church at Crystal Springs, it was a Baptist church, but my mama was Methodist. My sister was baptized. My mother was Methodist, and my mother couldn't take care of us at two churches, and I waited until I got married because I wanted to do what my mama said to do, and I came on up here to Ruby and I joined the Baptist church up there called Saint John's and was baptized in the river. That's why I was happy, because they sprinkles, you know, the Methodists. I wanted to be buried and I wanted to go in that water. I wanted to go in it. But you see, Mama, she couldn't take care of us in the Methodist and [the] Baptist, and so I went along with my mama. And when I got married I came to the Delta and joined Saint John. And I was buried in the Yazoo River.

I reckon it might not have been [any difference between sprinkling and immersion], but you know the Lord walked so far to be baptized by John in the River Jordan. You see? Well, that's where we Baptists get it. Christ walked so far to be baptized in the River Jordan by John the Baptist. [Now the Methodists] told me if I would go ahead on and join the Methodist church they would bury me, but they didn't. They didn't. I had to stay on like I was until I got grown and come on up here and was baptized. And I been happy, happy, happy ever since.

When anybody died in our day coming on, you had to bury them the next day. We didn't have no burials. No undertakers. And the people would go and sit all night and drink coffee and put this person on a cooling board, you called it. Have some planks. And put him on there and put nickels over his eyes. Put nickels over his eyes and put a little old dish of something with some salt in it over the mouth. Keep them from purging from the mouth. Then the next morning we buried him. . . .

And then my mother used to go—if somebody passed tonight, they would always get her to come and give this person a bath. If it was a woman, Mama would always go and give that person a bath and comb their hair and get them ready for the funeral for tomorrow. That was at Crystal Springs.

When we had flu or pneumonia or something like that, they would

Charlotte church annex in the early 1900s. (Courtesy of Burke DeGrandval, Charlotte, North Carolina)

use tallow. They would save tallow when they killed cows. They would use this tallow and get a piece of red flannel. You call it red flannel and you grease that and rub and heat it. We had a fireplace. You heat that flannel and just grease it, [rub] the bottom of your feet and all like that, and it would heal.

We had another tree. We called it sassafras, where they would make teas. That's for to use through the spring. And then they have something they call poke salad. You eat some poke salad through the spring and that was to help you, you know. You could mix it with your vegetables or you could cook it by itself.

And they had another thing you called simmer leaf. We'd make tea. Mama would put that down by the fireplace. We'd pour some hot water on it and then when we'd get ready to go to bed at night, well, they'd give us some simmer leaf tea. Well, that would help you [to get] your bowels moving. Then it would help you otherwise. Called it simmer leaf.

I had an auntie. She held this baby here. My baby. In the early twenties. She was a slave. She lived to be 115. That was way back. And she had [a scar] where they beat her, you know, as slaves. Looked like a little old titty or something would be hanging on her back. She was our auntie. Our great-aunt. We called her Mammy Sue.

We were small, real small, and she would tell my mama [stories], but we couldn't remember all she said. But she would tell us how she was beat, you know, beaten in that time. Well, that was the only auntie that we knowed. That was my grandmother's auntie. That was our great-auntie. It looked like a little titty on her back where she was beaten when she was in slavery times.

They were just mean to her. Just mean to her. But I'm so thankful that our foreparents prayed that we wouldn't have to go through what they went through. See, my mother didn't go through that. My grandmother didn't. That was our auntie. She was in it. We wasn't.

LAURA DONALDSON

Even though Laura Donaldson's mother and father died when she was a young girl, they managed to imbue their daughter with a strong sense of identity and justice. Born in 1923, Laura Donaldson, like her husband, Henry (who appears in chapter 5), harbored a strong distaste for Jim Crow. When the federal government moved to purchase the family's land in North Carolina to construct a military base, Donaldson drew on the memory of her father's toils to argue for a fairer settlement, not only for her family, but also on behalf of a white woman facing the same difficult situation.

When my parents married, my daddy bought this 15-acre plot. Then, when the first child came along, this of course was all before my time, he bought a second plot. Then in the latter years he bought this additional 80 acres of land. And to show you the change in things from then and now, both of them were dead when the government took over this property. When we went to settlement for all that property we got less than $1,000 for all of this property. My daddy after he stopped teaching he did a lot of building and he also had a blacksmith shop. I think we were about the only one in that area who had what is known as a forge. Some call it a bellows. You turn this thing to make the flame and he used to shoe their horses and repair their carts and wagons and things like that. We didn't have money, but I would say because of his having taught for so long and with his being such a needed person in the community, if it were a chimney he knew how to lay brick. If it were a mechanical thing like needing a tire repaired or the rim on the cart or something, this metal thing that goes around it, he had this forge that he could weld this thing and put it back on. As the Bible says, he was well known in the gates because he was a person who was needed in the community.

Looking back it was an interesting time. It was a painful time because my mother died when I was young and then suddenly [my father] was killed just before the takeover of this property. He was standing by the side of the highway and [a driver] veered off the road and struck him and killed him instantly. Looking back, some of the memories are painful like losing both of them. When we went to settlement this was before I married Don [Henry Donaldson]. We had to go back to Jacksonville because the government was taking over all of this area. They started at Camp Davis then they moved on up into the Verona-Jacksonville area and took that in for the marine base. So I was in school here then. I had to get out of school and go to Jacksonville about this property because all the heirs were supposed to go. I remember this lady's name: Miss Allen. But when we went they wanted for all of this property, they wanted to give us $200 and I said no and my brother was trying to shush me up because then if you were black back then they didn't call you black unless they did it in a derogatory way. You were a Negro or nigger which I didn't like but I accepted the classification of Negro but I could not abide nigger. But in most instances you got called this.

When I stood up the judge said, "What!" And I stood up and I said, "I refuse to accept this." "Gal, what do you mean you refuse to accept this?" I said, "I refuse to accept giving away the property that my father worked so hard to leave for his children for $200 when we have over 120 acres of land back there." He said, "What do you mean?" I said, "I just told you." So my brother's pulling on my dress. "Sit down, Sis." He called me Sis. "Sit down, Sis, sit down." I said no. He said, "What do you mean?" And I said, "I resent you telling Miss Allen [who] has a big farm and her husband is dead and left her with all these children and you're going to tell her that she can only have $300 for her farm." My brother said, "Sit down Sis! Sit down." And [the judge] said, "What do you know about property?" I said, "I know that my daddy worked too hard for it, and I know that Mr. Allen worked too hard for his." So he said, "Well, we'll call a recess." And this was the first time.

Our community wasn't as racist as some. We had grown up playing with the white children and we were used to them coming to my house where we were living in the country. But this was the first time that an adult white person had ever embraced me. And then I was afraid she [Miss Allen] was going to drop some of the snuff. She dipped snuff, this brown stuff. But she grabbed me and she said, "Honey, thank you so much. Thank you so much. I didn't know how to talk to him like that but thank you so much and the Lord's going to bless you because I didn't have nobody to talk for me and I couldn't afford a lawyer. But thank you so much for telling him for me." I don't know how much she got but when she came out when they went back, she was happy. I didn't know what we were going to get. They notified us months later by letter. But he got up off the little bit that he was offering and we came out to like about $1,000, which still wasn't enough but it was more than we would have gotten. But with my brother with him being older, being the oldest one in the family, and he knew about Jim Crow. I was too young really to know because we had not been exposed. We younger children had not been exposed as he had.

But with my daddy's background of having taught, I can remember when the white people because of his educational background would come if they had a business letter that needed to be written; they would come and ask him to write it for them. And as time went by I can remember them coming under cover of darkness because as I grew older I could imagine how humiliating it was that here is someone you consider beneath you, but because they had the perseverance to push forward and to learn, you have to come to them. But on the other hand they were friendly with us in a lot of ways because we kids played together and thought nothing of it. But when it comes down to you've got something of importance that has to be attended to, here you have got to come to someone you consider beneath you to do your correspondence. But so be it. This is the way it was. I never felt superior and by the same token I did not feel inferior, but I felt that we're equal. My daddy always told us you are just as good as anyone and don't ever let anyone tell you that you are not just as good as the next person. So I grew up with that feeling that I was just as good. And even though they were with me for only a short time I appreciate and pass on to my children the things that my parents taught us. So end of story.

THREE

FAMILIES AND COMMUNITIES

After Emancipation, former slaves faced enormous challenges on every level of life, but one of the most poignant was their search for "lost ones," as mothers, fathers, sisters, and brothers tried to locate other kin separated during slavery. Up until the late 1890s, black newspapers published "lost ones" columns to help individuals find family members. But many were not so fortunate to be able to hold out hope for a reunion. Writing in his autobiography, Frederick Douglass describes a separation so absolute that he lacked even a memory of his mother. What he knew was that he had had a mother, but they were separated "when I was but an infant—before I knew her as my mother."

Seeking to overcome this legacy of inhumanity, freed people and their posterity created and sustained fundamental relationships, building families and kinship networks, forming supportive communities, and organizing economic, educational, political, and religious institutions. Self-help and mutual aid in the raising of children, caring for the sick, and in helping the destitute were crucial for the survival and advancement of individuals, families, and communities. The spirit of responsibility quickened as African Americans were denied equal citizenship and were all but excluded from access to mainstream financial institutions. In the face of oppression, they forged a moral economy, creatively fostering racial solidarity, progress, and equality.

As Jim Crow laws multiplied in the early 1900s, with lynching on the rise and political rights wiped out, some 1.7 million black Americans decided to leave the South, emigrating to the North in what would be remembered as "the Great Migration." Others, choosing to remain, tried to find ways to create all-black towns, such as Mound Bayou, Mississippi, totally separate from the dominant white structures. Yet, the majority of black people in the South did not migrate, nor did they build all-black townships. Instead, they remained, living in rural communities or moving to larger towns and cities in the South to find work and education, or simply to take their chances far from the plantations where their ancestors were enslaved.

In towns, the landscape reflected African American disenfranchisement and poverty. For G. K. Butterfield it was impossible not to see the racial characteristics of southern cities and towns, where the lines of segregation were visible even to a newcomer. "When you live in the South and have been in the South all your life, you could find [places to eat and sleep] instinctively. . . . Southern towns are laid out in the same fashion, basically, and you could use your senses and sense where you are and where you're not." Decayed buildings and dirt roads were primary markers of a person's entry into the black section. While African Americans paid taxes, they did not reap the benefits of civic improvements.

Within these enclaves churches were vital centers of African American culture. True sanctuaries, they ministered to the spiritual and temporal needs of the community and were places for affirmation and celebration. Church revivals were great religious and social events, often drawing the whole town. Baptisms brought family and neighbors closer. Indeed church membership framed almost everyone's daily life. In churches many young people met the men or women whom they later courted and married. Churches also were safe spaces for political activities, and they often housed the earliest meetings of the local National Association for the Advancement of Colored People.

Fraternal organizations formed another center for mutual aid. Initially established as burial societies, lodges became safety nets for their members' families. Members cared for the sick and helped feed and maintain the households of ailing members. They provided resources for members who had experienced almost any kind of loss. Reflecting on the need to pool resources, A. I. Dixie talks about his fraternal lodge and the role it played in the lives of his neighbors. "Like if you was a farmer and your mule died and you belonged to the Emancipated Order," Dixie remembered, "everybody that had a mule had to give you a day's work, until they could get you another mule."

Black homes and neighborhoods were not fortresses in any sense, but they did provide some level of protection. LeRoy Boyd of Mississippi remembers how blacks in his community banded together in armed self-defense of his uncle, who was at risk of being lynched by an angry mob. Wilhelmina Baldwin recalls a similar effort of neighbors to protect a black soldier returning from World War II, who had accidentally brushed against a white female and was being hunted by a lynch mob.

Black men and women, confronted by brutal racial stereotypes, struggled to find ways to assert their dignity in the face of humiliating treatment. Women were frequently subjected to sexual insults, but within the African American world they found respect. Mary McLeod Bethune believed that women were the moral role models in the home, community, and country, and she emphasized the role of black women in the uplifting of the race.

Many communities also embraced the strict sexual and social mores of the times, aspiring to middle-class standards of conduct, dress, and speech as part of uplifting the race. These aspirations expressed the ideals of "the New Negro," of well-brought-up men and women whose behavior was impeccable. As Georgia Sutton remembers, "It was unheard of for a young lady to get an apartment. You stayed home until you got married. And if you didn't ever get married, you were just home." Like most older Americans recalling life before World War II, African Americans in this chapter tell about a morally stricter yet at the same time more supportive community that was rooted in knowing one's neighbors and watching out for each other.

Treated as second-class citizens, African Americans found strength in family and community. The institutions they created and nurtured formed a political and economic base to challenge Jim Crow laws and practices. Thus did earlier generations, against the grain of segregation, lay the groundwork for the civil rights movement of the 1950s and 1960s.

MAGGIE DULIN

Maggie Dulin was born in 1924 and grew up on her grandparents' farm in Muhlenburg County, Kentucky, near the town of Depoy. Recalling her father's and grandfather's baptisms, Dulin illuminates the significance of religious revivals and the role of religion among rural African Americans. She demonstrates how these occasions were times for witnessing and also served as opportunities for community bonding and sharing.

During World War II, 19-year-old Dulin followed many women, black and white alike, in going to work for the war effort. She spent six months working at a factory in Chattanooga, Tennessee, before returning home to help her ailing mother. Upon her return, she was courted by an old friend, Buckey Dulin, and she recalls their courtship and life together as a young married couple, deeply in love and struggling to get ahead in the immediate postwar years.

Even as a child, I can remember thinking that my grandmother was just too good. Everybody came to her house on Sunday, and the preacher and the people from way out in the country came and ate Sunday dinner. They came from Rhodes Chapel, which is out from Greenville, and they would come there and eat dinner. Every Sunday. And the preacher ate there every Sunday. They would get ready, that was a big thing on Saturday, killing chickens and getting the meat and everything ready for Sunday dinner. So she talked [about] the Lord so much, you know. She'd talk about "the Lord will take care of this" and "the Lord will do this." In the church, you hear the other people talking about the Lord. Until I thought—oh, I guess I was about four then—I thought one of these days, He's going to come and eat dinner too. And I'll get to see this man that they're talking about!

And everything that happened that was good in the community, she'd say, "Oh, Lord, the Lord did that. If it hadn't been for the Lord, I don't know what we'd do." You know, I'd hear them say that and I thought, "Well, who is this?" I can remember thinking that.

You were going to join the church. You were going to be a Christian in those days or else they were going to worry you to death with fear. Every revival within a certain range, you were going to go to it. And you

Riverside baptism in eastern North Carolina around 1940.
(North Carolina Collection, University of North Carolina at Chapel Hill)

were going to go until you were converted. And they didn't care how long it took. You were going. They had mourners' benches then. And everybody that was a sinner in the church had to go up front and sit on that mourners' bench and hold your head down. You didn't raise your head up. You held your head down. Why did they do that?

They called it a period of mourning, I guess, because you're supposed to be Godly sorry because you're a sinner. The preacher would ask [if you were a sinner] and you wouldn't tell no lie. Nobody would tell no lie. You were going to church. But, of course, my grandmother, when I went in the door, she just led me on up there and sit me down on the bench. She didn't wait until the preacher asked.

At that time, they wanted you to be at least 12 years old and they say you'd know what you were doing and all that stuff. And Christ was baptized and all this stuff at a certain age. And we had to kind of do like Christ do. At 12 years old, He was of God and whatever. And of course, they kind of went by that. And my grandmother said, "Now, you're going to be a Baptist. I don't care what church you go to but you've got to be a Baptist because Christ was baptized." That was her reason for being a

Baptist, that Christ was baptized. And you're going to have to get baptized in the river because the river will wash your sins away. The river runs and the ponds and things didn't.

But anyway, when I go in the door, every revival somebody would say, "They're having a revival over at Powderly this next week too." And I thought, "Oh, my Lord, I got to go to revival and sit on the mourners' bench!" And I started going. I guess [my grandmother] started taking me up there [to the mourners' bench] pretty young, about eight or nine years old anyway. Or ten. But she didn't worry too much about me not getting up until I got to 12 years old. She said, "Well, you're going to go to every revival until you accept the Lord into your life."

And so this little church—it was what they called a union church. At a union church, the Methodists would have services one Sunday and the Baptists would have services one Sunday and [both] the Methodists and the Baptists would go every Sunday. Now, why did they have to have a Methodist and Baptist church? Why did they have to say Methodist or Baptist? Why don't they just say church? But everybody would participate in everybody's services. And I thought, "Well, you know, you would think the Baptists would stay home on the Methodists' Sunday," but they didn't. And everybody would go hear everybody's preacher. But one thing the Methodists did, they sprinkled. And of course, the Baptists frowned on that. And so, I guess that's the only difference that they made in the church was the sprinkling and the being baptized.

But I went to this service. I was 12 years old this time and my grandmother, she really gave me a good talking. She said, "You're 12 years old. If you should die, you'll go to hell." She said that. "If something happen to you and you should die, you'll go to hell. You're 12 years old and you're accountable for your sins." And she said, "You'll go to hell." Just as plain as that. I thought, "Oh, Lord! I don't want to go to hell!" [Laughs.] She said until you were 12, they believed that your mother and father was accountable for your sins but after you got 12, you were accountable and if you died, that was it. And I had seen a lot of people—one man died and they said he was a sinner. And everybody was just all disturbed, where we lived, they were so disturbed because that man died a sinner. And I can remember people just went around in a gloomy state for, I don't know, weeks after that man died, worried about him being in hell, you know.

So I thought, "Well, I've got to do something." But anyway, I didn't quite understand. I didn't want to get up and didn't know what I was doing. The Lord, I guess He knew what I was thinking. I really believe in God like my grandmother. And I guess He understood that I wanted to but I didn't know quite what I was doing. And it was a lady there in the community, a bad lady. What they call a bad lady. All the men was crazy about her. Listen, she pointed the way to God to me. She came up and she told me, "Maggie, you just believe." She said, "You do believe there's a God, don't you?" I said, "Yes." She said, "That's all you have to do is believe, and get up and tell the church that you believe in God. That you want to be a Christian. That you want God in your heart." And [she] said, "It's just that simple. It's nothing that you have to do. You don't have to make a lot of noise. You don't have to shout. You don't have to do a lot of things."

Now that shows you that the Lord can use anybody that we call "bad." He can use anybody to do a job or do something that He wants done. Now that lady was supposed to be bad. She was a beautiful attractive lady. But she was supposed to be one of them wild ones! Because we all heard it as kids, and everybody would whisper then. You could hear things. But they didn't want kids [to hear] too much, but I'd hear things. But she was the one that pointed the way and explained to me more in a simple-like, child-like way than the preachers were able to do. I thought, "Well, if that's the way, you know, it's all right." I just thought maybe you had to get up and go to shouting and doing all these things. And I'd see the old people shouting and I thought, "Well, I don't feel like doing that. I don't even know how to do it." I thought you had to do something like that.

We had to be on that mourners' bench in Sunday school. All during that revival week, you had to get on that mourners' bench, every night, and it ended on Sunday. And so, Sunday after Sunday school, I just got up and that's where I accepted the Lord. And I never will forget it. This is what I won't forget. Mr. F. Hawkins was the preacher and he was a lovely man. And he loved "The Old Rugged Cross." And I didn't like that song. And he started singing that song. After I was converted, it was the prettiest song I ever heard in my life. It was different. And that's the way, really, I knew that I was saved. That song was different. And I thought,

"Well, why does he sing this every Sunday for?" He had a lovely voice. Right after I got up, he started that song. And I never heard anything as pretty in my life. "The Old Rugged Cross," so despised by the world. He would sing it every Sunday. I think he wore me out singing it. It was his favorite song, I think. But that Sunday, it was simply beautiful. It was just beautiful.

And oh, and my grandmother was sitting in the back somewhere over on the other side. And Lord, of course, you knew He heard her shouting! Oh, yes! Everybody shouted as if to say, "Lord, the hard sinner has gotten up!" [Laughs.] There were about 30 or 35 people baptized at the time I was baptized. And a man 80-some years old was converted.

Well, I was telling you about the river. They had a lake. [We] didn't get to go to the river for some reason or another. My grandmother didn't like that too much. Nooo! She didn't like that too much. But they had lights all the way around this lake because at the top of the hill [above] the lake, there was a horse stable. That's where the horses that they used in the mines [were kept] and that's where they'd come and drink. And they had lights all around there and all around the stable. So they baptized us at night. One of the most beautiful baptizings you ever saw in your life. The water just glittered. And it was beautiful and warm. It was just beautiful. And the man that baptized us, he was a really noted singer. And he started singing "Wade in the Water." Oh! And that was the prettiest thing I ever heard in my life. And then, you had to be baptized in white. And you had to have something white on your head. They tied a white scarf around your head and you had on a white robe. It was the most beautiful baptizing. I wished I had a picture of it. Wouldn't it be wonderful to have a picture of that? Then, people didn't have cameras and things. Oh, I would just love to have a picture of that. Beautiful. And we was all standing there waiting to go in. And he was out in the water with his arms stretched out singing "Wade in the Water." We were supposed to walk slow out into the water. And he was singing, "Wade in the water, children. God's going to trouble the water." Beautiful, beautiful, beautiful. I never will forget it. Beautiful.

[Nowadays] they baptize in pools around the church here. My grandmother wouldn't like that! No! She would think that [was] awful! See, we didn't have pools and things then. And that preacher better get your head under that water. I can remember once somebody's head didn't go under there. They had to be baptized again. They discussed it after[ward]. Everybody was watching to see if your head went under that water. And the older Christian people discussed that after that baptizing. "He didn't get his head under that water." That was a crime! And they said, "Well, what are we going to do?" They was whispering. And the mother came over and she was worried. "Didn't get my child's head under the water. And what are we going to do, Evvie?" [Laughs.] Well, the boy didn't want to go back anymore but they said, "Well, there's nothing to do but just take him back and make sure his head goes under." [Laughs.] A few Sundays after that—they didn't want to hurt the preacher's feelings. . . . They told him they knew it probably wasn't his fault. [The boy] was a good-sized child. And maybe he was holding back or something happened that you didn't get to get his head under there. And we just think you should have another chance to get his head under the water. They fixed it up nice. I thought, "I'm glad he got my head under there!"

So they carried the boy back. He was a good-sized boy. I guess about 16. And they carried the boy back and they got his head under the water. And everybody started shouting and clapping their hands. They got his head under there that time. But you had to get your head under the water. Yes! You're going to have to have that whole body under there. Just a little part of his head didn't get under there. [But] all of them saw it! Because they were standing there staring when you were baptized, to make sure that your head went under the water.

At that time, when I was baptized, my grandfather wasn't a Christian. And he was a good swim[mer]. He was noted to swim across the Green River in different places. The people that were sinners, mostly then they would go to church, take their wives and the baskets and stuff like that, participate. But they hadn't been converted. And it was a long time before he would join the church because he was such a good man. And some of the people in the church wasn't doing exactly like he thought they ought to have been. And he thought, "Well, they're just not right and there ain't no need to [join]." He had that for an excuse. But he hadn't joined the church at the time when I was baptized. He was so afraid they might drown me or turn me loose or something would happen to me, that he went to my baptizing and sit there, right close as he could get, where they were baptizing. He was going to jump in and get me. He wasn't going to let them drown me!

I never will forget, I saw him getting ready and I thought, "Well is he going to the [baptism?]" [My grandmother] said, "Yeah, he's going, baby. He thinks he don't want nothing to happen to you and he's going." So she didn't tell me [about] the drowning, she was scared that would scare me. I didn't know. I thought, "Well, what is going to happen?" I found out later he thought maybe they might turn me loose. But he went, and I guess it was 200 or 300 out there, had come for the baptizing. From Greenville, Depoy, and Powderly. The singing was so beautiful around that water. Everybody joined in singing that song, "Wade in the Water." And we had to walk down slowly until we all got down in the water with our white robes on. It was beautiful, beautiful. And so we were baptized. And after that, we went back to the church. And we were voted into the church. Whatever they had to do, they had to do it all that night because in case you died that night, you'd be already in the church. You wouldn't die a sinner out of the church. They were going to do it all that night. And they finished it up that night. So we were in the church. My grandmother was a happy person. I heard my grandmother above all the shouting. Every time somebody would go in, everybody's folks would shout, or somebody would shout. And among all the shouting—which was a lot—I could hear my grandmother's voice above everybody else's voice. Oh, she was pleased when they put my head under there.

One Sunday, I never will forget, [my grandfather] told [grandmother], "Evvie," he said, "I want you to [brush my suit]." He had an old suit. Nobody had very much, just one old suit. They'd reach up and dust it off and an old hat and dust it off and wear it to church every Sunday. I don't guess they ever had it cleaned. But he told Evvie to clean his suit up. You know, she got the brush and got it on the ironing board and cleaned it. Kind of pressed it a little bit. And so he told her to get his suit ready and everything, he was going to church. And so he did. He just went to church that Sunday and went up and joined the church. He done made up his mind. You know, he didn't have to have nobody tell him when to go. He'd go when he got ready.

The preacher asked him did he want to be baptized and he said, "Yeah." [The preacher] said, "When?" He said, "Anytime you get ready,

I'm ready." So they didn't lose no time. They didn't want to go all that week. The next Sunday, they baptized him in the pond. There was a great big pond they baptized him in. Oh, my grandmother cried so. She really did scream and cry. She just cried. You know, he was just a good solid, firm person, believed in what he believed in. He wasn't emotional. He just got out of the water and put his clothes on and came on home. Everybody was hollering and petting him and patting on him and hugging him and everything. And he would just do a little grin, you know, as if to say, "So what's the big deal? I've done it." But I never will forget him. I was watching. Everybody was just, "Oh, Hollie, we're so glad . . . oh, we're so happy." And they were just crying, you know, the old women and everything. They was just crying. And the men was shaking his hand and patting him on the shoulder. They was crying. Everybody was so happy because they loved my grandfather. And so he came on home and the preacher came on home. I could tell he was a changed person, though, because he seemed relaxed and happy, a different happy. He was a good man but it was a difference in him that day. I can remember so well. It was a difference in him that day.

[Both my grandfather and my father] were a lot better men at heart than a lot of the men that were in the church. And they looked at that [and thought], "Now this man is a Christian. He's supposed to do this and he's this and he's that and he's done this and he's done that." They expect[ed] them to be better than they were, the people that were in the church.

I was worried about my dad. Daddy was 62. Yeah. And I got kind of worried about him. I got to thinking about it so one day I called him down here and I said, "Dad, I want you to come down here." So he came. He didn't know what I wanted. So we sat down at that table. And I told him, I said, "Daddy, if you should die a sinner, and we have to go up and look down on you and you haven't give your life to God, it would kill every one of us." I said, "It would just kill us." And when I said that, I broke down and cried because I really meant what I said. And then, when I cried, he dropped his head. He done like that and looked down and didn't say nothing. And so I went on [and] finish[ed] talking to him and everything, what I was saying. He didn't say a word. He just got up and went out the door and said, "Well, I'll see you later." And I said,

"Okay." And he went home and told [my sister] Mookey to get his suit ready and everything that he was going to church.

And she got his clothes ready and she called me. She said, "Daddy called me." Said, "Daddy's going to church Sunday." I said, "He is?" She said, "Yeah."

So he went on to church. I wonder[ed] should I go with him. And I thought, "Well, no. Let him go by himself." I thought, "Well, if I went with him, maybe it would encourage him or something." And something just told me not to go. And so he went to church. And when the preacher extended the invitation, he got up and went. They like to tore down the church up there! He joined the Browder church. Yeah, I was really happy he did too. So they baptized him on the Sunday after that, I think. And I was worried. They baptized him down here in our pool at our church. And I was scared to death, baptizing Daddy. Daddy was a big guy to get baptized. Well, now, Reverend Harker is a big guy himself and he's strong. He was a young preacher. And he's strong and he was big. It seems that [my husband] went down in there with him. I done forget. But they went down to help in case he got down there and couldn't get him back up.

So anyway, they got him under there and they did get his head under the water. So my grandmother [would have been] happy. She was gone [by then]. Bless her heart. She would have liked to know that. She was crazy about my dad.

I had my first boyfriend—I didn't know he was a boyfriend. I didn't know anything about loving the opposite sex at that time. I liked the girls as well as I did the boys. Just whoever I was having fun with. But this boy, he knew some way or another he loved me. [H]e knew that he loved me in a different way, but I didn't realize that he was a boyfriend or a special somebody. Anything that he could ever do for me, he would do it. Then the boys and girls went to the woods and got hickory nuts and walnuts and stuff like that. And he would always go get a lot and he would bring me sacks full at school. And they had begun to sell candy there at school. They would have candy to sell and he would work and pick blackberries and make money and stuff like that to buy me candy. [H]e just gave it to me and I didn't know not to take it. I just thought he was just a friend or something. I didn't know he was wanting to be my boyfriend. But he was really kind to me and he really did love me. He really loves me, I guess, [even] now because every time I see him he has a different expression on his face when he looks up and sees me. He always gives this certain smile.

And I hated to hurt him and I did, I guess, hurt him. Well, really, I didn't have no special friends and I wasn't serious about anybody. And he still wanted to be a special friend and he wanted me to marry him when we got old enough to get married. And also his family did. His family was awful crazy about me. And they just loved me in a special way. But I just couldn't love him. I liked him as a person and I thought it was nice for him to be nice to me, but I just didn't have special feelings for him and I thought it was wrong to lead him on. And so we broke up, I guess, but he never did give up on marrying me someday. He never did give up until I got married. And then when I got married, he started drinking a lot. And he got to be an alcoholic and he never did get over it.

Oh, my parents was crazy about him. He was the onliest boy I could go anywhere with when I first started being able to go out. I had to be about 16 anyway. You didn't go out very early in those days. And I couldn't go out with anybody else but him. But they would let me go to the movies with him. And they were right. They knew a good boy when they saw one. And they knew that he was going to take care of me. And they were right. Because he was kindhearted and good. And he wouldn't have ever done anything to hurt me or disgrace me in any kind of way. So I could go out to the movie with him but see, they wouldn't let me go out with who I wanted to go out with.

We were able to go to the movies down here at Drakesboro when we lived at Browder. The blacks went upstairs and the white was downstairs. It was 10 cents to get in, I think. And you got a hamburger for five cents and a bottle of pop for five cents. So if you had about a quarter, it would do it all. Well, you had to have 50 cents, a quarter for the girl and a quarter for yourself. Oh, I can remember.

Central City was the same price too. And the school bus used to take us Saturday night to Central City. It was 10 cents to ride the bus, 10 cents to get into the theater, and five cents for the pop and five cents for the drinks. [T]he bus driver owned the bus, and he would take people to the theater on Saturday nights. And, of course, he'd have a bus full. He would carry us to Central City for 10 cents to the theater. And we had a place down there below the theater [where] this man made these great big hamburgers in a great big skillet of grease. And he would put these great big hamburgers in this big skillet of grease, and put them all on these buns, onions and pickles and everything for a nickel and a nickel for a soft drink. And so that's what we'd eat after we left the movie.

Central City was really a better place to go; [it] had lots more things than Drakesboro. Drakesboro didn't have anything [at] all but that little movie at that time. And of course, Browder didn't even have that. Just a coal mining town. Central City had stores and the town area and, of course, they had dancing places down there; we sure wasn't permitted to stick our heads in there. A lot of the black people ran places where they would drink and dance and have fun, and they'd have small bands sometimes. We knew about them! And we wanted to [go]. A lot of the kids slipped off and went. When they got to be teenagers, they'd slip off. But Dad said, "If I ever hear of you going in those places. You better not ever go in those places." And of course I didn't. I was afraid to go. But I sure did want to. I wanted to go just to see what it was like. I think if I knew what it was like, I would have been all right. But to dance and have fun, I thought, oh, that would be a lot of fun. But I wasn't permitted to go there.

Listen, they knew where you were at all times, and just before it got dark, you better be in the house. You couldn't be out at night. Sometimes they would call us, and we wouldn't be in, and then you got a lick or two when you went in the house. Said, "You know you're supposed to be in here before dark." So you weren't out at dark. You weren't out at dark when you was maybe 15, 16 years old. You came in. You could sit on the front porch, but you couldn't be out in the yard playing or up the street anywhere. And you couldn't go to nobody else's house without asking. You had to ask, "Can I go up and play with so and so?" They would have to know the parents up there. Our parents would have to know if the parents up there wanted us to come. If they were busy and didn't want us, we didn't get to go. And so we had to ask when we went to somebody else's house. We just didn't walk over in somebody's yard or go to somebody else's house. And if you went to the store or anywhere, you had to ask to go and they had to know where you were going and what you're going for.

When we moved to Browder it was at night. Mostly it was dark and we didn't get to see anybody that night while we was moving. The first person I saw the next morning was Buckey. He was 12. I looked out the window and I saw this young boy, 12 years old, going down the street with an iron. [T]he people that he stayed with, she washed and ironed for different people, and he was walking in front of her with the iron, going up there where she was going to wash and iron. He had on a little cap and the cap was wrong side out, and he was the first person I saw. Isn't that the funniest thing? And that was going to be my husband and I didn't know it at the time.

[H]e never was interested in me and I never was [interested in him], I don't guess. But I think he really was [interested] because he liked to tease me. And I think that's the way he knew how to maybe get next to me or close to me, by teasing me. He didn't know how to approach me. I believe that's what it was now that I remember. He used to tease me a lot, and I just hated him for it, and I never would have anything to do with him.

A lot of the boys would come to the house and see my brother. Or they'd come sit on the porch and talk to me. But he never would come too much. For years, we were there in the same town together, and we'd see each other, and he would speak or something like that. But one day, after we got older. . . .

Well, I went to Chattanooga to work. I was about 19. It was during the war time [World War II]; and we went to work at a plant up there. I didn't stay over six months or something. At first I was just in there doing a job, and then I got to be supervisor over in the cutting area of parachutes. But anyway, I came home about three months after I was up there and saw how the family was and the children were, Mama was sick, and things weren't too good at home. I went back and worked three more months to save some money to buy some things that they needed there at home. I wanted to stay longer, but they were in pretty bad shape, so I came on back home, and then spent what money I had to buy things that they needed there at the house. [I] stay[ed] with the kids because the babies were small. A lot of the children were small, and Mama wasn't well. She had had this stroke. So I just came on home and I was home ever since.

When I came home the first time, Buckey said to me, "When you go back, don't get married while you're up there." And I thought what difference does it make with him? I'm not going to marry him. So I just went on and never said anything. Didn't say "yes" or "no" or whatever. Then when I came back, that's when he saw me at the store one day. He asked me if he could come up there to see me and just sit down and talk with me.

And I said, "Well, Daddy might hurt your feelings."

And he said, "I don't care if he does."

So he came on up there that afternoon, and when Daddy came out the door, he was on the porch, and Daddy asked him with this big heavy voice, "What are you doing up here?"

So he told him, "I come up here to see Maggie, if you don't care." That's what he said. He was very meek. [Laughs.] Daddy didn't say anything. He just went on off the porch and went where he was going, and he didn't say anything. Of course, that got Buckey's toe in the door.

All the boys there were afraid of my daddy because one boy hit a girl one time, and Daddy found out about it. He told them all, he said, "If any of you all, anybody, ever lay a hand on my daughter you better look for me." Well, of course, nobody wasn't going to hit me. [Laughs.] Ohh, noooo. They wasn't going to come near me because all of them were afraid of Daddy. See, Daddy was about the biggest, tallest guy there in the mining town, with this big heavy voice, and he'd stand behind what he'd say.

[So Buckey] comes to see and visit me. That was about a year before we got married. We got married about a year after that.

Well, after we got married, he was working in the mines. He was making $8 a day in the mines. He had just got a job. When we got married we moved here to Drakesboro, and we lived in a three-room house across the railroad track, and it was full of holes and cracks and everything and very cold. If we hadn't been in love, we'd have froze to death. But anyway, we went down there and so the woman said she would rent it to us for $15 a month. We thought, "Fifteen dollars! My goodness! How high that was for rent!" We said, "Well, we guess we will take it." We took it. We nailed stuff over the cracks, and we put heavy wallpaper over the cracks and then we put the other kind of regular wallpaper on top of that, and fixed it up real cute. Painted it, and put linoleum down. We had linoleum on the floor at that time which was wonderful to have because they made them in different patterns and different colors for the kitchen and the living room, whatever. I fixed it up real nice. [Buckey] worked in the daytime, and I did most of the work while he was gone. It was an older fellow down the street that helped me paper the ceilings of the house. We fixed it up the cutest you ever saw. And so after we got it all papered and painted and the rugs down, we went to buy furniture.

Of course, when Buckey asked me to marry him, I told him that we couldn't get married unless we had some money, and so he gave me $500. At that time $500 was a lot of money! That was our first bank account. I'd taken it to Central City, put it in a bank. And we saved money until we had $3,000. Every payday he would give me so much money. Where he lived, he stayed with these people that reared him, and he would give them a certain amount. Then he would bring the rest of it, except what we would go to the movies [on], and give it to me. And I'd take it and put it in the bank. So finally, we saved $3,000 before we got married, and I told him that we needed to do that so we could get off to a good start. He said it was fine with him. So he just brought his money up there and gave it to me.

I had a lot of quilts that I had pieced and I had made feather pillows. My grandmother gave me some feathers to make pillows. He bought me a trunk to put all this stuff in.

So anyway, after we got married, we went and fixed up the house and all. Then we went to Central City to get our furniture. We got three rooms of furniture for $800. Kitchen, refrigerator, stoves, bedroom outfit, living room outfit and everything. All the rugs on the floor. Everything came to $800. [The salesman] looked at us [as] I picked out everything, and he was looking at us all this time, thinking, "Well what are these two black people [doing] down here picking out all this stuff and haven't got a dime to their name!" And we were so young. See, the grown people then didn't have that kind of money—$3,000! But anyway, he looked at us and said, "Well, how you all planning on paying for this?"

I said, "Well, we're going to write you a check for it." And I tell you, that man, I think he almost fell on the floor.

He said, "Where you got the money in the bank?"

And I said, "It's right up here at the First National Bank here in Central City."

He said, "Before we deliver, I'll have to verify your check."

And I said, "Okay. It's fine."

And so he did [that] before he delivered. We told him what day we wanted him to deliver the furniture and he said, "I'll have to get an okay from the bank to verify your check."

And I said, "Okay. It's up there." And he went up there and got it and brought it. And he brought that furniture and he gave us a receipt for it or something when he delivered it and everything. And he looked at us. He would drop his head almost as if to say, "How did you all come about doing that?!" He couldn't believe it was true. And [that was] a lot of money in 1946 for people living in a little mining town and didn't have anything, making $8 a day.

I just decided one day. I had just paid the $15-a-month rent. I told Buckey when he came home, I said, "Buckey, we're just not going to pay rent the rest of our lives. We're going to get us a house of our own." And he said, "Well, Maggie, just don't go too fast." He said, "We got to wait until we're able to get a house." And I said, "We're just not going to do this all our life—pay $15."

They had a large house up there at Browder where we lived. It was a great big two-story house. And they were beginning to tear down the houses up there. And they were selling these houses [for lumber] because they wanted the land for something else some way or another. I don't know what. But they were going to tear down this big house and I heard about it. I went up there to the company store. We were still trading with that store up there. And I went up there to the company store to get food that day. And I heard that they were going to sell that house for $200. So I decided that we could tear that house down and build us some kind of house if it wasn't but like the three rooms that we had. I said that way we won't have to pay at least $15 a month for rent. So anyway, I asked the man about it and he said, "Yeah, you can have it." I said, "Well, I'll talk to my husband about it tonight and see what he says." He said, "Well, you let me know because somebody else will [buy it], but I'll save it until you let me know."

I talked to Buckey about it and he thought, "Oh, this is terrible.

Maggie, what are you going to do?" We didn't have any ground. He said, "Where [are] you [going to build]?"

I said, "Mr. Lucien"—that was the man that he stayed with [before we married]—"said he'd help us to tear it down." And my brothers were teenagers then. They were at home and Lonnie said, "Well, I'll help." And Mr. Lucien said, "We'll tear it down." And there was a man out in the country, I think he had an old raggedy truck of some kind. He said he would haul it for like $10 or something like that. And so Buckey said, "Well, what are you going to do?" And I don't know why I thought I could [do this]. I think that would scare me to death to do that [now].

Well, anyway, I had the $200. [I] went and paid for the house. They started tearing it down. Buckey said, "Where are you going to put [the lumber] at?" They stacked it up there as they tore it down. He said, "Where are you going to put it?" So one day, I walked up through [Drakesboro]. I said, "I'm going to walk up through here to see if we can't find a lot." The mines was right up here and we were going over here to get some poke salad at the mines. And when I passed by here, I said, "That's where we want this house. Right here." So I knew who owned it. Mr. Tom Isaac. And so I went down by his house on the way home and asked him if he owned this lot. He said, "Yes, would you like to buy it?"

I said, "Well, that depends on how much you have to have for it."

He said, "Well, I'll let you have it for $150."

And I said, "Well, I'll talk to my husband."

Well, after I told Buckey, he said, "Maggie, I just think you're going too fast. You sure we can do all that?"

And I said, "Yeah, we can do it. We've got the money." Because we hadn't spent but $800 so that left us with a little over $2,000—$2,200. So I told him about it and he went and got the deed and everything. We signed, we bought it. They brought the lumber up here and stacked it up here. Then, we had to think about how we were going to get it built. How much would it cost to build. I didn't have no idea of what it would cost to build a house. And I said, "Well, we have the lot; we have the lumber. If we have to save up some more money, we will, before we get the house built."

So there was a man down here. Everything was just falling in line. He told me, "The man that built my house, he lives right over here. He didn't charge me very much at all." And so I didn't want to ask the man how much he charged him because I thought that was too personal. So I went over there and found the little old man and he said, "I'll come over and talk to you." I drew the plan off on a piece of paper. And I said, "This is what we'd like to have." And he said, "Well, I'll come over tonight after supper and talk to you about it." So we looked up and here the little old man came walking in the yard. He was a very little fellow. He came in the yard and sat down and talked to us. He said, "Where are you going to put it?" He asked all those questions and all and about the lumber. We told him we had tore down an old house and that we had all the framing and stuff like that. [He] said we'd probably have to buy doors, floors or something like that, and the roof, stuff like that. And so he sat and talked for a while and then he sat. I thought, "Oh, Lord, I wish he'd hurry up and go on and tell us the price." I was just sitting there on needles and pins.

He said, "Well, I'll tell you what I'll do." He said, "You get all the nails and furnish everything, buy the nails and whatever we need in the hardware area." And he said, "I'll build it for you for $450." I almost fainted. I was so happy I didn't know what to do. $450! And he said, "You won't have to pay me a dime until I'm finished with it." And he said, "That's completed." Can you imagine anybody doing that for $450!

And I said, "Well, Buckey?" I was wanting Buckey to tell him we wanted it done. And he said, "Well, we'll think about it tonight. We'll come over and let you know tomorrow." I said, "What do you have to think about?" I thought it would be $1,000. I thought getting a house built for $1,000 would be good then. But when he said $450, I didn't know what to think.

And so Buckey went over and told him that he could get started when he wanted to. And so he came up here and I showed him where to put it [and] he staked it out where I wanted it. He said, "Meet me up there tomorrow morning." He was right here. He started digging the footing and everything and got started on it. And built that house for $450. He started early spring as early as he could. It might have been about April. We moved up here in August.

[Buckey and I] were so happy then. We were just so happy doing what we was doing and how we did it. We were so in love. And we were just absolutely happy. We helped each other. I'd help him do the work he had to do around the house and he'd help me and we just was happy. Very, very happy. That's the best time of our lives, when we were doing those things and trying to get ahead. It was a good place to be. Of course, I wanted to do better, or build [the house] bigger. Buckey wouldn't let me. But that's all right. I never was afraid. Buckey was a little bit more cautious than I. I wasn't afraid when I could see what I [was] doing. Well, it might have been because I wasn't making the money either. But, I wasn't as cautious as he was.

I was thinking all the time that we'll live in this house and save up some more money and then we'll go to Greenville and buy a lot and build a real fine home over there. But I never did get to do that. He never would do it. I never could get him away from here. This was his first home. The first place that he ever lived and bought and owned himself. And I think it was very dear to him. It was a very personal thing to him. And I never could get him away. So after we got older, I stopped nagging him about it. I was nagging for a while to see if I could get [what I wanted]. He would always say this: "Maggie, you're not grateful, for anything" to get me to stop talking. I said, "Buckey, I am grateful, but if you can do bigger and better, you do it." And he would say that every time to make me feel bad to stop talking about it. So I finally stopped talking about it.

But he was a wonderful guy. And we had a good life together. Buckey was a nice person. He was a very kindhearted, good-natured person. He didn't have to try to be good. I have to try to be good. I've got a little of my grandfather [in me]. [But Buckey] was better by nature than I am with trial.

DAVID MATTHEWS

Born in 1920 in a community eight miles southeast of Indianola, Mississippi, Reverend Matthews believed that "freedom is preserved by eternal vigilance." A minister and an educator, Matthews explains how the economic pressures of poverty challenged moral values and shares the moral lessons he gleaned within his own home. He describes a community marked by mutual aid, where neighbors not only shared among themselves but, in their determination to educate their children, came together to retain teachers and prolong the limited four-month academic year of their local school. Matthews remembers how, in the 1950s and 1960s, community activism changed not only educational opportunities and facilities within the black community but also spawned an interracial committee whose efforts enhanced local job opportunities for African Americans.

I was born January 29, 1920, and I grew up in a rural community. My mother and father were Christians and they were laborers. We were sharecroppers. My father was a sharecropper. We had high moral values in that they taught us against stealing, robbing, or taking anything that was not ours. They were very strict on nonuse of alcohol and gambling, fighting, carousing, the bad house, they call it those days. Juke joints, they were against that. They also taught us to do a day's work for a day's pay and be honest with people as we go from day to day.

We were in a rural setting where we had four-month school. We would go about four months and then school would close out. Through the courtesy of some of the parents, the teachers were retained for maybe another month or so, but even at that sometimes the parent would have a problem with the bosses on a place. They wanted a lot of children to work in spite of the fact the parents were responsible for the teachers being retained. [To keep the school open additional months, parents] would scrape up money or vegetables or milk, butter, eggs, flour, and those that had a little money would share a little money with the teachers, and the teachers who were interested in our plight would dedicate themselves to serving on a month or so because of the needs of the children and the interest of the parents who would give enough to retain them there for that one month, which was a real sign of dedication because they weren't getting much. I think some of them would get $40 or $30 a month, something like that. It was very little. However, the prices were cheap but still that was a low wage in any area at any time. They were dedicated. They'd stay there and share with us.

We had one retired teacher's husband who gave my brother and I some books. We would come in at twelve o'clock and sit out on the porch and read those books. When we got to something hard, there was a professor in the community who had [been] retired for years; his name was Abraham; he would come along and he would show us something about algebra, you know, if we didn't understand. He'd share with us and give us some pointers on arithmetic and that kind of thing. But we'd come in after we worked that morning, come in that noon hour and spend that noon hour, after we'd eat or before we'd eat reading books. Then if we had some spare time, rainy weather or something like that, we would grab those books and start reading because they were gifts to us, English, mathematics, and whatnot. We had to study whatever spare time we got because we were laboring, raising cotton and corn.

To come out of that community was sort of like climbing out of a pit without a ladder. Like you can jump up one step and fall back two. My brother and I came to high school here, but we had to use the family car to get to high school because there was no transportation, about eight miles. We would fix flats and buy a little gas and come to school. In the eleventh grade I was called into service and I went and my brother remained here. He finished high school, and then he started teaching and going to school in the summer and finally finished college and became an administrator, a principal. He went to Delta State and got a master's degree. I came out of service and went to Morehouse and graduated Morehouse in 1950. I attended Atlanta University in 1950 in the summer, and Delta State University later, and Memphis Theological Seminary. I was called to the pastorage here, and I started teaching, so I did a dual job. I taught and I pastored for quite a few years. Those were rough days. The whites in the community were bused into school and blacks had no transportation and very short school terms. They were given nine months, we were given four. Now the school here in town ran nine months. They called it "Rosenwald" in those days. Those who were in town had access to it. Those who were out could come in, but you had to have your own transportation if you were accepted. That's how we got through high school, but it was a rough go you know.

We worked on the plantation and we got paid 75 cents a day and the day was from sunup until sundown. Not no eight to twelve or nothing like that, but as long as the sun shined you worked. They used the term from "can until can't." Time you can see it until you can't see it. That was the rule of thumb. However, during those days of struggle and poverty the so-called black community was pretty close-knit together. There were problems, but they were closer together than they are now because we had to share. Borrowing one from the other, sharing one with the other. Whatever you had you shared it. We didn't have much but we didn't have to worry about anybody taking that little because nobody was taking from anybody. It was a rarity for somebody's house to have been broken in because most of the times they weren't locked. We didn't lock the church in those days. The churches remained open and the homes remained unlocked. As a matter of fact, in the summertime with no air-conditioning, no electric fans, people could sleep on the porch and be content and nobody wouldn't bother them. But it was days of poverty.

Most farming was done by horsepower not tractors. We gathered the crops by hand. We planted by mules and horses. We had to learn to live pretty close on the farm. We got a little money by day work and got a little money by selling some of the produce as vegetables and chickens and eggs and that kind of thing. And clothes were a rarity because we were not able to get them. We kept plenty of food because my father would grow it, but he couldn't grow clothes. [Laughter.] So we had to struggle to buy a few clothes, and we didn't get many of those, but we made out with what we had. But I do admire them for several things. One, they gave us a name and all of us had the same name. We were given the honor of having a mother and father and they loved us. They were uneducated but they gave us some fundamental moral principles that will stand today. That has meant much more to many families than just academic education because many of them have received the proper education academically and then go wild otherwise. So we've been blessed to that extent.

Segregation was the order of the day. [C]olored waiting rooms were everywhere. White and black even in the courthouse [where] they had a little window where you go in and get your tag, a little dark corner. They would issue tags to the whites way out in the bright lights, and every once in a while they would see you and wait on you and wait on a white. You were discriminated against severely along those lines in public places. They had a colored fountain and a fountain for whites.

We had different ways to improvise to survive and that's the way we got along. We didn't have electric lights. We had lamplights. Later on we got electric, but we had to study by lamplights. We didn't have lights all over the house to see how to get along. It was days of poverty. There were some who got along pretty well because there were those who didn't respect the law. They made this corn whiskey, and they got along pretty well you know. [Laughter.] They made corn whiskey and they'd sell it, and they'd buy them cars and stuff like that. But I give my father credit, no matter how well they got along he would not deviate. He would not make whiskey or sell it, and he wouldn't encourage us to do it. He said, "Live right and eventually the Lord will bless you if you work hard and live right." That was his philosophy. So he never did get into that kind of thing, gambling, whiskey making, that kind of thing, he didn't do it. He gave us a good example of a good life, you know, a decent, moral life. And that stuck with us you know. So in spite of the poverty there were some things he wouldn't do.

There were several churches in our community. There was Saint John's Church of which we were members. We lived right in the yard almost. There was Morning Star above us, I guess about a half a mile. Then there was a Methodist church back on the place. They usually had service in the school that was built [there]. We would go to those three churches. There were others a distance away, but those were close around, in walking distance. We would go to Saint John's every third Sunday, on the fourth Sunday maybe Morning Star and maybe the first Sunday we'd go to the Methodist church in the community. We just interchanged because each church had service one Sunday, but you had prayer service every week, and Sunday school every Sunday, and they had choir rehearsals maybe two or three times a month. [On] Friday nights they had box suppers. The way that operated, the ladies would fix a box and the man would be responsible for buying it. And then they would have fruits and they would sell on the side, and this was an activity at the church which was a wholesome activity that gained some money for the church and [was] an outing for the youngsters.

We had revivals. Usually revivals would come after the crop was laid by in July, August, and first of September. Most of the time they would be over by the first or second Sunday of September. They were greatly attended because the ministers were fireballers and they preached damnation as well as salvation. They gave it all they had, and people would

Community grocery store in Alabama in the late 1950s.
(Courtesy of Sandy McCorvey, Tuskegee, Alabama)

fill up the churches day and night. And on Sundays they would fill them up day and night because there were not as many things to detract as we have now. They didn't have anything like riverboat casinos and that kind of thing and special TV programs and all of that. So the church really got the attention of those of us in the community at those revival times and also [during] regular service. Parents were more in control then than they are now because most families were close together, close-knit. The father was there and the mother was there unless death or something. Rarity for a family to have a divorce situation in our community. They would stick together. We ate together, and we went to church together and programs, [and] whatnot together. So there was more togetherness then. Fathers of the house were there and the sons couldn't get out of line because the old man was there, and it made a lot of difference. However, some women controlled the place they lived too, but, you know, not all of them. But the father and the mother were there. That made a difference, made a lot of difference in the discipline. And I guess the second thing, the broad perspective was that the community observed the actions of the children, and if they were out of line then any citizen in that community would be willing and ready to call you back in place. And of course if that didn't do they could even spank you, and nothing would be done about it when you'd go home except you'd get a second one. [Laughter.] But now you look for a lawyer and a court order. But it wasn't like that then, so you had a more close-knit community.

[Members of the black community] were admirers of Minnie Cox and what she accomplished. She was appointed under Teddy Roosevelt as the postmistress here in town, and of course she had to go through a lot of pressure because many of the persons would not receive mail through her. They would go out to maybe the next place rather than get mail from the post office here. They would go somewhere else and get their mail, and there was a kind of uproar you know. But they had a home over in the white community and the offspring had the home—that was the Cox residence. Wayne Cox was the husband, smart man. The originator of the Penny Savings Bank here in Indianola, and he did fine. The way they got rid of that bank was that the bank was low in funds. You know you've got to have so much according to the reserve, and they came in on them. They were able to borrow the money from a bank in Memphis, and when they came and checked them, they were in good. Then, when they would check and they'd sent the money back, they'd double right back on them and caught them with not quite enough in there. They intended to close it anyway, and they closed them out. But that Penny Savings Bank was historical. And the first bank we've gotten since that [time] is in Jackson, First America. [The Coxes] were wise people. I didn't know them in person but I've talked with some of the older persons who did know and who were acquainted with them and who had been in their company and saw how they performed and how they bought land and acquired it and retained it. It was just remarkable what they did under those conditions because the conditions [under segregation] were not favorable for that kind of progress [by black people].

Well what we really wanted, we wanted good schools and good principals, and at that time we were not pushing so much for integration in the beginning. We were asking for good facilities. We didn't have student lockers in our schools. We didn't have lunchrooms in those days. So we had to push for lunchrooms and lockers and libraries and science labs, and you know the things; we pushed for those things in those days.

At that point in our history we were not pushing so much for integration as we were for quality education as we had observed it. So they
[Mississippi's white school administration] sent special committees out,
not just because of us but because they were trying to get around this
integration and the committee made a study of Sunflower County and
recommended [building a new high school]. They had one good high
school in the southern part and one good high school in the northern
part of the country, and Gentry was planned, and they recommended it
so they built Gentry High School and placed a cafeteria, and finally they
came up with a gym later. We didn't have a gymnasium and lunchroom.
But finally they came up with a good library, pretty good library. These
were some of the objectives we were seeking during those days. Because
[of] my experience, I went through a colored high school, when I got to
Morehouse, I didn't know anything about the nomenclature of a com-
pound microscope. [Laughter.] So you know, you don't want kids leaving
out of school and not exposed to the basics that they should have, and we
were concerned about those things in those days.

I think part of [our success in acquiring a black high school and
better facilities] was the ruling of May 17, 1954 [*Brown v. Board of Education*]. That ruling also spurred up a lot of action on the part of the
white community to actually come up with some decent educational
projects [so] that we would not have to go to their schools and they
wouldn't have to come to ours. But those of us who had been exposed
were concerned about better schools; we were concerned about giving
teachers an opportunity. See, if you got a master's degree, you had to go
to Tennessee State, Atlanta University, or Southern University, out of
state, you know, Louisiana, Tennessee, over in Georgia or somewhere
else, or New York. There was nowhere in the state [of Mississippi] that we
could get a master's degree to qualify. And someone said, "Why didn't
you go to such-and-such a place? They've got a master's degree; they've
got bachelor's and doctorate degree, triple A." We didn't have anywhere.
So we started crying for some kind of institution where we could be qualified and certified to be good teachers, and eventually they evolved with
a master's program at Jackson State and Delta State and Valley State. Of
course, they downgraded Valley, but Valley's coming back. Valley State
was there to help to give us the baccalaureate program, and later they

increased [with] the master's program. Those were some things we were interested in because of our experience. You know teachers had to go way out of state to get anything to qualify, and white teachers could stay right here and go right to Mississippi State, Ole Miss, Mississippi Southern, or wherever. Those were not open to us in those days, and it was a pretty hard way to climb out.

We did sort of a unique thing. There were some good people in this community, white people I mean. We formed a group; we sat down and negotiated and talked about what needed to be done, what improvements needed to be made. We came to the conclusion that we were going to have to work together in the community if there was going to be a community, and we formed what we called a biracial committee which is still intact. Biracial committee, black and white, and of late we've made it male and female, but in the beginning it was just black and white male. We would sit down and talk about different things because we actually didn't see eye-to-eye, because there were some on the committee to say, "The only thing I've ever known of black folks was menial work. You know farmhands and chopping cotton and driving tractors and baling hay and sweeping the streets." He said, "I've never sat down with a group of intelligent black folks." He told us that to our face. He said, "I've never known that ya'll had these desires or thoughts"—[so that's] to let you know how important it was to sit down and just talk, just to understand that there's aspiration in black as well as in white and that there are some qualified blacks as well as qualified whites. He didn't know that until we sat down and talked together. Out of that connection [and] communication we got many things. I kept crying about I want something we can put our teeth in. I want something tangible. Ideas are all right, but there needs to be something tangible. I think the first thing we did constructive, we worked hard and got a young man on the post office. We didn't have a black in the post office work at all. Then we asked for fellows to be able to read the meters, the water meters, the electric meters, you know, because they didn't do nothing but dig ditches and didn't do any kind of work like that. So we asked for that kind of thing, and they started giving us those requests. And we started asking that some consideration be given qualified persons to work in these offices, in stores and that kind of thing, and they started gradually hiring folks in the various positions.

Mr. [John] Harper asked me to work part time as a deputy clerk in [the] chancellor clerk's office. I was also asked to work on the polls and that was unheard of because when I started working on the polls, I was the only black, and I was called Uncle Tom by the blacks and the object of nigger lovers by the whites. [Laughter.] Some blacks said, "How did he get on there?" And white folks said, "Nigger lovers put him on there." I was nice to them. I didn't explode. Some of the elderly white women, I would help them, and they finally got used to me. But I couldn't be the explosive type and get the job done as we were trying to do it. So we were successful then. After I worked so many years then, I got off it and on the election commission. I'm still on the city election commission. I was one of the first to assist in voting, and it was a first because we were just getting started, and [I was] the first to serve on the election commission. I wasn't so much worried about being first, but the thing about it [is] we wanted to get something done that you could see with your eyes, and it had to be done by the community. Even though the government may put an axe over your head, you had to perform the job. So we got a lot done without the federal government coming in to do it for us through that biracial committee. The biracial committee, I believe we started that committee in the 1960s. Now we met together before the 1960s, but we didn't have that committee intact. We met together several times.

A. I. DIXIE AND SAMUEL DIXIE

In an exchange with his brother Samuel, Florida native A. I. Dixie shares his thoughts about the social history of lodges and fraternal organizations. Such organizations offered not only the financial means to bury the dead and avoid the humiliation of seeking assistance from landowners, but also offered relief during times of economic crisis and physical illness.

A. I. Dixie. [The Knights of Pythias] was strong [in the twenties], all the mens that thought of themselves as anybody joined it because it was told that it was going to be a brotherhood. They had a song that they used to sing, "[David is your master] and steward for right against the wrong." Meaning if your brother was wrong, you were going to stand with him;

if he was right, you were going to stand with him; but with the wrong you would do it undercover. [White people back then didn't want them to have secret meetings.] For a long time [black people] couldn't have church at night. Have it in the daytime, but at night everybody was scared.

You had about all the colored folks [joining the lodge], because [the lodge] was giving you [help]. If a person of the Knights of Pythias would die his widow got $500, and they buried him. They had their own [funerals], and they would have a long march, and once a year they would have a celebration called a turnout. And they had a big temple in Jacksonville. And the man, his name might come to me, but anyhow, I was [in their grand lodge], and they said that they covered Florida "like water covered the sea." And [the lodge leader] had a lot of money. It's going on now, but it's no more strong like it used to be because they don't pay a $500 policy no more. They used to pay $500 and bury you. [In the 1930s Depression] folks got to where they were making 75 cents a day, and you was paying $2 a month [to the lodge] and sometimes you didn't make but two days and wasn't but 75 cents [for the whole month]. It was rough in Hoover times. There's a lot of things that went [under like the lodge]. The American Woodmen used to be strong here, too, but it went out; it went out way after then.

I joined [the Order of the Emancipated Americans] in the thirties. It's strong now because I hold a gathering now. It's not strong as it used to be because folk [are] making more money. See, you just paid 75 cents a month, [and they] give you $200 in cash when you die. But when it was start[ed] up, it wasn't paying that. If you was a farmer and your mule died, and you belonged to the Emancipated Order, everybody that had a mule had to give you a day's work, until they could get you another mule. And if your house get burned down, they would chip in and help you get shelter. It wouldn't be a fine house, but now with the folk making money, we ain't got the members we used to have. "That ain't enough money for me," but I tell them every year, "What money?" It was the strength that you help me, and I help you. It was originally if a member got sick the lodge just send a brother, two brothers to sit with him if it's a man, and if it's a woman, they would send two ladies, because [we] didn't have hospitals, just had to sit around. This here was a demand from the lodge;

this was out of their ruling. He could say, "You go stay with so-and-so." They would send a different person every night, two different people every night. I had went and stayed from first dark to five o'clock, time enough to go home and get my breakfast and get prepared to go to work. When we went there the family then could go on to their room and sleep, because they had to [stay and care for] him all that day. Some of them [lodge members] would go there every night. But now they got hospitals so—as I was telling the people—I say, "You all don't understand it like I did." That's what they were doing. If a man's mule died, and he was a member, and his crop need plowing and he'd make it known, and this brother go down and give him a day. That's how that thing got started. See, folk on a tobacco farm, they'd have to go up to the boss to get a casket for their people. And one or two wise men said, "Why can't us put us little might together, and save us from having to stand around somebody else's [the bossman's] house, when somebody die?" So then they would give you that cash, and you could go get your casket.

SD: Back in those days people was more considerate.

AD: Well they had everything in common. But when folk went to prospering they . . .

SD: They [swung] away from that.

AD: Yeah. You could join [the lodge]; they got folks what didn't own nothing to join just for their protection if somebody got sick. See, if you was on the farm you was a laboring man, and it had been time when folk would say, "Put him in the bed and come on to work. I got to get my tobacco." There were certain times they wanted you to work. I knowed a man was sick, he said, "I need you to work, yes sir," because [he] was sitting in the house, laying in the bed.

I joined a lodge when I was a young man. But, as I take it, in the Depression, our president, he built a temple there. He had an undertaker, barbershop, and a store. And he was running that under the lodge name and running it so many years that when the city filed on it for taxes for what he was doing that killed that concern. And he runned away by night. Now I wasn't living [there], but I know that he sold this insurance to a white company and the white man drove to my house and wanted me to take up the money and send it to him. But I didn't know nothing about him because he just come to my house, and I told him that

I wouldn't take a part in that. There were several lodges, and a lot of folks lost their place because of bad crops and you had to give up.

They [white people] burned down [the Knights of Pythias's lodge in 1920?]. That was in River Junction. The man that was the head of that [lodge] was named T. S. Phillyaw. He was a preacher. They got on their knees and take an oath to stand by a brother [in] case something happens to him. Get in distress, they would go to him but it wouldn't be openly. See, if they helped a brother get away that was just agreed to be betwixt them. But Phillyaw told me that when [the white people] told him they don't meet no more in private meetings, he called the members; he said, "We took oaths, brothers. Let's have lodge meetings." [They] had an inner guard at the door, and then they had an outer guard [and] he just walked around the building. But he [Phillyaw] told me the outer guard sold him out, because they [the lodge brothers] give him a gun and said, "If you see anything coming, you shoot and get out the way." But he told me this outer guard run, and they saw the bottom of the fire. So when they looked and see'd it [their lodge building] was on fire they couldn't go down the stairway; they had to leap out. And Phillyaw lived in the country further than any of them, and they [the whites] caught him before he got home that night, and they put a good whupping on him. Well, he had to leave, but well he was of [mixed race], and he went before the governor [of Florida], and he went back and he stayed there until he died because the state bought his farm. I was a small boy in the twenties when that happened.

I started in the church when I was 14 years old and T. S. Phillyaw was about one of the [few] with education because he wrote up a paper for us. [When] he wanted some deed made to some property, [that] we [Union Missionary Baptist Association] bought, the lawyer told him [why didn't] he make out the deeds, and he say "If I was a lawyer I would, but it require that a law man must." But he had it all copied out. And the man said, "You got it." Typed it and put his seal on it. They bought some property and they still got that property out on south side of Chattahoochee and they named it. They build a private school there; well, it was a [denominational] school. Didn't have a high school then in the county for black people, and these churches decided that they would build a high school, but it had to be a boarding school. And the next year after they built it, they built a high school here in Quincy called Dunbar, so then

Triune Lodge 130, Ancient Free and Accepted Masons, Birmingham, Alabama.
(Courtesy of Blanche Davis, Birmingham, Alabama)

folks said, "Why [should] I send children to pay school when they can walk to school here?" [T]hat property [of the Union Missionary Baptist Association] is still there. I went [and got] the abstract of it a few years ago because some of the folks wanted to sell it, and I told them as long as I live it would never be sold, it had to stay in that association name.

LEROY BOYD

LeRoy Boyd was raised in a small Mississippi Delta town in the midst of the Great Depression. The African American community that Boyd grew up in tried to buffer its members from the worst effects of rural poverty and white supremacy by sharing food with each other during times of scarcity and resorting to armed self-defense when their neighbors fell prey to white depredations. While these efforts were not always successful—and Boyd would eventually leave the community for Memphis—the lessons he learned about collective self-sufficiency during the Depression served him well as a union organizer and civil rights activist in the 1940s.

I was born in Mississippi, a place they called Blackhawk. I attended school in Mississippi. Of course, it was quite difficult for us to get an education down there at that time. We had to walk miles to school; I'd say about five, six miles. Come up a rain, we'd have to go further than that because we'd have to go around a creek, because the creek would be up [from flooding]. And of course, we walked right by the white school. The white children was being bused to school, and they passed us in the bus, you know, coming to school and going home. So the kids made fun of us. They'd call us "black birds." And in fact at times we'd holler back at them. We'd call them "red birds," you know.

I'm from a family of 10 children, and I came to Memphis in 1945. My father, in the olden days, before he owned his own land, would sharecrop or rent. And he would pay standard rent, you know, so much per year for that land. So I never have had the experience as some of the others, you know, [of] white [landowners who] was over them to tell them what to do. The only person I had to look to was my [grand]daddy, my mother, and father. [My father] owned some mules [and] my granddaddy owned a place. After my granddaddy died, then my daddy paid the halves out the place.

We didn't have the best house. It was an old, wooden house. Sometimes you might look down, you could see some of the dogs under the house, coming through under the house [because of a] hole in the floor. Same with one of the corners you could look out and see daylight. And they tape a patch of cardboard over the windows, help keep the air out. [It's] just what you get used to, and we just had [to get] adjusted to it. Of course, we had big fires in the house. We cut plenty of wood and we had a big fire. The people from the city used to come down there and say: "God, y'all burn up in the front and freeze in the back." [Laughter.] That's how we kept the house warm.

We had two rooms. We had a fireplace in the front room and the bedroom. Had a big fireplace in there and a big fireplace in the next room. Wood wasn't no problem. Just go out there and cut wood and keep a big fire all night. So the house didn't get [freezing]. Well, if it got *real* cold, it gets cold enough for water to freeze, you know, in the bucket. It got below, I would think, 32 degrees because I would lower the dipper in the bucket. See we had a cistern, you didn't have running water, and we'd catch our water from the house top. Had a big system, real big. When it rained, had gutters around, to pour the water right off into the cistern. That's what we used for drinking water. Every so often during the summer, if it got real dry, the cistern got dry; we'd clean it out. Clean it out real good, hoping that it would rain, while we went somewhere else, and we had to tote water, you know. Some people's place around there had a well. Then we'd get the mules and wagon and draw water [from their well] until it rained.

There were other black families around there, [and] quite a few had land. Blacks above us, they had land. They appeared to have got along fine. Of course, in later years, [in] Blackhawk they [had] a little trouble, you know, with some of the whites. But it never did develop in a lynching or nothing. At that time, if a person had a little land, he had some kind of old gun around the house, see. Those type people wasn't afraid to speak up for [themselves] if they thought they was right, although they know that they could be lynched. But they kind of stayed to themselves.

I remember one of my uncles, he got into [trouble]. I think it was a white man over at Blackhawk there. He asked [my uncle] about taking him somewhere. He told [the white man] he had his wife out there. He didn't want to take him. He had an old Model-A car. He say the man went out there and looked in his car, and the wife was in there. He said, "Why you tell me a lie?" Say, "I didn't have to tell you no lie." So he just turned his back. And the white man stood there. He picked up an axe handle and busted him.

The white man busted him. Hit him right along there. And he turned around and grabbed him. That kind of knocked him down there in the store. So, the white man's place that he was living on, they said they were going to [get] him out, probably get him at night. Well, all the Negroes, they got their guns and stay out at his house that night. Didn't nothing happen. The [Negro] was scared then. I think some of them were scared, but they was trying to go to the aid of [one] another.

That's one thing about my daddy. He wasn't afraid to speak up. Because I remember one time, this old guy, he came by there. He was working on a cookstove, he told my daddy, "I can fix that stove there where it won't take over three or four pieces of the wood for your wife to cook." So he kept talking with Daddy and he agreed to let him fix it.

Boundary Street, Charlotte, North Carolina. (Courtesy of Burke DeGrandval, Charlotte, North Carolina)

He going to charge him so much for a pound for this stuff that he put on there. Daddy seen what he was doing. See, he going to make some money off [of him] because he going to pack a lot of stuff up on there, see. It was one of the woodstoves. And [Daddy] asked what he was doing. There was little old cracks in there he was fixing to hold heat; the heat wouldn't come out, see. My daddy raised his voice, "I ain't going to pay you for you packing all that stuff up on there." Say, "I know what you doing." That was one time I learned that he wasn't afraid to speak up for his right. I was real small, but I remember him because my father, he would growl. He growled when he said it then. You know how it is when you been taught about the white man.

We moved on [and my daddy] searched around until he could find someone that they could agree on the rent. So he did. We moved on another man's place by the name of Mr. Streeters, and I remember him telling him one day that the man saw him over at Blackhawk. "LeRoy, I see you walking around here. Everybody I see [is] in the field." And [my father] told him, "Look, if I don't get one lick, the only thing you looking for is that [rent]," I think the rent was $300 a year. "The only thing I'll be giving you is your $300 if I don't stick a plant in the ground." [Laughter.]

So he got him off his back. I remember him coming back telling my mother, "I seen old Streeters over Blackhawk come telling me, 'You walking around here and all the other Negroes in the field.' " So we stayed down there until my grandmother wanted to get out from under. She told my daddy she wanted him to come up and take it over. He paid all the others' halves out of there. So we've been on the land, ever since then. That was around 1941, I believe.

Well, my mother, Lilly, she was the mother of 10 children. And she would cook for us. Get up and cook breakfast, get us off to the field. Then she'd come to the field, and she would quit around ten, eleven o'clock, come home, cook dinner, and we'd come home at twelve; we'd eat dinner. Then she'd be able to come back to the field maybe about two o'clock after she got the house straightened out. If she had any girls, well, they would help wash the dishes. Then you head off back to the field, chop cotton, pick cotton. During the first of the season it was chopping time. She would be the last one to come to the field, the first one to quit to go to the house, prepare dinner. And sometimes she'd put a dinner on that night. She'd cook them peas and whatnot, put the pot on. She wouldn't have that much to do then. She come to the house, just cook some bread. That's one of [the] other things, we raised most of what we eat. That's how we survived.

Mighty few people around the country make up sorghum syrup. That's what we used to do. Everything that we had to have, but sugar and flour, we raised. Corn, put it in the crib. Shell a couple of bushels of meal, take it to the mill and grind it, make meal. We had bread. We had cows giving milk. Hogs for the meat. Plant peas. Well, in the wintertime, we didn't have the deep freeze we have now to put them up green. We let them dry. Get them out of the hull. Take and put them in a sack and beat them out. You got a little pea. You let them stay in the hull until you get ready for them. Then put them in a sack and beat them out of the hull. You put them in a big stack, get you a stick, fill it full of peas and beat it. All of them peas come out of the hulls in the bottom. You just take the hulls out and you got peas. So they pick the peas and put them in the pot and cook them. You got some pepper left from your garden, put some pepper in there, put some piece of meat in there, you got peas. We didn't know—talking about soup lines. There's always ways that you can survive. In fact, it's the same thing now.

My daddy raised cattle. He raised hogs. He raised corn, and we can carry that to the meal. The only thing that we didn't raise was flour, sugar. We had a big lot of hogs. I know we've killed as high as eight. They be big hogs. And that wouldn't last way up in the summer. My daddy used to go to work on something, at that time they called it a WPA. And that's where he would make a little extra money to keep from having to borrow money, you know, so [that] what he made that year was in the clear.

People back then would share. If you was a neighbor and you had got behind, my family would just go and help you [for] free. When we kill a hog, we'd share the meat. It wouldn't be no whole lot, but we'd send so-and-so a big mess of meat. They would do us the same way. But we had cows; we had hogs. We'd kill a [cow] during the summer. The only thing that we didn't have then was refrigerators, like people have now. I don't know what they'd do. They fixed meat someway that it would keep for a long time, kind of smoke it. I guess they were drying that blood out of it. But we'd keep it a long time. One time it come out pickly. I don't know what they did to it to pickle it to keep it from spoiling. But now I do know they used to put salt on it. Salt would keep it for a long time. It wouldn't spoil as quick.

We wasn't around [whites], that was just the black families [with whom we shared]. Really, I never was around a lot of the white families that was sharecropping. Only white I was around was landowners. The one that we rented from, he had 400 or 500 acres. Sometimes he'd be two miles or more away from us. And we never did see him that much, no more than to go over to Blackhawk to the store there.

My sisters [were] the oldest of the family. The biggest responsibility fell on them until we, the boys, got large enough to share the responsibility of cutting wood. We were the last one to go to school, first one to quit. In fact, the onliest time we had school open [was] sometime around September. And well, we had to finish gathering the crops. After we got the crop in and just around November, then we'd go to school. Or sometimes my dad say, "We got to get some wood up for winter." So by time we got there it was getting close to Christmas. Around March we got to

[go]—I said the last one to start school and the first one to quit—We got to quit the school. Time you getting good in learning, you had to quit and go start farming, breaking land. So that was the reason at that time [that] children [were] deprived of an opportunity to get an education. Kids now ain't got nothing to worry about, but just go to school.

My daddy was [a] good provider, and he was a good manager. He was able to keep his head above the water. By what I said "above the water," he know he didn't have enough income coming in; he get out and make money to support his family, see. That's some of the things that he taught us how to do. We work by the hour for some of the whites cutting wood to make some extra money. See, you can't just sit down and look for something to come to you on a silver spoon. So that's one of the things that I always believed in.

My mother worked right with him. That's one thing I can say, they was a team. My mother was a hard worker, too. My daddy wasn't the type to make a living and take it away from home. What he made we spent it, he brought it home. During the Depression, I was real small then, the onliest thing I can remember, I know there had been times that I didn't have the shoes then. I had my shoes but, you know, the sole about to come off the bottom of it. And we didn't have the best food to eat anymore, peas. My daddy was a big hunter, too. In the fall of the year, he'd get his gun and go kill rabbits, kill squirrel. So he might kill five or six squirrel. My mother cooked them, put them on the pot there and, man, we had a big eating. Rabbit the same way. He was a good marksman. So as I said, he was a good provider.

GEORGIA SUTTON

North Carolina native Georgia Sutton remembers her mother being adamant that she and her sister receive an education. Sutton, who later went on to become a teacher and then a full-time librarian, recalled the pressures placed on female educators by the black community, who relied on them to serve as the moral guardians of their children. The guardianship of children, however, was extended not only to parents and educators, but was shared by all members of the community. Neighbors frequently helped to chaperone, tutor, rear, and discipline neighborhood children, transforming neighbors into what Sutton labels "the extended family."

I was born and reared in New Bern, North Carolina, and I've lived here all of my life, except I went to school in Durham, North Carolina, which was North Carolina College at the time I attended. And then my first job was in the state of Georgia, as a teacher-librarian. It was in Quitman, Georgia, down near Valdosta, Georgia, and I stayed there three years until I married, then I moved back to North Carolina and I got a job here at home.

At that time it was a segregated school system and jobs were very, very hard to get. [I began teaching] maybe '53 or '54 somewhere along in there. The state of Georgia attracted me because of the way they paid [their salaries over 12 rather than 9 months], and then too I felt that I had grown up, and I sort of wanted to be on my own. Of course, then it was unheard of for a young lady to get an apartment. You stayed home until you got married. And if you didn't ever get married, you were just home. I had a room with a family, and it was almost like being at home, really. There were three of us living there and [the landlady] really protected us and looked out for us.

It was a requirement when I started teaching that you must visit the homes and get to know the parents. When I first started teaching, the theme was you must teach the whole child, and part of your duties, you had to visit the children in your class. In times as they are today, I don't think that would work. That was a segregated situation. [Back] then teachers were a leading part of the community. They were well thought of, and when I first started to work, a teacher had to be very, very careful about social life. You just could not go and do certain things and then [go] to teach in a classroom. For example, let's say you might like to go to clubs. If a parent saw you out there and it got back to the school board, the chances are there would be some repercussions. Maybe you might not get fired, but you'd certainly get called in. You were expected to attend church in the community. Whether you joined it or not, you didn't always have to join if you did not want to, but you were really expected to be role models for the children. I cannot say that every teacher did what they were supposed to, but basically on a whole, the teachers were well

Delta Sigma Theta pyramids, Fort Valley State College, Fort Valley, Georgia,
sometime between 1945 and 1949. (Courtesy of Laura Blount, Albany, Georgia)

thought of, very well respected. You were an important cog in that machine. [These "rules" were] mostly for females, I'm afraid. The men usually do what they want to a point and without any repercussions, really.
So men usually went where they wanted and did most of the things they
wanted to do, but it was the ladies who had to be careful.

When I first started, I didn't think [these social rules] were very reasonable. I thought that as long as you did what you were supposed to do
in the classroom that the community did not have any right to demand
certain things of you on your free time. But I do think that teachers need
to be a role model to a certain point, because when a student can walk
up to you and tell you about what you are doing, then you don't have the
respect of the student.

It took them some time to implement [the decision of *Brown v.*
Board of Education], and as time passed there were some changes within
the systems. I knew that with integration the black children would be
exposed to all of the things that the white children were exposed to.
Under segregation and especially in the South, there was a tremendous
difference in how the schools were set up, the materials that were used or

given. In fact, when I was in school, I remember when the white children had the new books and the old books were sent to the black schools. I remember that vividly. I resented it. I highly resented it. But that is the way it was, and my mother used to tell, "Remember, what you need is to get an education." And I always remembered that. Of course, it wasn't easy for me, because my father died. And my mother who did domestic work instilled into the two of us [my sister and me] that an education was necessary, and both of us went to school. She said, "You study. You learn. And I want you to always remember, nobody can take whatever you learn away from you." What I think she was trying to say is [there] is nothing you can do about it, but you learn [and] you will be able to take care of yourself in later years.

My mother was an only child and her parents died when she was young and she was reared by an aunt. We were and have always been a close-knit family. [We lived in] what is known as the Duffy Field area [in New Bern, North Carolina]. You certainly could not say that we were well-to-do, nor wealthy even, and we certainly were not professionals, but it was a decent neighborhood. There is one thing that I do know that we have lost as a race in most cases, the extended family. For example, I had a neighbor who lived next door. If my mother were working, I knew very well that I was not going to misbehave because she was going to tell it as soon as my mother got home. The neighbors and the people around you meant a lot because it kept you from getting up on the wrong path. They really did. We looked out for each other. And to tell you the truth, I'm sort of glad that I grew up with that. Of course, during that time you were chaperoned well. You were not allowed to go just loose to this place [or] the other place without being chaperoned. And it wasn't the ideal that any adult [would do], it had to be someone that your parents knew. We had hours to be at home. For example, when I was growing up, if I went to a friend's house and especially after I started school, my mother would say, "You be back before that streetlight comes on." And I can remember many, many afternoons, I was running to get home before that light came on. But, parents kept close tabs on children.

I think maybe I was fortunate. My neighbor [Betty Blount] was not a teacher, but I'm sure she had a high school education. I stayed with her during the day while my mother worked, but she taught me how to read.

She taught me to write and she taught me math. And I've been reading since I was four. And when I started school I could read and write, too. A lot of the other families didn't have any choice but to work. But somehow or the other things have changed to such a point wherein children are looking out for themselves, and that's getting back to the extended family. When someone worked, and I can remember that once in a while if the children were old enough, they would leave them there by themselves, and the neighbor would look in on them.

[I went to] Sunday school every Sunday. Some Sundays my mother worked, but there wasn't any doubt about where we were going. In fact, the same lady that I mentioned was a Sunday school teacher and her husband was a deacon in the church. And when we were small, before we could go by ourselves, she'd always come by the house and pick us up. And my mother would always have us ready, if she had to go to work and then we'd go on to Sunday school with her, and we stayed for church. As time passed, we were in the junior choir and whatever. The church was an important part of the household.

As I think back on it, one of the things that really used to stand out in our mind would be the programs that they would have at Christmastime. All of the Sunday school classes would participate and they would have a program, and it would depend on the Sunday school teacher as to how her class was going to participate. If you were fortunate enough to be able to sing, there would be solos, but it was always a big Christmas program. What we really looked forward to was that each child would get a gift at Christmas from the Sunday school. They used to have several programs. There would be Children's Day programs, Easter programs, and there was always the junior choir and other activities. During the summer, every summer, [there] was something else we looked forward to: The church always had a big picnic, and at least it was for the Sunday school, and since we are near the water they would always take the Sunday school children to the beach. The Sunday school would always prepare lemonade and whatever, but we mostly took our own sandwiches and that was always an enjoyable day, too. We looked forward to it. And parents really would work hard to see that you got to go on that beach outing.

When I grew up there were several little neighborhood stores. I can remember when I was growing up you could buy almost enough groceries for a week for a dollar. In the black community, we knew how to survive; those storekeepers knew there was very little money available. They sell you five cents' worth of flour. Measure it out. Five cents' worth of meal. They knew that the average family didn't have very much and that is the way they had to sell it and that is the way they sold it. And you could take almost a dollar and a quarter and buy probably everything you need. And that is how they took care of the black community, helping each other.

You talk to just about anyone who grew up in a segregated situation, you're going to find those people [were] readily adaptable to certain situations. You had to have strength in order to have survived. My mother used to say, "That lady that I work for is foolish enough to believe that I really like her. I'm not thinking about her one way or the other. Just pay me what she owes me." What I am saying is that it has been in recent years that the average white has discovered that blacks do not love them per se because all along they thought years ago, "She's just crazy about me. She works for me. She does this for me, and she's this, that, and the other." We've learned over the years to survive. And I learned, too, that I could smile on the outside. My mother told me, "Nobody ever knows what goes through your head. You can afford to smile on the outside. Get what you want and go on." In other words, she was telling me, "You need to work. You've got to have the money to go to school. You do what you have to do [to] earn the money." She said, "Then when you earn your money, go where you have to go, do what you have to do. You don't have to tell anybody, 'I'm going to scrub your floors.' "

[This] used to be an interesting thing to us. Mama would always come home and tell what she said and what she had done [at work] and have a big laugh about it. It'd be a big joke to us. But my mother learned to survive. She had two girls to rear and she did what she had to do. It was a big joke to us. But you see, that's a side of black life that whites never see. They never felt that a black was a thinker. Never thought that blacks thought about anything, but you can sure believe they did. And a lot of them who worked in their kitchen laughed about some of the things that went on. And they'd laugh about it and say, "Didn't I fool her?" It was always a big joke to us. And I used to enjoy it. Well, it used to sort of make me feel better about some of the things that I had to suffer.

Couples at a social club in the late 1940s. (*Courtesy of Leola Mott, Newton, Georgia*)

That brings back a situation where a white owner had a café, and he only sold blacks food out the back door. I remember distinctly, my mother told us, "You better not ever take one penny of my hard-earned money there. Even if you can't go in there and sit down and eat, he could let you get it from the front door." She'd say, "You better not ever—I better not even hear that you go there. You don't have to. He doesn't have to spend your money." I never forgot that, and I never went there either. Even as time passed and he let us in through the front door, I still wouldn't go.

Over the years there's been some things have been really amusing to me—[in particular] for people to assume that most blacks do not think. My mother used to always say, "Don't ever let anybody beat you thinking. You have a head, use it." And right now I find myself thinking, "Why did she say that? Why did she do that?" And I'll sit back and think it out. And if you're not careful, I'll have an answer for whatever has happened. Not always right, but most of the time I can figure it out: what a person actually means when he says certain things to you. Sometimes they don't ever say what they actually mean. We were brought up that way. My mother put it like this: "Use that head for something other than to hold a hat."

GEORGE KENNETH BUTTERFIELD JR.

G. K. Butterfield Jr. lists railroad tracks and street corners as among the symbols of Jim Crow segregation. Railroad tracks mapped not only transportation routes, but routinely marked a racial junction, the divide between white and black communities. In Wilson, North Carolina, the street corner operated as an employment turnstile, the place where black men seeking work waited for white farmers to pick them up and hire them for field labor, while black female domestics waited for white employers to drive them to work. The racial landscape that Jim Crow produced made the layout of southern towns not only familiar to people traveling from one town to the next, but readily traceable. According to Butterfield Jr., travelers usually knew they were entering the "black section" of a particular city or town based on increasing signs of "blight." And Wilson's 23 miles of unpaved dirt roads (compared with less than one mile in white communities) became a marker indicating the "black section."

I came from a traveling family. My family liked to travel. That was my dad's hobby, if you will. He loved to travel, and I traveled with him. I have very fond memories of trips, and plus he was a dentist, and he would attend all of the dental conventions. And then he was active in his fraternity. He would go to all of his fraternal conventions and NAACP conventions, and he integrated the North Carolina Dental Society, which was the white dental group. And he felt that it was important to go to their meetings, so we did an awful amount of traveling. In the old, old days, we would have to stay in rooming houses. We would go into a town. We would find a black community, and we would find the local boardinghouse and that's where we would stay. Hotels were unheard of for black people. That was basically in the South and in the Midwest. In the northern cities, there were selected hotels that would overnight black guests. Selected hotels. Not all of them, but selected ones. And so when we would go to Washington, Baltimore, Philadelphia, and New York we could find a hotel. If we went to Atlanta, Birmingham, Nashville, we would have to find a boardinghouse. When we needed to eat, we couldn't just pull up to a restaurant to eat. We would have [to] come off the highway and drive into town and find the black community, and find the local black café, and eat and talk for a few minutes, and get back on the highway, and continue on.

When you live in the South and have been in the South all your life, you could find [places to eat and sleep] instinctively. Right now when I go into a strange county to hold court, I can go straight to the court-house, and [I] have never been there before. Southern towns are laid out in the same fashion, basically, and you could use your senses and sense where you are and where you're not. And if you keep driving, you can see the quality of the housing decreasing and blight setting in—abandoned cars and people hanging on the streets and then you can begin to see blacks. You know you're getting closer to the black community, and you can just go right in and find it. You may have to stop and ask someone: "Where's the boardinghouse?" And you may be a block or two from it. It wasn't hard to find. You could find it instinctively.

We have a railroad in Wilson and the railroad has always been the line of demarcation between black Wilson and white Wilson, between east Wilson and west Wilson. That railroad has been the proverbial di-viding line and when you cross that railroad you could tell that you were in another world. I served on the Board of Adjustment one time here in the city, and a nightclub was trying to open up on Nash Street in down-town Wilson, and the lady came up and she said, "Please don't give this place a permit to run a nightclub. I would never have dreamed of a night-club being on Nash Street. Please protect our Nash Street." Been night-clubs on black Nash Street as long as I can remember, but she didn't even think of that as Nash Street. Nash Street to her began at the railroad and came in this direction.

But I said, "Just a minute. You said there never has been a nightclub on Nash Street."

"There has? I been here since 1915. There has never been a nightclub on Nash Street and I don't think it needs to start now."

I said, "Ma'am, you're wrong. Dew Drop Inn." Said, "You ever heard of the Dew Drop Inn? You ever heard of Mid-Town Lounge? You ever heard of the Stop Light Grill? I mean these are clubs that are—"

"Oh, oh, oh. I know what you mean."

Then she was embarrassed. And so that railroad has always been [the dividing line]. And street corners, early in the morning, if you need a job for the day, you would congregate on the street corner in certain places, and white farmers would come by and pick you up and take you out to their tobacco field for the purpose of harvesting tobacco. We called it "cropping tobacco." So to go down the street early in the morning, you'd see old and young blacks just sitting on the corner waiting for the truck to come by to pick them up. There were also black women basically who worked domestically. They called it "in-service"—"in-service" meant "I went, I worked in service with a family, serving the family." And so you'd have a lot of rich white women every morning driving into the black community to pick up their maids. And they wouldn't allow their maids to sit in the front seat of the car. They would have to sit in the backseat with them. There were a few progressive-minded white employers, female employers who would let their maids sit in the front, but most of them had to sit in the back. But whenever the husband would bring the maid home, without exception, the maid would have to sit in the backseat, because no white man wanted ever to be seen with a black woman sitting in the front seat of his car with him. So invariably, the maid would be in the back. So that was a symbol in the black community.

WILLIAM J. COKER JR.

William J. Coker Jr. grew up in Norfolk, Virginia, in the 1940s. His father worked at the U.S. Naval Shipyards and later at a paper plant. His mother was a custodian at a white public school. With steady employment and help from adult relatives who lived in their household, Coker's parents were able to provide their children a secure and loving environment that some neighborhood children clearly envied.

My father was able to shelter us from ugliness. He and my mother worked hard. When I say worked hard, it isn't that they drained themselves, but they did work hard to get us the things that they wanted us to have, to provide for us in a manner that they wanted to provide. He bought that huge house, plenty of space, and some of the gang that I grew up with, now when we talk about old times, that's one of the points they refer to.

We were raised—if there's a word—rather princely. We were a

planned and loved family of children. We had the extended family. When we moved to Norfolk, my grandfather had died, my grandmother came, and soon after, my aunt came, who was a schoolteacher in the North Carolina school system. So we had the extended family.

For quite a while they lived with us. Eventually, my grandmother went blind, but until then, you can imagine the goodies—you come from school, and you've always got some goodies waiting for you. In the morning, having breakfast and classmates in the neighborhood stopping by to get you, and they come in the house, and we're finishing up breakfast. It didn't mean anything. Only in adult years have some of the less fortunate playmates of ours mentioned that feast-like manner that we ate in. You know, children don't pay any attention to that. I can hear my grandmother's voice—of course, Mother had gone to work—so, you see, that's the benefit of the extended family. I can hear her voice now saying to the children who had stopped by, "You all want some breakfast?"

It was mannerable to say, "No, thank you." Only a couple of children who probably needed it or wanted it more would sit down and eat with us. There was one girl, one of my sister's friends, who lived within an eighth of a mile of the school, would walk back to our house so she could eat breakfast with my sister and then walk back to school, [and] she had to pass her house again.

That remind[s] me of something that happened. There was a vacant house in the neighborhood, and in the latter part of World War II, some people moved in it, a lady with a whole lot of children. I'm speaking of six, seven, eight children. I started playing with them. I think one of my brothers, my older brother, started playing with them, too, and we became friends. My mother got clothes that we had worn, and I think she asked one of her friends if she had anything that she wanted to put in it, too, and carried several trips of clothes over to this lady, and she was so very grateful.

Surplus food—the school had leftovers. Since my mother worked there, she asked for it and they gave it to her. She gave that to them, because we didn't need it. They remain friends of ours, lifetime friends. That's a part of what I meant [about] doing what you can within the infrastructure of the group. Then if you have to go to city hall and say, "I want this or I want that," this means that you've done all you can do.

It's missing [now], because another factor has come into play. It's many things, but this is one of the factors, and perhaps one of the most important ones. Urban renewal has not lived up to the promise. As bad as things were in the bygone days, we wouldn't have survived if we had not had a stout infrastructure, institutions within our group that were strong, and it kept your identity and your focus. You knew who you were, regardless of what others may say. You knew you weren't inferior. The infrastructural institutions were there.

HARRIET V. WADE

The Depression of the 1930s drastically reduced the already limited number of jobs available to African Americans because of segregation. Born in 1928, New Bern, North Carolina, native Harriet Wade describes how the Vail barbershop, the first African American barbershop in New Bern, served generation after generation within the community. The barbershop was much more than a business; it was a gathering place where politics, gossip, and information could be shared and exchanged.

My grandfather's first barbershop was downtown, [back] then it was South Front Street and now it's the uptown part, this new South Front. The oldest man in New Bern would probably tell you he went to Vail's barbershop, and he took his son and his son took his son and his son took his son. [It was begun] in the 1800s because my uncle was born in 1899, my dad was born in 1901, and Granddad had a business at that time. We had a barbershop and beauty salon combined. My uncle and father and cousins were trained by their father [as little boys] standing on boxes, and I feel sure they were Pepsi-Cola boxes and they got their training under their father. [For my grandfather] I believe it came natural.

Now the understanding I have [is] when Granddaddy's barbershop was downtown he cut everybody's hair [black and white]. I believe he was the only barber in the town. I believe without doubt we had the oldest business in New Bern going back to the 1800s until 1984 when I sold my business. Right after the Depression my family, the men, the barbers, my dad [included], went to New York because there was no work here, and I have a letter that's got to be 43 years old that my dad wrote my uncle asking about me, and my mother was expecting my sister. All of them ended up there, the brothers because times were hard here. The men went to New York to work, and the women stayed here, and [they] sent money back. [The men were working as barbers on] 125th [Street in Harlem].

We had a big 10- or 12-room house over on South Front Street, L-shaped porch, first telephone in the neighborhood. I believe Granddaddy built the house. Through all the hurricanes and storms the house did not fall. This house was on the water. I can truthfully say that my family was considered wealthy. The house on South Front Street had three backyards. The last yard, well the middle yard, was a pecan orchard. The front yard had the toilet and my dad's workshop; and the backyard [had the] waterfront. We had a walk and motorboat and a car, which was something in those days. But they tell me my aunt, my dad's sister [Leola Vail Howard], was the only black girl in New Bern who had her own horse and surrey. And that was the same as a Cadillac today.

I grew up here and Baltimore, in [the] 1940s. I was born in 1928. My life growing up was without cares. My mother came from Pamlico County in Bayboro. My father always said he married a country girl because he loved to eat and he knew country girls could cook. But my mother wasn't happy I guess with the marriage, and being young she left my father. In leaving my father that left my uncle's wife [to care for me]. But growing up I had everything but love. My mother left my father, and of course I grieved and she went. The wives in the family did not have to work. They tell me that never was my father in the street without $100 in his pocket. You know, secure. And there were very few black businesses at that time.

Later on in life [my mother] went into the profession. Now my uncle's wife, [Alberta Vail] in the 1920s took it [professional training] in New York [at a beauty school]. Later in life the women became beauticians. Now I believe it was in the 1930s they combined the barbershop and beauty salon. This went on until my uncle retired in 1976, and he was at the age of 84 I believe. Everybody in New Bern knew him, black and white. He rode a bicycle and had his box jacket on. Everybody called him

Uncle Bub, B-U-B, [although his name was] Seth, Seth Allen. And that bicycle was his means of transportation. He never learned to drive.

I guess it was considered a modern barbershop at that time. But his wife, Alberta B. Vail, [managed the beauty parlor]. The barbershop was in the front and the beauty salon was in the back. The sons and then a grandson, which was my daddy's brother's child, worked in the barbershop. And then I was the last one to come along, and no doubt this is the end because no one else is interested in the profession.

I can remember the beauty salon being in several places, but the barbershop [was] on Broad Street. [There were] about five chairs, a dirt floor in the back, but the barbershop itself did have a floor. The back room, where the toilet and everything was, was dirt. And in the window at the front there was a shoeshine stand, and I believe there were four or five barber chairs. After my mother left my father, he had to find someone to take care of us. There were three of us at that time, three girls. And I remember we had a housekeeper who wouldn't comb our hair, so he took us out to the barbershop and cut our hair off. Cut it off. That was my first haircut.

We'd sit, I sat on the shoeshine stand and listen at the men talk. It was more of a meeting place. We had a doctor here, Dr. Mann, and Dr. Mann's son was the first black football player for the University of Michigan. I was just a little girl, but I had a crush on Bob. It was something that wasn't ever known, but it just thrilled me to sit and listen at them talking about Bob's touchdowns and what Bob did. And the ladies would pass and the men would whistle. And of course, during that time Friday and Saturday, Saturday was the big day, people would come in town from the country on their horse and wagon to get their hair cut, do their shopping. Some would get drunk and fight, you know. But everybody in New Bern knew us. They respected us.

The beauty salon and the barbershop were gathering places for information like the newspaper is now or like television. People spoke of their accomplishments, bragged on their children, and talked about how hard times were. Believe me, before television people were closer. Communication lines were open. Now during that time people go to work, come home, and the men would walk out to the barbershop. And that was their entertainment. In most barbershops, they played checkers. It was rare that a woman went in and got a haircut.

IRENE MONROE

After teaching in rural Lamar County, Alabama, for nine years, Irene Monroe joined her brother in starting the Madison Nightspot in Bessemer, Alabama, in May 1940. They named their club after the Madison stop on the streetcar line and continued to operate it until it burned in 1967. The club attracted a number of entertainers who later became famous, including Ray Charles, James Brown, and B. B. King. Monroe also describes her work promoting these musicians and suggests how important music and dancing were for black southerners as a form of self-expression and emotional release. Her interactions with whites, who came to the Madison Nightspot for barbecue and beer, reveal how complex race relations in the South could be, as does her story of one New York band, the Sweet Arthurilles, who were not quite what she expected.

Anybody would stop out there [at my club]. I didn't care what color they were. I had a lot of white customers. I had them come in convertibles and back up to the door, and they would sit there and eat about two or three barbecue pork sandwiches, and then bring them beer. I served them.

And then Mr. Jesse Edwards, he was the [white] mayor of Brighton over there, and his mother, she didn't care nothing about it. She'd come on in there and sit down on one of them stools, just as big, and tell me, "Irene, fix me a slab." She'd bring a basket. "Fix me a slab of ribs and cut them all apart." Let it be whole, but just slice it down, where she didn't have nothing to do but pull it off. I'd fix her barbecue sauce in a jar, mayonnaise jar, and wrap her bread separate. She would say, "I'm going to eat about two or three pork sandwiches." She'd sit there and eat two or three pork sandwiches, and then she'd carry the ribs with her, and drink her beer, and I didn't have no trouble.

I served beer on the curb out in the front. They'd park out in the front, a man and his girlfriend. They'd back up to the door with the top back, and they'd sit right there and eat pork sandwiches as fast as I could make them.

The whites would come in. I didn't turn nobody down. The blacks didn't pay them no attention. Some of them would come in a truck, gang of boys, and they'd sit around that truck on this side of the bed and that side, the ridge of it, and put a case of beer down the center of it, and they'd sit out there and drink it. You could drink it on the curb, and they didn't bother you.

Everything was cheap. Coca-Cola was 6 cents. Barbecue pork sandwich was 15 cents. I started off selling beer was 10, 11 cents a bottle, and that was 92 and Cooks and all like that, but Budweiser and Schlitz was 15 cents. But you could buy beer for 10, 11 cents a bottle. They wouldn't come in and ask for a bottle of beer. They'd come in and order a case. If it was four or five of them, they'd come in and order a case, put half a case on the paper now and let the other stay in there and be cold and then bring the other half. That's the way they would buy it, and they'd drink it all.

Them little old houses out there—[there] was the barn where I stored my beer. Billy Smith, what used to run the Blue Bird up there, he and Brother bought a car, one of them boxcars that come on the railroad track. They'd buy a car, and they'd have a truck go up there and unload it, Keeler's Half and Half, and put it out here. I furnished several houses with bootleg. I'd sell them a case of beer, especially on the weekend. They'd run out on Friday night. They'd come down here on a Sunday. They'd put one in their trunk and go on about their business. I had several houses in Inez, over there in Titusville. I had two or three houses I furnished beer by the case.

When I first started, I got some contracts was $300, some $350. I paid Ray Charles, Little Junior Parker, James Brown, Ivory Joe Hunter. He's from Louisiana. I don't know how many bands I had out there. But I'd book them from New York and from Houston, Texas. Houston, Texas had B. B. [King] then. That was my sure hit when I wanted to make some money. He'd been there a lot of times. Yeah, he'd been there, and James Brown, too, and the Five Royals and Ivory Joe Hunter. He had a lady here, a lady playing the piano, Vanetta Howard. She'd sit sideways on the piano and look to the people and get up and twist, and they'd just holler. I had reserved seats down at the front and a fence around it. Other people sat in the booths and outside. They'd come out to dance, you know. Up in the front was the café, if you wanted a sandwich or whatnot.

We'd be open every night. I had eight waitresses on the floor. They made $8 a week and tips. The men [who] worked the club, I think I didn't pay them but $5. They worked on tips. They'd make good money out there in tips.

I didn't have no trouble. All these people out here [would say], "Irene, they can park in front of my house. I ain't going to let them steal nothing off it." They'd be just watching the cars for me, not stealing no tires off them. I had that lot up there. I had them parked on it, and then they'd be parked all up the street. They'd say, "Just open that window where we can hear that man play that guitar."

I had a big old window on this side, and I'd open that window. And they'd say, "That man reminds me when I was down in the country trying to get my row out. Let him play that horn." B. B. would get on one of them songs with a guitar, "Lucille" and "Had a Little Girl." Boy, he would flail that thing, and they'd just jump.

Brother said, "Lord, Sister, don't let nobody else in here." They'd be out there in line trying to get in when Louis Armstrong [played]. I said, "I can't let nobody else in. It's standing room [only]."

"I don't want to sit down. I just want to get in there."

I'd let them all in there, and they was all up in the café part, dancing. We had to hand them your sandwich over like this, and get your money like that. The same with a Coca-Cola. They'd have their bottle in their pocket and their cup in their hand and the Coca-Cola in their hand, just dancing, just like that. They had a good time.

I had B. B. [King] and Ray Charles. That's when I got that little old building out there as a motel. I had to fix a place for them to stay, because they couldn't stay in the white motel, and they had to stay in there. They stayed out there and played out here. You'd have to buy about four or five dates on them. I went to Montgomery. I had three places in Montgomery, I believe, the Catfish Club and the Sawmill Quarters and another place. I played B. B. down there and Louis Armstrong. I played Nat King Cole down there the first time. I lost money on him, the first band I played up there. That was his home, Montgomery.

I lost money on him, because, see, they're supposed to advertise for you. I'd carry them placards and give them advance sale tickets to sell and put them up and everything. But see, the people never got used to going. They didn't know about them back then. You were promoting things like that. After then, why, I didn't have no trouble. I'd go to Selma to the Elks. I'd carry them to Selma and another little old place in Tuscaloosa. Them people had beer. I don't know how it was fixed, but they had it in the wall. You'd go there and they'd put the cup up under there and they'd run it out of there. They had the whiskey like that, too. They didn't have no bottles in the place. They had it fixed in the wall, and they were just selling all kind of whiskey and stuff. They would give me the door [receipts] to get to sell to the people. They wouldn't charge me no rent. They'd just bring a big crowd to their place to get to sell to them. That's the way they made their money, selling food and drinks.

Every night I'd have somewhere to go to play the band. I'd get a little shut-eye, strike out that evening about five o'clock. I'd always leave early to get in town and let them know that the band's there. I'd come back that night when it was over with. We'd get back home here. The band would come back here because they didn't have nowhere to stay.

I had the Sweet Arthurilles. They were white girls, and I didn't know it. New York folks send you a poster. They don't tell you whether they're white or black. They just see an artist and they want to come, why, they just come. They send them on. When they got here, they was white. I had them out there in the motel [and] I said, "I didn't know you all were white."

They said, "It ain't no different."

I said, "Well, will you all mind putting on a little pancake makeup?"

They said, "No."

I got some pancake makeup and made them brown skin, light brown, put it all over them. But they had on little white blouses and little bow ties, and that girl was blowing that horn, and she got hot, and she turned it loose, she opened up. One fellow said, "She's white! She's white! She's white!"

I said, "Shut your mouth." I said, "Shut your mouth, nigger," just like that. [Laughter.] I said, "What you care about what she is."

She was blowing, right. She was blowing that horn. They were dancing. He come up there and point up. See, the stage was up kind of high. They couldn't get up there. He went up there to it, and he was standing up there looking at her blowing. She was just tearing that horn up, and she unloosened her little blouse. It had a little round collar and a bow tie, little tie like that. She took it loose, she was hot, and you could see that white down there, and she was brown up here. He said, "She's white! She's white!"

I was standing around. I just walked the floor. I said, "You shut your mouth, nigger. I don't want to hear you say that no more. What difference does it make? Ain't you enjoying it?"

"Yes, ma'am. I'm having a good time."

I said, "Well, you go on and have a good time or else you'll be out of here."

They stayed out there. I mean, they played their dates, and then they left. I had a big crowd. Them girls could blow them horns. Yeah, they could blow.

B. B. had a lady, a black girl from Memphis, the first time he came here, Evelyn. Her name was Evelyn. I never will forget her. She could blow. She'd take that solo. She could blow that horn.

But the best blowing I ever seen was, I don't know if it was the Five Royals or not. That fellow was kind of crippled. He couldn't sit down in a chair. He had to have a stool because he couldn't bend. He was on that stool up there, and he'd take that solo. Them people, they stopped dancing and just get around and look at it. He played that horn. He could make it talk.

RUSSELL EVANS BLUNT

In the account of Russell Blunt of Durham, North Carolina, sports were a fundamental part of African American community life, as well as a pleasurable leisure activity and entertainment and spectator outlet.

I've been all over the South, but sports are more or less a universal thing. And the black community used sports as something to lean on. We had good times. As a black man if you were an athlete and you wanted to play baseball and you were good, you had to play on a black team and you played against black teams. And some were better than others. That's when the Negro Baseball Leagues started. All these great athlete baseball players. There were some great black baseball players. I saw Satchel Paige pitch in Boston with a black team, and they had to go play a team in Atlanta the next night.

The athletes were important because what are you going to do for entertainment? The community would get together. My mother is from Sunbury, North Carolina, and my father is from Hillsborough, but they met up in Massachusetts and married. When I would come home to visit my cousins down here in Sunbury, I was a fairly decent baseball player and they put a uniform on me, and I'd play for Sunbury for the two or three weeks when I was down here. And they made their own field. They leveled it off. A little bumpy and stuff like that, but on those Saturdays when they played ball it was a great day. It was a great gathering of the community, you see. And they played another town, and everyone would follow when we traveled to play in another town. The whole town would come out in most of these places. Down in Baton Rouge it was the same way.

MERLIN JONES

A full half-century after he left his hometown of Canton, Mississippi, to serve in his country's armed forces during World War II, Merlin Jones tells about the building blocks of the community of his youth and contrasts these early years of African American communal solidarity with the unfamiliarity of urban Memphis. Mr. Jones remains a vigorously active participant in his church, the Congregation of the Temples of the Living God, serving as an elder, a superintendent of the Sunday school, and secretary of the trustee board.

I was born in Canton, Mississippi, an only child, my father a carpenter and small contractor, my mother a seamstress. My mother had a tenth-grade education, my father an eighth-grade education. And my family, even back to my grandparents, owned their own home, and our whole family, as a matter of fact, owned property. I grew up in the Methodist church. I can't remember when I started attending church because it was an age I don't even recall. All my life I've been at church. My mother taught Sunday school, and moral values. I was taught self-respect, to respect the lives of others, and also that, as my daddy used to say, "treat others the way you want to be treated and you'll get along fine."

Unlike a lot of only children to come up I wasn't allowed to be self-ish. My mother said, "I'll beat the devil out of you if you try to grow up selfish." I had to share with my cousins, my playmates, my what have you when I was small. I attended the public schools there, and this was perhaps the first time that I was aware of segregation per se, because the white elementary school was on the street where I lived, and we had to walk past that to get to our school, which was approximately five blocks further. So consequently you can see, I asked my parents why, and they never gave me what I thought was a satisfactory answer. They just said, "Well this is their school and that's your school," something like that. But my dad did, in fact my parents always did teach me this: "Nobody is better than you, and you are no better than anyone else." That was something that was instilled in me. That "God made us all, and we are all made equal."

Even though I lived in the town I was a member of the 4-H club. And I could raise chickens, and I had a hog one year that I entered; it didn't win. But one of my chickens did win a blue ribbon. And [we did] things like that, and people [were] staying busy, and you didn't have time for crime because every boy had work to do when he came home in the afternoon.

At first we heated with coal, my dad would buy his wood in the sum-mer, stove wood, he had a house we called a wood house, and he would buy this wood, and I would have to stack it like this to dry. And after it had thoroughly dried he started buying it in the spring, and by this time of year I'm beginning to stack it in this wood house. Laying it flat like this on up as high as I could reach, so we had dry stove wood all year for cooking. Used very little wood in the house because we heated with coal. But [we had] this coal house, [and] the man wouldn't bring his truck in. He said, "I may get stuck in the yard," so he dropped the coal here, and I got to pick the coal up, and I got to carry it over here another 20 yards to the coal house. And so consequently I didn't have time to get out and get into trouble.

In the afternoons I'd come in from school; I had to feed the chick-ens. This is when you could have them [in town], then they passed a law where you couldn't. Well, I had to feed the chickens, feed the hog, feed the dog, get in the coal, get in the wood. That was my job. And in the winter by that time, it's dark. So, the next thing, lessons. My lesson was checked every night, and so I had to give some satisfactory results, or I didn't go to bed. Whether it was seven, nine, eleven, whatever it might have been, my lesson was checked. Even when I got up in high school, my parents checked my lesson. It's strange, my dad only had an eighth-grade education, but I never will learn as much algebra as he knew, I don't know how he learned it.

One thing, like I told you before, some of the people were so terrible, some of the white people, that my mother wouldn't let me work for them because she knew it meant trouble. I can remember one time when I was about 14, 15 years old. I had just gotten a job working at a 10-cent store against the knowledge of my parents. My mother found out I was work-ing, and she said, "You won't work there because that man [Francis] has a habit of," and I'll quote her, "kicking those nigger boys' asses." She said, "If he kicks you, I'm going to shoot his legs off." She went down and got me out of work. "Well," Francis says. "No," she said, "because I'm going to show you, just like I always say, you've got a habit of kicking little nig-ger boys' asses, and if you kick his, I'm going [to] shoot your damn legs off." [Laughter.] That's the way she would speak up. It didn't matter who, nor what, nor where. They say she was crazy. And even when I got older [they'd say], "You're crazy like your mama."

Life in a small town is quite different than in a city, and in a small southern town you really have two towns in one. You've got a black town and a white town. With their different, shall we say, "folkways," because there are certain traditions in black neighborhoods and certain traditions in white neighborhoods. I don't know whether the white peo-ple believed in sharing, but the black people believed in sharing. In my opinion, I think they have a closer relationship with one another in small towns because they're so concerned for the neighbors. And I don't know whether the whites do or not. But I have seen a lot of white people, if a white person is [in trouble] it's just too bad. That's the way they look at it, you know. But the people in our neighborhood, there was nobody [they wouldn't help]. Say, if you were out of work, you didn't have to worry about not having food. Heat, the utilities working, because somebody was going to pay it. And I have heard that sometimes, even two or three times during a month, somebody, two or three people trying to pay somebody's utilities, say, "It's already been paid!"

And I think that's one thing that helped. And out of our little group that came along, the group that I grew up with, there were one lawyer, oh I don't know how many teachers, social workers, mechanics, one railway porter. One of the guys I grew up with was singing with some choral group in New York; there were three of them that had their own construction business; others have gone away, worked various jobs, but I know of none of them who ended up in jail or prison. Not one. And the girls in the group, I don't know of them having any illegitimate children; nobody's been involved in any drugs. So I think we came from a pretty stable group.

Religion has always been a key thing in the black community. Most of the black people, in fact all of the black people in my neighborhood were either Methodist or Baptist. We went to three different Methodist churches, two different Baptist churches. But they were still either Methodist or Baptist. I say most of them, not all of them, but most of them went to church every Sunday. Most of the children went to Sunday school every Sunday. And they were active in church, not just going but active. I've always been active in church. I can remember we had a community choir; it was made up of the young people of all the five churches I mentioned. And we were pretty good. There was a couple of ladies and one man, Mr. Garett, used to work with our group, and we stayed together for about three years and we would sing at various churches. And the money raised stayed at the church; we got nothing out of it, we didn't even want anything out of it. But it was just the idea of doing this. Once a month we would sing at one of the churches. And the people started turning out, naturally as we sung together longer, we got to be better. And it eventually got to where we would have a full house every time. That was something I think that helped to bring us together because not only were the people of our neighborhood there but this brought in the people of the whole town together. No matter what section of town that you lived in, you had somebody in there from that section of town. Consequently that was something that helped to unite the people, and it brought the churches closer together.

When we were building our church, the students were building it, and the other churches put on programs and so forth to help our church. There was another church, it was a Baptist church; they built their church, [and] other churches put on things to help them put up their church.

Half of the people there, more than half were born and grew up right in the house that they lived in. Either they grew up there or when they got married they moved there, and that was where their children grew up. So you didn't have this rivalry like you have now [when] you've got people here [you] don't know. I know one neighbor here, one neighbor over there, one down there. That's all I know, that's the neighborhood! The rest of these people walk out here, I wouldn't know them! I don't know their name, I don't know their faces. But where I grew up, I knew everybody. I could tell you just about everybody's age, and maybe their weight, that's how well you knew them. Because you saw them every day.

The people there, they had a white fairground, and a black fairground. A white fair and a black fair. However, on one day, I remember at the white fair, the black people could go. And on one day, when the black fair was there, the white people could come. [Laughter.] It was crazy! I don't remember what day it was, but it was one day during the fair. This was in the thirties and forties. They'd have the white fair, they'd have this white parade; two weeks later, the black fair, the black parade. [Laughter.] When I look back on it, it was all silly, you know? And, everything was [on] Hickory Street, this was a street here, this was all black. The cafés, the dance hall, two funeral homes, mmm, what else, pool room. On Hickory Street, this was the black business street. And that was where the black businesses were located primarily. And so on Friday night and Saturday night, that's where you'd find most of the black people; they'd gather down there around the cafés and various places, and there was one place, a dance hall.

When I was talking about the relationship between the people in the neighborhood, the people there, it was a very stable neighborhood. To give you an example, when my father died he was 94; there were one, two, three, four people died during that year, and he was the youngest one. Mr. Thomas was 102, Mr. Elvis was 98, Mr. France was 96, my dad was 94. And they had all grown up together in that same neighborhood.

Men's meeting on "Black Billy Sunday," Mt. Calvary Baptist Church, March 20, 1912, New Iberia, Louisiana. (New Iberia Parish Library, New Iberia, Louisiana)

You're talking about a stable neighborhood. All of their children had grown up in that neighborhood, and some of their grandchildren had grown up in that neighborhood, as a matter of fact some of their grandchildren and great-grandchildren still live in the houses where they lived.

I'll go back further to the 1930s. I told you my mother was a seamstress. During the Depression, in the thirties and after the Depression, my mother sewed for these people, and people who sew buy cloth to make dresses; they have scraps left over, and they would give it to her. She would take that and make little dresses for neighbors' children. I can remember her telling me when I was small that during this time she made dresses for 15 cents. Fifteen cents for a dress, and she would work and make two and sometimes three dresses a day on a sewing machine that you had to pedal; it wasn't any electric machine. And when my dad couldn't get work, that's how we survived. With my dad raising hogs and chickens and a garden, and all the people in the neighborhood did likewise, and that's how we survived. And say you had an abundance of pole beans, you'd [tell] all the neighbors, "Come on, my beans, I can't keep up, come on and get you some beans." And they would go into the garden, and they would pick what they needed for that meal. Somebody else said, "Well I've got a lot of tomatoes; I've got okra," and they would just do that. Now sometimes for some of the older people in the neighborhood, they would pick it and take it to them. This system [was] like that, and nobody starved, and nobody was hungry because they shared. And this time of year they would can. I can remember my grandmother canning. She had her garden; in fact she called it her orchard because she had pear trees, apple trees, plum trees, peach trees, and we would have to go out and gather this fruit, and we helped her. We would peel peaches or apples or what have you, and they canned fruit. They made jellies, preserves, and just much more than they were going to need. And if there was a neighbor whose house would burn or something, and their food supply and canned goods would get destroyed, then the neighbors would pitch in and help replace it. I can remember one neighbor, and my mother said, "Well, I've got two mattresses on this bed. I can give her one; I only need one." Took one of the mattresses off and gave it. My dad and some other men helped to rebuild the house. Didn't charge them anything. There were some of the people at the lumber company, they were white but they were pretty nice, they gave some of the lumber to help to rebuild the houses. And that's the way the people got along.

My mother made dresses for some of the children [and] I'm going to show you how things work. Some of these same people that she made dresses for when they were growing up [in Canton and] I was here, [in Memphis and] my mother had grown old. She was living by herself; my dad was dead. Some of those same people [in Canton] helped to see after her, and didn't charge her anything, and didn't cheat her. They would take her to the store; they would go take her to pay her bills; she was independent: "You can take me but I have to do it for myself." And, she had a stroke when she was 85. She had been sewing that day, and that night she had a stroke. And they found her, she was trying to get to the phone. They said she was a little over a foot from reaching the phone, and that's where they found her on the floor. She had a heart attack and a stroke, and she stayed in a nursing home for 17½ months, and she was unable to move or speak, and so she was there but I went to see her every week, and the whole time I was going down there for two winters I never had any bad weather. God just fixed it that way. We ran into a thunderstorm once right down here near Coldwater, that's the only weather that delayed us.

So in the neighborhood, in the town in fact, the people worked together. It was more or less what you would hear about the old western days when people pitched in to help one another. I've seen my dad pay people's rent, pay their utilities, and sometimes my mother would fuss. He said, "Oh, well I won't lose anything." And he didn't. I remember there was a lady whose husband had left her, and she had four children, and my dad paid her utilities; my mother made some dresses for the girls. There were three girls and a boy, and one of the other neighbors brought her some food. They eventually helped her find a job, but that's the way people would pitch in and help each other. I guess because it was, as I said, a very stable neighborhood. There were no strangers in the neighborhood and there was no turnover; everybody stayed there. We grew up together, I mean, when I say grew up together I mean it. From birth to adulthood, I guess if World War II hadn't come along and separated us, we would have still been stuck together. But we were always from birth on up to college together.

I tell you one thing we used to do though; we used to frighten people. I lived here on this corner, this street went into the cemetery, this street went straight through, this was where my grandfather and a lot of my relatives lived up in here. This went through and it turned this way, and went on out to the rural areas from there, and they used to come through in wagons on Saturdays coming to town; they'd go back on Saturday night. And we used to get in the cemetery and get behind tombstones and make weird sounds, and they would beat those mules and horses. [Laughter.] So, I mean the negative didn't affect us because that was a play area for us. This was a very large cemetery; I guess it went for a quarter of a mile in either direction, no a half mile I'm sure one way. And we knew every inch of it. And we would get in there, and we would get behind those large tombstones; we had a lot of fun doing that. And one guy would get out and get a sheet on a moonshiny night; he'd take a sheet, a pillowcase and put it on a stick and wave it, make that sound, and those people would think—we really had a lot of fun doing that. Until one night a man came and started shooting at us, that just about stopped us. "Damn, I came ready for them this time," I mean he was shooting like mad! But we always protected ourselves; we stayed behind the tombstones. It was really funny how they used to run. I was telling my wife about this, she said, "Y'all should have been ashamed of yourselves." We were very devilish; we weren't bad, we were devilish.

I can remember one year at Halloween—I told you about the janitor at the school? His grandson got his keys one night, went out one night, and Mr. Snodgress, an insurance agent, had a Model-T Ford, a coupe. I don't know whether you ever saw one or not. Real sharp little car. And we got that Model-T and we pushed it for, I don't know, eight or ten blocks to the school, and we unlocked the school, pushed the car down the hall, down the aisle; you know how the cars were narrow then. We went out the shop, got some lumber and pushed the car up onto the stage and closed the curtain. We got dust mops and wiped up all the tracks, put the lumber back, and locked the school up.

The next morning we went to school. Mr. Rogers had chapel every day. He went in to open the curtain at our chapel and here's this Model-T Ford! [Laughter.] You had to see him! Mr. Snodgress had called; his car was missing; he didn't know where it was; he was inquiring about the neighborhood. They didn't call the police back then, they inquired [about] the neighborhood, somebody stole his car. "Did you see anybody borrowing my car?" And they found the car on the stage. It was really funny! Mr. Rogers said, "If I knew who did this you would be expelled; you would never go back to school!" He had an idea but he couldn't prove anything, because we were the devilish people. We had another case. The shop teacher we didn't like, he was the one before Mr. Patton came, and he went out and we nailed his chair to the floor. He was one of those people you've seen who liked to snatch his chair and sit down on it. He snatched up the chair, the chair wouldn't move! [Laughter.] Everybody got busy. He's standing there cursing and fussing: "If I find out who nailed this damn chair to the floor, I'm gonna beat every devil [out] of you!" That's the kind of stuff that we did. We didn't go out and bother nobody's houses. But devilish stuff like that was what we did. And it was a lot of fun, it didn't hurt anybody, and we didn't do anything that would really damage anybody's property or anything. We didn't hurt Mr. Snodgress's car. So to get the car off the stage, they didn't know how to get it off. The shop teacher came up, he said, "I've got an idea." He said, "I saw some 2 x 10 that had some tire tracks on them. I have an idea how it got up here." He went back there, got the wood with the tire tracks and put it on and brought the car down. It was really funny though; the Model-T didn't weigh that much, it only weighed, oh about 1,500 pounds if that much. So if you ever seen an old Model-T coupe you'll know what we were talking about. It had a steel top; it was a two-passenger car. Maybe you could squeeze three in it, but it didn't have but one seat, and two doors. And it was straight up just like that, the windshield straight up.

[And Mr. Snodgress] was one of the nicest people I know. As a matter of fact, when I went to college, he was one of the people who wrote me the nicest letters of recommendation.

I told him later [about the car and what we did]. He said, "I had a feeling you boys did that but I didn't want to get you in trouble." He said, "I just took it as a good practical joke." His daughter knew about it; she saw it. But she didn't tell anything, she didn't tell it. And I said, "Janice, why didn't you tell your dad?" "Uh huh, I just got busy." She got up the next morning getting ready for school; he was looking for the car. She said she didn't mind walking to school that day! But she couldn't tell anybody what happened.

WILHELMINA BALDWIN

Wilhelmina Baldwin relates the story of an African American soldier returning from World War II who, in choosing to assert himself and defy the emasculating etiquette of Jim Crow, found himself in a struggle for his life. "[Y]ou just didn't look at a white woman if you were a black man," Baldwin confesses. "Don't touch her any kind of way."

As the story demonstrates, help within African American communities

*took the form not only of providing food and clothing, repairs to homes,
and tutoring for neighborhood children, but also refuge from racial
violence.*

I know there was one fellow who had come, he'd been in World War II.
He had been wounded. He was a man of small stature. I cannot remember his name. We knew him at Boggs Academy, and his name just
escapes me. One Saturday he was walking down the street with a friend
of his. A white guy and his wife were coming, and the man should have
been on the outside in the first place, but his wife was. The man was
walking close to the buildings, and the woman was in the middle of the
sidewalk. This guy was talking to his friend, and the woman kind of
bumped him.

He tried to be a gentleman and said, "Oh excuse me, ma'am." This
[white] guy says, "Don't you put your hands on my wife." [The soldier]
said, "Wait just a minute, I apologized, she's walking in the wrong place
anyway. You should protect your wife on the inside of the street." [The
white man replied,] "You don't tell me what to do!"

This little guy all of a sudden jumped on that white guy and knocked
him out with two [blows]. He hit him twice. And all that anger he had,
and fear, frustration he had when he was in the war, just came out of
him. He hit that guy twice and knocked him out cold. And he walked
away, he didn't run.

This other guy took him around the corner and said, "Man, don't you
know you're in trouble?" He said, "Well they can come for me anytime
they get ready." He had one hand grenade that he had brought from the
army and some other stuff. And this guy says, "I know where I'm going
to take you. You going with me." And he brought that guy out to Boggs
Academy, parked his car in the barn. This guy was in one of the rooms
over at the boys' dormitory, stayed out there.

We sent his meals over to him and everything. He stayed out there
for almost a week, until he made contact with his people in Florida.
And he went to Florida. That was the year I left Boggs. But I heard that
he had been back to Waynesborough twice and nothing happened. His
wife said that the man did not run into her intentionally, and that he did

Page from a family album. (*Courtesy of Margaret Nelson, Orangeburg, South Carolina*)

try to apologize. But she said that her husband had a hot temper, and he jumped on that guy.

The [white] man was really wrong to take it that serious, but you just didn't look at a white woman if you were a black man. Don't touch her any kind of way. I guess that still happens. But that was a frightening time for me because I was still at Boggs Academy, and I tell you, we didn't know what was going to happen, but we knew we had him out there. We didn't want him to come out at all. The sheriff came out to see if we had heard of him, if we knew him, the last time we had seen him, you know. Nobody on campus, some of us knew him, but hadn't seen him in a long time, didn't know about his whereabouts.

We prayed real hard that they wouldn't do any searching because it wouldn't have been hard to find him at all. But they would have had a time finding that car because the barn had bales of hay and a lot of tools. A tractor was up there and an old truck. So after they pulled his car in and piled the hay they put the truck across the front of the barn. It was just sitting there with tools on it, like it had just been sitting there for a long time.

But when that guy left going to Florida we took up a little collection for him, so he could have gasoline. But he had that hand grenade with him and two guns. He had a long rifle, one of those things with the bayonet on the end of it. He was ready for war.

FOUR

LESSONS WELL LEARNED

Immediately following the Civil War the masses of ex-slaves sought to secure education long denied them by their former masters. Missionary schools such as Hampton Institute in Virginia, founded mainly by northern Christian organizations, first answered the newly freed slaves' call for learning. But northern and southern whites were determined to direct and control black schooling, even as they built segregated schools for freedmen and women. They came with various educational philosophies for their black students; most meant to prepare them for a life of subservience to whites. As a result, deep divisions quickly emerged among whites and blacks regarding the intent and purpose of formal education. Within the black community this conflict has long been identified with two prominent black educators and intellectuals, Booker T. Washington and W.E.B. Du Bois. Their opposing views came to represent the polarities of the argument.

Washington, a Hampton graduate and president of Alabama's Tuskegee Institute, advocated agricultural and industrial training for blacks, who were sorely in need of economic uplift. He proposed that African Americans train themselves to perform jobs that white Americans would allow them to hold, thereby making them not only an invaluable labor force, but independent property holders. In contrast, Du Bois advocated a curriculum that focused on the study of literature, the arts, philosophy, and the social sciences. His interest lay in developing a well-educated cadre of leaders for the black community. Those he called the "Talented Tenth," who could then devote themselves to the uplift of the race. White southerners and philanthropists mainly envisioned Washington's model, encouraging his brand of instruction to create a black underclass of laborers.

Fargo Institute in Arkansas represented one school that closely followed the Hampton-Tuskegee model. Here black students who sought a higher liberal arts education had to choose from narrow options. Besides manual crafts, they followed a preparatory course for teachers. Similarly, in Historically Black Colleges and Universities (HBCUs), postsecondary academic institutions founded before 1964, the curriculum often forced students to navigate between industrial and liberal arts. These were not easy decisions for students.

As we will see, the type of institution one attended significantly shaped a student's experiences and opportunities. Many students attended publicly funded schools, which were frequently poorly financed by state or local governments. In contrast, in privately funded schools such as those built by the Rosenwald Fund throughout the South, black principals and teachers frequently had more leverage on curriculum and discipline (although ultimate oversight of such schools was sometimes in the hands of the local white elite).

The lessons that Jim Crow taught to black children were numerous and easy to comprehend. Children learned that they were not allowed to attend the same schools as whites. After a short while they saw that only white children received a bus to ride to and from school, along with new books and desks. They learned too that only white students had decent libraries or science labs. Census statistics by 1910 in Beaufort County, South Carolina, bear this point out. While state expenditures per white pupil averaged $40.68, the average black pupil received $5.95. The average value of a white school was $30,056, and $3,953 for a black school. Similarly, Macon County, Alabama, spent $57,385 on 1,435 white students and only $27,813 on 7,145 black students—the majority of the school population.

Even as they learned these lessons, African Americans struggled to transcend impediments set before them to attain decent educational opportunities. They improvised and found ways to supplement the meager resources they were allotted. They devised innovative means to improve the poor educational opportunities that southern states afforded them. Many simply learned methods to cope with the harsh realities of southern apartheid; they were determined to survive and live lives of value to themselves and their communities.

In an effort to fill the void left by public school boards that neglected their care, black schools became institutions carefully nurtured by black parents and communities. Braving unequal opportunities and facilities, they supported black schools from their own meager resources. When there was no wood to heat the schools, parents would send children to school with timber to fuel the heater. If schools offered industrial education, the community's laborers not only donated the tools and materials to furnish the classrooms, but also volunteered as instructors. In Canton, Mississippi, the town's black brick masons and carpenters taught boys those trades.

Although the segregated school symbolized inequality, it also came to represent a degree of space and autonomy for black communities. Subjects like black history, which were ignored by the white teachers and administrators who defined the official state school curriculum, were covered in black schools. When the curriculum did not call for African American students to learn trigonometry, their teachers taught it anyway, endeavoring to level the disparities between white and black students. Often teachers found in this independent space the freedom to teach in unconventional ways. Arlestus Attmore, a teacher in New Bern, North Carolina, inserted black history into his lessons. He remembers "that in our history books we were only introduced to a smattering of people of the black race such as George Washington Carver and other blacks that stood out. We did not know about Mary McLeod Bethune or those people that were not mentioned in the book. I would do research in the libraries and collect all of the materials that I could to let the children know of the accomplishments of the people of their race." Black teachers like Mr. Attmore, moreover, taught well beyond regular school hours and the regular curriculum, staying after school and offering subjects not covered adequately by the state curriculum.

Despite these efforts to provide the best education possible, the segregated school still worked to engender feelings of inferiority among African Americans. Indeed, beginning in the 1930s psychologists and social scientists such as Howard University professor Charles H. Thompson began arguing that segregation stigmatized black students. Their research armed the NAACP's counsels—from Charles H. Houston to Thurgood Marshall—to argue that segregated schooling both harmed black children psychologically and denied them the "equal protection" mandated by the Fourteenth Amendment. In its 1953 appellants' brief, the NAACP reargued these two claims and the Supreme Court agreed. Its 1954 *Brown* decision pointed out that public school segregation had "a detrimental effect upon the colored children," who were being "deprived of the equal protection of the laws guaranteed by the Fourteenth Amendment." Still, for many African Americans, even a Jim Crow education helped to transcend humble beginnings. It gave hope to many; it represented a place to affirm black children culturally and prepare them educationally. Segregated schools were integral to white oppression while simultaneously promoting black liberation. Schools endeavored to teach African Americans how to negotiate their harsh and oppressive reality, even as they caught a glimpse of how to overcome second-class citizenship.

ANN POINTER

During the era of legal segregation, African American children rarely had access to public transportation to and from school. To make matters worse, black children frequently had to walk past white schools on the way to the more distant, segregated institution.

As they trudged long distances to school, African American children often experienced harassment at the hands of white children, as Ann Pointer, a native of Macon County, Alabama, relates.

I tell you, I had to walk to school every day and back no matter if it was storming. We could not ride the buses although we were paying taxes. But we couldn't ride those buses. Nothing rode the bus but the whites. And they would ride and throw trash, throw rocks and everything at us on the road and whoop and holler, "nigger, nigger, nigger," all up and down the road. We weren't allowed to say one word to them or throw back or nothing, because if you threw back at them you was going to jail. Now that's one of the things, that's the only bitter spot in my heart, and I shouldn't have it, but you know, you can't keep from thinking. We were paying tax, but yet we could not ride those buses; our school was the only [school for blacks]. We didn't have nothing at our school. They give the teachers some chalk and a couple of erasers for the board, but no kind of supplies. Not even heat. If your father didn't bring two loads of wood to that school, then they made you go to the woods and gather wood and you, you were not going to sit by the other children's fire. We were told, "All who ain't brought your wood, go to the woods." We had to go out there and walk up in water trying to find wood to help heat the school.

THOMAS FRANKLIN VAUGHN

Thomas Vaughn of Pine Bluff, Arkansas, shares a remembrance that adds a nuance to our understanding of how plantation owners controlled the access of African Americans to education. In a seeming departure from customary patterns, a plantation owner offered to drive the young Vaughn to school during periods of inclement weather. Vaughn's unwillingness to accept this proposal illustrates the caution of African Americans in their dealings with whites.

Even plantation owners would sympathize with you if you were really trying to do something. One walked up to me one day. It was snowing. It would snow a while, then sleet. I'm trying to make up my mind to walk the railroad track or use the gravel road. They didn't have blacktop, just gravel, and so I'm trying to determine whether you need to walk the railroad [or] to walk the gravel road. This plantation owner walked up to me and said, "Where are you going?" I said, "I'm going to school." He said, "Why are you going?" I said, "To better my condition." He said, "Don't you know you'll catch yourself a cold?" I said, "That's a chance I'll have to take." He walked on inside his store and called his grandson, and said, "The boy is up here and he's going to school anyway. So, anytime you

Young boy feeding chickens, Tallapoosa County, Alabama, sometime between 1939 and 1942.
(Courtesy of Sandy McCorvey, Tuskegee, Alabama)

see him standing up here in front of this store, you pick him up and take him on down to his school." So I'd ride to school sometime in the [Packard]. The big car then was a Packard. But I didn't wait there too many times. I was too independent. I was afraid one day they'd say, "I'm tired of carrying him," you know. So the [weather] had to be extremely bad, before I would stand out there and wait on him.

WILLIAM J. COKER JR.

"This is going to blow your mind," William J. Coker Jr. asserted before launching into a description of skin color prejudices among African American teachers at his elementary school in Norfolk, Virginia. In Coker's view, prejudices of this sort made it all the more difficult for black children to overcome the educational disadvantages imposed on them by whites.

You see, when we say education today, we think of formal education and the classroom structure. During that day, there was a responsibility of survival, and the men and the family, if they were any good at all, they had to prove themselves by providing. With my grandfather, on my grandfather's farm, he had three sons. Of course, they had to work the farm, and in my father's case, he worked both the farm as well as a regular job. That's simply the way it was. If I remember correctly, I believe he told me that he and Mother both went to the sixth or seventh grade. I'm not sure.

But you see, there's something else about that day. Your main education, as well as the reinforced education, was done at home. The reading, the writing, and the arithmetic, as they say, both started in the home and was reinforced in the home, and the formal part of it was sort of an in-between thing. There were always books in the home. And of course, Bible-reading was a great part of it. My grandparents, as well as my parents, you could sit and talk with about almost anything. They wouldn't live a day without [reading the newspaper]. I recall the *News and Observer*, I believe it's called, and there's another paper. Seemed like it's the *Tribune* or something that's coupled with North Carolina papers. This is what they subscribed to. They didn't know much about the *New York Times* or the *Philadelphia Inquirer*. [Laughter.] That would have been another world.

I was able to ease into school at five years old, but I got the whooping cough. This was before we moved to Norfolk. I got the whooping cough, and didn't finish the year. So when I came to Norfolk, well, I was six, I started in the first grade. The first school [I attended] was Waterford Elementary School in South Norfolk, Virginia. This was an eight-room building without a library. We had books without backs on them, pages torn out of them, and some of the pages were marked and a part of the book marked. What we got was the books from the white schools, which they had probably used for four or five years and then passed on to us.

We never got a new desk. We had a basement cafeteria, for a small school—except for the fact that it was very hot down there. Kids are resilient. Kids don't complain. But today no parent would send their child to that kind of thing.

The teachers were a mixture. They were all dedicated, I'm sure, but some of them—how shall I say this to be delicate? Some of them did not treat the lower-class, for lack of a better word, children in the best manner, and I was very aware of this. As a child, I was very aware of it. I guess I've been a fighter for the underdog by being an underdog all of my life. Children from certain neighborhoods, children who did not have the advantage of being able to dress in a reasonable manner, or maybe even children who didn't have that 10, 15 cents in their pocket for lunch—by some teachers [such children] were treated atrociously in my way of thinking.

This is going to blow your mind. I've only started talking about this recently, and the reason I'm talking about it is not to lambaste anyone, but we must assure ourselves on an intragroup basis that this must never happen again. We can't expect [help from] external forces. You must learn to do some of the things that need to be done for your particular grouping yourself.

First grade. The very first day the teacher placed you in what was to be your permanent seat. All of the little fair-skinned, curly-haired girls and boys were placed on the first, second, then maybe some of them in the third row, according to how well they dressed and their skin complexion. There were no dark-skinned children on these three rows. Even if they were from wealthy families—and there weren't that many wealthy families, but there were some who did better than others.

It was very well stratified. Being middle complexioned and being well dressed, I was on the fourth row. For the next three years, I would be on the fourth or fifth row, which naturally meant that the [teacher's] attention would presumably be given to the children closer to her, since her desk was in the front.

I remember a girl, and I haven't seen her since 1950. [She] had black velvet skin, coarse long black hair. A beautiful girl. Quiet—subdued into being quiet, perhaps—and brilliant. Okay? She was never called on. She was almost voiceless. Her seat for [the] eight years I went to school with her was the seat nearest the door. So when class was over, she can get out of that door and get home and will not have to be called names. Of course, since the teacher didn't do anything to—we're kind when we say "build her self-esteem," but that really wasn't a question. Something was projected to this girl.

She didn't dress in a stylish or elaborate manner, but her dresses were starched like cardboard. She was a beautiful kid. She was an only child, and her parents were quiet churchgoing people, and you never heard anything negative about them. There wasn't any reason for this girl not to have been one of the leading students in the class, called upon, looked upon, and so forth, but instead she was treated as a reject.

There was a neighborhood, a very rough neighborhood, of boys and girls—A Avenue, B Avenue, several other avenues. They all centered around hip joints and gambling houses, and of course, kids were born. If you want to speak of absolute rejects, those were the children. They couldn't have bought their way past the sixth or seventh row in the class, heading toward the back. Very few of them made it through high school. Most of them dropped out after the eighth grade.

This has been stuck in my craw for a very long time. It's painful. It hurts, because I was the kind of kid who was outgoing and I played with everybody, I talked with everybody. I'd get on my bicycle after school and go over to another section to talk to guys and girls. I was never interested in sports. Music, reading, and just going and talking to people, were always the things that I was interested in, even old people, believe it or not.

After the eighth grade—we didn't have a high school. There was a [white] high school within a mile and a half from my house. They bused us to another town, from Norfolk to Portsmouth, which is about 10 miles, and named the school Norfolk County High. Now, what they did was purely political, because they didn't know which way the integration [issue] was going to go. So good political minds of the South said, "We'd better build some high schools, some black high schools," and that's precisely what they did.

But in the meantime, we've got all these kids, what are we going to do with them? Now, you can imagine, before 1952, in South Norfolk, Virginia, there was no high school. People lied and claimed to live in Norfolk [so they could attend Booker T. Washington High School]. If they had an aunt or cousin, anybody, they used that address. That's what my sister did. And there was St. Joseph's [a private high school]. They did the same thing. [South Norfolk] had what they called a high school, which was based on the old-time standard of two years. At any rate, that was the school they had.

By the time I came around, by the time I finished the eighth grade,

Senior class, Florida Agricultural and Mechanical College football team, 1936.

(Courtesy of Sue Kelker Russell, Tallahassee, Florida)

there was a political issue called the desegregation of the schools on the docket. They knew they had to do something, or they didn't want to take a gambler's chance of not doing anything. So they decided to build some schools. [George Washington Carver High School] cost $350,000, thereabouts, and when it was completed—a year after they started building Oscar Smith [a white school], which at the time cost more than $1 million.

So [meanwhile] they bused us to Norfolk County High School, which was in Portsmouth, Virginia. There were government buildings that were built over there during World War II for the Navy, and these were the buildings that we were using. Cold in the winter, hot in the summer, but they bused us over there, and we went to school there in January of 1950, I believe it was. We stayed there until, '50, '51, and [then I] started to Carver High—George Washington Carver High. They completed our school in South Norfolk.

Still, it was furnished and supplied by the old system, and no library again. There was a library room, but apparently no allocation for it. So they just grabbed some old books that may have been floating around at several of the other schools and threw them in there. You see, this was all a part of the system that you're not 100 percent proud of. My dad paid as much taxes as any workingman there, and yet we did not get the benefits of it. I say my dad, but hundreds of other people did likewise.

The school was built and supplied in a manner that [said], "Well, now they got their school." Okay? But the school was not a school, a high school, as we know a high school now. We were in no ways comparable to Oscar Smith High, which was the white high school.

It's sad. It's sad, because it was a place you go to in the morning, and you leave in the early evening and go back the next day. The school was supposed to be second to home and church, but it wasn't. It wasn't. I think in systems like this, we lose too many good people. We lose too many people.

I walked past an elementary school that was exactly two blocks from my house, and walked a mile to school, from the first through eighth grade. You talk about paying dues. What mother will take as a choice of putting her six-year-old son or daughter to walk a mile to school, across traffic spots and so forth, in the rain, in the snow, in the cold, etc., etc.? Not many. So anyone who would take the stand of, "Well, you people have to work harder," as someone said a few weeks ago, doesn't know. You've given blood, sweat, and tears, the best of everything that you have had *traditionally*.

Now, what more can you give? How much longer do you have to wait for your slice of the pie? It is not a gift. Your slice of the pie would not be a gift. It would be the same thing that all men get, and the same thing that the cattlemen get in some regions of the country, and other industries, and other groups, as a matter of fact. There is no greater welfare than the tax breaks and all the considerations that's given toward business. So "welfare" has become a dirty word, and certainly it needed some changes. It never should have drifted to this, but why penalize the recipient? Because they're the ones that's locked into it and least likely to be able to do anything about it.

MERLIN JONES

A native of Canton, Mississippi, Merlin Jones recalled attending a high school that received only the slightest amount of financial and material assistance from the local school board. He tells sarcastically of the generosity of white administrators who did little to furnish the school, and relates the ways parents in his community came together to provide more for their school.

Our school for a small town wasn't too terribly bad. It went from grades 1 through 12. There was no kindergarten. White children had it; we didn't. But most of the parents taught the children at home before they started school. So consequently we started off fine. When I started school I could count, knew colors, and basic stuff, what they teach to you in kindergarten. And, we had, I think, 16 teachers, which was very good in those days for a small southern town. The people in the community did challenge the school board on this and won. There was 10 acres of land across the street from the school, and the PTA went to the school board and said that if you'll help us buy this land for a playground, we'll pay half of it, the school and the board will pay half of it. And they bought it. Which gave us a very adequate playground. Some of the people who owned grading equipment graded it off, and made a beautiful playground, and that was our playground, which was directly across [from the school on] a little side street. I can remember when I started school. There was a two-story frame building, wooden building, and we had an iron potbellied stove. You've heard them talk about the potbellies? That's what we heated with. We had coal. We had a janitor at the school, a Mr. Smith, and the larger boys would help bring coal in the afternoon and bring coal in during the day. But, the smaller boys, we would come in the morning and Mr. Smith would have the fire made especially for the people in the lower grades. And when I got up, I guess I stayed until I was what, sixth grade before we finally got another building.

Sometimes we would get to school early, it was real cold, we would go real early, and help him light the fires in the various classrooms, and the teachers, I realize now, really most of them didn't have the grades. They had one, two, three years of college, but in my opinion, they were better teachers than we have now, with the master's [degree], because they were interested, they taught the child. Now, you teach the book, because you've got X amount of material you must cover, no matter who learns and who doesn't. Then each child learned because each child was taught. You had a better relationship between the parents and the school than you have now.

The teachers were all black. The school was in the middle of a black neighborhood. And this area, the one the school was located in, was next to a mail carrier. A doctor, a painter, the school principal lived in that area, and incidentally, the PTA, our people were just something. They bought the property, the house for the principal to live in. The school didn't buy it; the people bought it, the parents. The house that the principal lived in had at least six or seven rooms, adjoining the school property. He would just walk through his gate, out his back door, right on across to the campus, to the walk, and straight on into the school.

At first there were no walks on the campus. Each [graduating] class, I don't remember what year it started, put down a section of walk. The first one led from the street to a walk in the center, but [there] was a building across the lot in which there was cinders and gravel, [and] you had to track mud in. So one class put the walk in this way, another class put a walk on that side. The next year somebody else put in a walk, I remember my class had a walk put in that went from the north entrance of the high school building to the north entrance of the elementary school building. They were both on the same campus. [The elementary school] was a large two-story building that had a lab and nine or ten classrooms. That was built when I was about sixth grade. The other building, which they called the high school building, had one, two, three, four, five classrooms, the principal's office, an auditorium, and I can remember distinctly the auditorium seated, what was it, 650. They used to always say that they had a larger auditorium than most of the small towns. Most of the small towns, if they had an auditorium, it wouldn't seat but two or three hundred people, and we had a large stage with dressing rooms on either side. [It] was a pretty big school, and we had a library. But the parents had to furnish it. The school board gave the space, period. The shelves, and that's all. This is your library. I think, they gave a couple sets of encyclopedias.

Let me tell you about the science lab. You know what they gave us? They gave us a regular chemistry lab: they gave us one Bunsen burner, two beakers, a funnel, a strainer, and something else, and that was it! That was it! That was what they equipped our lab with. Oh, and one microscope, about what I gave my boys when they were in school. [Laughter.] The parents had to make up and equip the lab. The parents had to do that. I came from a town where the people didn't take "no"; they didn't sit back and wait. We can't. They had an attitude that we need it, and we're going to do it, which helped all of us. It helped us to be a bit aggressive in life. We didn't sit back and wait. Incidentally, I think that we had a very, very high rate of students that went on to school beyond high school. Most of the students either went to a trade school, technical school, college, or what have you. Incidentally, out of this lab, there was one boy, David Harris; he lived over in the section with the cinder streets. His dad had been a cabdriver; his mother worked at a furniture factory. David graduated from high school, and he was in college. He came to Tennessee State the same time I was there; he was younger, much younger than I. He graduated from Tennessee State with honors in chemistry from this little lab that I told you about. And that wasn't all—he got a full scholarship to Harvard Medical School! And he graduated from Harvard with honors. So I, I told people, it isn't the school, it's the students, because the school that we went to, when I compare with today's schools, we weren't supposed to learn anything. Outdated textbooks, untrained teachers, overcrowded classrooms, I've been in many classrooms in which we had 36, 40 children. They had the old-fashioned seats, with the desk in it, which was designed for one child. With the inkwell. They were designed for one student, we sat two on a seat. When you wanted to write, I always tried to find me a left-handed buddy, so we would have no problem.

The black parents and the black teachers made the difference. Because the system was set up I think to comply with the law. "We have given you a school. Here's a building. And here's some people. Now, it's up to you." But we did it.

For our shop, every boy grades 9 through 12 had to take shop. The principal said that everybody who comes out of this school is going to know how to make a living. Every girl had to take home economics. She had to learn how to cook and sew. Every boy had to learn either carpentry, brickwork, painting, something, a part of the building trade. They gave us a little shop that was perhaps the size of this dining room, that was our shop, it might have been a little more depth but it was no wider than this. When I was in the ninth, tenth grade, we got a shop teacher, and he said that this won't do. And again, the parents and some of the people who owned the lumber company there [who] gave us some lumber built our shop. We built our shop, the school board then at that time was a little more generous, and they gave us some of the equipment for the shop. Saws, planes, we had; they gave us some tools, and my dad [and] some of the other people gave tools, hammers, squares, things that they weren't using. And Mr. Bull, who was a brick mason, he and some of the other brick masons gave trowels and stuff like that. They gave free lessons in brickwork. They would come over a couple of days a week for boys that were interested in brickwork, and give them instruction in brickwork. Same thing for the painting. Those who were painters would do that, and my dad and some of the others in carpentry, they would come over and help Mr. Patton the teacher. Most of the boys were interested in carpentry, and he would have to try to teach everybody.

Incidentally, while we were there, when I was in school, we built a church, and we built a shop for another school, a county school. We received no pay, and the county school got no benefit, except that they had a shop we built them. We built the church that I was a member of, the St. Paul A.M.E. Church. It's been torn down now and replaced by another church, but it was a large two-story church. We built it with the ground level as a basement, with a kitchen, dining room, and so forth [on] the upper floors; the upper floor was the main part of the church with a stairway going up the side. That was during the early 1940s. You see, they still hadn't started giving us any money. The Methodist church that we built this for gave the school some equipment in return for building the church. But we saw it as an opportunity to learn some practical woodwork. We learned what we had studied and done in shop; we had cut rafters and so forth. If you're cutting a rafter, you've got to make it fit, and it paid off. There was one guy I remember, I just saw him a few weeks ago, he is a contractor, and he has something like 12, 15 men working for him. He owns lots of equipment, a big company. He learned right there.

Brenda Quant's second-grade class, 1952. (Courtesy of Brenda Quant, New Orleans, Louisiana)

JOHN W. BROWN

John W. Brown was born in Portsmouth, Virginia, in 1917. He remembers the second-class status of black schools and black citizens in Portsmouth. Nevertheless, he makes it clear that the dedication of individual teachers and his own perseverance enabled him not only to make a living, but also to work at the U.S. Naval Shipyard in Norfolk. Brown served as deputy equal employment officer for 10 years, from the late 1960s until his retirement, helping to improve job opportunities for women and minorities. He also climbed through the ranks himself, retiring as a GS-13 on the federal government pay scale.

At I. C. Norcom High School, there was no gym. The football team was equipped with the used and leftover football equipment from the white high school, Wilson. The books that were furnished were used and leftover books from Wilson. The only thing that was equal was the caliber of teachers that we had. We had dedicated teachers that went beyond the unequal requirements, because the white schools had [a] curriculum quite different from the black schools. It was not intended that we be taught things that we were taught at I. C. Norcom, because it wasn't in the curriculum. But we had teachers who taught it anyway. I can think of one in particular; that was trigonometry. It was taught in the white high schools. It wasn't taught at Norcom. But we had some black teachers that slipped it in. I remember that distinctly because I liked math.

The other inequities were quite visible. Anything that was public was also white. For example, the public park, the public playground, they were white. They had some little Mickey Mouse playgrounds, but they were what they called exclusively colored, as if it were worth being exclusive. Then for the same fare, it was back of the bus.

Stores [were] another place of inequity. You pay the same money, but don't expect to get the same goods, because the stores that were exclusively yours didn't have the same goods. If you were bold enough to go to a better store with the money to buy the better goods, we were told often that, "We don't have your size." Of course, there were other stores that were not as subtle, and they had signs out front, "Niggers and Dogs Not Allowed." Right here in Portsmouth. Now they're more subtle. They don't have your size. The conditions are somewhat improved now, and, in my judgment, it came about through equal employment opportunities and education.

I'm retired after a total of 41½ years of federal employment. At the shipyard, I had completed an apprenticeship in mechanical trades and worked for a little over 15 years in the pipe shop as a pipe fitter. Then I was promoted to the design division as a—I'm trying to think of the term they used—I was a draftsman. I was in [the] design division for approximately 12 or 13 years, and I was promoted to engineering technician.

It was not difficult to get into the shipyard; it was difficult to get into meaningful positions. The way shipyard employment was handled was that you entered upon satisfactory completion of an examination, but then when you arrived there, it became subjective. You were placed in positions not according to your merit, but according to your color. That began to change with the advent of Equal Employment Opportunity back around 1969 or '70, somewhere along in there.

So when I took the test for apprenticeship in the shipyard, I was told by many of my black people who were very happy with their position in life that, "You don't need to be taking that; that's a white boy's job." But I took it anyway, and I remember [the apprenticeship exam] was given in a

high school in Norfolk, and there were 5,000 candidates for that apprenticeship, and I scored fifth highest of the 5,000. I was extremely proud of
that, until I reached Norfolk Naval Shipyard, when I was asked—I want
to get it right now. When I reached the shipyard, the subjective part of
it became evident, because I had applied to be an electrician. Well, when
I got over there, I found out that the electrical shop, mechanics' appren-
tices and mechanics, were all white. They didn't have any black electricians and they didn't intend to have any. So they offered me [a job as an]
apprentice plumber, hoping that I would refuse it. I accepted it.

So I got to the pipe shop, the second obstacle thrown in my way was,
"When you want to come to work?" That was on a Thursday.

I told them, "I'd like to start the first of the week. I'd like to come in
Monday."

"Well, you don't want to work, do you?"

I said, "You didn't ask me that. You asked me when did I want to
come and I told you Monday."

"Well, you be in here tomorrow morning."

So I started work on the last day of a pay period, Friday, at Norfolk
Naval Shipyard. It was made very clear to me that I was not wanted,
which made me more determined to stay. I stayed there for over
40 years—41½ years.

I was promoted from apprentice up to general manager, GS-13,
during my career there. I retired as a GS-13. Head of my office. I'm
proud of that, because they tried every way to make me quit. I used to
tell them that, "You can make me mad, but you can't make me mad
enough to quit."

My last 10 years in there, I was deputy equal employment opportunity officer, and I'm proud to say that I participated in many, many
changes to the advantage of minorities and women at Norfolk Naval
Shipyard.

DELORES THOMPSON AARON

*Delores Aaron was a lifelong resident of New Orleans. Her remem-
brance of her childhood in this city complicates our understanding of the*

racial and class divisions operating during Jim Crow. An educator, school counselor, and former assistant superintendent of schools, Aaron began teaching in the late 1940s.

[There] was a variety [of people from differing economic backgrounds] for instance, [and] it was not necessarily what you'd call run down; it was just a different variety of people. You had people at the highest strata. I think the neighborhoods were not so pronounced at that time; there were also white folks who lived in that neighborhood. During my young years it was very *common* to have white folk living next door to you, who would speak to you, be very polite with you, would walk to school with you and continue on to their school because all of us knew the schools were segregated. Yet, when I think about the children like the Longeaus who lived up the street from here, the Longeaus walked to school. They walked me to [and] from Conti and Praro [streets] because their mother had a grocery store, and the grocery store was right next to us.

When we came home, we [competed] with those children who were in the same grade. Oh yes, we used to compete, we used to brag on what we knew because that's what we did. We used to play school, and it was a good interchange. You know, now that I'm grown, I'm positive that they learned some things, and we learned some things from each other. We watched the radio together at night. We could sit outside and at that time [they] weren't locking doors and all that, so their front door would be open. If there were black kids on the block whose parents didn't have a radio, then all of us congregated on the Longeaus' steps. And we would sit, and there would be no light in the living room of the Longeaus. All you could see would be the front of the TV *light*, and we would sit and actually *listen* to the radio, and the man would say something like, "That's right, that's exactly right," and somebody in the group would say, "That's Alexander's Ragtime Band," and the man on the radio would say, "That's right," just as if he heard you, as if he were answering you, and we would just get so excited. I remember how we used to compare lessons; we compared books, and that's how we knew that they got new books. I never remember one of the Longeau children displaying a book at the beginning of the year because you want to know what book you're in. That competitive spirit came from our parents, and also our Sunday school teachers. Our Sunday school teachers were always preparing us to do a better job and always using white people as the standard. Please, white folk have always been the standard, and this was not necessarily *always* the best thing to do, but that's what black people did. That's what I mean when I said that I believe that many middle-class black folk [were] sort of condescending. [They] just made us feel like if *we* can just do what *they* do, then we're okay. But we're not to expect them to accept us. But at least be able to do much of what they can do.

[We had] good teachers, good teachers, teachers who *taught* skills. For instance, in English, all of us make mistakes in grammar; it happens to the best of us, but when checked you knew what was correct. You know that way of saying, "What did you say?" and then you say it correctly. It's because you know it. You couldn't say it correctly if you didn't. Well, teachers taught skills, all of us had a foreign language. You didn't finish high school without some knowledge of a foreign language.

At McDonogh 35, you were taught again that ladies wore stockings, so every girl had to have an opportunity to serve as an office girl. At McDonogh 35 you were selected to serve as an office girl where you wore stockings to school every day, and you did that just to let you *know* that ties would not choke boys and stockings would not heat girls to the point where they would faint. But, when you talk about the extra things, for instance, [take] the symphony, if you go to the opera in your city, the persons whom you're going to *see* [at] the operas were usually older people. During *our* time we were not only *taught* to appreciate the opera, but we were taught, "Don't just say it's nice to go to opera." You *learn* the story behind the story, so you wanted to know if so and so was *singing*. At this time you had someone who would say to you, "Well let me see if she sings it or he sings it as well as so and so." And, if you notice, we compare the people who sing; we compare because we know the roles; we were *taught* the roles and started right there. We learned that in school. *Every Friday* you had music appreciation for three to four hours. You learn to sing out of that *Twice 55* book. And I keep *telling* these people, if you notice, that children who get in trouble least are the children who are truly part of some Protestant church's choir. Watch those kids; the bulk of those kids go to school; the bulk of those kids sing; the bulk of those kids have a

Bricks School, Enfield, North Carolina. (Bricks Club, Enfield, North Carolina)

knowledge of literature, a *knowledge* of history to some degree. You can talk history to them, and they have an appreciation for it because they learned the songs, and the person teaching the song gives them the *background* of what happened as a result of this song evolving so they know the story, so they feel good about themselves. And that's why I said that if we can get them to sing together like we used to, we *always* had something in common whenever we were in school.

[Y]ou took it for granted that you just didn't teach a child for three hours, that you were responsible for doing some of the other kinds of things in order to broaden [him]. We kept talking about teaching the whole child. Well, you can't teach the whole child from nine to three because you're too busy dealing with the academics. So in the afternoon we taught poise, we taught good manners, and we know we did that; we took the children on *trips*; we did a whole lot of things. For instance, that's when I started raising funds at the high school. All of my children who were on my cheerleading squad—now when you got on a cheerleading squad you had to say when you wrote on that little application that you wanted to go to college. Those were the ways that we encouraged children to go to college. Colleges wanted children who were well-rounded, so this is what we told the children. You had just a slew of kids coming out for cheerleading, for basketball, for whatever, because we encouraged them because we knew that the colleges wanted kids who were well-rounded. We actually thought it was *our* responsibility to get these darn kids ready, and we *got* them ready. That's why when I walk the street, or I'm sitting here or any other place and the kids [say], "Miss Aaron taught *me*, Miss Aaron," the kids are going to *brag* because we *did* go beyond. But as far as feeling like it wasn't the thing to do, or [to] lie [that] we were being put upon—my truthful answer is that I had no knowledge that I was even going beyond, and I feel strongly that the others didn't either because I wasn't there by myself.

[W]e had a lot [of students] and they came to you with so little. There was just so much that you couldn't take for granted. You could only compare them with your *own*. For instance, like study habits, there were kids who once you discuss something with them, you could tell that from the first few days that you gave homework [that] they didn't come in with the homework. Then you knew that they either didn't *want* to do it, or they didn't have anybody at home encouraging them to do it. You could compare them with *your own* because with my own child I had a schedule. So what did I do? I just did the things that I did with William; [that's what] I did with these other people's children.

GERALDINE DAVIDSON

Born and raised in Zent, Arkansas, Geraldine Davidson attended the Fargo Agricultural School located in Fargo, Arkansas. Founded in 1919 by Dr. Floyd Brown, a graduate of Tuskegee University and follower of many of Booker T. Washington's educational philosophies, the school stressed character development and the development of a strong work ethic. With the motto "Work Will Win," Brown attempted to educate the heads, hearts, and hands of his students with a curriculum that included traditional subjects like math, history, and science along with industrial and home economics courses. Brown also shared his wealth of knowledge about black history with his students and left a marked impression on them.

*Davidson arrived at the school in the 1940s. At Fargo she developed
a greater sense of pride in herself and her community. Now the curator
of the school's museum, Davidson relates how the Fargo school became a
bulwark of that community and describes its day-to-day operations.*

When Floyd Brown came here [to Fargo] and built that school, my father's mother knew about him. So I've known about the school ever since
I can remember. I had a sister that graduated in 1936. I had another one
that would have graduated in 1939, but she passed away. I had another
one that would have graduated in 1942, but she decided to get married.
I had another one that would have graduated in 1943, but she decided to
get married. So I graduated in 1947. So we've always known about Fargo
Agricultural School.

It was really a community-based school. Dr. Brown would try to
interact with the community, because the community is the one that
accepted him and believed in him and his dream. During certain holiday
festivities that he had, after he became established, he would send his bus
into the community to pick up the community people to come and join
in the festivities on the campus.

I remember when we played basketball, the last year I was here we
won the state championship. They were having the farmers' conference
down here, which was something that Dr. Brown had organized for
all the farmers in the nearby counties. They would come together and
talk with one another about how they could produce more and better
food. This particular time, we had to go and play in the tournament.
He needed that bus to go to different points and pick up the people in
the community. He chartered us a Greyhound bus to take us down to
the championship game in Pine Bluff, which was AAMNC [Arkansas
Agricultural, Mechanical, and Normal College]. Now it's UAPB [Uni-
versity of Arkansas–Pine Bluff]. That is just what the community meant
for him.

When we were on the campus, he would take us to different communities in Arkansas, like Holly Grove, Clarendon, De Witt, Ethel, or
Trumann. He would pick out one Sunday where he would take his choir
to go sing at the church. He would let us go up to Union Baptist. If he
wasn't going to be [at Fargo] to have vespers, he would tell Mrs. Brown

Mrs. V. W. Montiero's sixth-grade class, Lincoln School, Norfolk, Virginia, 1922.
(Courtesy of Josephine Linyear, Norfolk, Virginia)

and two or three chaperones to take the girls up to Union Baptist Church. Once I got up there, my uncle was a deacon there, [he] would always want me to take up a collection [for the school]. So Dr. Brown and his school really networked with the community. Whenever we played basketball, the community was here to support us.

Mostly everybody in the community went to school here if they were in high school. The people, the parents, anytime that Dr. Brown gave something down here, everybody would come to see just what was going on at the school. They were interested, because if their children wasn't here, they were thinking about putting their children in the school. So the community played a large part in Dr. Brown's activities, like at Thanksgiving. At Christmastime didn't anybody come down because Dr. Brown would let all of us go home for at least two weeks for Christmas. We would leave around the 18th of December and we would come back New Year's Day.

He would have the farmers' conference, he would have the tournaments down here, he would have celebration on Thanksgiving, and he'd have the baccalaureate Sunday. It was just when anything went on at

Fargo everybody knew about it, and they would be coming in wagons, walking. They were coming any way they could come.

Dr. Brown sometime would send messages to all the churches. He would send announcers. He would send an announcement, and then the people in the community would read it. Sometime his announcement would be printed up, and the community would know about what was going on down at Fargo.

If it was too muddy for us to come down, there wasn't [highway] 49 then. It wasn't even named. Later on they named it 39, and after that they named it 49. But it was a mud road, and if you couldn't come down there to go to the school, most of us would come down on the train. When you got off up there near the highway, the railroad would have gravel on down here.

I was real tiny when I entered high school. I think I was 14 years old and I didn't weigh 100 pounds. My uncle told me, "Now, don't you tell them you're 14. You're too little." I think I weighed about 95 pounds. I sort of stayed tiny because I walked from the home of a lady my father let me stay with, our organist. She wanted someone to stay with her, so I stayed up there, and I stayed tiny all through my ninth grade. When I was in tenth grade, that's when my father told me, "You have to go and stay in the dormitory because you have to learn to live with other people other than your family." See, and I didn't want to obey that lady. She did help me with my algebra. She said, "You know it. I don't have to help you with that. (Because she was a teacher.) You know that." [Laughter.] But she was a sweet lady. Her name was Miss Annie B. Cowan.

When I came to live in the dormitory my second year, which was the fall of 1944, we would get up in the morning. The matron would wake you up about six o'clock. You had to be dressed, your room had to be in tip-top shape before you could go to breakfast. Your room was inspected by the matron and the other teachers, and then you could go to breakfast.

After breakfast, if you did not have a chore to do, you had to go back to your room, and school started around eight-thirty in the morning. But if you had a chore to wash dishes, sweep up the dining room, you had to really rush, because you had to be ready to leave the dormitory about 20 minutes after eight o'clock in order for everybody to be in their class-room and where they were supposed to go at eight-thirty.

If I went to home economics in the morning, which was taking sewing and cooking, handicraft, I spent four hours there. The boys, while we were in the cooking classes in the home economics department or sewing classes, they were either in the shop or on the farm or attending the chickens and the cows and doing the milking.

In the evening, my classmates that worked out on the farm and us that worked in the home economics department would come together and go to our classes and have our academic subjects, and that's the way it was all through that year, the tenth grade.

Now, in the next year, I might have gone to my academic subjects first and then go to home economics in the afternoon. It was divided into two sections. You had what Dr. Brown called common sense, where you were taught how to sew, how to do handicraft work, how to cook, how to be good homemakers if you chose to do so after you left there. I thought that was real good, because in a sense they were educating the head, the heart, and the hands.

History was my favorite subject, and my music teacher was the history teacher. She taught me history and she told me, "If you go to college, try to major in history. You talk about history as if you were there." That was my favorite subject.

I liked math. Any kind of history I was just crazy about it. I was pretty good at math and algebra. We had algebra, geometry, and math. I was pretty good in that. I had English literature, pretty good in English. But I was super in history.

We had black history every year. You never graduated from black history until you left the school. We studied about Carter G. Woodson, Marian Anderson, Mary McLeod Bethune, Phillis Wheatley, Paul Laurence Dunbar, Booker T. Washington, George Washington Carver, W.E.B. Du Bois. It was a lot of black people in history that I learned about at Fargo. As a matter of fact, I knew about some of them before I came to Fargo.

We had in our little country schoolhouse, two-room schoolhouse, we had a little book about that thick and it taught us about black history. The community and the teachers had gotten together and ordered these books to teach us. It wasn't what the superintendent of schools wanted. It was something my aunt and another teacher thought of.

In that little book, it told us about Phillis Wheatley, Paul Laurence Dunbar, Booker T. Washington. I knew all about them when I came to Fargo. And when we came to Fargo, we were having some of the same subjects, and I knew about that. So they ordered it, and each household had one of those little blue books. My auntie was a schoolteacher, my father's sister.

We never could start school until about the last of October because you had to harvest the crops, and you would go until about May the next year. But when you were finished putting in the crops, you could go two months, out of the summer months you went two months, and that made up the school term. You had a split school term.

Algebra [was my least favorite subject]. I always asked them, "Why do we have to take this?" They said, "It's a required subject and it helps you with your math." I found out that it did. I just couldn't get ready for algebra, but I finally did.

The other subjects, I liked home economics, but I really liked setting the table, making it look pretty. I didn't care too much for cooking. I liked to do the handiwork, like crocheting, embroidery, and weaving the basket. I liked that. I didn't care for a pattern, and Mrs. Brown knew that.

And I didn't care for cooking. She knew that. So what she did, she made me do a lot of handicraft work. Then she would tell me sometime, "Okay, Purcell, I know you've been studying. I know you're wondering why I haven't called on you. Now, all next week you're going to have to cook the teachers' breakfast and serve them, and you will be graded by that."

She would have my menu made out for me. I would get my cap and my apron and put it on. It was about six or seven teachers I had to cook for. Just the breakfast, nothing else. She would ask each teacher how was it, that's how I was graded, and how did I serve it.

It was very challenging. She never smiled. I know once I was a junior and we had to make our commencement uniforms. My class color was pea-green and pink. We had beautiful white skirts, pleated all the way around, with a long body, and we had the pretty pea-green blouses, with a ribbon running through the sleeve and around the neck. I had to make my skirt so each pleat was the same. It took me three days to do that.

She'd watch me, and then she would tell me, "Don't ask anybody anything, Purcell. You study your pattern and you will learn how to do that. But I don't want you to ask any of your classmates. I'm not going to tell you. Look at your pattern. Study it."

And I did. What I was doing, I forgot to measure, take the measure [of] each pleat. She said, "That is why math is very important." What I did, I found out how much material I had to work with and then I figured out how wide each pleat was supposed to be, and the third day I got it right. And then I looked at her and she looked up at me, and I could tell she was pleased, because it was in her eyes. She would not smile. But she was one grand lady.

I learned how to play basketball when I was in grammar school. I had a cousin that taught me when I was in grammar school. She was a student down here, and she taught me how to play basketball. By the time I was learning real good, she married someone and they moved to Brasfield. I was really upset. I wanted even to go to Brasfield and stay with her, because she had taught me all about basketball. Then she told me, "You can't come with me. They're going to have a basketball team up there, so you just do what I told you." See, I was a guard. "Just do as I told you and you'll be all right."

She went down to this school where she was teaching at, Brasfield Elementary School, and she had her own basketball team. She brought them up here, and they beat us good. We went down to play them and they beat us by one point. She took me aside, "You see how good you are? If everybody would have played like you, you would have beat our girls."

When I came down to Fargo the first year, they asked everybody to come down and try out. I tried out, and I made the second team. The next year, I made the first team, and I played on the first team for three years.

The basketball players had better food, too. We couldn't have sweets, but we had good food to eat. We could not eat with our classmates anymore. We were pulled and put at a separate table. We had special privileges. I was glad when they would send a note around to your teachers, whatever class you was in, "If anybody is on the basketball team, will they please meet at the gym at a certain time." Then we would get a chance to get out of the class to go practice.

But it really worked as an advantage and disadvantage, because in the morning we had to get up at five o'clock, maybe, go to the gym, take laps. Now, the rest of the people's sleeping, and we had to run, come in at six o'clock, take your shower, and be ready for breakfast at seven.

I would be so sleepy sometime on the court. See, the reason why she would do that is because that night we would be going someplace to play. She had to get the practice in, and we probably wouldn't have time to practice during the day.

I really enjoyed playing with my schoolmates, and the coach would always tell us, "You can't win unless you play as a team." One of our sayings before we start playing, we would put our hands on top of one another and say, "All for one and one for all," because you couldn't win by yourself. You had to have that networking as a team.

When we traveled Dr. Brown would send the coaches and maybe another chaperone with us. We would use the school bus. Sometimes we would go to Helena, Marianna, over to Corbin High in Pine Bluff. We would travel to Stuttgart at Holman High. We would play sometime at Lincoln High and Forrest City. I'd say we would travel around a 50-mile radius, no more than 75 miles, to play.

Dr. and Mrs. Brown were our parents when we were on the campus, and they only wanted the best for all of us. Mrs. Brown never smiled too much, because she came in contact with the girls and she could not let one person have more attention than the other. She had to divide her time between all of us.

Dr. Brown was a very jovial man, but he's stern. He would tell you, "If you can't go to college, whatever you're going to become, become the best." He said everybody will not be able to go to college. He said it's not a sin and it's not anything to be ashamed of. He said, "What you have to do is remember your roots and your family values and what Mrs. Brown and myself have taught you here, and if you work, work will win. We're asking everybody that leaves our school after graduation to go out into the world, but don't forget your roots here, either."

He always was telling us when we was in school not to be ashamed of where we came from. Like if your family was poor, don't be ashamed of that. That is your heritage. And then like he said, he was part of our heritage, too. He said, "I don't ever want you to forget about Mrs. Brown

Tuskegee Institute kindergarten.
(Photograph by Charles D. Robinson, ca. 1920–21. Courtesy of Dora Anderson, Tuskegee, Alabama)

and myself." And I have not forgotten about them. But I never would have known when I was in school that I would be the one to come back and keep the legacy going.

KENNETH YOUNG AND MAI YOUNG

Married for more than 60 years when this interview was conducted, Kenneth and Mai Young recount numerous occasions where they challenged the boundaries between accommodation and resistance to Jim Crow.

Both Kenneth and Mai Young attended private black academies as primary and secondary school students growing up in Alabama and Georgia, respectively. These institutions, which enjoyed a greater degree of autonomy from white control, also boasted an important advantage over the county schools for black students. They operated eight-month terms compared with six months or less for the black county schools. After high school, Kenneth Young went to college and earned a bachelor's degree. He returned to Alabama to become a teacher and a school administrator. In his capacity as a school principal, Mr. Young had to walk a fine line between providing the best possible educational opportunities for his students while bowing to the whims of white school superintendents who placed a much lower value on African American education.

Kenneth Young: Old Dr. Backey. I'll never forget him. My mother's folks were very poor. They didn't even have a horse and a buggy. So they sent me down to the station to meet Dr. Backey on the train. Dr. Backey got off the train and had his suitcase, looked around and said, "Who's here to meet us?" I said, "We're here to meet us." [Laughter.] I said, "My grandfather hasn't got any horses and buggies on my mother's side." Now my father's folks had money as black folks went. He had some money but mother's folks didn't have a thing but religion and plenty of that. So he took us and talked to us, but she started this school and she ran out of money, and she wrote to the Lutheran board that she was working with and told them she was out of money, would they care to help this black school. So they said we'll be down and visit your school. So Dr. Backey came down, I'll never forget it, big old six-foot white man, crippled, limping.

Dr. Backey kept asking me how did we get home. I said, "We walk." I said, "Grandpa hadn't got any horses and buggies; [that's] my mother's folks where we are going." Now my father's people were what you'd call well-to-do black folks. They had money and land. But my mother's folks didn't have a thing but religion. They had a plenty of that. [Laughter.] So we got in the road and walked home, went to my grandfather's house. He told Dr. Backey, said, "We'll stay here tonight but tomorrow I'm going to carry you down to Mr. Lee Bonner's house." Lee Bonner was the captain from the Army, had retired there and was the owner of the land in the community. "I'm going to carry you to Captain Bonner's house but you're going to stay here tonight and we ain't going to talk about it." Black folks won't going to stay in white folks' houses and white folks sure won't going to stay in your house. "So we ain't going to ever tell anybody you stayed here and don't you tell it." The only way you can stay here is if some storm or something would catch you and you couldn't get out.

So the next day we went down to the big store that Captain Bonner owned and ran and introduced these Lutheran friends. So they went to explaining to the captain who they were. Mr. Bonner said, "We've read up on your credentials. We understand who you are." See when they first came in there they'd ask him, "You going to teach these niggers to read?" Some of the teachers said, "If we can." Said, "They're kind of slow to learn." "That's what I figured." Said, "But some of the white folks back at home are afraid ya'll are going to teach them to read and that's going to ruin them." So this black uncle of mine said, "Don't worry about that, they're like your folks, they're dumb, they ain't going to learn fast." [Laughter.] So I stayed and went to school there for some 10 or 15 years.

The black folks learned early their place in life and you got along fine as long as you didn't step over the line. You knew who was white, you knew who was black and you don't make a mistake. In other words, white men and women were addressed as "Mr. and Mrs." You didn't address blacks that way. And don't make a mistake talking to a white person about a black person and call him "Mr." I know when I first came back home to teach I'd been away four years to boarding school, and I had northern teachers while I was away. I picked up a little northern brogue. I was talking about some black woman who was supervisor of the schools for black folks and I kept saying "Miss So-and-So." Finally, the white woman stopped me and said "Young, that woman you're talking about, is she black or white?" I said, "She's black." "Well, don't Miss her to me then. Just call her by her first name. Don't ever Miss a black person to me." I said, "No ma'am." So before we'd get very far I had an occasion to say "Miss So-and-So" again. She stopped and looked at me: "Told you about that!" "I won't make that mistake anymore." So you had to watch your tongue. White folks Mr. and Mrs., blacks by their first name.

Very seldom [did black folks break those rules]. Sometimes they'd do it without thinking but very few deliberate attempts to ignore the southern custom. We all lived here together, and I know when I went to be principal there in the southern part of the state [in 1930] the superintendent of the school system had come from my home county about 100 miles up north. I went to see him. They'd sent me to him when I got here. He said, "Oh yeah boy." Never called a Negro man a man, it was always boy. "Yeah boy," [he] says, "I know you. Your daddy's name is Sam Young." "Yes sir, he is." "Well, I'll be damned. Ain't that something." [Laughter.] He said, "I told them you'd get along fine because you knew the white folks." "I sure do." What he meant by that, you know the customs and you will not ignore the customs down here. "You've been up north?" I said, "Well I went to Tennessee, that's not up north but from Alabama that's a long ways." He said, "Well you know the customs and you aren't going to do anything that's against the customs." "No sir." So I didn't. I stayed within, you know, the boundaries as long as I was there.

Mai Young: I never shall forget, our youngest daughter was downtown. We took her downtown to buy some shoes so she was trying on the shoes. When she got through trying on the shoes, I guess Pat might have been about two years old, she got up and threw her arms around the [white] salesman and she couldn't say a word, she just had to—that kind of thing was unheard of you know at that particular time. And then we went to Columbus to take the children for something, buy them some clothes I think. We adopted two children at the same time and we took them over there and Pat wanted some water. Pat said, "Why can't I have it?" I think he [gestures to Mr. Young] gave her some.

KY: They had one cup up there and the white person drank. White person drank out of the fountain, had a cup hanging there and you had to drink out of that. So I had my youngest girl, and Pat, [who] was about two and a half, three years old, said, "Daddy I want some water." She was standing, and I put her up to the fountain and let her drink. This is a white fountain. This white guy ran over there and said: "Can't you read!?!" The sign said white only. Said, "Can't you read!?" I said, "The baby can't read." I stood and looked at him. I didn't move. First thing crossed my mind [is] I'm going to die here today because if he'd snatched that child away from that fountain while she's trying to drink I'm going to hit him. He just turned and walked on off. I guess he looked in my eyes and saw death because I'm going to kill him today. So when Pat got through drinking, I wouldn't drink myself, but I held my baby and she drank. He ran, "Can't you read!?" I said, "The baby can't read."

MY: We had an experience like that down in Montgomery. We had gone to a game I believe, and I went in the restroom and the guy at the filling station came and knocked on the door. Kenneth said, "Don't you go in there."

KY: I was outside. He saw her go in but he ran to the door, bam, bam. I said, "My wife's in there mister and don't you go in!"

MY: "She's not supposed to go in there."

KY: I said, "I don't care if she's not, she's in there and don't you go in!" I said, "If you want some trouble you go in now and I'll die here today." Turned around and said to somebody: "That's a fool." Anytime a Negro outside and you didn't do anything about it they considered you a fool. So he told us, "That's a fool." But I said, "My wife went in there and don't you go in."

MY: I heard him outside. I was almost afraid to come out.

KY: I took a stand.

MY: [Laughter.] And we got away from there as quickly as we could.

KY: I said, "I'm going to die here today." I said, "Don't hurry, take your time. I'll be here when you come out."

MY: I'm telling you, those were the days.

KY: Eating together and using restrooms the southern white, he would die before he'd let you do it.

MY: And this generation coming along now, they just can't even visualize.

KY: Sometimes I say to my friends "I guess the law was in the plan to end it like it did to get it died out. But sometimes I wish we'd fought like hell. I wish they'd burn the whole damn South down." I told a southern white man one time, I said, "I'm sorry that we closed out the segregation like we did." He said, "What do you mean?" I said, "We just let it die out." He said, "That was the best." I said, "We were humiliated so many years and nothing we could do about it." I said, "I wish we had fought." I said, "I would like to have burned the whole damn South down." And I meant it. I said, "I wish we had burned the place down."

They did everything they could to make you feel inferior. They didn't miss a trick. If they had two fountains they'd put another cup up there for the blacks. Everything they could do to make you feel inferior they did it. And when it ended you can't find a single white person who remembers it. [Laughter.] I swear you can't. You can't find a single one who remembers the days of segregation and those who talk about it, they're so mad about it. Those white folks were so low down and dirty. I'm glad they're dead.

MY: And you know there was a time when, well I remember it in Alabama, I don't remember it in Georgia because we had our own black doctors in Georgia, and you didn't have to go to the whites. But I remember at the time they had separate waiting rooms when you went to the doctor, and they'd serve all the white patients and then serve all the black patients. The last white patient might be served, and then they'd serve blacks.

KY: I carried my mother to a white doctor in a place called Selma about 40 miles from home, maybe not quite that far. I didn't have an appointment. I figured he'd get a chance to see her. That man saw every white patient he had. As long as they came he'd see them, and as they closed, we'd been there since nine o'clock in the morning, and around four-thirty the whites stopped coming, then he turned to me and said who wants to see the doctor. I said my mother would like to see him. "Well, come on." He saw her then. Been sitting there since about nine-thirty.

The southern white man, somebody asked me one time: "K.B., do you think these southern white folks are going to hell for the way they treated you all?" "No, they aren't. They're not. No." I said, "They can't go to hell, it ain't big enough to hold them." [Laughter.] "Some of them will get in, the rest of them won't get in because hell will be too little." He laughed. I said, "Say boy, there were some mean southern white people. Everything they could to make you feel inferior they did it." Every now and then you'd meet one, he'd be so different from the rest of them you wouldn't want to believe he was from here.

MY: We had an experience down in Brewton [Alabama] where the reformed church supported [our school] and we had, they didn't call them teachers they called them missionaries. We had a white teacher who came down to teach Bible, and the whites got it into their heads that the white teacher was out there teaching at the black teacher's school and they said she had to go. She could not stay there. Not only that, they wouldn't even trust him to take her to the airport. They came out there and got her. You remember that? Came out to the school and got the teacher.

KY: I told her, whatever her name was, I said, "Don't say you're a

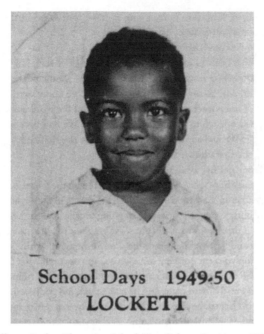

Schoolboy at Lockett Elementary School, New Orleans, Louisiana, 1949–50.
(Courtesy of Philomene Allen, New Orleans, Louisiana)

teacher for anything. Just say you're a missionary. They won't be too up on what a missionary means. You're going to have your same work, same pay but you just say missionary." She laughed.

MY: Boy it circulated there.

KY: "What's this I hear ya'll got a white teacher?" I said, "No ma'am, we don't have any white teacher. This is a missionary." Some of the men knew me said, "Oh, Mr. Young you can't fool us, now we know that's a teacher." "Un-uh, she's not a teacher she's a missionary." But the word got back to the whites we had one white teacher on that faculty. We had how many teachers, about 25? We had about 25 or 30 teachers on the faculty, had one white one. That's the first one we had, only one.

MY: They got her away from there.

KY: Yes sir, they came back and told me, "Young, she'll have to go." I said, "Well, I'll get her to the station." "No, you'll get her . . . to the airport today and you're not going to take her." Says, "I'm going to take her, put her on a plane myself. It's not that I don't trust you but we've got some mighty mean white folks around here and between here and that airport they could think any kind of thoughts. Stop your car out here somewhere. You can't tell what these southern whites will do about it. That's a white woman you've got riding around in your car." So I told him to come and he came there and got her, put her in his car and carried her to the airport. The South has been a mean, mean place.

I remember when I went to south Alabama to take over a school, my first school I ever had as principal, and the superintendent was talking to me about the school. My initials are K.B. He said, "K.B., you can handle them niggers." He called the blacks "niggers." "You can handle them niggers down there. You've got enough white blood in you to handle them." And we black folks who had that white blood we were proud of it. Proud because it meant extra privileges for us. I remember being out at a little country store near where I was working. I was working at a black school operated by the Presbyterian church, and one of the principals was practically white. You couldn't tell him from a white man. [He] came from Virginia, had that Virginia brogue. Just to hear him talk you'd never dream he was a black man. So he came in the store and everybody respected him, but the white man who was visiting didn't know he had black blood in him. So he said "yes sir, no sir" to him as the whites did to each other. They were courteous to each other. After a while this black minister left and this visiting white fellow said, "Williams, who in the hell? I don't know that man, who is he?" Williams started to laugh. "What's so funny?" They were laughing because "You thought he was white, didn't you?" "I sure did thought damn well he was white. Ain't he white?" "No!" "Well, I'll go wipe this hand." He was shaking hands with a black man [laughter] which was against culture. He said, "That's a nigger?" "Yes, sir. And you will find plenty of them just like that."

It tickled us because we could always tell them. Just something about a black person, I don't care how much white blood he had in him, you could tell him. His ways and actions gave him away. That's a deadly sin to pass for white and you were not white. But some did. I used to have a boy who drove the principal around school where I worked, the principal.

His home was in Virginia, so once or twice a year they'd drive up there and this black boy would drive them. His name was Loving. Loving's a good friend of mine, always told me what was happening because the principal talked to him. So Loving said: "Mr. Young, when we leave here in this community where everybody knows us, we aren't black anymore." He said, "I'm black because I'm the driver." But his children, when they leave here, they're white.

MY: They were as white as white.

KY: I thought [people who passed] were smart as hell. Sorry I wasn't quite light enough to pass myself. [Laughter.] I figured they took advantage of us and used us so we could take advantage any way we could of them. So I thought those guys who could pass, they were smart. But I was going with a girl once, she was just as light as you. I quit on that account because I hated to go with a girl that everywhere I went white folks would stop and look at you, like you got a white girl. That's the worse sin in the world, that white girl, and I didn't particularly want to explain her all my life so I just weaned her off. . . . But I was down to the little local store one day and this girl and her, somebody from the school, the school was a black school, with some of the teachers. They were black and knew it, but some of them were so white they could have passed. This girl came in the store, and she was speaking to the storeowner, who was a Mrs. Byrd. She was just as polite to Mrs. Byrd, and Mrs. Byrd felt inferior around her because although she was a black person she had more sense than Mrs. Byrd and better looking and more intelligent. So after she left old Mrs. Byrd said to the other white person, "You know, that's a shame that Arthur Williams's daughter has got to be a nigger." I'll never forget she said it. She didn't count, didn't count black folks. She talked about us and to us like we didn't exist. Said, "It's a shame she's got to be a nigger. She's just as white as you or me." And she was. "It's a shame she's got to be a nigger." So just for meanness, I said, "She ain't a nigger anywhere but here." I had a white fellow tell me after segregation ended, we were down further south of Alabama and we came back here to live in Brewton. This man said, "Young, we often said if we're going to end segregation we sure wish you'd be here, because I think you would get along with the whites better than this crowd coming in now." I knew what he meant. He meant that you probably would let us do kind of like

Mrs. Dorcas Washington and students in their one-room schoolhouse,
between Paxville and Silver, South Carolina, in the 1940s
(Courtesy of Mamie Washington Carter, Summerton, South Carolina)

they'd been doing. I didn't say anything. I said to myself, "Un-uh." I said well, Mr. whatever his name, I said, "It's going to be hard to change. It's going to take a good long time." But I said it never will go back the way it was. I said you don't want it to go back there. "No, no." I said, "Well I'm glad you don't because it never is going back like it was." He said, "I guess you're right."

We had one old lady who was the supervisor of schools for blacks, Mary Davis. She was supervisor of black schools. She was a mean old something. She didn't want the black schools to have anything. Her favorite expression was: "Well, Young, we don't even have that in the white schools." Ask her for something: "Young, we don't even have that in white schools." So one day I said, "Mrs. Davis, do you plan to have everything you want for all your white schools before you get something for us blacks?" I said, "That county school where I'm principal, that's the best black school in this country, and you want your sorriest white schools to have stuff better than we're having." I said, "I can see how you might want us not to try to beat your white high school, but we don't plan to have a school behind your sorriest white school."

Grinned all the time I was saying it. She said, "Young, go ahead and get what you want." I joked her because that was a fact. She didn't want your school to have anything until every white school had some of it. You got the leavings. So I told her, "Mrs. Davis, you don't plan for your poorest white schools be better than our best black school."

"Go ahead and get what you want, K.B." I kind of got away with her that day.

MY: Lots of these youngsters now don't remember. They really don't. You tell them things that happened, they just can't believe it. That's why they can't appreciate Martin Luther King because they don't know what happened. They really don't know what happened during those days. Hard to visualize it.

STINE GEORGE AND DORIS STRONG GEORGE

Southern black schools were segregated and administered by white officials. With the power to hire and dismiss principals and teachers, white administrators held considerable influence. They hired principals and teachers not only for their ability to teach but for their deference to whites. Through such hiring practices, they created a network of informants, coercing "loyal" black employees to report any subversive sentiments to the administration, and helped create a sense of apprehension and mistrust among the faculty. A native of Georgia, Stine George and his wife, Doris, were admittedly an exceptional couple in their hometown of Moultrie. Both were college educated and held graduate degrees. Stine worked most of his life as a high school instructor, and his wife was trained as a mortician. Both had gone to the North for their graduate education because Georgia did not offer such training for African Americans, and they were not permitted to enroll at the University of Georgia (or "The Holy Ground," as Stine referred to it) because of the color of their skin.

Stine George. They didn't ever have black superintendents all over this country. All superintendents were always white. White superintendent

Charles Rousseve, author of The Negro in Louisiana: Aspects of His History
and His Literature, *published by Xavier University Press in 1937.*
(Courtesy of Mrs. Charles B. Rousseve, New Orleans, Louisiana)

always picked the least of the evils of all the blacks. In other words, he
never picked the blacks who he thought would do a good job of teaching and educating the black kids. He got the ones who were strong and
ugly, who he thought would keep the kids in place. Now this is true, ask
anybody, and all the superintendent's offices up through the 1960s were
always in front of the courthouse.

What he would do is pick his principals by having [the candidates]
all come at the same time. They'd get out of the car out there. He'd look
at them, how they walk and how big and burly they were, and he'd pick
them from out there. But they all would come in, but he'd done [already]
picked them from out there. Didn't worry about any brains. He just

wanted somebody, just a person there. That's what happened. That's how it went. We do good to do as we are because we had no voice in choosing the teachers.

Doris George. They didn't worry about the children learning because they didn't want anybody that asked a lot for your kids.

SG: They didn't allow the principal to do that. The principal couldn't ask for nothing. I mean, yeah, they'd get him see. Therefore, once they got the principal, everybody else was scared to do or say anything. Now there were some communities where the teachers were [Uncle] Toms themselves. They'd go tell everything on the principal just to promote themselves. But, in general, like in Donalsonville particularly, that superintendent was a racist cracker.

I'll never forget, we are taught how to deal with a racist, you know. [During a job interview, the interviewer] asked me, said, "Who's your superintendent?" [He was] talking about back home, and I hadn't been there in four or five years, six or seven years. I knew his name; I said, "Mr. Adams." I knew to say "Mr." because if I had said his first name he wouldn't have given me that job, see. But I was just humble like he wanted me to act see.

I wouldn't have got my first job unless I was humble like he wanted me. He said, "Yeah, R.D." My principal was named R.D. He said, "R.D., we'll let him sign a contract, and I expect you to respect him because he's the one I expect information from." He said, "I don't want ya'll to bring me any information, all the information you got [to] come through R.D." You know, talking about my principal. And that's how he did that thing, and, of course, teachers in there didn't go down there and tell him anything. But I'll tell you, that principal, he was scared to death.

So anyway, you asked about college. I went to Fort Valley, did my undergraduate work there. The bad part in Georgia was once you graduated from college there was no institution in Georgia that would let you attend. You could not; they had no higher education in Georgia for blacks. In fact, that was true up until 1970, about 1972. Even the University of Georgia didn't let blacks in there. Autherine Lucy integrated the University of Alabama. Charlayne Hunter and Hamilton Holmes were the first two blacks at the University of Georgia, and they rioted and they had to slip them out the back door when they tried to go to school there. That was probably 1968, 1969, or 1970, somewhere along in there. So we had nowhere to go. We had to go out of state to do advanced studies.

DG: [The state] would give you the difference between [the cost at] the University of Georgia and at the school you'd go to there [in the North]. University of Georgia tuition was so cheap. I got the whole thing, room and board and tuition, even transportation to go to Chicago, to keep me from going to the University of Georgia.

I could go to any school that would take me. University of Georgia, see, they had to provide education for blacks and whites alike. They didn't have any state school that offered a master's degree in anything. You didn't have but three [colleges] for blacks. That was Fort Valley, Albany State, and Savannah State. They didn't have a graduate program. They had to give you the same opportunity. So rather than let you go to the University of Georgia, they'd rather pay you to go to any school, just pick your school, any school anywhere that would take you; you could go and they would pay all of it. They'd do anything to keep from integrating the schools, even lose money.

ARTHUR SEARLES

A native of Albany, Georgia, Arthur Searles suggests the variety of forms that education could take for African Americans from the 1920s to the 1940s. First, he entered a black public school, where his ability to read propelled him directly to the third grade. Then, after attending high school and normal school, he found himself teaching other African Americans in the New Deal's Civilian Conservation Corps.

With the help of the CCC camp director, Searles was able to attend Tennessee State University, completing his bachelor's degree and staying on for two years as superintendent of buildings. His memories of Tennessee State's president, William Jasper Hale, and other faculty members and students offer a glimpse of the social scene at a black college in the late 1930s.

In 1940, Searles returned to Albany to teach high school, a job that his mother essentially secured for him by asking her white employers to use their local influence. In 1943 he was drafted into the Army, where he was again involved in adult education through a special training unit designed for soldiers who had not completed the sixth grade, as many black soldiers in World War II had not. Thus Searles was again in a position to help others in the same way that he had been helped by Hale and other mentors. As his gratitude to these individuals makes clear, the lack of state support for black schooling in the Jim Crow South made networks of supporters absolutely essential for any black person to achieve academic success.

My birthday was on September 20, and Albany State College usually opened around September 3, and, of course, I was still 15 years old when I started Albany State. When the 20th came, I had moved up to 16 years old. But I started college—it wasn't [called] Albany State then; it was Georgia Normal. My mother had been a schoolteacher, and we always liked to play school in my house. I started elementary school when I was five years old. In those days, if you were potty-trained and you didn't mess yourself all up, they would let you go to school. When they found out that I could read and write, I sat around waiting for them for two weeks—they finally put me in third grade. I had never been to first nor second grade in my life.

Of course, that meant I could get out of school pretty early. However, after I got out of school, well, I went over to Dr. Holley, J. W. Holley. That's a character we've all grown to know. He was the founder and president of Georgia Normal College. That's Georgia Normal and Agricultural, GNAC is what they called it. I suppose I did two years with them. Of course, it was a normal school and that was as far as you could go. I couldn't get a job teaching or nothing like that. So I was going around here. My father was already dead, and I wanted to be doing some sort of work.

They had a work relief program called the Civilian Conservation Corps, CCC, and I signed up for that although I'd had two years of college. It was '33, I think. Something like that. Now just about all black folks who had at least one or two years of college training would join the CCC. It wasn't looked on in any favorable nature but that was my plight, and when I got into the CCC camp, they knew that I had had two years of college. Ninety-five percent of the people in the CCC camp could hardly read or write. So they put me in the education department to teach the young men how to read and write.

The camp advisor was Dr. William E. Lightfoot. He was the director of the CCC camp at Fort Benning. I guess they had about 600 or 700 young men. Yeah, that was Old Roosevelt's thing, the CCC camp, and a lot of white folks went in too. Of course, it was segregated. But Fort Benning is the largest military reservation in the world, and they could have three or four CCC camps on the reservation, and the two or three never would meet each other. But we did play in intramural baseball and drove to one of the other camps and one of the other camps would come over to us and have baseball games. That also helped me when I was in the CCC camp. I was a pretty good baseball player.

I was there one year. The fellows who were in the CCC constructed firebreaks and went all over the state of Georgia where there was a whole lot of forest. You know about firebreaks? They cut a piece of land, a space of land about 10 feet wide or 12 feet wide so that if you had a forest fire, when it got as far as that clearing, it wouldn't spread on over. It wouldn't burn the forest. They called them firebreaks.

Well, anyway, Dr. Lightfoot sent letters to some 12 or 14 black colleges. Now there was *no* black state-supported institution in Georgia or many of the other southern states. But Georgia particularly because it was the one I was concerned with. If you wanted to get a degree, you had to go to some other state because we couldn't get one. I always could go maybe to Clark College or some of those schools in the Atlanta area, but I'm saying state-supported. Clark was supported by one of the churches. Morris Brown was supported by the AME church, and all around like that, see. So, we didn't have any. But this fellow wrote Tuskegee, and he wrote North Carolina A & T, and he wrote several colleges, and the only one that answered his letter [was Tennessee State]. They sent it directly to me, saying that they understand from Dr. Lightfoot that I would like to continue my education and he recommends you so highly that we're going to try you out.

So I went on up there and to my dismay, the first thing they told me was that in order for you to make the three years, you're going to have to take just about a half of [a course load]. At that time 18 hours was a full load. But if you were a work student, you couldn't make but 12 hours.

So, I'd talk with them about the thing. I said my mother's back in Albany and I want to get on out and go to work so I can help my mother out. I'd like to make a deal with you. Any class that I make under a B, you can put me back on the work/study program. But if I make an A and B in all my subjects, then you just have to let me stay. I'll be doing just as well as anybody else. So they agreed to that. And I made the As and Bs.

I finished Tennessee State in '38 and I worked there for two years [as superintendent of buildings]. Then my mother got with her good white folks, and they decided to give me a teaching job here in Albany, teaching at Madison High School.

Then, my mama got it in her head to bring me home. There was no man in the house. I had two sisters still alive. My father died at least 10 years prior to that, prior to 1940. Must have died in 1930 then. He was much older than my mother. [My mother] went to these white people. They were Jews. And Mama told them she wanted her son home and so they went to [a city attorney and said], "Let that Searles boy have one of these jobs." Prior to that time, in all the colored schools, the principal, Mr. Holmes, put high hopes on Atlanta. He had finished Atlanta University and he just thought that the best teachers would come from Atlanta. The year that I came here they had a complete sweeping away of all Atlanta teachers. They hired me, and they hired a fellow named Robert Seller. We were hired at the same time.

So [my mother] begged me to come home because I would be the only man in the house. She said that she'd hear noises and things like that around the house, which was right on the corner. When you walk down the sidewalk, you get close enough to hear a noise out there. But, I came in that day just to come home and pay her a visit. When I got there, the principal of the black high school, Mr. Holmes, came while I was there. He told my mother, "I got some good news for you, Mrs. Searles. I'm sending a letter to your son to tell him that we hear he's been accepted as a member of the faculty." And she said, "Well, you don't need to send a letter. He's right there in the other room." And she called me. "Clarence, come on up here." I knew Mr. Holmes already. "Come on up here," and I saw Mr. Holmes.

We sat on the front porch and we talked for at least an hour. I wanted to ask him so bad how much was he paying me. It looked like he was fixing to get up and go. [Chuckles.] So I had to go ahead and ask him. I finally asked him how much was he going to pay me. He said it would be $50 every month for 12 months. "You have two months that you don't have to work at all, maybe three months." I said, "But now, Mr. Holmes, you're paying me $600 a year for 12 months and I don't care whether you pay me $75 a month, when it end up, it'll still be but $600." I was making $125 as superintendent of buildings at Tennessee State, $125 a month. And I said, "I just can't accept it. I can give my mother $75 and I still have $50 for myself. You see what I'm talking about?" So he said, "Well, I'm going to leave it here with you, and you and your mother settle that."

That very same night my mother was brought home in a funeral home hearse, because black folks didn't have any ambulances at all. So they brought me on home. She said, "Come in here son. I need to talk to you bad." She said, "I had promised [the man who helped me] that if he gets that job for you, I'd be mighty grateful to him." She said, "And I hate to go back and tell that white man"—that's about what it amounted to—"that you said you weren't going to take the job. I guaranteed it that you would take the job." She said, "I think if you go on back up to Tennessee and not take that job it'll kill me." Of course, you know, that was just like putting a pistol in my face. Yeah, I wouldn't have that on my conscience, that I killed Mama. Well, I accepted the job [and] I must say to you for the record I have never regretted coming back home. People said we got one of *our* boys. You know, I was one of their boys. [Laughs.] And it does make a difference.

Let me try to go back and do some of my life story. I have not included enough people who aided me along my way. At Tennessee State, I think I told you that President Hale was the president of the college and he was Dr. Hale, William Jasper Hale. He was very instrumental in helping me. He even called these people down here [in Albany] and told them to get me a job.

You know, I told you I had a flair for showmanship. So I got the [Tennessee State] building crew, and I gave them enough money to buy me a briefcase. I said now I want one of you all to present me a briefcase as a going-away present. Just as the chapel was getting ready to end, they said that they wanted to make a presentation to Mr. Searles who's leaving tomorrow for a new position. They gave us time to make this presentation, and when they gave the presentation to me, I said, "There's a sign out on the library that says, 'Grow or Go.' You must grow while you're here or you must go away from here." I said, "Well, I'm fixing to go so I can grow." And what did I say that for? The president of the college jumped up from his seat and came up to the stage in a hurry. Of course, when the president comes by, you know, everybody quits, and Hale was that kind of a fool. You're talking about a dictator. President Hale was the dictatorest dictator I've ever seen. I didn't cross him any way. I just wouldn't do it. He got up there and he says, "Young people, you hear him say he's going to grow. He's going down there in Mason, Tennessee, where rattlesnakes and everything have a good time, and he's talking about he's leaving this big city of Nashville, going somewhere to grow. You can't grow here, you can't grow nowhere!" [Laughs.] He chewed me out. He said, "Now, I'll be honest with you." He said, "I'll be honest with you. People say my wife's crazy about him. She doesn't want anybody to move her typewriter unless it's Searles. And tell you the truth about it, if he wasn't so doggone ugly, I'd be jealous of him." He tells 2,000 people sitting out there in the auditorium that he'd be jealous of me if I wasn't so ugly. [Laughs.] Of course, everybody laughed, you know. But I didn't think it was all that funny. Didn't tickle me. I was embarrassed to the nth degree. But President Hale was quite a good friend of mine. All the teachers liked me. One of the reasons why all the teachers liked me was the president was crazy about me. You know, that year they told me I had to make a B average or above to carry a full load, President Hale told the teachers, "If he doesn't make a B average, you give him a B average." Now that's wrong! I understand that, but I appreciated it because I wanted to get on out of there.

The dean of the college was Dr. George W. Gore. He became later on the president of Florida A & M. He was my journalism teacher, and he said I was one of the best students he'd ever taught in journalism. He went on down to Florida A & M, and he invited me down there to speak to the journalism class, and his wife was very kind to me too.

The author of a black history of Tennessee, Dr. Merle R. Epps, was very instrumental in molding my career. As a matter of fact, he told that girl right there [Searles's wife], "Girl, you're nothing but a fool. You better catch that man. You better catch him." [Laughs.] I had a lot of help from [him to] get her. Of course, I needed a lot of help. I went to see her one night, and I think there were five other fellows there waiting to see her.

Ugly as I am, I've been able to attract people with my words. I remember [on] the same night that I was telling you about when five other fellows were there to see her, she had told all of them that she was sick and that she couldn't see any of them. I said I was on the faculty then; I was a staff member; and I could take her into the faculty reception room, see, and I told her all this and I said, "Now, all illnesses are a matter of the mind. You've heard of Christian Science people? They say, they tell themselves every day I'm getting better and better." I said, "Now if you come on down here to the faculty reception room"—and that means a whole lot to a student, you know. She was going to be the queen. [Laughs.] And I says, "Now, just trust me. When I whisper sweet nothings into your [ear] like I did, you'll forget all the illness you ever had." [Laughs.] I had a pretty good line among them days. I don't think they hold good now but that doesn't dissuade me from trying.

So I won her away with me that night. Some of them tried to hang on, but I was a little too heavy for them, and the president had gone out to her people, her father. Her father owned 800 acres of land in middle Tennessee. I could see myself, even if we had some children, they would eventually get some of it. She was good-looking, now, don't let me—I'd have got her if she'd been penniless, if I could have. But all this added to it, you know. He had him a car. That's back in '38, '39, '40. Very few black folks had cars then. It was almost Depression time. But Papa—everybody called him Papa—Papa loved me dearly. He's dead now too, and she's dead now too, but the president went out to his farm. He was named the farmer of the year in Tennessee one time while I was courting, and they gave him a sack of Booker T. Washington's half dollars, silver dollars. You never heard that, had you? He won the Booker T. Washington farmer of the year award. Of course, I had my paper going. When we married, I mean. I don't mean when I met her. I didn't marry until I came back here in Albany. Then when I did get the paper going, everything was all right.

The big change that I made in my life was to come back to Albany. Truthfully, I did not want to come back to Albany because the pay was so low, but my mother wanted me home so badly, and I didn't mind at all being home with my mother. She had gotten up in years, and I wanted to show how much I loved her by staying here with her and helping her in every way I can. My years here with my mother were very near and dear to me. One of the first things though that she did was to let me go ahead and get married. I was teaching in the high school, at Monroe High School; I was teaching the business courses. Economics, business math, business English, and I think I had about five classes a day. Now the classes were small because we didn't have but a few children going to high school. It was a pleasure to teach them. In those days, parents helped you to teach their child. You better not go home and tell your mama or anybody in your class that Mr. Searles had to chastise or to punish the parents' child because of disorderly conduct or speaking up to the teacher or anything like that. That was not only true in my classes but in all of the classes. So it was a pleasure to teach school, and I thoroughly enjoyed the years that I taught at Monroe High School.

It was named Madison High School when I started teaching there and in 1943, we had already started the war with Germany and the national draft was going on. I was drafted along with thousands of young men. I, again, found myself at Fort Benning as a soldier. I was again lucky to not even have to go out in the field at all. I spent my three years in Fort Benning and could run home most any weekend and see my family. I rose to the rank of a battalion sergeant major for the special training unit, STU. The special training unit was to help people who had not completed the sixth grade get their academic hours up. I did not teach. I simply was the administrator of the outfit, but it was quite a good experience for me too. I had already started my teaching career here in Albany.

So I met so many people who assisted me along the way. So many. I wish I could name [more] of them.

EMERY L. RANN

Emery Rann's family moved from Bluefield, West Virginia, to Charlotte, North Carolina, in 1927 when he was 12. After graduation from

Johnson C. Smith College, where his father was a professor, Rann taught in the Deep South for a short time and coached high school sports. His reflections on his experiences traveling with his teams suggest how relatively sheltered his life within Charlotte's educated black middle class had been, despite his attendance at poker games and dances where bootleg whiskey flowed.

Rann volunteered for military service in World War II but was rejected because of high blood pressure—a mistaken diagnosis, as it turned out. He then seized an opportunity to pursue his life's dream of becoming a doctor. As he explains, he was able to put himself through Meharry Medical College in Nashville because he was willing to "hustle."

My dad came the year before [to Charlotte], and we were still in West Virginia while he came down and cleared the way for us to come in the next year. He was a teacher here at Smith. He was a teacher of mathematics, of English, of history, and was librarian at various times. He had taught at Bluefield State. One of his former coworkers had come here, and recommended him to the president, and he was brought here. I don't know much about West Virginia, except that I'm glad we moved. West Virginia is such a primitive place now as far as I'm concerned. The whole industry is coal, and it's just bottled up in that. I don't think Dad was too happy in his work there at Bluefield, and, while my mother went to school there, I don't think it was very progressive at all in education. I don't know the detailed reason for their moving or their wanting to move.

We stayed [in the Biddleville neighborhood in Charlotte] about two years, I imagine, and then moved down to the campus, and we stayed here for a long time. The building has been torn down. It was three doors down [from] where the Education Building is. It was interesting [living there]. Mrs. McCrorey had a distaste for anything, really, including my younger sisters, two of them, and Mrs. McCrorey would pick on those girls. They'd skate on the sidewalk, and they'd catch the devil, or they'd walk across it, and they'd still get the devil. It was really horrible. But all the students knew us, and we got along well with them. While we were here, they brought in the girls [coed students] starting with the senior year, junior and senior, and then eventually taking in everybody.

Cyrus Nero, right, and classmates, high school graduation, Greenwood, Mississippi, 1937.
(Photograph copied by Robert Jones, Mississippi/North Carolina Self-Portrait.
Courtesy of Melving and Gwendolyn Loper, Jackson, Mississippi)

I was in the ninth grade when we came here and went to Second Ward School, and it was shocking because we had been in a private school in West Virginia [at Bluefield Institute], a model school, more or less. The school was really a proving ground for the students. Students in education would come down and teach the classes, and of course we had the professor of education who acted as the principal and oversaw the work that was going on. I remember so well Mrs. Fannie Cobbs Carter. I do not [know] how I remember it, but she was the professor of education, and she was a remarkable woman. I was talking to a group of my family in West Virginia at one of our reunions and mentioned Fannie Cobbs Carter, and everybody remembered her. She was just dynamic, just full of herself, full of education, and she loved us. That was a big thing.

[Second Ward School was shocking because of] the state of poverty, the lack of morals, and the pugilistic attitude that so many of the kids had. It was shocking after being in that closed environment [in Bluefield]. I'd never heard any cursing. These kids would cuss without any compunction.

Central High was our greatest rival. It was all white, and Second Ward was all black. It was the only high school for blacks and we would get the hand-me-downs from Central. That is, the football, basketball uniforms were all used from Central, and they'd wear them until they wanted new ones and then pass these on down to Second Ward.

One interesting thing happened though. In my junior year in high school, a man came here to work and saw that we didn't have a band and he felt that we should have one. So he organized and taught us the fundamentals of music. For two or three years we had a band made up from the students who were interested, and this man was teaching us. It is really gratifying now, looking back on it, to see how this man came in and gave of himself to make us aware of music.

When we moved here, [my mother] was the principal of Woodlawn School, which was an elementary school 10 miles from here, and I recall how she would sometimes walk to school and back. Some of the theological students who had cars would drive them. Mama and the others who taught with her would drive her to school and bring her back, but so often it wasn't possible. Well, the car might not be functioning or the streets might not be passable. So they would walk it.

My dad was a farmer. He would come up and teach. Well first of all, he would get up in the morning and go out and work in his garden. Come in, dress, come to Smith, and teach, then go back and work in the garden. The thing that I remember most about that was how much I hated it. He wanted me to come out and work in the garden with him, and I hated that. It was traumatic to me because of the fact that the rest of the boys would be out playing, usually tennis, but anything, and I just hated it because I wanted to be out with them. That thing has followed me all my life. I don't like farming. When I was a kid he used to let me grow squash, and I'd take it out in my little wagon and sell them. A lot of people bought them just because it was me, not because they needed it. I put it down as soon as I got able to say no. Really, I had so much else to do, I didn't have time to fool around in the garden much.

After coming to Smith in '30, I was so tied up in things on the campus that it's hard to name. Everything on the campus, I was in. I was in the glee club, on the quintet, which was the official singing group of the campus. I was in drama. I was active at the Y, [and] my fraternity, Alpha Phi Alpha, and the Pan-Hellenic Council. Just about everything except debating. My dad wanted me to be a debater, but I didn't have the interest. And social clubs, of course.

At that time there were four groups on the campus, nonfraternity, and there were a similar number of clubs in town. Every week in the spring, there would be a dance, and I have wondered very seriously how in the world during those Depression years we were able to decorate, hire a band, and dress up and go to these parties every week, and yet we did. The places where we had them are ill reputed now. For instance, I've forgotten [the] name of it, but [it was] downtown in an old soft drink building where we'd have to get the crates of drinks and pile them up out of the way so that we could dance on the floor. Athenian, I think they called it the Athenian Ballroom. We would have our dances, and the four clubs would have them. LCE, the bachelors; RSOT, Royal Sons of Tut; Sons of the Nile; Les Chevaliers Elegants; and something else. I've forgotten the fourth one. But all of the old clubs in town would entertain as well as those of us who were here on the campus. Of course, the Serenaders played for us at all these dances until they left and went to New York. The fellow who took them up there found that they didn't have enough money to really give them a good backing, and so they came back to Charlotte.

I lived right here [at home during college]. I'd sneak up to the dormitories and play poker. My dad didn't like gambling, but the gambling we did was practically not gambling because we didn't have any funds. Penny ante, stuff like that, you know. Another very poignant thing is our buying whiskey for these affairs. There were bootleggers all around this area, and one in particular over where one of the old girls' dormitories has been built. Right next door to it was a bootlegger. We'd go in and buy a 50-cent shot. Throw it down and then gasp for breath for about five minutes. Most of it was of the bathtub variety.

I don't know whether you'd call them shady areas or not, [but] there were some areas where you didn't frequent. Places in Brooklyn [a

Charlotte neighborhood]. My dad was quite adamant in my [not] going to the show on Second Street, which is no longer in existence. A lot of bootleggers were on that street and some legitimate businesses were there. The AME Zion Publishing House was in the corner. The library, public library, was in that corner, in that section. The doctors' offices and drugstores were all in that area, but there was still that element that wasn't too conducive to people coming in.

After leaving [Charlotte], I went to the University of Michigan and got a master's degree and had a series of teaching jobs in Georgia, Alabama, Texas, and Charlotte. Well, the South was the South, and I recall so often so many experiences that I had. I had bitter experiences in practically all the places that I went.

In Georgia, first, I got that job because Mrs. Gregg, who was the wife of the principal, came up here to a study session that they had here at Smith. I hadn't taken any education at all. I just had a pure science major. I was intending to go to school, but at that time the money became quite a problem, and I couldn't go. So I went to Georgia. I taught about five different subjects, unrelated, coached football and basketball with no equipment whatsoever. I wrote to Auburn College, Auburn University, to the coach, and told him what the situation was. You know he sent me enough equipment, balls and uniforms, to equip my team. We had one game and that was in Atlanta, and it was on the spur of the moment, and they didn't have time to really get ready for our team. But the coach said he would give us dinner after the game, and of course, we'd have to leave. They didn't have facilities for us to stay overnight. We played them. Our boys didn't know a thing about football, but the score was 12 to 6, I believe, and they made their last touchdown in the last minutes of play. It was very interesting.

In basketball, we just cleaned up. One experience we had though was at LaGrange, which is about 30 miles from Newnan where I taught. We had them beaten about 30 to 12, something like that, and, during the half, these white men came and sat down under our goal, and said the first that makes a basket is going to get shot. So the score ended. We had 30. They had 32. We didn't get a basket. [I told my players] don't shoot. You joined the program. You went along with it, if you wanted to live,

Bryant Edwards, Helen Marie Washington Parker, and John Hope Franklin, left to right, at Booker T. Washington High School, Tulsa, Oklahoma, spring 1930.

(Courtesy of Fred Parker, Los Angeles, California)

because those guys didn't have any compunction about you. That attitude existed in just about every place we went.

When I was teaching in Alabama, I carried a basketball team over into Mississippi, Okolona, Mississippi. The boys said, "We don't want to stay here overnight. Let's go on down to"—oh, what's the name of that school, the state college for blacks then in Mississippi, whatever it was. I went down to send a wire to the coach at this school, and the owner of the drugstore where you made your call said, "Where is the place?" I told him where it was. "Do they have a phone there?" "Yes they do." He said, "Do they have a phone there?" I said, "Yes they have a phone." "God damn it, nigger, when you talk to a white man, you say 'sir'!" I said, "Sir," and went out of the door, and lo and behold, there was a group of white men waiting, and I ran and jumped in my car. I mean I didn't run, but I made haste to my car and left that town just as fast as I could.

I was 20 when I finished college. Taught one year and then went to Michigan. I think I was too young. I think I should have had more experience and have developed more, but I took it as it came. My last experience in teaching was back at Stillman College in Tuscaloosa where they were nagging me to come and join the Army. I would get various persons to say that I was essential, and consequently got out of it. Finally, I just said, well, I'll go ahead and join and get this thing over with.

So I went to Fort Bragg, which is the area here, and it's a long story. After my examination, I was in this long line waiting to talk to one of the officers. There's a naval officer, army, all the specimens, all the men in the various sections of the armed services were there. And as I walked up to the naval officer's desk, I saw him reading a University of Michigan bulletin, and I said, "Pardon me, sir, are you a Michigan man?" He jumped up and said, "Yeah, are you?" I said yes. "Where did you live?" I told him, and it happened that the Alpha House in Ann Arbor was right across the street from this guy's house, and we used to sing dirty songs to each other. We'd get together and sing Michigan songs. We were just having a good time, but when I got to the Army man, he stamped rejected, and I was quite upset because I didn't have any idea that I was sick.

So I came back to Charlotte and went [to] my doctor. I told him I had high blood pressure, and he said, "No, you don't have high blood pressure," 120 over 80, which was perfectly normal. That was my situation. I volunteered for several positions, but the people said no, there's no place for a colored man in that field. You can go to Tuskegee and join the Air Corps, the Army Air Corps, and you won't have any problem at all. I told them, no, I don't want [to] fly. So, I gave it up. Got with the war price and rationing board, and while there I took my examination to go to medical school, and passed it, [and] was accepted.

I had wanted to [go to medical school] before, but with four of us to be educated, I didn't press at all. It was part of my rearing. The four of us heard from the time we were large enough to understand what was being said that we had to make sacrifices. We don't have the income, and we just can't afford all the things that we want. I think that had [been] a very, very keen part of my growing up, the idea of sacrifice. That hurt, too. Because even in the band that we had here at Second Ward, I wanted to play the saxophone, but I chose a bass horn because they furnished the horn, and I didn't feel like asking my dad and mother to give me a saxophone so I could learn to play it.

I had always wanted to be either a medical missionary or a doctor, and at one of these schools I decided I didn't want to be a minister because the ministers were so rotten. I just didn't want to be associated with a group like that, and I would prefer being a physician. With this opportunity, I decided I'd try medicine. So as I said, I passed the examinations to go into medicine, and I saved every penny I would make in the war price and rationing board, and went to Meharry. I chose Meharry instead of Howard, and the first semester was fine. The second semester, books, tuition, room and board, everything, went up, and all of my funds were just wiped out. So I got several teaching fellowships, and that helped me through.

One of the things which was really griping to me was that so many of my relatives said, "Oh yes, this is my nephew, my cousin, or whatever, who's a student in medical school. He's really doing well." [But] when I wrote to them and asked them for maybe $100 or something, [they said,] "Oh, I'm sorry. We don't have the money." That's the way it was.

Meharry is right across the street from Fisk. The main street is Jefferson Street. On the corner below Fisk and Meharry was Gene Price's pharmacy. I contracted with Gene to live in his house, which was upstairs above the drugstore, and I had a roommate. One day I was in the drugstore at twelve o'clock, and the place was just overflowing with people. People from Tennessee State and from Fisk and from Meharry were there getting lunch. So I took off my coat and got behind the counter and started working. After we were through with the rush, Gene came up to me and said, "I sure appreciate your help. Can you come down every day?" So I said yes, and I came down every noon to work in Gene Price's pharmacy.

When I went to pay him my money, he said, "Well, listen, I want you to continue working with me at noon, and you won't have to pay anything on your room rent." His mother used to bring him his lunch and dinner, and after a little while, she started bringing me a plate. Pretty soon, I had no board bill. So I got room and board free for the three years after that first year that I was there. Hustle! [Laughs.]

[Gene] was, I guess, about 10 or 12 years older than I. He was a very good friend of Jimmy Lunsford. That's before your time. He was one of the Duke Ellington, Count Basie equivalents. He had a wonderful band. On the weekend we would take in all the shows. Kept the job, serving the tables, and we'd hear all the plays and all the shows, see all the shows. Still hustling! [Laughs.]

FIVE

WORK

Most African Americans in the Jim Crow South toiled for white employers. While segregation's power could be mitigated in their own churches, lodge halls, and homes, such communal protections withered on the job. Segregation relegated African Americans to the lowest-paying, most menial and hazardous forms of labor, yet black workers did not always accept these terms of employment.

In the wake of Emancipation, many freed people hoped that they would be compensated for generations of unpaid toil with free land. As the vision of "Forty Acres and a Mule" faded, however, sharecropping became a way of life for millions of landless African American farmers. In this system, landlords or furnishing merchants provided land, seed, and other agricultural implements while sharecropping families provided their labor for a small "share" of the profits. Even though this system developed as a "compromise" between former slaves and slave owners over the terms of agricultural employment, people remembered the system with loathing. More often than not, sharecroppers would end each harvest season deeper in debt after their supplies were deducted from the landlord's ledger. Questioning the judgment of the white boss meant risking eviction, violence, or even a lynching. No wonder that Sarah Campbell's brother's fellow workers emerged from North Carolina's sweltering tobacco fields singing in an effort to raise their spirits. When asked what kinds of songs were being sung, Campbell replied: "I believed they called them blues."

By the end of the nineteenth century, African Americans increasingly looked to the New South's burgeoning cities as a land of hope. But here too African Americans were increasingly segregated from better-paying jobs. White southerners refused to work under black supervisors and most white craftsmen strenuously opposed the hiring of African Americans in the skilled trades. As a result, the cadres of black carpenters, bricklayers, barbers, and other skilled African American workers—who had plied these trades during slavery—began to lose ground. By 1900, most black southerners were not only frozen out of skilled employment but denied jobs in the region's booming textile mills. A small number found employment in mines and tobacco factories, but during the age of Jim Crow the majority of African Americans labored on the land.

When African American laborers fell into debt or were convicted of petty crimes, they often found themselves ensnared in the system of convict labor and debt peonage. Forced labor flourished in the New South, entrapping thousands of black laborers on plantations, turpentine farms, road-grading crews, railroad gangs, and in coal mines. Southern states passed laws designed to tie African American laborers to employers in relationships that were at times barely distinguishable from slavery. These laws included "anti-enticement" statutes that penalized labor recruiters who offered workers higher wages, and "after dark laws" that made it a crime for sharecroppers to market their produce away from the watchful eye of the landlord.

W.E.B. Du Bois argued in *Black Reconstruction* (1935) that oppression in the workplace was fueled by the desire of the New South's ambitious but capital-starved employers to keep African Americans as powerless as possible. Du Bois wrote: "The lawlessness in the South since the Civil War has varied in its phases. First, it was that kind of disregard for law which follows all war. Then it became a labor war, an attempt on the part of impoverished capitalists and landholders to force laborers to work on the capitalist's terms." From Du Bois's perspective, this was the linchpin of Jim Crow.

Of course, not all African Americans labored for whites. Most urban and small-town black communities could boast of a small middle class made up of doctors, lawyers, teachers, business owners, and preachers. However, Jim Crow severely hampered most African American businesses, which suffered from a lack of access to credit as well as an impoverished clientele.

Chronic low wages and the constant need for more help in the fields compelled many African American families to send their children into the labor force early and often. Essie Mae Alexander went to work in the Mississippi cotton fields at age nine, three years later than her brother who started fieldwork at age six. Thomas Chatmon started working in the fields when he was four years old. Hard-pressed parents had few options. White employers and school officials colluded to take black youths out of the classroom and place them in the cotton fields. Noted sociologist Charles S. Johnson observed: "Literacy is not an asset in the plantation economy, and it was not only discouraged but usually forbidden. The belief that education spoiled the slave carried over with but little modification for many years into the belief that education spoils a field hand." Black working families struggled to improve their material conditions as well as the educational opportunities of their children.

White supremacy shaped the terms of black employment. Maids were required to enter the rear entrances of their employers' houses as a reminder of their subordinate status in society. As they had during slavery, women domestics often fell prey to sexual exploitation by the husbands and sons in their employers' household. For African American women, poor working conditions were not rewarded by higher wages.

Adding insult to injury, the millions of African Americans who toiled in agriculture and domestic work were excluded from workplace protections that other Americans relied on in the wake of the New Deal. Workers in domestic service and agriculture were denied coverage under the Social Security Act, the Fair Labor Standards Act, and the National Labor Relations Act. While U.S. citizens now looked to the federal government to provide a minimal safety net, the millions of African American men and women who were relegated to these low-wage jobs had to fall back on their own resources or rely on the whims of their employers to survive. The federal government effectively turned its back on much of the country's black labor force.

African Americans fought back against racial oppression on the job.

Resistance took many shapes, including leaving work, slowing down, and striking for higher pay and union recognition. In the opening months of 1934, African American laundry workers, waitresses, and coal miners struck for higher wages in Birmingham, Alabama. Commenting on this activism, the *Pittsburgh Courier* remarked: "The alleged docility of Southern labor is not in evidence around Birmingham these days." African Americans seized on labor shortages during World War I and again during World War II and left the rural South in search of higher-paying industrial employment.

At times, resistance took the form of performing heroic—even dangerous—feats of labor, confounding white stereotypes about the work ethic of African Americans. John Cooper, part of the first cohort of black city firefighters in Memphis, Tennessee, in the 1950s, expressed pride at being able to outperform his white counterparts. "I'll tell you," Cooper stated, "when they first come on, they say we 'Niggers couldn't put no fires out.' So in a way we proved that we could put them out just as well as they could and better." In spite of the dangers and difficulties they faced on the job then, African Americans took pride in their work and sought to make their occupational lives as meaningful as possible.

Black industrial workers occupied a strategic place in the American economy. Toiling as miners, longshoremen, steel, and railroad workers, African Americans were at the center of the New South's project to create an urban, industrial economy in the twentieth century. African American workers in these industries often provided the earliest and most sustained support to the nascent industrial union movement that emerged in the Great Depression.

Jim Crow hampered African American workers' efforts to organize. White coworkers jealously guarded the higher-paying jobs that their white skin gave them a monopoly over. As a result, black union activists had to fight a war on two fronts: first, against employers who sought to crush collective bargaining gains; second, against white workers who identified themselves with white management rather than with black laborers. Like nationally known labor leader A. Philip Randolph, black union activists in the South tried to make the American labor movement a vehicle for democracy and a voice for all workers, regardless of race.

LILLIE FENNER

Lillie Fenner was born into a sharecropping family in Halifax County, North Carolina, in 1907. Fenner's father and mother—like their parents before them—never owned the land that they farmed. As sharecroppers, the family was subject to the rules of white landlords and had to move frequently during Mrs. Fenner's childhood. At the same time, the family displayed an intense resourcefulness and pride, growing much of their own food and cooperatively pooling their labor with neighbors in order to survive.

[My grandparents] didn't own [their] land. They rented and they share-cropped. They had peanuts, cotton and corn and soybeans. Every one of us [children] worked on the farm. We picked cotton. Shake peanuts. They didn't have no tractors and things like that. We worked with mules. I used to take them and plow and break ground. I used to run rows with them and plant corn because that was something that I would love to do. Then I would get on the back and ride them up and down the rows. Sometimes, we had a store not far from us, I'd get on the horseback and ride it to the store and get what I wanted to get and come on back home. Sometimes I'd hitch them up to the buggy and ride on the buggy. That's the way we come up. [Women] would go out and plow to help their husbands out, let him rest a while while they plowed. Yeah, a lot of them did that. And I was helping my father out.

My daddy would have a pen full of hogs. We owned a cow but we never owned no mules or no plows or nothing like that. And we had chickens. We didn't have to worry about buying no eggs or chickens or no meat. We'd have all of that. We raised cane to make molasses. We had to buy a little something like sugar and rice or something or other like that. Other stuff we always made at home. About two weeks or three weeks before Christmas we would always kill hogs. Salt it down, put salt on it and pack it up and let it stay there about a month; then he would take it and wash the salt off and put some smoked liquid and hang it up in the smokehouse. He'd get hickory wood and smoke it. Then it would be ready to eat. It would be cured out then. [Neighbors] would come from other places to help out because most everybody that lived around

Farmer in Calhoun County, South Carolina, 1958.
(Courtesy of Cecil and Ethel Williams, Orangeburg, South Carolina)

in the community would kill hogs at that time. Like if we killed hogs today they would come and help my dad. If they killed tomorrow then my daddy would go and help them. They'd go around to each house and help them kill hogs. They would get women to help in the hogs. My daddy would have so many women and the other ones would have so many. They would help out like that in the hogs. Then when they finished they would give them so much fresh [meat] for helping them in the hogs. Sometimes they would give them a little piece of money. That's the way they got their pay. They said they had rather have the meat because they didn't have none. So my daddy would give them a whole lot of meat, sausage, and stuff like that.

We had a nice garden. We had cabbage, collards, turnips, salad, white potatoes, garden peas, butter beans, and stuff like that. [My mother] canned every year. She canned 300 or 400 jars of vegetables. Apples, peaches, anything she could get she would can to store it back for the winter. If it won't nothing else, we'd eat that. During the wintertime a whole lot of women would have what you call "quiltings" to quilt quilts. They would take the quilt and put it in a frame and swing it up in the loft. They would have women to come around and help quilt that quilt. They'd have peanut shellings. People would come at nights and help you shell peanuts. We would have little refreshments to give them drinks and cookies. You'd just sit and quilt and shell peanuts. They'd sit and talk until [it was] time go home and then they would leave.

They [the landlords] wanted to see you out in the field sunrise and sunset.

They didn't want you out of there one minute. Just wanted you to stay in the field working all the time. They didn't want you to go and get a cool drink of water. Tell you to carry your water in the field. You know when it's hot that ain't going to last long. It would be hot. We left from there. We moved around different places. But I tell you I can't tell you where they was. When we left from down there in that house we moved up in a place they call Dumplin Town. That's what they call it in them days. I was very small. We lived there for about two or three years. Then we moved back in the same house down there on that road. We moved back in that house and we stayed there two or three more years. Then we moved over on this other road over here called Simmons farm in a big house over there. That's where we lived there seven or eight or nine or ten years. When we moved over there we moved in a one-room house, one bedroom and a kitchen. All of us had to sleep in that one room when we first moved there.

Seemed like my daddy and the man he worked with couldn't agree on different things. So we would get up and move somewhere else. We'd stay there a while until it looked like they couldn't agree, and then he'd get up and move somewhere else. If they [black sharecroppers] didn't get up and go out early, he [the landlord] would ask them why they didn't come out early to work. My father told him he was waiting to get his breakfast and get straight around the house. [The landlord] would always tell him that they could bring their breakfast to the field. He told him he didn't eat in the field; he eat at the house. He would have a disagreement about that. He told him: "If you can't do like I say, you have to leave because I believe in my men being in the field at sunup." My father told him, "Well, I think that when I finish this crop I will move." So we'd move again. That's just the way we lived.

The happiest day to me was when I could go to school. That would be a happy day to me. And I would meet up with the children, laugh and talk and carry on with them. And sometimes some of them would come with me halfway home and say, "Sure do miss you from school. Be glad when you come back." It would be the same thing when I'd go to church. That was a happy day. But seems like then when I'd get back home, seems like I would be sad because I knew I couldn't go to school that next day and I knowed that I had to be working and doing something. I'd be thinking about school and the children but I couldn't go. I would be sad.

CLEASTER MITCHELL

Cleaster Mitchell was born and raised in the Arkansas Delta. A domestic worker like her mother before her, Mitchell learned early that resistance to white authority could have dire consequences. Anxious to protect her daughter as best as she could, Mitchell's mother taught her to be wary of white men in the household. Often, these men—husbands, sons, and acquaintances of white female employers—tried to extort sexual favors from black maids and cooks who, like Cleaster Mitchell, found creative ways to fight back against sexual exploitation.

My mother worked for all the people in Blackton. She cooked for those years of 1925 up until 1936. It was on a Christmas Day [in 1936], and she was cooking our Christmas dinner, and Mr. Roberts came. He was one of the merchants. He came out about 10:30 and said to my mother, "Mary, I come after you to go up there to serve for Mrs. Roberts."

My mother said, "Well, I can't go today, Mr. Roberts, because I am preparing my children's Christmas dinner, and I always fix them a Christmas dinner. If I had of known, I would have tried to make some kind of arrangements to have gotten started early and maybe I could have come served dinner [for] you all."

He was so mad. [He] left. About an hour later he came back out and called my mother to the car. My mother lived in his house. [He said,] "I want my house. I want you to get out of my house, and I want you out of here tomorrow."

She just told him, "Yes, sir." And when she got through with Christmas dinner, she went down to see Mr. Bennett. He had a house out here right off of Henderson corner. It was just an old vacant house out there, and the horses and things would go and stay in it. It was bad. We had to go out there and clean it out. But that's where we moved, all because she refused and didn't go because she was cooking our Christmas dinner.

See, that's what you had to contend with. You done what they say do or else you suffer the consequence. It was always a repercussion. It was always something.

From the time I was four or five, I went to work with my mother. See, you grow up in this. It's not like waiting and saying, "You're 15 now. You can go do some work." You done all of this work [before the] time you get 15 years old. You done worked for everybody in town almost. I've been self-supporting ever since I was really 12 years old. At 12, I knowed how to take care of myself. I could work for anybody at 12, because I was taught.

Well, one thing they taught you was honesty. They always impressed this in you. "Don't you take anything." They'd tell you, "Don't talk back." They would tell you to do a good job and all these things. They would sit [you] down and show you examples about them. Say, "Well, you know, it wasn't easy for me. And if they say thus and so, just don't say anything. You just go on and do your job. If you go up and do a good job and you be neat and you be clean and don't take nothing don't belong to you, you will not have a problem."

We automatically knowed you went in the back door. You didn't have to guess about that. You could work in the house all day. You could never come out the front door. [The] only way you come out the front door, [was if] you swept the front porch off. But to just come up the main walk or something, no. You was just trained like that. That was never a qualm with us. That's how come, I tell you, in some ways it was easier than people think it was, because it was just understood at an early age what you do and what you don't do.

I worked for one [lady] that was poorer than I was, but to get some recognition, some status among the white people, she got somebody to work for her. But she didn't have any more than what I had. I had more fun working for the one that was as poor as I was than the one that was rich. The one [who] was poor was more down to earth. We had something we could talk about and things, and she knew what hard work was. You worked, but she didn't worry about you killing yourself.

See, some of them you worked for, they worked you all day, and said, "When you get through with such and such, I want you to do so and so and so." Time you get through with this, "I tell you what. You know what I want you to do? I want you to do such and such a thing, and when you get through with this, do so and so." It was something all day long. In '43 when I was working up here, you know I was only making $2.50 a week. I washed. I ironed. I took care of the baby. I worked the garden. I mowed the yard. I took care of the chickens. I pumped the water for the animals. I done everything. I got $2.50 a week.

I've cried many a day. They accuse you of something. And if you try to say I didn't do it, they say you're lying, you did do it. And then here you stand and you know you didn't do it. I wanted to say, "I'm going to tell my mother," but you couldn't say that. Yeah, I cried a lot of times, because that happened to me, too.

Miss Miller, I was working for her. I was just a kid. I must have been approximately about 12. And see, they test you to see [if] will you steal something. So she goes in and she puts 35 cents down on the floor. So I goes in and I cleans the room. Well, I swept up a kernel. You know what a kernel in the wood is? It's wood in the pinewood. Sometimes it's a knot in the floor, and the kernel will break out and make a hole in the floor. So I had a dust mop, going up under the bed. And then when I got here and I pushed it over, by the money being heavier than the net, it went down through the house.

I never saw it, but she just swore by all means I took the 35 cents. I just cried and cried and cried. She said, "You're going to get that 35 cents," and she just raised all kind of [sand]. I kept telling her I didn't get it.

So that evening we went in there, and I was to change the dresser scarves on her dresser. She just stepped right over the hole and looked and she saw that 35 cents. It got a way with her so bad. She couldn't move. I come to see what she was looking at. She said, "What you do, sweep the trash through the hole?"

I said, "No, I don't sweep no trash through the hole. I take it up with the dustpan."

"Well, I see the 35 cents down here through the hole."

I said, "I guess it just fell in there when I was sweeping."

But see, she had really hurt me so bad about it. Yeah, you know, you get angry and stuff, but since, you know, you come up in this, you expected a lot of this, so you didn't let that make you a bad person. The only thing I can say, it did not make you a bad person.

[Another] one of the things that they instilled in you was about being approached by the young mens. It was terrible at one time. It wasn't nobody to tell. And a lot of them had children and rode right by them and didn't speak to them, and they knowed that was their children. Now, some of them, if the person was working for them and they had this baby, I know in a couple of cases that baby was actually raised in that house. You see, that's how come I know their wife couldn't do nothing about it. The lady he got the baby by couldn't leave and the wife couldn't do nothing about it and had to let the baby stay there. They was scared of their husband, too.

You could go to the wife and she'd say, "Oh, just don't pay him no attention. Just don't pay him no attention," because she's scared. You go to her because you think you were doing something. Most of the time, they know they was doing it, but they wouldn't tell you. They'd say, "Oh, don't pay Mr. So-and-So no attention. He was drunk. Don't pay him no attention."

A lot of people that worked and had jobs, they left on that account. It wasn't something you could—like I say, you had no alternative. To go to the law didn't mean anything. There wasn't no law [for] you [to] go to. And I'll tell you, one time in the South, it's bad to say, white men was crazy about black women. They would come to your house. They would attack you. They took it for granted when they saw a black lady that they could just approach her, that it was not an insult to her for them to approach her. But my mother taught us what to do and everything. She had to leave us at home a lot of times, and she said, "Okay, you all stay in the house. You see a white man or something coming up here, fasten the door. Stay in the house. And if they knock, don't let them in." See, she had alternatives for you to sort of protect yourself and stuff.

So when the grown person approached me, I just told him not to do it. "Don't put your hands on me, because I'm not here for that." And then if they kept at it, I said, "I'm going to tell your wife." I had a lot of alternatives. When I got up grown where I could really speak up for myself, then I had a lot of things I'd tell him.

Like I told Mr. Brown down here. See, he just took it for granted because I worked there for Mrs. Hettie. He just walked right in and I was putting up some glasses in the little shelf thing up there. He'd just walk right up here and just—he just walked up and he just put his arms around me. I was so mad. I told him, I said, "Listen, I been knowing you all of my life, Mr. Jim. You never knowed me to meddle you, flirt with you, or anything. I've been working here with Mrs. Hettie almost four years. You never seen me approach Mr. Billy or nobody, have you?"

"No, I was just—."

I said, "No, you wasn't playing. But don't you do that. As long as you live, don't you put your hands on me no more. I'll tell you why. Because if a black man done that to a white woman, you'd be the first to get here and find a limb to hang him to. So if you would hang the black man about doing it, you think I'm going to let you do it to me?"

From that day to this one, I had no trouble out of him. That really stopped him.

He said, "I wouldn't do it."

I said, "Yeah, you would."

This happened to me in 1943.

But every bit of this went on. That was no joke.

Well, I was working for [Mrs. Hettie]. I nursed her son in '36. I took care of him. I helped raise him. I washed and I was hanging the clothes out, and Wayne shot me with a BB gun. But he shot me on my spine right there, right up here. Right where that dot is, he shot me there. And I tell you, he done me so bad. He might have been real close on me when he shot me because it was bad enough. My arms just went like, you know, numb or paralyzed or something. And in a few minutes, my face was gone just like this. I don't know whether he ruptured a thing.

So I just left and went straight to the doctor. I didn't wait to tell them. I just left and went over to the doctor. I went over there, and he gave me a shot. Well, I had my own money. It was $2, about $2.50. I went over there and I just paid him.

So when she seen me coming back, she said, "Cleaster, where you been?"

I said, "I've been to Dr. Bradley."

"What did you go to the doctor for?"

I said, "Wayne shot me with that BB gun." So I just kept walking, because I was really sick.

"When you get ready to go to the doctor, you let me know. Don't go over there and make no bill."

By that time, that was all I could stand. I just walked right out and got me a change of clothes. I just walked right out. Yeah, there come a time you can't cope with it anymore.

HENRY DONALDSON

Unlike Cleaster Mitchell, Henry Donaldson was classified by the U.S. Census as a skilled workman, a brick mason. Yet, in spite of his relatively privileged occupational level, he lived with Jim Crow on the job the same as if he had been a common laborer. After serving in the U.S. Army during World War II, Donaldson left his home in Wilmington, North Carolina, and worked throughout the South on major construction sites with white coworkers. While Henry Donaldson was tempted many times to lash back against abusive foremen, he was chastened by the thought of facing unemployment or working at a job that paid even less. Here, he discusses how white supremacy was maintained at building construction sites, even at the cost of slowing down the work.

I'm a brick mason by trade. I'll tell you one of the most hurtful things [in] my experience on the job there in Atlanta. They had all white in charge of everything. We had a white foreman. He stood over us day by day. And the labor foremans were white. And believe me, they couldn't spell their name if they saw it in letters big as a brick. And their word was "nigger this" and "nigger that." But what would hurt me and here I am a brick mason, working on a corner, here's a labor foreman come up not even knowing how to pick up a brick hardly and he would come up [and say], "Nigger, you're making a lot of money." I wouldn't say anything because, you know, it intimidated me and I'm trying to work.

It was sort of hot like it is now, and we had one on the job, he just didn't like me because you see these khakis I have on, I've always liked to wear these because they're cool and they're clean. I'd always go clean on the job. So [the foreman] said one day, "Every time I look at you, you don't look like you're working hard." He said, "You're sweating but you're not dirty." So I said, "Why should I be dirty? I came to work and I can't stand odors, body odors and things like that. I wash every day." So what he did, I was building a corner and he was so stupid. Now, when you're laying brick it has to set up before it gets hard. So he took his foot and put it up on my corner and knocked it over. Well, right then I just got upset. I said, "Man, what you doing?" I said, "You're tearing the corner down. The other brick masons will be over here and I won't have nothing." "Shut up, nigger, and build it back!" And the supervisor came by and he looked. "What's going on over there!" I said, "This man come over here and kicked my corner down." You know what the supervisor said? "Go on boy and put it back. Hurry up. The gang will be over here after a while." Well then I got upset. I really did. I walked off. I walked off I guess about six or seven paces and the superintendent [said], "Boy you want to work?" And it came to me all of a sudden. Well, I'm down here. I need to work. I've got to work. So I told him, "Yes, I want to work." "What?" "Yes, I want to work. Yes sir." I said, "Yes sir." And I went on back to my corner.

But I'm telling you that thing really got next to me. Now here's this little old labor foreman and they were sort of funny to me. Every one of them would close their eye, one eye, and all of them chewed tobacco. I hated that stuff! They'd spit all over your work, on the brick. And you know, you have to pick them up and lay them. But you couldn't say anything about it. You'd better not if you want to work. And this fellow, it seemed like he just wanted to intimidate me all the time. But I had to swallow a whole lot of times because I was from up north, that's what they called North Carolina [laughter], "up north." But I stayed on that job until it finished. This is the thing that we had to put up with.

If you wanted to work, you had to stay there. I remember once one of the black bricklayers from Georgia, he was an older man, and he couldn't work as steady and hard as we did, but they gave him a fit on the job. Finally, he had to leave there because one of the supervisors said something to him. They were teasing him about being an old man and about how many girlfriends you got and this, that and the other. You know, just running on, teasing him. So he told them, he said, "In the first place I've got a wife and I'm too old to have any girlfriends so to hell with that." And he slapped him, this old man. This was a much younger fellow, this white fellow, but he slapped him. "Don't you say that to me!" And that man had to hurry up and leave there because they were going to hang him up and they told him, and we knew what that meant from hearing this, that and the other. When they said they were going to hang you up back during that time [laughter] you'd better get.

From 1946 through 1950 this is the kind of work that I did up and down the East Coast. When I came out of the Army I was discharged on the 5th of February of 1946, and I resumed my masonry after coming out of the Army. Construction work was scarce around here so I went to the Marine base in Jacksonville, North Carolina, and worked a while for $1.50 an hour. That was top wages in 1946 for a brick mason here around North Carolina and especially in this area. Then we got a 25-cents raise and went to $1.75 an hour. And about this time the work began to get scarce on that Marine base, so I left Jacksonville and Wilmington and went to Gadsden, Alabama, the first of 1947. Then we made big bucks, $2 an hour. That was the top wages at that particular time for masonry on that end of the road.

During this time [in Alabama] black brick masons and white brick masons did not work together on the same building. In North Carolina we worked together even though they had better breaks on the job. They could take a break but we could not. But on this particular job in Gadsden, Alabama, we would all go to work, blacks and whites would go to work at eight o'clock. About nine-thirty the whites on their building, they would take a 15- or 20-minute break for coffee or a drink or whatever. But the black brick masons could never have a break. We worked from eight until twelve o'clock. For lunchtime we had 30 minutes off for lunch. And the only time we could possibly get a break is when we'd go to the privy, as they called it, and we mustn't stay more than five minutes or else the foreman would come by and kick on the door. "You're not sick in there are you?" [Laughter.] "No, everything is all right." "Better get back on the job." Then he would go on. So we would go back.

We worked hard. Full eight hours every day. Maybe I'd say about 10, no more than 15 minutes for privy time. But during that time we were making a lot of money, and I had a real nice room where I boarded and my room and board was $10 a week. We got breakfast in the morning. We had two sandwiches for lunch. And then naturally we would have a nice dinner, supper we called it. And during this particular time in Gadsden, they had a curfew hour. No blacks were to be on the streets of Gadsden, Alabama, after eight o'clock at night. You had to be off of the streets. We weren't used to that around here, it was sort of tough with us. We would like to look around the foot of the mountains and see this and then sometimes we would run over. But then there was always a law officer and all of them weren't dressed in uniforms. In other words, if he had a white face, he was an officer. They called them auxiliary cops. But then you must be off of the street by that time. And even where you room and you boarded, you must be off of the front porch inside of that building by ten o'clock. You had to be inside. In other words, this was to keep the peace. Finally, the time that we lived down there, I got used to it because I didn't want to be locked up. And you would be locked up. [Laughter.] And one of our fellows, he [was] waylaid one night and they put him in jail, roughed him up a little bit to let him know, "Nigger, you are supposed to go by the rules and regulations. You're from up north, you don't do that up there. But we do it down here." Keep these "niggers" in line. So he had to stay in the balance of that night and half of the next day and that was Ed Thompson. And the supervisor from our brick job had to go and get him the next day at twelve o'clock or they wouldn't let him out. This was to teach him a lesson, and all the other fellows, not to be on the street. But we sort of got used to it and we stayed there until this job [finished].

They moved to another project in Atlanta, Georgia. We were building this project there and it was built out of brick. We had practically the same restrictions there working together and we never worked together. This was [laughter] sort of intimidating at times when we went there. The foremen were from Birmingham, Alabama, and they called the black bricklayers "black scabs." [Laughter.] "You black scabs get on this

building over here." We were unionized, had a union, but the whites controlled it. We could meet in the same building on union nights, but we
didn't have the same privileges as the white bricklayers.

ESSIE MAE ALEXANDER

*Born in Mississippi in 1927, Essie Mae Alexander entered into a life
of sharecropping. Rural poverty drove her into the cotton fields at age
nine to toil alongside her six-year-old brother. Alexander's family, like
many others in the Mississippi Delta, was constantly on the move in an
effort to better their way of life. Essie Alexander highlights the ways that
African Americans knitted together networks of mutual aid in the rural
South in an effort to survive poverty. Alexander emphasizes the example
of her mother, a woman who, though crippled by rheumatism, regularly
cared for the sick, walking seven and eight miles to offer help to another.
Claiming as her motto, "If I can help somebody as I travel along, then my
living will not be in vain," Alexander followed in her mother's tradition,
participating in the quilting circles and healing practices intended to help
others. The unpaid labor of Mrs. Alexander's mother served as the margin
between survival and starvation for many African American families.*

*Here, Alexander tells of the wage discrimination that prompted her
family's move from the Doppler to the Murphy plantation in 1938. A
plan hatched by Alexander's father and other sharecroppers to earn more
equitable wages unraveled in the face of the power of the white overseer.*

The reason we moved from the Doppler plantation where my father had
been renting corn land [was] because with a large family, you couldn't
afford to give half of your corn [to the landlord]. See, you had to give half
of everything, which [meant] really you was working for like a fourth
because all the expenses came out of your half. I figured it out—and
I told my father—we were working on the fourth. You farmed up to the
fourth. So he was renting corn land, and I think at that time the corn
land to rent was something like $3 or $4. All the men agreed that they
were going to make a decision that they would not rent the corn land on
halves. So my father and two other men were the only three that were

Edd Vann, a farmer, and James Vann, his son, in Vance County, North Carolina, in the 1950s.
(Courtesy of Andre D. Vann)

renting corn land. The other was divided, they called, by half. After they got there, everybody else backed down, and he said that that was his decision, he would not take food from us to give it [to the landlord]. A lot of the time the corn was just thrown out somewhere. If he couldn't rent it and get all of it, pay so much for rent. Well, it went up to $7 an acre for renting corn. At that time, you made a lot of corn on an acre of land. But then the man still didn't want to do that, so my father thought it was time for us to move on to somewhere else.

They planned it at our house, but when time came for them to face Mr. Jett, who was the rider, everybody else backed down. But my father said his word was his bond, so he kept his word, and we did much better after we left there and went to the Murphy plantation because Mr. Murphy didn't live on the plantation. He lived at Sumner, Mississippi.

We never went hungry. But I knew of some families had less in the family than we had. I guess because there was so many of us to work, it made it a little easier. My mother used to gather vegetables and what have you. We had chickens and things. She just fixed a lot of food, and everybody came by and ate along with us. And what we didn't have, maybe somebody else had. One thing, most of them shared—we had milk cows, and when our cows would go dry or either would have a young calf so we couldn't drink the milk, then someone else would share their milk and butter with us until our cows got back, and we did the same with them. And working, I guess we always got through first, because there was a lot of us to work, and most of them was boys, just two girls. When we got through chopping our fields or whatever, then we went to the next person and helped them to finish.

Each parent at that time would help rear each other's children. If we went somewhere, my mother and them, they didn't have to worry about what we were going to do. If there was another parent there, they didn't have to worry about it because if we stepped out of line, they stepped right on our behind. And when we got home, if we couldn't convince them not to tell it, we got another one. It's not like now, "What did you hit my child for?" But they would want to know, "What did you do so bad that they had to whip you? Now you just come on and let me give you a good whooping."

[My mother] formed a group of ladies that would go [and care for the sick]. In the daytime, when my mother and them wasn't working, like in the middle of July and August, until about the 15th of August, there wasn't any work for the women to do. The men went to the woods and cut wood for the winter, and the women just quilted and did whatever. So if there was sick people in the community, my mother would get that group of ladies and they would go and visit in the daytime. If there were men that were down sick—of course, the women took care of the men too. But at night my father and some other men would go and sit with that individual until a couple hours before time to go to work, and then they'd come home and get ready to go to work.

Women got together and [quilted]. If there was somebody in the community—if there was a lack of covering, they would share. They would get together and share that way. I still do stuff like that in the community, get together with ladies and do stuff like that in the community. They were missionary Baptists, and that was part of their mission to go and help people that was less fortunate or that was ill.

I have three children. I had one born in the hospital. The others were delivered by midwives. Really, midwives did a lot more than doctors, because the doctor, once that baby was delivered, unless you had to call him back, you were on your own. But the midwife would come back and check you and that baby until the baby got four or five weeks old, and if there were any problems, then they would report it to your family doctor. It wasn't many babies delivered back then by doctors. Most of them was midwives. My father's sister, she delivered as many white babies as she did black in the hills. People just couldn't afford doctors too much then, so the midwife would deliver the baby. If you had some money to pay them, it was okay, and if not, a dozen eggs or a chicken and they would go on about their business. That's what you paid them with.

I think a couple of my children got hurt and had to go to the doctor or something, but otherwise we used home remedies. [W]e used to use for cuts coal oil, kerosene—we called it coal oil. That's what they sold for coal oil, kerosene. That would get the swelling and the soreness out, and if you was cut deep enough were it to bleed a lot, you took the soot out of the chimney or out of the stove and sugar and put it in there and that would stop it from bleeding. For fever they had a type of fever weed, peach tree leaves and all of that. You had to nearly get your head cut off to have to go to a doctor.

For diarrhea we used to boil kookaburra roots. For sores, there was a weed they called milkweed. You broke it off. It had little fine leaves, and you broke it off. White stuff would come out like milk, and that's what you put on your sore. For colds and whooping cough, we made tea out of the hoof that come off the pig's feet. We put it in the stove or down in front of the fire and baked it real hard and put it in something and boil it, put a little sugar in it. For mumps and stuff like that, we got sardine oil to rub the mumps to keep the mumps from going down.

Some of them [the home remedies] were passed down from my mother and other people. But for me, things just came to me to try this or try this, because although I was a young woman living out there on the plantation, I had to take care of everybody else's children. When somebody's child got hurt or got sick, for some reason they would call for me, and I had to figure out something that I know that wouldn't hurt them, that would help. Nine times out of ten it worked. Then I was [a] real observing person. If I went to the doctor with somebody, and I heard the doctor—the doctor used to tell you about home remedies, too. If

I heard it, I kept it in my mind, and I wrote it down when I got home, what the doctor said. And just anything I would hear an old person say they used or what have you, I'd write it down. I tried it. And it worked.

THOMAS CHRISTOPHER COLUMBUS CHATMON

Born in rural Coffee County, Georgia, Thomas Chatmon was the second of eight children. He was forced to quit school for several years to help support the family following the death of his mother in 1936: "I was a part slave. I have worked many a day on the farm sunup to sundown for 40 cents a day, $2 a week," Chatmon recalls. While the local school system did not offer African American children an education beyond the seventh grade, Chatmon's parents desperately wanted the young man to have the opportunity to attend college. Among other things, the chance to receive a college education represented the difference between a future life of back-breaking labor and the ability to earn a better living. The odds were not in Chatmon's favor.

Now Broxton [is a] little town [of] about 1,500 people. And all the surrounding area was primarily farming. We did not own a farm but my father was a farmhand. [M]y first memory of growing up in Broxton—I was about four years old [and] my mother took me to the cotton field, and she taught me how to pick cotton. She made my sack out of a flour sack. You would find flour in 24-pound sacks, and that's what I used to learn to pick cotton, me and my oldest sister. [G]rowing up there, one thing I always love to emphasize is [that] we had a seven-month school, and my parents always saw that we attended school the whole seven months. Unlike some other parents that allowed the white people to snatch their kids out of school and start working on the farm, my parents didn't stand for that. My parents were both uneducated, but they always wanted their children to get an education. My mother didn't hesitate to tell those white people that, when they would come around and want us to go work on the farm during school hours. When you finished the seventh grade that was the end of that, that was as high as you could go. Then you would have to go off to school. My mother did send my oldest

Women at the Farmers' Fair, Penn School, St. Helena Island, South Carolina, 1939.
(Courtesy of Earnestine Atkins, Lula Holmes, and Louise Nesbit, St. Helena, South Carolina)

sister off about 24 miles to a place called Fitzgerald, Georgia, a private school that the Baptist church had built. GC&W High School is still there in Fitzgerald now.

I lost my mother in 1936. I was 16 years old, and she had always asked me to stay with my father just in case something would happen to her, and help him raise the kids. So when she passed in '36, of course, I couldn't go to school because I had to help my father. I stayed out of school for four years, as she had asked me to do, and helped him with the kids. When they got up a certain size I told him it was time to go back to school and he agreed. I went back then and finished high school, not in Broxton however. I finished high school in a little town called Ocilla, Georgia, O-C-I-L-L-A. That was in Urban County. That was about 25 miles from Broxton.

As I said, I was a part slave. I have worked many a day on the farm sunup to sundown for 40 cents a day or $2 a week. That was the going salary for blacks. I don't know about whites, but that's what we made during those times, and of course my father was making 75 cents a day and I was making 40 cents, me and my sister; they paid the adults a little more than they paid the kids. A lot of my kids now wonder how did my father feed eight or ten people with that money. We made it because we raised our food, always had a garden, had our hogs, had our cows and our chickens.

[M]y father learned to be a tobacco specialist. We lived on a man's place. His name was Currin, R. E. Currin. He was from the Carolinas. He was the largest tobacco grower in that county. He raised at that time 50 acres of tobacco. That's all he farmed with, tobacco, no cotton, no corn, no peanuts, just tobacco. My father was a supervisor of that farm of 50 acres of tobacco. Of course, now we didn't spend all our time with him. My father moved from there to another man's place. He was the biggest white man that I knew of in that county. He owned more land than anybody. Of course, we worked tobacco, cotton, corn, peanuts and everything on his farm. But [if] there was one thing unique about my family [it] was this: My mother insisted that we own our own home so that we could be a little bit independent. What we did, we had some cows, so she sold all the cows to buy a home. Therefore, the white man couldn't come around and demand that we be pulled out of school and work because we lived in our house, and not his house.

[T]he last year [I was] at home with my father. That was the year I was supposed to go back to school. I had been out of school until that year, and I worked the farm and my father worked turpentine so we could clear all the crops. My father would work turpentine to generate enough money to pay for everything until we gathered the crop, and we were going to clear all the crops, and I would have money to go back to school with. My father would have money to buy the kids clothes. So we did, and when we had gathered our crops and sold all the money crops like tobacco, peanuts, and cotton, my father told me that Saturday, "Let's go and settle up so you can get ready to go to school." I said, "Okay." And so we went up to Mr. Thomas's house, to the backyard as usual, and he came out onto the back porch. "Well John, I guess you and Bud came to settle up today." He said, "Yes sir." He got his book out. I had kept a record myself of everything we had gotten from that man that year and I know we didn't owe him, and we were supposed to clear good money. So he came out on the porch and he started thumbing through his book. Finally he looked up at my father and said, "John, you don't have any money coming, but you cleared your corn." Well, when he said that I reached for my book and my daddy stepped on my foot because he knew them crackers would kill you if you'd dispute their word. The first thing that went through my mind was "how could this man take *all* our money when my father had *six* other children down there, *raggedy*, no *money, winter* was coming and he's going to *take it all.*" So my father said, "Mr. Thomas, we don't have any money coming?" He said, "No, John, you don't have any money coming, but you're going to clear all your corn." So we said, "Okay," and we started back to the house.

We lived about four or five blocks from him on a country road. This was the second time I'd ever seen my father cry. He started dropping tears, so I told him, "Papa, don't worry about it. I'll make it. I'll go back to school. I'll make it somehow." But anyway, I had ordered me a suit of clothes and the suit was in the post office there in Ocilla. That's where I went to school. That was the county seat. And the suit was $17.25 to get out, and my father told me, he insisted that I take a load of corn. I had a friend of mine to come out there and pick up and take a load of corn and that's how I got my suit out. But when I left that farm I never did go back. My father would come to town every Saturday and bring the kids and I would see them, and I would give them money. I got a job working in a dry goods store, department store in fact you call it now. We called it a dry goods store. And I had a job picking up at the cleaners. I had three jobs and went to school every day and I was able to still help my father while going to high school. And every week he'd come I'd give him a little money.

When me and my father got back to the house I went in and pulled a pillowcase off my pillow, the little clothing I had I put in that pillowcase. I looked at my mother's children and I hated to leave them. I was just like a second father to them, and I started walking. It was 12 miles from where we lived to Ocilla. This man [Thomas Harper] passed me walking to town in a new Ford he just had bought with some of the money he took from my father. You know he wouldn't stop to pick me up and ride me to town. And when he came back from town that night he stopped by the house and blew his horn, my daddy came out and he asked my dad, "Well where's Bud?" My daddy said, "That boy's gone." "Well, tell Bud when he comes back, come on, and I'll let him have some money." My dad told him, "He ain't coming back." And I was a good plow hand, see, because I love farming. "Is he really ain't coming, John?" "No that boy ain't coming back." "Well I bet if I let him have some money. . . ." "Naw, he ain't coming back." My daddy told me about it when he came to town. Ain't been back until this day.

When I finally finished at Morehouse [College] and came back here to live, I had a classmate, Samuel Chatmon. I had told him so many times about Thomas Harper while we were at Morehouse [that] when he came to see me, he said, "Gee, I want you to take me to Thomas Harper's farm." I said, "Okay." I had just bought my wife a new Cadillac, '63. He got his pistol, he said, "I'm carrying my pistol because if Thomas Harper makes any kind of funny moves [laughter], then I'm going to let him have it." So we got in my wife's car and went on down [there]. He was still in the old house. But this time I didn't go around to the back. I went up on his front porch and knocked on his door. He came to the door and he looked up and said, "Yes." I said, "Yes, Mr. Harper, this is Bud, Buddy Chatmon, John Chatmon's oldest son." I said, "You probably don't remember me, but I used to plow Emma out here," that was the name of my mule. "Oh yes, Bud," he said, "come on in." I said, "No, I don't want to come in, I appreciate it." And I looked him in the eye and I said, "Mr. Harper, the reason I came out here, I just wanted to thank you for taking my farm. Because if you hadn't taken all I had, I probably would have stayed out here and got married and had a bunch of children and made your children rich. So when you took all our money, I left. Never did come back as you know." I said, "I want you to know that I thank you for that." "Oh Bud," he said. I said, "No, you see that Cadillac sitting out in the driveway?" I said, "I paid cash for that." I said, "I live in a Roman, big structured home in Albany. I want you to come visit me sometime and you won't have to come around to my back door."

Boy, that man turned all kinds of colors, but in the meantime my classmate, Gee—we used to call each other Gee—he was sitting out there fully prepared with his pistol in his hand. But you know what that white man did after I left? He went around the whole black community and told them what I had done. "Bud came back and told me how he felt." He had never had a black man to say things like that to him before. But I had to do it because it was in me, and Gee wanted me to do it with him, so we did. But it's things like that that my son has never had to go through. None of my children ever had a job with a white person from the time they were with me because I just didn't have that. My wife ain't never worked for nobody *but* me since I've been married. I told my father when I was a boy, "Father, when I get grown my wife ain't working for nobody, no." I meant that. And he said, "Well, I'm glad to hear you say that, now I hope you mean that. The only thing is that you might have to get an education." And I went to Morehouse, I worked myself the first two years through Morehouse. And of course I had to go to the Army in 1943. And when I came out I was on the G.I. Bill. That's how I survived. I came through the same process many black boys came through.

LEON ALEXANDER

In the midst of the Great Depression, working people across the nation forged new social movements for economic justice. Like many others of this unsung generation of activists, Leon Alexander traveled an arduous path to becoming a union organizer in Alabama. His father had been an activist in the United Mine Workers (UMW) and was blacklisted by area coal mines in the aftermath of the failed 1922 coal strike. In this excerpt, Alexander stresses the pivotal role that black miners played in leading union organizing campaigns in Alabama's coal fields. A man of large stature and possessing a booming voice, Mr. Alexander reminisces about his early working experiences in Birmingham-area coal mines, including conversations with the last group of convict miners employed by Sloss-Sheffield, encounters with black workers fleeing from debt peonage in rural Alabama, and defying the Jim Crow laws they experienced in the mines.

In 1922 up until the union was reorganized in Alabama in 1933, the union was outlawed. The way they broke the union was they went down the farms. The state prison system was leasing prisoners to the coal mining company. They replaced the miners who was on strike and used the National Guard to keep the miners away from the mine and to keep them from establishing a picket line to keep a strikebreaker from entering the mine. They used the National Guard to do that because the governor of the state had control of the National Guard, and he ordered them under the pretense of protecting the coal operators' property.

They set the coal miners who was involved in that strike—and these wasn't just black coal miners—they set their things outdoors because they [were] living in the company houses and ordered them to move before sundown. Now those things happened here in the land of the free and the home of the brave, and it didn't just happen to black. I don't want to just paint a picture [that] says they done something to me. They done something to just about every poor person in the South. My father lost his job because he was branded [as an] "agitator," and it got to a place where he couldn't get a job with no major company in this state. All they had to say [was] that you were an agitator and that sealed you and they pass your name to Woodward [Coal and Iron Co.], Republic Steel, and T.C.I. [which] later became U.S. Steel. All of these were the big guns in the coal mining industry, DeBarbeleben Coal Company which controlled everything in St. Clair County. They were the big wheels in this county. What they said went. I wasn't about 12 years old, but I know about the effects of it because I felt the pangs of hunger when my daddy couldn't work, and that is one of the things that galled me.

I was raised up under the so-called separate but equal schools. They were separate, but the equal part was a joke. There was no such things as the schools being equal. When I finished ninth grade in school, I had to come out and had to go to work because my mother and father had separated, and she had all of the children. She was trying to work and wash and iron. Back in those days black women would wash and iron for white families, wash their clothes and iron their clothes, and so my job primarily coming up was to deliver and bring them to the house. Mama would wash them and iron them. My job was to deliver them back to the families that she was washing for. I came out of school at 13 years of age and that was the end of ninth grade.

I'll tell you an incident when I went to work in Louisburg [in 1933]. They had signs posted all around the mine, "Not Hiring, No Men Needed," and I sat on the superintendent's porch on the office. I sat there on the porch all day, from that morning until he came out of that mine. Sometime after two o'clock that afternoon, his secretary told him when he came up. They called him "the superintendent's clerk"; he spoke to him as he was going into his office, and I'm sitting on the porch and I heard him say, "What that nigger doing sitting out there?" So that man said "He wanted to see you." He said, "What he want to see me about?" "About a job." He said, "Didn't you tell him?" He said, "Yes, he can read, and he understand what the sign said, but he wanted to see you about a job." So he came back out on the porch, and he said, "I understand you want to see me." I said: "I do. You the superintendent?" He said, "Yes." I said, "Well yes, I do want to see you." He said, "What you want to see me about?" I said, "About a job." He said, "Don't you see that sign there? And there's one over there at the bathhouse. There's one on the post out there [saying] no men *needed*, not hiring." I said, "Mister, you said no men needed, but I need a job." He looked at me [laughter] and you see he was outdone.

Now, there were things back then that was called "a white man's job," and "a black man's job." Ninety percent of the machinery that was operated at the mine was operated by white. The cutting machines was one of the few things that the predominantly black had because that was *really* some tough work. It was hard work. Moving under that low top was really a man killer, so they were satisfied for us to have that. But, if it was a machine where you was sitting down operating a machine, nine out of ten times if you saw that machine and saw somebody sitting on it, it was a white man sitting on that machine, and those are the situations that we learned to live with.

Not that we were satisfied with it. But it was nothing that we could do about it, because as I told you in 1922, they broke up the strike by bringing in National Guardsmen and going down in the country and hauling men in here by the boxcar load, and putting them to work in the mine to replace the men. I was a kid then. I wasn't large enough to work in the mine but my daddy was large enough to work in the mine and my daddy worked in the mine, but when they broke up that strike in 1922, the men who were involved in that strike was unable to get a job with *any* major company—Woodward Iron Company, Republic Steel Company, and Tennessee Coal Iron Railroad Company. Those were the *major* companies that was in Birmingham. Those men [who] wanted a job they had to leave here and go somewhere else to get it because they were blackballed here. And when I say they were blackballed, they actually were blackballed. Each of these companies had pledged to not hire any man that was involved in that 1922 [strike].

In 1933, the International Union, John L. Lewis [president of the United Mine Workers] sent organizers back into Alabama again to organize the coal miners. Each company then set out and organized what they called a "brotherhood" or a company union, and they put all black and white in it. But, now here was the catch in that thing: the black in the "brotherhood" couldn't sit in the meetings with the white. They had to go to a separate place and sit, and the whites would have the meeting and would come over and tell them what the decision was. When we first organized and I left Louisburg in 1940 and went back to U.S. Steel, we had the "brotherhood" thing there. That was in opposition to the union you see, they started the company union to compete with the union. We called those guys "popsicles" [laughter] because they had a picnic one 4th of July over at Highland Park, and a gang of us went over there and ran them off. And they had tubs of popsicles and things. And we started to call them "popsicle" and saying that the company had bought them out for a popsicle. But in 1942 we decided: we wasn't going to have no two unions and that's when we broke up the company union.

In 1942 we decided that we was *not* going to tolerate dual unionism anymore, and that's when we shut all the mines down and said no man who belongs to the "brotherhood" was going to work in that particular mine and we made it stick. Now they went and got the National Guard and brought them out and stationed them around the mine and said, "The mine was open." But we told the men, "The National Guard may protect you at the mine, but he ain't going home with you; you got to go home by yourself, and that's when you going to answer to us when you go home." And so none of them tried to go to work, but when the company saw that the majority of the men were out, they had a submachine gun mounted on top of the commissary at Edgewater Mine.

The company used this racial thing against both the black and the white. When they talked to the black, they said, "We give you this job now." They just said it to keep you in line. "But you see the white man, he won't work with you." And they sent me on a section [of the mine] and there was only two blacks up there. There was a man and another one, and they told me, "We just decided that we wasn't going to work with

Workers in a factory in the late 1940s. (Courtesy of Leola Mott, Newton, Georgia)

no blacks." And I told them, "I don't give a damn that you decided you don't have to work with me, because you can go out, but I am not going out. The same man that signs your check signs mine, and I'm not going; you're not running me from up here."

So I stayed. Gradually we talked some sense into them, and told them, "Our fight is not with each other, our fight is with the company." John Lewis came here and he spoke at a labor rally here in 1941, '40 or '41, somewhere in that time frame, and he pointed out to the white men that they [the coal companies] are *using* them and the black men as well. They are *using* you all against each other. That is what the company's good at. As long as they can keep you divided, they can hound you like they wanted to.

In 1933, I went to work in the coal mine for Sloss Sheffield Steel and Iron Company. This was the situation that they had. A white bathhouse and a colored bathhouse, and they were so designated by signs up on them saying "white" and "colored." Now the bathhouses were joined together. They were in the same building, but it was a wall between them. It was a door in the bathhouse, but the door both locked and unlocked on the white side. I'm not telling you a fairy tale. I'm telling you what actually happened. The white coal miners could unlock the door and come over on the colored side. But *we* couldn't open the door and go on the white side. Ironically they had hydrants—it wasn't no fountain—these were water hydrants where we caught our water [to] fill up our cans and buckets and move in and out of the mine. They had a sign here that said "white" and a sign over that one that said "colored." You couldn't even catch the water out of the same hydrant! If we were caught at this [white] hydrant catching water, automatically we were discharged.

We *did* challenge the colored and white fountains or hydrants. When I went back to work for U.S. Steel, I had a group of men all go to the white hydrant in 1942. The company always suspected that I'd done [it], but they never did prove it. I secretly took the handle or the key off the hydrant so they couldn't turn the hydrant off. And then we all had to catch the water [laughter] at the hydrant that was marked "white."

And the mine foreman came out and wrote out what was known as a "74." That was a discipline sheet, and they made out one of those noting that this was going to be part of our work record. Subsequently, if we got into any more trouble or caused any more trouble, we were subject to a discharge for it. And the mine foreman told me, "I *believe* you took that key off of that hydrant, and if I could prove it I would fire you right now." But he couldn't find *anybody* that said that I took the key off. Not only had I took the key off, I threw it in a cart that had a load of coal in it and they never found it.

I was a part of organizing of the mine because the international president John L. Lewis always maintained that the union was color-blind. A union meeting was called in the city limits of Birmingham, and [Bull Connor] had an ordinance passed when he became the police commissioner which said we couldn't even go in the same door [laughter]. In other words we had to go in the back door, and the whites came in the front door. You heard about Mr. "Bull" Connor? What made him famous? He was a baseball broadcaster. He didn't hide it. He'd be on the air there announcing. If a man would hit a home run, he'd holler, "Did you see that? *Way* back in the nigger bleachers!" Now that's what he was yelling [laughter] on the radio. And he used that until he died, to fight against what lawfully was ours to start with.

We were upset. We owned the building, our dues money just bought the building, but he had an ordinance passed that said that we could not go up the stairs on the front. We had to go to the back. We rebelled against it by just defying the ordinance and walking on in the front door, and they had police standing down there at the door to challenge us. Do you believe that? And [the policeman] said, "Where you going?" I said, "Where does it look like I'm going? I'm going past [you]." "You have to go around to the back." "Well, who says so?" "Mr. Connor." "You go back and tell Mr. Connor Alexander says he going up front, because this building belong to us. It don't belong to Mr. Connor." He said, "Well you defying a—a city ordinance." I said, "If that's defying city ordinance, it's totally fine because you count all them black faces out there. We all going straight up the steps." I said, "No more 'Mr.' And you tell Mr. Connor no more are we going to the back door, except we wants to go to the back door; we're not going to obey an ordinance that says we got to go to the back door." Then they said we had to sit on separate sides of the hall. We couldn't all sit on the same side [laughter], the white had to be on one side and the colored. It is laughable!

But in spite of all that we got going. In 1934, [union organizers] Bill Rainey and Walter Jones who was black came down here. *The Birmingham News* depicted a black crow and a white crow on the headline of their papers and said that "[t]he black crow is going to eat up the white crow by taking your job." That way they were keeping the white out of the union. It was so difficult [to organize]. [The organizers] was putting out some union flyers at Sloss Sheffield Steel and Iron in Louisburg. I got off the bus and Rainey and Walter Jones were sitting in a car by the highway and I sat by the car and they handed me a flyer telling about the union. They wasn't saying how *blacks* was being treated; they were saying how *coal miners* was being treated. And the whites began to realize that they were being treated just as bad as we were being treated, but they were being treated in a way to where they would use us to keep them subjugated. When I passed by the bathhouse window, the mine foreman was leaning up in the window. Now I had this flyer that the union organizers had given me. I went in the bathhouse and he said, "Give me that hand-bill." I told him, "That man in the car will give you one." I didn't have no children, no wife, no nothing, so it didn't make no difference. The boss said, "Don't you go in that bathhouse with that." I walked right on in.

When I went to get my lamp, he told me I wasn't going to work for Sloss anymore. So I went back in the bathhouse and took a bath because it didn't make any difference with me whether I had a job or didn't have a job here because I wasn't making too much money no how. When the men saw I was out there they asked me, "What was the matter?" Well, "[t]hey just fired me." And so the gang around me wanted to know what I'd done. I said, "Well I got a flyer," and I showed it to them. I wouldn't even give it to the mine superintendent. I wouldn't give it to the mine foreman. I wouldn't give it to neither one of them. They looked at it, and all of them pulled off their clothes and took a bath. Now, we didn't have no union but they decided that if they were going to fire me, they might as well fire all of them. After the whites saw that all of the blacks were not going to work, they were ashamed to go themselves. Not that they were supporting us because they had been indoctrinated against that, but they stayed out too.

Officially or unofficially we was on strike. Okay, the next morning when the day shift came they found out that the evening shift had struck the day before. Then the day shift refused to go to work. I knew people on the day shift, and they knew us. The mine foreman come in and told me that I didn't have a job there anymore. I was a "troublemaker, an agitator" [laughter], but nobody went to work. Bill Rainey called a meet-ing, and had rented a hall right across the road from the mine. So we all showed up there. Now, the union was negotiating with Sloss out on Thirty-second Street at their main office. The superintendent of the mine came over to our meeting and tried to persuade us to put the mine back in operation. I just knew I was gone then, but I wasn't the only one who was out. But Bill Rainey and Walter Jones got us our job back because they told him, "These men are not going to work unless these that you have discharged are put back to work; so remember, they was on the state right-of-way when they were given that flyer, not on company property; they had not gone to work so it wasn't on company time, and you can't discharge a man for what he do on his own time." They had to put us back to work.

We had a meeting hall right across the street from the mine. The hall belonged to the Free and Accepted Masons and they let [the union] meet in that hall. Everybody who was attending [was] black. *Finally*, some of the whites started coming over. We had been meeting, we didn't have a charter or anything. It was in 1934 before we could even get enough signatures to get a charter from the international union. And then after Louisburg, then Docena mine was organized. And of course [the coal companies] wasn't checking off any dues at that time, because they felt like if they didn't check off the dues that we wouldn't go, you know, to the [union] hall and pay our dues. But we fooled them and went to go[ing] in there [and] paying them. And it was in 1942 before we got a checkoff system out of them where they take the men's dues off through the payroll.

Walter Jones was black. He was the organizer sent here by the international union to help organize Alabama. He died here. But he was a powerful organizer, and he had a lot to do with changing the white conception of the union and proving to them that the company was using *them* as well as using us. [He did this] by showing them methods that the company was using. We couldn't be a foreman, couldn't be an electrician, all of those things. But when the company would want to bring pressure on the whites, they would promote *one* black up to an electrician or just any job that they normally didn't have, and that'd scare them to death and push them back in line and they wouldn't join.

Ironically enough all of these were mines where the state of Alabama sent its prisoners to work and leased them. They were leased to coal companies. When the court ruled that no longer could the coal mines operate the prison labor, they also ruled that the time that the men had already served was sufficient, and they had to be free. Now that wasn't a state court that ruled that because these big coal companies controlled the state courts and the district courts and all of that—that was the federal court. I worked with one [convict miner]. John Sanders had served 17 years of a 25-to-life sentence for something he maintained that he wasn't guilty of doing, killing a white man. On circumstantial evidence, they sentenced him to 25 years to life. And he told me he didn't know the man, never seen the man, never done nothing to the man. They didn't have to prove anything. They carried him to court and the all-white jury found him guilty. I worked with John Sanders for seven years at Louisburg. Hardworking man who said that he spent 17 years in prison for something he didn't do. Back then, if a white man said you did it, you were guilty before you ever went to court.

A whole lot of black men left the farms and came to Birmingham. The plantation owners that they was working for would come here and claim a bill against them. The law here in Jefferson County would arrest that man and turn him over to that man to go back on his farm. Now that's why a whole lot of them when they left they didn't stop here; they went on to Pennsylvania, West Virginia, or somewhere else because if they stayed here they would be arrested and carried back to the farm. I saw it happening. The money goes to the plantation owners, always.

In Alabama black folks was in the forefront of [organizing the union]. Whites didn't have anything to do with it because they was afraid of being branded as a "nigger lover." The [coal companies] put up posters all around saying that they—the white fellows that were joining the union—were "nigger lovers." The company branded them through the *Birmingham News* and *Birmingham Herald*. Those two newspapers done a whole lot to help the companies keep the union out.

There was only one thing that got me involved in union activity and that was: I was among the first to get fired in Birmingham because of union activity. I was fired back there because I took a flyer from Bill Rainey. It was the principle involved in the thing. You see, number one, you working like a dog—you ain't making very much money. People don't believe that I have spent 14 hours underground in the mine, and didn't make a dollar. That's hard [to believe] in this age of high wages. People can't understand that I moved rock out of the way where they could cut a place and start up a place where I could load some coal and it took me all day to move all that rock and when I got to moving it I was paid exactly nothing for it, and you multiply that by thousands of men. Now this didn't just go for blacks, that went for anybody.

People just wouldn't hardly believe, but coal miners both white and black are a close-knit group of people. They grew into one powerful bunch. This generation that's coming on now, that didn't have to suffer through what we had to suffer through, they don't know nothing about the company getting the National Guard to come out there and surround that mine with soldiers, with rifles. They'd use the Army, the National Guard. They did it at Red Mountain, they done it at Edgewater, and the governor would order the National Guard; they'd go say, "There's going to be trouble," and they'd stand there with guns to prevent you from going to your own job. This was during the thirties and forties.

We organized all those unions that you hear talk of, the international rubber workers union, the automobile union. We organized every one. United Mine Workers organized them all. We organized the smelter workers union; we organized the steelworkers union and supplied them with money and organizers that knew *how* to get the job done. *We* did that.

It was a lot of discrimination [against black coal miners] and it's not only in Alabama, it wasn't just in the South. West Virginia, Kentucky, Tennessee, Ohio, wherever coal was mined. There was discrimination in the hiring practice, in the promotion practice, in all of these things, there was discrimination in it. The coal operators knew how to play the game of divide and conquer. See in Pennsylvania they had a lot of Polish that came into Pennsylvania working in the coal mines. So they played them off against the other races that was working. By promoting them and giving them favored status, it made the other races mad with them, and they could keep you from getting together.

But we still organized because the persistence just paid off. You know, adversity wasn't anything new to us. We had lived under adversity all our lives, so having nothing wasn't a problem with us. When you hear [us] say, "I didn't know I was poor, until I went to work and got some money," we're telling the truth. We had no way of knowing. What we going to measure it by? The white man live in one part of town. You live in another part, and most of them that live close to you was just as poor as you were.

EARL BROWN

The black miners' struggle for equality in the mines did not end with unionization. As mechanization took hold in the nation's mining industry after World War I, African American workers fought to gain access to skilled jobs. Such jobs were reserved exclusively for white miners, with the tacit support of union officials. Earl Brown started working in the Mulga Mine in the Birmingham, Alabama, coal mining district shortly before World War II. He led a number of wildcat strikes in the effort to help African Americans to break into higher-paying, skilled positions. In the course of these industrial battles, Earl Brown met Leon Alexander, and the two men became friends and fellow organizers. A leader in the Birmingham black Masonic lodge as well as a member of the local NAACP, Brown stresses the importance of being active in organizations in an effort to create social change.

Segregation had a great effect on the black coal miners because they didn't have the equal opportunities, the equal rights in jobs. They were put in bathhouses that weren't kept [well], separate water fountains— white and black. You go down into the mine. In the mine cars they had a section for whites and a section for blacks, and coming back to ride out on the cage, they had separate lines. They'd take so many whites on this line, and then go down and take so many blacks on the other side and let them go down. Just wouldn't mix. So that was an effect. No job opportunities for advancement. You had a certain mold that you stayed in, and you couldn't get out of that mold. The best jobs went to the whites and lower jobs or the menial work went to the blacks. That was in the 1930s, of course. It didn't do too much better after the union got in control. Before the mines were mechanized, you had about 70 percent or 75 percent of blacks [working in the Mulga Mine]. That was loading the coal, carrying the timbers, but the machine that did it was whites and whites just didn't get in loading no coal. Mostly black, because the work was hard and menial. Therefore the black had nothing else to do but go out and go to work. Whites wouldn't do it.

It was tough. I almost didn't stay in the mine, because when that first rock fell, I ran from where it was, that roof falling in; it's something that you've never heard nothing like it. I ran out of there! The mine foreman caught me at the trapdoor as I was getting ready to go. He said, "Where you going, boy?" I said, "I'm going home." He said, "What's the matter?" I said, "I can't stand that, all that coming in." He said, "How long you been here?" I said, "About a week." I guess it was just meant for me to stay at the mine.

I was quite vocal when I went to work [in 1939]. Regardless of who was being hurt, I would take up for them. Because I was vocal they took me off that shift and put me on another shift. That was very painful to me. They could do that because seniority didn't prevail then. They told me: "Nigger, if you keep your mouth shut, you'll advance. But you got too much mouth." So that was one of the things, but that didn't stop me. [Laughter.] That didn't stop me.

They had a system there that the white motormen [workers who transported miners, coal, and equipment in and out of the mine] was getting overtime on each shift. The black motormen, they could not pull the man trip and they could not pull the head motor, but they were classified as motormen. We went to the motor boss and asked for some of that time to be split up because we were motormen. He said, "The hell with you, I'll do it like I want to." So the guys got around me said: "What we going to do?" I said, "We'll just come out" [strike]. There's one thing about the union back then regardless of whether you're black or white, if you struck they wouldn't go across your picket line. So I pulled them out, a wildcat strike. And the first day we was out, the mine foreman he [tried to] put us back to work. So we stayed out a couple of days. He called me. He said, "What's it going to take?" I said, "Equalize it, just like we asked." He still said he wasn't going to do it. Then the head office got ahold of it and they got on him. He called me. Since there weren't so many telephones back then, they sent someone to my house. Said he wanted to talk with me and I came down. And he said, "What's it going to take? I want these men back to work." I said, "Well, equalize this time. Put some of those lead boys on so they can get the equal time. That's what we're out for. That's what it's going to take." "But it's the middle of the week now. Would you give me a chance to start it off Monday?" I said, "I don't trust you [laughter] but I will since it is the middle of the week. If you do what you're saying I will ask them to go back to work." So we did. That's the only way I asked them to go back to work. I met with them, told them what the motor boss had promised. Said, "Now, we will do this, but Monday if he doesn't have it equalized that we all go on those same motors and make the same time that they do, we're back out of there," and they said, "O.K." That happened. That broke that up.

It might have been the late forties. The jobs was still divided. There was a job that came open. A helper's job. An electrician. They were all white, the helper, electrician, and white electricians, and they were separate. When that job came open, one particular fellow, a black guy, he began taking electrical work. Repair televisions and radios and whatnot. And so when that job was open I asked the mine foreman to fill that job with a black. He said, "No, we're not going to do it. We want skilled people." I said, "But it's a helper's job and a helper is trained by the electrician." "Well, he'd have to have some qualifications." I said, "He has some qualifications to make a helper. He had the potentials. I said he has went to school. He has a certificate." And I had the certificate and I handed it to him. "This here's his certificate. The boy has taken electrical work." "Well, I'm not going to fill it." I said, "Well, O.K." I was planning a strike, but another white boy came to me about two days later and said that they were going to cut out all the helpers and make everybody electricians just to keep blacks [from] getting infiltrated. He said, "I'll testify to that." I said, "You will?" He said, "I certainly will." A white miner. Young boy. I couldn't hardly wait until that morning when my foreman came by. Said, "I understand that you're going to cut out all the electrician helpers." "Yeah, we going to make them all electricians. We're not going to have any helpers." I said, "Is that because we asked you to put some blacks on there?" "No, it's not." I said, "I got someone to testify to your conversation with other mine foremen about what you're going to do." He said, "Who was it?" I said, "I have someone to testify. I said we can settle it here, but if you don't settle it, I'm going over to the main office and take this man over there." He looked at me, and he said, "What are you trying to do, integrate the bathhouse and everything!?" I said, "No. I just want the jobs. When you going to let me know?" He said, "Probably in a day or two." So the next couple of days he came back. He said, "We'll put in Leroy, Leroy Davis." I never will forget him. That's the first one that infiltrated. He said, "I'll put Leroy on the job as helper, but I'm going to put another white man equal with that." I said, "I don't care. We just want a break in there." That's another time that broke that ranks where it was one job, white.

The next time I broke it for myself. There was a lamp house job that came open. I was making good money, and I was running the motor, but the lamp house job came open, and I saw a chance there to further break this segregation. That's attending the lamps, capped lamps and electrical lamps, and repairing them, repairing the methane monitors, and keeping the bathhouse clean. There was a bathhouse for repairmen. No black had ever [held the job]. It always had been white! It's a good job. So I went to Mr. Kirk. He was superintendent at the time. I said, "I understand in about a month the lamp house man is retiring. I'd like to have that job." He said, "Earl, we need qualified people on that job." I said, "I realize that. If you can find a person that is qualified and wants that job, I don't have no problem with it. If someone's going to train for that job, I want that training and I want to go on that job." He said, "Earl, you got a good job. You'll be cutting yourself $20 a week to go on that job." I said, "I been out here on that main line for about 21 years. I've had wrecks and been covered up [by mine cave-ins] and have got broken up. I want to get out in the air." He said, "Well, we'll fill that job. We're going to fill it with a qualified person." I said, "As long as you do that, Mr. Kirk, it's satisfactory with me." Just about a week before the man was going to retire, he called me on Saturday. He said, "You still want that lamp house job?" I said, "I sure do." "You realize you going to be cutting yourself about $100 a month?" I said, "I want the lamp house job." "Come down on the owl shift Sunday night and get you some training. A week's training." I said, "O.K."

Sunday morning I was getting ready to go to church. The president of the [union] local called me. He said, "Earl, I know you're getting ready to go to church. I want to talk to you before you go. You got time?" I said, "Yes." So he came to the house and he said, "Mr. Kirk called me and told me that you was going on that lamp house job. You was coming off the main line. Do you know what happened when you asked him three weeks ago about coming?" I said, "No I don't." "He turned and called the main office and told them that you had approached him for that job." At that time the civil rights movement was pretty heavy, you know, through here. New Orleans, a part of Montgomery. It hadn't hit Birmingham real good then. And that was NAACP, you know, had all the cases and schools and what's going on there. So, when he called he told them that

Stevedores loading cargo in the late 1940s. (Courtesy of Clement Knatt, New Iberia, Louisiana)

"Earl Brown wants that job up there," and they said, "We'll see about it." Said they turned around to MacDuff who was the chief investigator. Said, "We want you to investigate everything about Earl Brown." They found out I was a member of the NAACP. Said, "You better give that nigger that job." That's what the president of the local told me. Said, "He's going to come out there. He's going to try to integrate the bathhouse and he's already done made his self vocal in too many things that he's going to integrate the bathhouse and whatnot." That's what [the president of the union] said. He was afraid of that his self. He said, was that what I was trying to do? I said, "No. I just want the job." And I was the first black on that job.

I figured because we all were working or laborers down there we should have been treated alike. I didn't want to go in their bathhouses. I wasn't going home to eat with them, but if we were on that job, we done the same labor, we should get the same pay without any derogatory remarks about "nigger this" or "nigger that" and all that. That burned me. I was very vocal about it. During that particular time I think the first time the union people saw that I would stand up they elected me to what you might call a shop steward at the mine committee to handle their problems. I worked there many, many years before I came over here [the district union office] at that mine.

The one that worked with me in different ways was Leon Alexander. Everybody know Leon. White and black. They know Leon. He could get your attention. He talked real slow, but when he'd get heated up he'd just go out there and he could say some outlandish words. [Laughter.] We were having a meeting I believe in Wyler Union Hall in Wyler and it was over a district-wide issue when all of the unions were meeting there. And, Alexander, I heard the voice. He's got a voice you never forget. Rather deep and loud! [Shouting.] And he was giving somebody holy hell over what they done up there. He was big and tall. That's my first remembrance of Alexander. I was on the grievance committee up at the mines. That's when we first got to really know each other. You know, get acquainted, but later years we got to know each other because he worked with me on organizing or whatnot after I got into the district office. But he's quite a character. He's quite a character. But yes, everybody knew him all over the district and we'd go to conventions and he did the floor. One of those mikes. And the way they had it lit up when he spoke out of that mike everybody could listen. [Laughter.] When he spoke, everybody listened. [Laughter.] Yes sir. He was at a TCI mine at Edgewater at the time back then. That's when I first knew him. He and I would meet together. We'd be strategizing because the same problems were all over the South in coal mines.

Really, my fight began in trying to get equalization of jobs. Now I guess everyone that I went through it with was a tough fight, but it was an accomplishment. And, the last one I think that got Mulga really integrated and broke down was through a new mine foreman that came to Mulga, old man Dobbs. I was on the mine committee at that time. At that time all machines was run by whites. The whites would strike and no work could be done. I was a mine committeeman on a grievance committee. They didn't want those other [black workers] on the job and they'd strike. Old man Dobbs came and we had a conference. He said, "Earl, we got to stop this. Whites get a problem, they know no blacks is on these machines. What do you suggest?" I said, "Begin training them." And, he began to ease some of them as helpers on those machines and this is the first time the union split and that was a fight with me over the black and white. When they struck, I told those blacks, I said, "Get on those machines. We stopping this mess what they're doing!" I went to Mr. Dobbs and I said, "They going to run the machines. They going to stay here and work because what they're going out for is purely discrimination against someone else and we're not going. We're going to break it up right now." Then Mr. Dobbs, he said, "Well, we'll try it. We can't run the full shift on that because we have a limited amount of people." I said, "Run what you can." So we worked about two shifts that way, and those whites come in there jumping on me. "You letting them work that! We union!" I said, "Yeah, but y'all ain't union. You come on back to work like you supposed to. You on a wildcat and I know what you out there for. They going to continue to run it." So they came back. That began integration in that whole mine. That's my toughest fight.

I wasn't there too much longer after that because I'd gotten the attention of the international [union] and some of the district people. Had many times in our union halls where we'd meet for our union meeting and I was very vocal about that. I would tell them, "If you allow the company to do that to the black what he done, he'd do it to you after a while." And they get mad with you. "It's a necessity that we all be together on any issue." I said, "To me you're just members. You're not black and white. You're just *members*. And when an issue comes up you just as much involved and I'll fight for you just as much as I fight for the black, and you need to do the same thing."

After more than two decades working underground in the mines, Earl Brown was appointed to a position at District 20's union office in Birmingham. Soon he talked his supervisor into allowing him to lead an organizing campaign that challenged Jim Crow on many different levels.

He said, "I just want you to be physically around the office or doing something here." For about a week I did that and I told them one day, I told Hollyfield, I said, "Mr. Hollyfield, I was hired to do a job. I want my share of the work." He said, "Earl you know how the Ku Klux are." I said, "I don't care. I was hired to do the work. I'm not afraid of the Ku Klux, because I know how to treat everybody." He said, "Well, we got some [union] organizing to be done in Tuscaloosa County." That's where Richard Shelton was. He was the chief of the Ku Klux. That was his home. He said, "Do you want to go?" I said, "Yeah." [Laughter.]

I went down to the local union hall in Tuscaloosa County. It was full. I mean it was *full*. Nothing but a sea of white faces. When I walked in the door, Mr. March looked back and said, "Yeah, here's Representative Brown I've been telling you about." Said, "Come on up. Come on up front." I walked on up front, and I could feel those piercing eyes, you know, in the back. [Laughter.] When I sat down and turned and faced all that sea of white faces, none of them was friendly. And Mr. March, after he opened up the meeting, he got up and said, "This is our new representative. He's going to be down here to help us organize. He come well recommended. He's a religious person. He knows *how* to treat people and we're happy to have him." Said, "He's going to stand up and tell us something tonight and let's give him a hand," and nobody clapped but him! [Laughter.]

I got up slowly and I began to give my background, where I had worked at, how long I had worked. Some of my experiences on the mine level as a mine committeeman. And then I went back into the background of the United Mine Workers, how it had come and how organizing was very important for us. Told them how in this area you have more *scab* people working right here, taking your jobs, what you supposed to be getting. I told them, "You'd have the higher rate of pay if you would get it all organized." Practically I spelled there, I guess, about 45 minutes, an hour. When I sat down, everybody got up. [Claps.] I never had no problems out there. Took them under my wing just like that. Never had no problems. Some of these guys when they go they got their pistols, their knives, but I never had a handgun or a knife taken with me nowhere. So, that's some experience I'll never forget, either. [Laughter.] At that time, I know some of them sitting up there was Ku Klux. But I just had a way. I was positive, and I just wasn't afraid at that time. I was young, and I was pretty muscular.

I never will forget it. During that time I was down there going into various places, on Christmas I never had to buy any cakes or nothing. No sir. Those ladies would bake cakes, some of the best cakes for my

Christmas. Those peoples was very nice to me. They had the confidence that I would go in there. On an organizing drive, we'd go in there. You had to make strategy. And I remember one [white] guy, he said, "Come on up here to this table and eat!" I said, "I'm not hungry." He said, "You going to eat with me." And we sat there and he'd break his cornbread, you know. He don't cut his bread. "Take that bread and *break it*!" That's the type of thing. It was a little embarrassing because I always cut my bread, you know. But he said, "Breaking bread." [Laughter.]

Oh yes. It's been a struggle. It's been a struggle, but it's never taken me down. I always had an upbeat [attitude] and right now I guess I got more people that know me and trust me than any in this district. This is my twenty-seventh year here and every four years they have to have a vote. *Everybody* been moved out of here, but I'm the only one that consistently has been [elected] here since I've been here. Ain't nobody that stay here over four years or eight years. They gone out. The changes have been made, but I haven't left this office since I came in. But I've had some experiences, some good experiences, and bad experiences.

One thing I tell these youngsters when they come in, I try to tell them, above all, first of all, don't tell a man what he want to hear. Tell him the truth. Don't tell him a lie. And know your [union] contract, and if you don't know, tell them you don't know. You'll get the answer. I've never politicked for a person's vote. If he didn't have nothing, I'd tell him he didn't have nothing. He'd get mad. "I'll vote you out." That's all right. I'm still not politicking. And I never told one of them a lie about anything. The majority [of miners] know me for what I am, and that's somebody that they can depend on when they call for something. And somebody told me, said, "You can stay in that office as long as you want to. Ain't nobody going to beat you." I said, "Well, I'll stay until I feel like I want to get out."

But I can just see that all that passes what you build up in people and what people believe in you and what you stand for. And if you're going through this life, you have to have that. Some like you, some dislike you. But my philosophy, I didn't have no enemies to punish, no friend to reward. Just treat them all right if I couldn't treat them all alike. That's the philosophy I had, and it paid off.

WILLIE ANN LUCAS

Willie Ann Lucas is a third-generation midwife. She earned her mid-wife's license in 1945 at the age of 24. During the Jim Crow era, midwives played an important role in African American communities, delivering babies, dispensing home remedies, and caring for the sick. Here, Willie Ann Lucas describes the work of midwives in detail, noting in particular the differences between her experiences and those of her mother, who encountered fewer state regulations and less supervision from doctors prior to World War II. Lucas notes that while doctors gained greater control over health-care delivery in the countryside, midwives were called on to provide care to the indigent who did not have the resources to pay for doctors' services.

My mother was a midwife and a schoolteacher. My father didn't teach school. He was a logger and a farmer. My mother strongly believed in an education. My mother had ten children, and I'm the eighth. She had nine boys and one girl, and we all got some form of education. I got married and later went back and got my college degree, and I followed in her footsteps as a midwife. I was a licensed midwife for the state of Arkansas from '45 to '72. I [also] taught school here in Brinkley for 23 years until I retired.

My grandmother was a midwife, my mother was a midwife, and I guess I took it up from my mother. But I had to go to school a year, to class, you know, to learn all about it and everything, and after that I had to go out with an experienced midwife, which was my mother, to deliver babies. The first one that I went with her that she delivered, they named their child after me. My first delivery, the lady named it after me.

It was a requirement that you go to school a year to learn it, so I did. Of course, that was in the forties when I started. I think I got my license in '45. But back in those days, you delivered a baby for $5, and sometimes you didn't get that. I remember before then, in the late thirties, my mother would deliver babies and they would pay her with corn. Corn was 50 cents a bushel. Pigs were a dollar. They would pay her in corn, pigs, and you'd get half a calf sometimes for $5, and that's the way she got

Bakery owner Elmer Bradshaw, father of Bernice Caldwell.
(Courtesy of Bernice Caldwell, Charlotte, North Carolina)

her money most of the time for delivering babies back in the Depression days.

In my mother's days, they would just engage you to deliver the baby. You know, if they got pregnant, they would come and ask you if you would deliver the baby for them. But in my days, I had to have what they called a blue card. They would issue them to me from the health office, and I would give them to the patients when they come and engage me to wait on them. They would have to take them to the doctor, and every time they go to the doctor, the doctor would fill out this card with their blood pressure and whatever else on there. And if they had any danger signals, like feet swelling or high blood pressure or something like that, they wouldn't recommend that they have a midwife to deliver, and that was the difference. Back in my mother's days, they just delivered the baby. But when I come along, you had to have the okay from a doctor. When they went for their last checkup he would mark whether they're safe or unsafe for a midwife to deliver, and if anything happened, then he was responsible. He had to come if I called him. That was my backup. He had to come.

Back in my mother's days, a midwife was almost the same as a doctor. When World War II broke out, well, then doctors were scarce and everything else. And I don't know, you just didn't have no problem. They just knew you was a midwife, and they'd just come. Wake up twelve o'clock at night and you'd hear this wagon coming down the road, and she'd just get on up out of the bed because there wasn't nowhere else for them to be going but coming after her. They'd come in the wagons. They didn't have any cars. She would come in sometimes when it was raining in the wintertime and her clothes would be frozen stiff on her. She'd be standing up there, and I said, "Oh, I'd never be a midwife." And bless goodness, before I knew it, I was one.

You had a suitcase, briefcase to carry. In this briefcase you had a set of towels and you had masks. You were required to have a mask. You carried your own pan because that's what you had to sterilize your scissors with, and you would put that on and boil your scissors and sterilize them in order so when you cut the navel cord, umbilical cord they call it, then it wouldn't set up infection or anything. And you had to carry this tape, umbilical tape that you'd tie the cord with before you cut it.

But the only thing about it, you didn't use gloves. They didn't require you to use gloves. I don't know why. Because one thing, you didn't do any examining. You didn't give any medicine. You weren't allowed to give medicine.

In that [briefcase], you carried everything necessary. If they didn't have anything to put on the child, you had something in your bag that you could dress the baby with. Back in those days, you had what they called a belly band. That wasn't really the name they call it now, but they don't use them anymore, and that's why you see so many babies have a hernia because the band kept the navel from protruding.

The most difficult ones were breech first. Breech is where they come backwards. Instead of head first, they come folded up and their rear first, and that was the most difficult and the most dangerous. But [my mother] never lost a patient, but it was just more difficult [if the baby was breech].

The only [medication] that I can remember that they used was quinine, and quinine was used if they were in labor and [they were] having them little old piddling pains. They'd give them some quinine; it would cut them [pains] off if it wasn't their time. And if it was their time, they would heed them up, and they'd go ahead on and make the labor pains come closer and harder, and they would go on and have the baby. Some midwives would give the patients castor oil, but I never did that. That's about all they were allowed to give.

Of course, when I started, I learned a few more little techniques in it, things you could do—using a hot towel to keep them from tearing, things like that. I got my license for a practical nurse, and that helped me out a whole lot, too, with my midwifery, but, see, that came after I had gotten my license.

They'd come to you and ask, "What must I do? I'm hurting here. I have aches." But most of the time, [the midwife] still didn't give any medication or anything. She would refer them to the doctor, tell them to go to the doctor, because you were never allowed to even be giving aspirin. You weren't even supposed to give anything. They just had normal childbirth. And up until 1972, I wasn't allowed to give anything. I couldn't give an aspirin or anything for pain. Therefore, a lot of them, that's why they went to the hospital if they could afford it, because they thought, when they got there, they were going to get something for pain. And then when they come out, they'd had the first one over there and they come back home, and the next time they say, "They didn't do anything for me there. I might as well have a midwife." And so I'd get a chance at them the second or third or something like that because of that. They thought they were going to get some help to stop those pains, but they didn't.

[Older generations of midwives learned] I guess by just going with somebody, just picking it up from some of your relatives or somebody that was interested in going around with them and all. Now, like my mother, along in the forties, she had to go take classes. She lived in Marvell, but she'd have to go to Helena once a month and they'd have classes. That was teaching you all the danger signals and everything else that you should know about a patient because, see, if they had swelling in the feet, you didn't deliver them because that was a kidney problem. Some of the feet would just swell. Well, that was caused by kidney infection, and you didn't dare deliver one with kidney infection. They would teach you all that, things to avoid.

With the blue card, they had to be approved by a doctor. The only thing, I was delivering twins, and one we thought was dead and one wasn't, and the lady said, "Stop fooling with that one and try to take the other one that's alive." By that time, the baby gasped, and we knew it was alive too, because they'll be in a sack, and that sack didn't burst, and therefore it was in there with all that fluid, what's called a water bag. That's probably my scariest experience was working with that one.

To me, it was just natural. It wasn't anything. I didn't get afraid. Nothing scared me or anything. I could still be doing it, but they got all these health clinics now, and they said they didn't need the midwife anymore because they had enough health facilities, health clinics to take care of all the OB patients. And so that's why I'm not doing it today. I would still be doing it. I loved it. It didn't bother me one bit.

Most of my deliveries were at home, but most of them was in the rural areas, you know, out in the country on farms. I had some in town, you know, city, but the majority was from rural areas.

When I started doing midwife work, we had telephones. And then, when they called and asked me if I would wait on them, then I would tell them you have to come see me, and I have to talk to you, and I have to give you a blue card, and you will have to take it to the doctor every time you go and let the doctor, after he examines you and everything, fill it out. He put the date on there and everything when you visited him. So that was the difference [over time], you know. I had to have proof and my mother didn't. They just would come to her house and say, "I'm pregnant, going to have a baby, and I'd like to get you to deliver it for me," and that was it.

Some doctors, when World War II was going on, they sent them to my mother. They would send them to her to deliver. I guess they didn't have any money, and they wasn't going to be paying. And I had some to do me that same way here in Brinkley. They owed the doctor, and the doctor said they wasn't going to wait on them because they owed

Midwives Association, left to right: Mary Pratt, Mary Guant, Mrs. Prezeal Simon, Virginia Compton, Mrs. Laninia, Mary Traham, Mary Anthony, possibly Mrs. Farrington, and Patsy Moss, sometime between 1930 and 1940.

(New Iberia Parish Library, New Iberia, Louisiana)

them; they didn't pay them. And then they would call me and ask me if I wanted to wait on them. They didn't pay me; maybe they'll pay you. And I have some that still owe me. At that time, it wasn't but $15.

[I delivered] both black and white. I delivered quite a few white. But like I say, it was kind of the poor whites that didn't have much money, not rich whites. And the same way with the blacks. Not the rich blacks that could afford to pay. Well, they paid, and so did the whites. But I delivered a lot of white babies.

Back then in mother's days when she was delivering babies, doing midwife work, I don't think [the doctors] had any problem [with midwives]. The doctors, it looked like to me, was glad for them to get a midwife to deliver because we just didn't have any money, in the first place. Just like I said, they'd pay with corn and hogs and whatever, cows, whatever they had, and she would take that for money. But see, the doctors, he didn't need that stuff, and he'd be glad for them to go to a midwife.

But I have people today saying they wished the midwives was still active, because they'd rather [have them] but, see, you got so much stuff now. You got the hospital over there in Little Rock, where they take you if you don't have any money. [If] you don't have anything, then you can go to the hospital and you don't have to pay anything. All you've got to do is just get there. Then they got all this other stuff. You're on welfare and getting all that money and you can afford to go to Little Rock. So most of them now, the doctors will send them to University [Hospital] in Little Rock. That's supposed to be the free hospital. If you've got money, you have to pay. But if you don't have any, they take you anyway.

They just stopped renewing the [midwives'] license. They wrote me a letter, and they said they wouldn't renew my license because they have enough facilities to take care of the OB patients. They don't deliver them here at the clinic, but they will send them to Little Rock. They'll take care of them. They get their prenatal care here. But then when it's time for them to deliver, they send them to Little Rock. We used to have a hospital here [in Brinkley], but we haven't had one here now since about '60-something.

In the thirties there weren't [any types of prenatal care]. Now, I got married in '42. I don't know, I had a lot of pain in my sides, and other than that, I don't think my mother would have ever taken me to a doctor. My husband was in the service. I never would have gone to a doctor if I hadn't had so much pain in my side, and that's just the way it was. If you didn't have any problem or anything, you didn't go to a doctor. But see, I was having a lot of trouble, and so she finally decided to take me to the doctor. Of course, with my second one, I didn't have any problem and I didn't go to a doctor.

When my third one came along, [there was] about eight years difference in him and my two girls, because he was born in '51 and my daughter was born in '43. Of course, I fell out the back door, and when I fell, I guess I did some harm, and I ended up in the hospital. So I had to go to the hospital, and that's where they delivered my baby. The last one was in the hospital. But if I hadn't of fallen, I guess I wouldn't have even gone. But it was just, if you did all right, you didn't have to go. But if you had problems, then you'd have to go to the doctor. That was back in the forties.

IDA BELL ALLEN

Born in South Carolina at the outset of World War I, Ida Bell Allen reflects back on seven decades of household labor. Work has played a dominant role in Allen's life. She and her young peers were called out of their schoolhouse in Pine Hill, South Carolina, to labor in the cotton fields. Allen's narrative is also a reminder that the extensive, unpaid labor performed by African American women was a key to forging what she refers to as the "family tie" that bound black communities together during segregation.

I'd go to school at Pine Hill, used to go four months. That's all the long we went because we were farmers. We'd start planting and then we didn't go to school until it was about the last part of October or November until the crops were just about gathered, especially the cotton. Then we'd go to school on through there until time to plant. Well, in March you had to start for the farm. Well, the brothers would plow and till the soil and all that; we girls could go on to school. A lot of things you had to do by hand then. You didn't have machines to do it, like scatter, which is called compost now, but we used to call it manure because we used to take it out of the stable. We had to scatter that up and down the row. And then the fertilizer, we'd start that to plant the crops. Well, we girls, we had to stay home from school then to help put that down. After that then we'd go back to school again. And then school closed out about the first of May because you'd start then to chopping cotton and whatnot and go on. That's how you'd do it.

There was no fighting and carrying on like children now. We was glad to see each other. Tried to help each other, help them carry their books. The little ones had to walk too. We helped along with the little ones, took them by the hand. It was a good life and I learned well. Because, see, my real mother died when I was in school two years. Then after, my father married the second time and she was just like my mother. Now she learned me everything mostly I know. This is my stepmother. She'd teach me how to do my domestic work and stuff like that and take care of children. Now, she'd teach me that. I always give her that praise.

She was just as good as any mother. She wouldn't [tell] all the little bad things we'd do; she was so good; she wouldn't tell our father we need to get a whipping. She was kind of a young woman and, you know, she went right along with us. We got along fine. Had a good life. Then, after I married, she still was a mother to me. When I give birth to my children, she would come and stay with me a month. Wash, keep house, and cook for me, and then she would go back. She would put me on my own and then she would go back. So I had a good life.

One thing that always I was blessed with after I married, we owned cows. So we had butter and milk for our children. So we didn't have to buy that. We always had that until all of them got grown. The toughest time along was the six boys was in school at one time. It was a little rough then. Boys is rough on clothes and whatnot. And then you couldn't buy clothes for little boys in the store. I had to learn to sew, to make pants and shirts for them to go to school.

The worse I would say suffering through segregation and whatnot was in World War II, really when the war lasted so long. I had four children along in that time and food was scarce. There wasn't no big farms. Then I had to go to the store for a lot of things that we couldn't raise on the farm. My husband just started over again, put a little farm there after he come from the factory. So it was a little tougher on me then because a lot of things they'd put on the shelf, and they'd say they were going to have it on there tomorrow, and you get there and they're all off the shelf, it's just a clean shelf. Then you had a family that you had to feed. So that was about the toughest time going through that, and segregation didn't make that, just the economy made that because they'd feed the soldiers. But somehow or another I raised our children; they were healthy. We did the best with what we had, and they stayed fat and happy.

It was a little rough but I didn't give up. I didn't give up. I always had hope for different changes. And sure enough it was, and after that then they said there was peace, declared that. Then my baby started to school when he was six years old, and that gave me a chance [to] do some domestic work. I worked at Shaw Field. It wasn't Shaw then. It was an Army base then out there. I worked there about 10 years to kind of help because the children was in school and I didn't have to stay home. Well it wasn't too much money in that job. I'd be back, and then he was working at night. When I was at work he was home. He'd go to work in the evenings, and at that time I was on my way back. So that's the only way to keep them together, the six boys together. So it wasn't so tough. So I would say we was wonderful blessed. I know many friends of mine cannot say that.

I used to make a lot of [quilts] when I first married. The scraps were left off of material and whatnot, [and I] used to buy it in bundles, scraps and things from the store. Then [in] these ladies' homes after we stopped having children, we'd piece up, put them together and put it in this long strip, and then after that we sewed all of it together until we'd get it wide enough for a quilt. Then we would go to one house to visit and we'd put it down on the floor and we'd get to admiring it, get the cotton and pad it out and put the cotton down and pad it out then spread the top over it. Then we'd get on our knees on the floor and baste it on like that. Then we'd roll it on an ironing board, a long board we used to have, a long ironing board. Then we'd start sewing the quilt as we'd get it together. Go out to one another's house and help and do things like that. When the children gets married, we knew what we had to do when we'd get an invitation and whatnot. We'd bake cakes, make quilts and give them, stuff like that. Buy dishes and stuff would go on like that.

This [was] a family tie back then. You know what they need. I [watched] a lot of mothers' children. They was working and I had children. I had to stay home. Those little children would come with their little sandwich, and they'd stay with me until their mother would knock off of work, stay there and play with my children under the tree shade and whatnot and their mother would come and pick them up and go on. But now you can't get nobody to do that. They'd treat those children just like how they'd treat their own. If they'd get sleepy, none of the kids didn't get in the bed. They'd get a big quilt and spread it out on the floor, and everybody would lay down on this floor and sleep, have their nap. Then they'd wake up and then they'd have their lunch and they'd go on back outdoors and play. Happy. It hurts me now to see just how far our black race changed from their inheritance. That's what hurts me. Because really some of our race have really tried to be white. They thought they were above others who didn't have the education or whatnot to get into these places. Regardless what line of work they do, you ought to remember your inheritance. I'm a Negro. Always remember that. I don't care how bright you is, if one fellow's black and the other one's white, you're a Negro. I went to school with a lot of them, and I was raised with a lot of them. I was educated to that. That's why I know they think that they was more than I was.

God just helps me to keep it because He knows that's me. That's just me. And I pray God just keeps me this way until I die. I don't have nothing burdening me down. I sit out there on that front porch and I feel just as free as I can be. That's how I was raised. I didn't care what you have, didn't worry me. Only what I had. The only thing I was jealous over, you couldn't beat me working, and you couldn't beat me doing domestic work, keeping my place clean, keeping my children clean and healthy to go to school.

I tell them I'm blessed with my six boys, and I ain't never had to went down to the courthouse, you know, court. They didn't get into nothing. When they finished Lincoln High School, there was six. Our family now was real poor. You can't send anybody to college. Five went in service. And that's how when they come back then they went to different techs and got their career in electricity and working for the telephone company and different things. They went to school and learned that. I let them know when they finished we wasn't able to send them because we couldn't send six. We knowed that.

RALPH THOMPSON

Ralph Thompson toiled in the molten heat of International Harvester's Memphis factory foundry for over two decades. During that time, Thompson became a union activist and elected official of the United Auto Workers (UAW) Local 988 in Memphis, and eventually assumed the presidency of the UAW's national Foundry Workers' Council. Working in tandem with other African American factory operatives, Thompson fought to open up skilled jobs at Harvester to black employees. The road to improving job opportunities and wages for African American industrial workers in the Jim Crow South was a long and difficult one. Corporate supervisors and white coworkers often colluded to keep black laborers at the bottom of the job and wage scale. In this passage, Thompson discusses a far-reaching net-work of black labor organizers who turned to each other for support and, at times, self-defense against white violence.

Thanks in large part to the work of these activists, African American workers began assuming higher-skilled positions only to witness a national wave of plant closings that devastated black working-class neighborhoods in Birmingham, Memphis, Chicago, and other core urban areas between the 1950s and the 1970s. In this excerpt, Ralph Thompson begins his narrative with a discussion about how segregation undermined educational opportunities for the members of his generation, and, hence, limited employment opportunities.

We did reading and writing, but we didn't go beyond that. And I guess that was part of it [segregation]. And, to see other [white] kids that could play baseball and had baseball diamonds and things like that and we were denied. We didn't have it and nobody could furnish it for us including our families and all. That was a little hard for us back then. But I think the biggest thing that stands out in my mind was the burning of the school. Maybe the next was us having to buy the school bus. Those are two of the things that really stayed with me and I really get upset when I hear people talk about "busing." When we would walk home in the evening down a gravel road and when the white bus would come, the driver would get up in the center, you know. The gravel would pile up in the center and the wheels would cut tracks in the road and it would pile it up. And he would get up in the center for those rocks to shoot out from under the wheels. And I can remember having to turn our backs in case a rock might come out and hit you in the eye. And if you were walking home from school and it rained and there's a low spot and you happened to be coming by that low spot and you could hear the motor on the bus rev up because he's going to speed up cause he's going to hit that water as hard as he can. How can a person be so cold? And we would run, and we would turn our backs. And I'd say how can a person be so cold that would try to wet us down and try to put our eyes out and things like that? And those are some of the things that when you look back today and you see how mean people could be to a kid. They didn't know us. We didn't bother them. And they would ride right by us and those kids was

Malvin E. Moore Sr., right, with employees in Moore's Tailor Shop, Pine Bluff, North Carolina, 1930. (Courtesy of Malvin Moore Jr., Durham, North Carolina)

going to Millington at the time, and we were out there for a year, and nobody tried to help us or get us back in school for a whole year. And I hear people talking about "busing" and they used to bus them right by us. The only time we got on a bus was when we bought one. Mr. Charlie Smith had a '46 Chevrolet bus, and we went to school so regularly if we weren't there he would wait on us in the morning and we'd come. We'd see the bus. We'd take off running. But the things that stand out in my mind, that bus coming trying to, with the rocks and it rained, hit a water puddle. I'm talking about going out of his way to hit it. And we knew that, because we turn our backs. If we couldn't get beyond, we'd get off the road as far as we could and we'd turn our backs. And that's what it was like. That's what it was like and you didn't have nobody that you could turn to help you say, "Hey, bus driver, don't do that." See? And going home telling your parents, you can imagine how frustrating that is. They'd tell you to turn your head and little things that they could tell you to do, but you couldn't fight back because you didn't have no way of fighting back.

When I got out of high school, I went into the military in 1954. I volunteered, and I was right on the tail end of the Korean War although I didn't see any action. I was stationed in Albuquerque, New Mexico, and I was a military policeman. After being discharged from the military, I just had little haphazard jobs and finally got a job at International Harvester which was one of the bigger manufacturing companies here in the city. And that was in 1959. So it took me almost two years to get a job. I found minimum-wage jobs, but this was one of the better jobs. When I went in, they hired about 50 people that day. I was the only black person in the crowd and I can remember that guy coming into the conference room and he looked over and saw me in that crowd and he said, "Did I call your name?" And I said, "Yeah." He asked me my name and I told him, and he went and looked at his list to make sure that I was on that list. And I guess out of a 100–150 [applicants] they only hired about five blacks. This was in 1959. And naturally, I had some business college, but I had graduated from high school, so I ended up working in the foundry for most of my time there, because it was segregated, and when you went into jobs they were basically "white jobs" and "black jobs." And black jobs were basically in the foundry. You went anywhere else, you were either disqualified or you were given such a hard time that you had to leave, you know. You would just give up and you would give in.

And over the years we just kept fighting and pecking away and finally we started getting some jobs. Even their worst jobs were decent-paying jobs, but I'm talking about running machines and drills and things like that. We couldn't drive cranes, overhead cranes. Finally we got to where we could do that. We couldn't run no machine. They didn't let us do that. You couldn't get no office job. All you could do was the hardest job.

In the cafeteria, they had a chain and the whites came in one door and we came in a different door. We came in the back door. We would come to the steam table and the trays would divide us. We'd get trays off the same stack. They would go to the right. We would go to the left. And they had two cashiers. They had a white cashier and a black cashier. The black cashier couldn't work on the white end, but the white cashier could work on the black end. So finally, I forgot what year it was, but they came in, the government came in, and they had to take the chain down. And just out of habit we still went in our separate ways. So the government came back in a year or so later and they had to change it around where everybody had to go in the same direction in the cafeteria.

And I remember in 1969 I went on a milling machine. On a cotton picker they got a picker bar and the spindles will stand out like this and they rotate. And that's what pulls the cotton out of the boll. On the end of that bar you had to grind it out because you got to put a "O" ring. And you had to rough it out and then you had to finish it out. And then when you do the finish grind on it, it's shiny. And you got a little triangle tool. In the corner of it was the thing that actually would do the cutting. And the tool itself had to be soft because it wouldn't keep an edge, but it was the top of the picker bar on a cotton picker is really what I was grinding out. And that's what I was doing. And for some reason I just couldn't run the necessary parts. And what they [white supervisors] were doing, I didn't know it at the time, they would give me a tool that wouldn't keep an edge. You know, it was cut and I had to keep changing out, because it would burn up so fast, you know, it would get dull so fast. And I can remember as it happened yesterday, the supervisor, when they disqualified me, they put a white person on that job, and I can see that supervisor reaching in his bottom desk drawer on the right-hand side and giving this guy a tool and he could just run it. And I transferred away from that department back to the foundry and I ran for an elected [union] office, because I made up in my mind if I didn't do anything else that I would make sure that the people that I represented would get a fair shake in this place, in this environment. And over the years I was elected I guess on two years some five or six times, and overall I must have stayed in office about 20 years.

I ended up a laborer at International Harvester and what they were paying back then was fairly decent money, and I could take care of a family on that. And what got me into the labor movement, working and seeing people, things happening to people and a couple of things that happened to me, and I started getting active. And one of the things that some of the guys that I worked around couldn't read, and I could read. And they would kind of play off of me. I guess I was their eyes. We'd get

a handbill or a flyer from the company or union either way, and we'd
be sitting there on break or lunch or something, somebody would say,
"What is this? What are they talking about? I don't have my glasses."
That's the excuse they'd always have. "I don't have my glasses." And instead of saying anything, I'd just read and say, "Oh this is such and such
and such." And that started people to talking because I was younger and
I'd come to work on time and things like that. And they said, "Why, you
ought to run for office," and I started running for the by-laws committee
in summer school and things like that. And I worked myself on up and
I got as high as vice-chairman of the bargaining unit. But now when you
get to vice-chairman, that wasn't elected from the total group, that was
elected from the committee. But I held an office that represented about
1,000 people. And I worked there until I got appointed to a staff job.
I wasn't a supervisor. I was a group leader. And I ran the department
where they received all the steel, the pipes, bars, and sheet metal and stuff
like that. And that was it. And I worked in other departments. Now that
was, like I explained to you earlier, about the chains.

They had what they call a merry-go-round over in the molding department and it was a chain and it was flat and you put your molds on.
You could put two on each cart. And you had your machines lined up.
And what they would do if they had a white person over there, they'd
always put the white person on the first machine because the person
down here by the time these carts get to him they're full. Two more's on
this one. Two on this one and two there, and he might not have known
where to put his mold. So he could run, let's say, like a third of the molds
you have to run. And that's the way they would do things. And then after
they changed, they had it where blacks was working together, teams, two
guys, and whites were working together. And I was a union rep at that
time, and I couldn't figure out why blacks were always being disciplined
and suspended and whites weren't getting any. Not that I wanted white
people suspended, but something ain't right with this. And I discover one
day they had two books and let's say you had an infraction, they'd write
you in this book, and the next time they'd put it in a different book. So
when you opened the book whatever you were he could always pull that
book up. I guess he'd go look at it and see where you stand, and pull that
book up. And I accidentally stumbled up on those books and I brought

it to the company's attention. And I took a position as an union official that in the future when a team broke up, some guy transferred out and an opening came, the next person in line had to go there. We can't swap up. You got to go to that spot, and if you don't like each other, you got to learn to like each other. If you don't like each other, fine. You still got to work together. And I found that a lot of that problem went away. Because if you got a white and a black working together, then they're together there and it's kind of hard to pick one out and show favors and don't show favors for the other one. The other thing I found that the heavier molds began to move around through the group. Those were some of the things that we dealt with.

I'm not going to sit here and tell you that I satisfied every person that I represented. I didn't, but I tried my best to be honest and fair with them. Because we were always into arguments and fights and all where we were concerned. If it was black, it was very easy, seemed like, for them to suspend us. It was very easy seemed like to suspend us. And that was one of the things, some of the things that I experienced in the years I worked there. The cranes over in sheet metal and all that. For a long time we couldn't run it. A simple thing as a saw and all you got to do with a saw is nest your pipes and stuff here and count them and however many you got in the nest and run it up and take your rule and set it. And we couldn't run those kind of machines. They wouldn't let us run it. They'd disqualify us. They'd do all kinds of things to disqualify us. And we had to try to make it. And it was a never-ending fight.

First of all, [white coworkers] wouldn't help you. They would do little things to you. You would have to watch your machine. Somebody might come through there and loosen a bolt or something up on you. You have to watch that real close. But they kind of stayed in the background and management would deal with you, disqualify you, say you can't do the job. If you had a problem, wouldn't nobody help you, and if they put somebody with you they'd show you a little bit, but they wouldn't really show you. And then they'd say to the management, "He can't do it." And the management would watch you, and most of this work is incentive, and if you couldn't get up to snuff you had 40 hours to get up there. But like I was telling you about the job I had, if I had to keep changing the tool out, and the tools were new because I was taking them out of the package, but they were soft. I found out in later years just by observing that they were soft and they wouldn't keep an edge very long, and I had to change them out and I couldn't keep up. And this might sound strange, but on this particular job that I can remember this, from my station to the end of the line they had two shifts. And from my station back they had one shift. So the supervisor's name was Jones. He told the guy that I couldn't keep up. I couldn't run enough to keep up, but they had two shifts down here. And being green, I didn't argue with that and didn't see it, and then I was disqualified. And I can remember some jobs over there you couldn't even think about going to. You were disqualified before you even got there.

I found that some of these [white] people didn't have high school education, but there were systems and ways to carry them. You take a set of machines. You make a setup in the morning and just before that guy leave in the evening, he'd make another setup. The guy come in on the second shift and he'd run it as long as the machine would run. The guy come in on the third shift, the first thing off, he'd make a setup. So the guy in the middle didn't know how to set it up, but because he was white they fixed a way or found a way to take care of this guy. And I really don't fault you to that degree. It's just that when somebody talks about a level playing field, if you get out there in the real world you'll find that it ain't no level playing field. The system don't allow this playing field, because when I went in, I passed the test. When the guy looked and saw me in this crowd of 50-plus people, there weren't but like 55, 50 people he didn't take my word and say he must have a right to be in here. He asked, "Did I call your name?" I said, "Yeah." He didn't take that. He went and looked on the list and looked my name up. It ain't no level playing field. That's just the way it was. The person that was over payroll just had a high school education! I'm not saying I could come in and do the same job, but I couldn't even be a clerk in that department. And I couldn't be the person that used to bring out time cards and production cards with part numbers on them and all you had to do was put it in the file cabinet. Now I'm down here as an incentive worker, pieceworker. I can go over there and pull the cards out of the file. Look up the number and pull it out, because I'm down here at the foundry and I'm working. But I can't come out of the office with these same cards and put them in that file cabinet, but I can take them out of the file cabinet. See what I'm talking about? They didn't let us have those jobs because there were ways to disqualify us and that's what they did.

It was a guy that came up through the Pullman Porters, George Holloway, and when I came in 1959 it was like five or six of us. I was young and I could read. And he stayed on me about participating [in the union] and telling me and he just kept pushing me, and pushing me. And that's what got me started. George Holloway was the driving force that dealt with the [Jim Crow] signs where he could go in doors; even though he was a representative, he couldn't go in certain doors. He couldn't go in the hotel in negotiations. He had to go up the service elevator and things like that. And because of his union background in the Pullman Porters and all, he was just a union man. It was in his blood. You could just talk to him and it was just in him. And he kept pushing us to do better and support him, and he needed us when certain things was going on, and he kept us informed, and [started] breaking down some of the barriers. That's what George Holloway wants and some of that rubbed off on some of us. And when he moved up to the [UAW] staff, then we started running and we tried to do the Jackie Robinson, you know. Everybody wanted to be George Holloway, see, but his role was bridging the gap between us and the other side. The other side being the white company and the white side of the union. He had to deal with all of that. So he was that guy. He was that spokesman for us. I didn't do it, but I can remember the stories about them having to escort him home at night to protect him. I can remember them talking about how somebody shot in his house. I can remember those things and that made me want to do this. I knew how that came about. I can remember the signs. I can remember the water fountains. I can remember being denied jobs and things like that. So that made me want to make it just a little bit better if I could. And if my little two cents meant that it was going to be better then that's what I wanted to do.

We had people that was in the background that was pretty active that came to the union meetings and the people that didn't take an active role as far as running for office, but would kind of circle the wagons around Holloway when he was in trouble and people wanted to kill him. Keep them from beating him up and things like that. Then there was a group

Female mechanic at work on trainer plane. Tuskegee Airfield, Tuskegee, Alabama, in the 1940s. (Courtesy of Ernest Henderson, Orangeburg, South Carolina)

of people that would do that. Then you had other people that would run for positions and all. So it was quite a few, but we were all active and we all followed the leadership of George Holloway because we knew that he was the guy that would level with us and was leading us in the right direction. And he needed our support. But we had quite a few people that were very active. Back then the bulk of our people were in the foundry because that's where they would put us, and it was very hard for us to get out and make it somewhere else. So that was our nucleus.

And when we could get somebody out and in a department or something, then we supported that person in any way, you know, moral support. We didn't have no money or nothing like that, but we would support them that way. And encouraging people to take on assembly jobs. And I can remember Larry Bingham going into welding and they [whites] would put exploding firecrackers in the welding booth. Here's a guy couldn't make it at International Harvester welding and taught welding in one of the vocational schools back then. One of the schools that veterans went to and he taught welding, and it's strange. I can't think of the guy's name that was an electrician, couldn't get in the electrical department, but supervisors and people that worked there would call this guy and have him to go over to their house and do electrical work. Grady Terrell, electrician. And I can remember how you kind of supported him by slapping him on the back and encouraging him and all the things that happened. Jimmy Moore, when he went in the crane to drive the crane and they [whites] had the wildcat strike. Those are some of the people that you had to look at as pioneers and trailblazers, if I can use that term. And Holloway was that guy, and he was encouraging you to do this and all. And he was pushing me to go to union meetings and participate and all.

But those are some of the trailblazers. If you're talking about leaders, you had a group of those. You had people that kind of protected you from violence, Holloway in particular. Then you had the trailblazers like Larry Bingham, and Jimmy Moore, and Floyd Price, and how he had to order [them to give] a checker's job [to a black] in Department 65 in Sheet Metal. They [whites] didn't want him, because this was a job where you were walking around with a clipboard and stuff like that. And finally, when we started getting in there and you looked up it was black. As a matter of fact, my brother was in there. And you had to talk about the OD and the ID of a tube, and sheet metal and gauge whether it's 18 gauge or whatever and how to measure and all that kind of stuff. And we were doing it, but how we had to fight to get there! I can remember all that stuff as it happened just like it happened yesterday. And I can remember in later years we had a guy, he was in a department and he was sweeping the floor. I went to industrial relations and argued with them that it was a maintenance job posted in the maintenance department, and if he was in the department, he could sign the posting and get the job as a skilled tracer. But the department wouldn't let him go. They had him out there sweeping the floor, and after I raised the issue industrial relations had that guy, Perkins, had him moved into maintenance. And that's how he got into the maintenance department. We had all of those kinds of fights and arguments and you had to go. When they hired the first black nurse, when Miss Butch retired, Martin came to me and said, "Why don't we have a black nurse?" I went to Gene Kenum and I said, "Gene, this is a golden opportunity if the company means what they say about equal rights and things like that. Here's a golden opportunity to hire a black nurse." They did. And I can't even think of her name, and if she talked to you today, I'll bet you money that she wouldn't even know how she got that job or she'll tell you, "I got that job on my own." But it was some pushing behind the scenes and we never talked about it.

I think we [the UAW] represented somewhere in the neighborhood of 200,000 foundry workers throughout the country and Canada. That was Ford, GM foundries, Caterpillar foundries, International Harvester foundries, John Deere foundries, all of the foundries that was represented by the UAW. [In the foundry] first of all, you're dealing with scrap iron. You're dealing with molten metal. I think there's 2,800 degrees for it to melt and it's running like water. In the summer time, if it's 100 degrees outside, it's like 115 or 120 inside. It's heavy because they're using sand and they got whatever they put in it, it's black so you got all this sand. You sweating and it's sticking to you and all. It's heavy work. It's incentive so that means it's fast. And it's just so rough. Back then in those days it was a rough, tough job and you had to be tough to do it. Because you got metal running like water. Once it's set up it's still 1,200 degrees or better. It's red hot. The molds now, they are hot. They are steaming. You got gas coming off of the molds, because of the ingredients you put on the sand to form the molds. Then you got noise, because you got metal banging against metal. You got grinding wheels that's running. You got sand coming in the back of the building. You got people making cores. You got people making molds and the casting. You got people grinding those castings. You got furnaces up there where you put them in heat treat. All of this is in one building. And to heat treat something you got to bring it up to 1,800 degrees. Although it's in a furnace, if you bring the inside up to 18, you know you're going to get some heat outside. Not a lot, but you're going to get some heat outside. So here's a situation: In the middle of the building you got iron being melted at 2,800 degrees. You got these molds out here on the deck and steam and stuff and dust from that. You got people grinding it and the particles coming off from the grinding wheel. Little particles of iron coming off of that. Although you got goggles on, that particle will find a way to get in your eye. Then once you get through grinding it, some of it's going back through heat treatment and all of that's right there together. And that's extremely tough. We survived it some kind of way. That is the reason why the

Dining car cooks taking a break during the 1940s.
(Courtesy of Larry Henderson, Birmingham, Alabama)

foundry workers through the [UAW] council here argued and won special treatment [for foundry workers,] because our life expectancy was shorter than a factory worker. So that's why for every five years that we spend in a foundry, they give us one year credit. So when I get to 25 years I got the equivalent of 30 years, and I can walk out with full retirement at 25 years, but I'll call it 30 years. The factory worker's life expectancy was longer than mine and that is why and how that came about, because of that conference right here. We brought up problems and talked about issues that was unique to the foundry. The things that happened to us that didn't happen to factory workers.

[During the Memphis sanitation workers' strike of 1968] on our side, our side meaning the black side, seemed like we were unified. We didn't knock the union, and we met at the UAW hall there at 1190 Walker. The community people, the NAACP people, and all used to come there and meet because that was one place they could go meet in a group and didn't have no problems and things like that. And the community was behind the sanitation workers. [Mayor Henry] Loeb [was] in a sense the enemy for lack of a better way to put that, and everybody rallied around

Day laborers pick cotton on the Milestone Plantation in the Mississippi Delta, November 1939.
(Photograph by Marion Post Wolcott, North Carolina Collection, University of North Carolina at Chapel Hill)

the sanitation workers. We remember the [trash] tubs on their heads, and they [sanitation workers] used to be sent home and didn't get paid if it was raining and things like that. It was just [about] some dignity, and then when Martin Luther King came in here, that just put a little more I guess class, that ain't the word to put to this drive. And everybody, you know, was getting on the bandwagon. At that time Walter Reuther was the president of the UAW. He came in here and he gave $50,000 to the sanitation strike. He gave $50,000 from the UAW to the sanitation workers. And if Walter Reuther said, "You UAW people," especially among black people, "you need to support something," we tried to do it because we believed in Walter Reuther. He was a union person and we believed in him. When they were getting involved that meant the local union had to get involved. But the community rallied around the sanitation workers, you know, back then. But since that time, you know, we're so anti-union now, I mean, you're almost afraid to wear a union label in your shirt. But I'm not afraid.

Harvester was a good place. It must have been a good place. I stayed there 30-plus years. I retired from there. Of course, you might say: "Why didn't you quit?" Where, what am I going to do? Jump off the world? I can't jump off the edge. I got to figure out a way to live in this system. I got to try to find a way to make it better if I can. All of this [came] from Holloway telling us to get involved. See, I can't accuse the company of something and [be] raising sand with somebody else if I'm not willing to go out there and bite the bullet and stand right up to it and talk about it trying to get some relief. When we talked [about] the nurse earlier, the nurse never had to wait on me for no reason. She never know until this day, because I know I didn't tell her what went on, but we made the company conscious that they had a golden opportunity to hire a black nurse. Now whether they were going to hire one anyway, I don't know, but I do know we made the company conscious of the fact that there was a golden opportunity. And that's how we did some of these things, and all of it came from our relationship and talking and George Holloway's teaching.

SIX

RESISTANCE AND
POLITICAL STRUGGLES

By the 1890s, throughout the southern states, white officials and lawmakers had written Jim Crow legal statutes that regulated nearly every aspect of black life. These statutes dictated where blacks could eat, which seats they could occupy in theaters and on buses and trains, which jobs they could perform, where they could live, which water fountain they could use, and which beaches and parks they could visit. In Florida, "after dark" laws even prohibited black sharecroppers from selling produce at night.

Beginning where statutory restrictions ended, Jim Crow customs and racial etiquette seized every opportunity to belittle and humiliate African Americans. A racist code of social conduct and customs reserved the use of the titles "Miss" and "Mister" for white men, women, and children; disparaging epithets were reserved for black Americans, including, but certainly not limited to, such words as "boy" or "gal" regardless of the person's age, "auntie," or simply "nigger." Whites expected black household workers to enter white homes through the back doors, black pedestrians to step off sidewalks when whites passed by, and under no circumstance was a black man to glance, let alone stare, at a white woman.

The routine, mundane quality of racial oppression created opportunities for African Americans to express their opposition to Jim Crow in their everyday lives. The strategies blacks employed to resist racial oppression had to remain creative and adaptable, as the laws and customs with which they were expected to comply varied from place to place, circumstance to circumstance, and day to day. Resistance to Jim Crow could mean anything from joining a civil rights organization to sitting at a whites-only lunch counter. Parents defied landlords who tried to force their children to leave school to work in the cotton fields. Workers threw down their tools and struck when employers tried to lower pay scales. Individuals tested the boundaries of Jim Crow by talking back to white men, challenging white landowners for a larger share of the profits during "settling up" time, and by finding ways to insulate their families from white coercion.

Black household workers challenged Jim Crow when they refused to enter the back door of an employer's home, as Olivia Cherry of Norfolk, Virginia, tells us in her experience: "I worked for a lady one time in town that refused to let me in the front door, and I [would] go to the back and call her and come back to the front door. I refused to go to the back door. . . . I knocked and rang and called her. She never did come, because she was determined for me to come to the back. I went home and went to bed, and that was the end of that job." Other African Americans refused to patronize restaurants and shops where the owners and employees did not treat them with the same respect afforded to white patrons. Georgia Sutton of New Bern, North Carolina, relates a strong admonition from her mother, who forbade her from supporting such businesses. Similarly, Wilhelmina Baldwin of Tuskegee, Alabama, refused to buy clothing from a shop that would not allow her to try on merchandise.

Marie Fort of Memphis, Tennessee, relates an incident in which her son and his friend drank from the white water fountain at a Sears department store. "Sears had a sign up over the two water fountains, black and white. Well, my boy just went on and started drinking [from the white fountain] and this other little boy came up to drink, and the man said, 'Don't you see that's for white boys?' This little Jones boy said, 'I get white when I get thirsty.' "

Sometimes African Americans engaged in acts of armed resistance to defend themselves from hostile whites during especially intense moments of racial conflict. When Police Chief Petty inquired about Thomas

Chatmon's safety and promised police protection when he was targeted by Ku Klux Klan violence during his run for city commission, Chatmon replied, "I ain't worried, Chief. . . . All my friends [are] out here with shotguns."

Contesting segregation also required blacks to confront the bureaucracy of white political power. They established organizations such as the National Association for the Advancement of Colored People and the Universal Negro Improvement Association, seeking justice through litigation, demanding their right to vote by protesting the literacy or poll tax, and attempting to register.

In addition to undisguised challenges to Jim Crow, African Americans also dissembled, speaking in a manner that conveyed accommodation, while keeping their true feelings and motivations to themselves. Black southerners frequently engaged in acts depicting the image of the "contented Negro" that defenders of Jim Crow tried to nurture. Henry Hooten of Tuskegee, Alabama, tells us: "Most times we would use strategy rather than use force. Be very kind. Use psychology on them. That would be the first thing the white man thought you knew less about was psychology." This technique often defused white rage, allowing blacks to avert injury, self-hatred, and despair.

Whether overt or disguised, African American resistance to white supremacy was costly. Rarely did whites allow a challenge to the color line to go unanswered. Blacks who sought to undermine or temporarily check the system had to weigh the unlikely prospects of success with the certainties of violent reprisals. Evictions, firings, lynchings, or mob attacks quickly followed on the heels of black protest against injustice. This grim reality weighed heavily on their minds as black people considered the consequences of protesting for their homes, families, and livelihoods. In the intense climate of racial hatred in the Jim Crow South, African Americans knew that the price of resistance could be their lives.

EDGAR ALLEN HUNT

African American parents employed a wide range of tactics and strategies—limiting their children's encounters with whites,

302 REMEMBERING JIM CROW

challenging unjust laws, lobbying to improve their schools, and feigning accommodation—to shield their children from the bitter truths of Jim Crow life. Edgar Hunt of Memphis, Tennessee, describes his father's use of physical force to protect his children, and the reprisals that followed quickly, after an incident in rural Arkansas during the 1920s that his father told him about when he was a boy.

[My father] had six kids and he was looking for work. He told me that he was on some man's plantation sharecropping and my two older brothers was out there picking cotton, you know. And he was picking cotton—he could pick 400 or 500 pounds a day, he could. But he said this white fellow whose plantation [he] was on come out there with a whip and said the boys wasn't picking enough cotton. And he was going to whoop them.

My daddy told him, "Well, these are my boys and I'll do the whipping. You know, they pick cotton, but they got to learn. They still young."

And [the white fellow] said, "Well, I'll go to whoop them. When I get through whooping them, they'll pick more cotton."

And he said, "No, don't hit them boys." Said he drew back that whip at them and my daddy come out with this little pocketknife and cut him. So he had to leave there running, you know. He went and hid in the woods, and they kept dogs looking for him for three weeks. He said he [was] eating hickory nuts and whatever he could get out there in the woods and go on up in trees and stay in there at night, until they kind of relented in the search.

He said after three weeks of staying in the woods and getting away from wild boars and things like that and climbing trees to get away from them and all that there, he sneaked back in there one night and got my mama and the children and left in the middle of the night. He said when he left there, he'd went [to] talk to my grandfather. [He] wanted him to ride up on the wagon with him because he was there, too, but on another plantation. And he said [it was] three o'clock in the morning. He went and got his mule and wagon and sneaked in there and left all the furniture and everything—just got the family and left in the middle of the night. And so that meant Grandpa had to leave, too. So he wound up in Blytheville [with] all of [us].

BRENDA BOZANT DAVILLIER

Born in 1941, Brenda Bozant Davillier calmly refused to remove herself from the front pews of a Louisiana Catholic church to the two back pews designated for African Americans. Responding to a letter from an archbishop promising the end of church segregation, a teenage Davillier staged a front-pew sit-in that challenged a social climate of racial hatred so intense that white members preferred to leave one side of a church empty and stand, rather than sit beside or behind "colored" congregants.

We went to Corpus Christi Church, which was a black, colored church. We didn't have any integration in the church because nobody white came to the church. When I was in the tenth grade the priest [at Corpus Christi Church] read a letter from the archbishop stating that there would be no more segregation in Catholic churches, that whenever you went into the Catholic church you sat anywhere you wanted to sit. That summer I went to Slidell to visit my grandmother. It was the summer after the tenth grade. Most of the African Americans were Baptist or another denomination. The Catholics in Slidell who were not Anglo-Saxon were few and far between. So we had the last two pews in the [Catholic] church [in Slidell]. I told my cousins, "We [can] sit wherever we want to sit in church now. We don't have to sit in the last two pews."

The way things were then in the country, we'd walk that mile to church and then if you wanted to go to confession, you'd go before Mass and go knock on the rectory door and ask to speak to someone to hear your confession and he would do it. The church was always open like an hour before Mass. So I got my two cousins [who were] younger than me—I didn't want my older sister or anybody else to know what I was doing—and some of my other cousins. All of them [were] younger than me. I said, "Now we're going to go to church early [and] we're going to go all the way up to the front and sit in the first pew, and if anybody tells you to move, don't move." I told my cousin, my good friend, "You sit on that end and I'm going to sit on this end and don't let anybody out." I said, "If anybody tells you anything, just sit there and say your prayers and don't even look around." [We went into the] church. Nobody was in there. We sat in the front row. Two ushers came early. You could hear them talking in the back. They came up and talked to us and said, "You have to move." We didn't answer. We just sat in church and didn't move. They couldn't make us move.

Well, it was summertime. There was no air-conditioning and people came to church and, as I told you, we had all colors in our family. So we had all colors across the front of the church. Nobody would sit behind us. So there was one whole side of the church empty and people were standing up all in church. A couple of people fainted because they wouldn't sit behind us. I was in tenth grade. My cousin was in about the eighth grade and some of the other ones were younger than that. The adults—colored, Negro, African American, whatever—none of them came and sat up there with us. They sat in the last two pews.

Needless to say, our parents found out. The only one who could go to church after that with me was my cousin, the one who sat on the other end. But every Sunday we'd go up to the front of the church, either the first or the second [pew], as close as we could get to the front of the church for the whole summer. And gradually people began to [change]. They wouldn't sit with us. They might leave the pew behind us empty, but they had to eventually start sitting behind us. When Father came in for Mass, why he couldn't say anything because the bishop had given his letter. But he was a big man. He was fat and he was big, Father Tim. He was out there. He was glaring at us. It looked like he was about to explode, but he couldn't do anything.

One of the Sundays I went before [Mass] because we'd always go to confession about once a month. I knocked on the rectory door. "Father, could you come hear my confession?" He slammed the door in my face.

WILHELMINA GRIFFIN JONES

Wilhelmina Griffin Jones of Tuskegee, Alabama, born in 1915 to farming parents, identified herself as "Miss Griffin" to a white police officer, an act of defiance that required Jones and her companion to appear before a judge. During the 1943 court proceedings, Jones remained indignant, refusing to adhere to racist protocol, while her companion

Drafted soldiers bound for Camp Pike, New Iberia, Louisiana, 1917.
(New Iberia Parish Library, New Iberia, Louisiana)

used veiled compliance and prevailing stereotypes to manipulate public officials.

This was in 1943. I had come to Tuskegee in 1942 to work at the Tuskegee Army Airfield. On a Saturday afternoon another couple who were friends of mine and another male friend of mine decided to ride up to Opelika, Alabama, that afternoon. We got back into Tuskegee just about dusk. As we drove north on Main Street where the Alabama Exchange Bank is now located, just before we got to the median on Main Street, and of course I was driving the car, we heard a whistle blow. My friend who was riding in the back with his friend said, "Wilhelmina, I think the police is blowing for us, and maybe you had better stop."

Well, I had seen a man standing in the middle of the street at the median with a lantern, but so many people at that time would try to hitchhike from the city back to the Tuskegee Army Airfield I really paid him no attention. I thought it was someone trying to get a ride back to the Tuskegee Army Airfield, and I drove slowly past and my friend said again, "I think he wants us to stop, so you'd better stop." And I did. When I stopped he got on his motorcycle, which was located down by the Alabama Exchange Bank, and drove on up to where we were. He drove over to the side where I was and he asked [if I saw] that man standing there with a lantern.

I told him, "Yes, I saw the man, but I thought he was trying to get a ride back to the Tuskegee Army Airfield."

And he said, "Well, no, he wasn't trying to get a ride back." There had been a fire across the next street over and there was a fire hose stretched across the street.

I said, "Well, I certainly didn't recognize that, and if it was [a fire hose] it felt just like one of the ridges in the pavement."

So he talked on and in a few minutes my friend in the rear of the car said, "Officer, if we have done any damages, or if we've done anything that we shouldn't have done and there is a fee or whatever, we're willing to pay whatever is necessary."

So he said, "No, you're going to have to come down to court on Monday."

And my friend still tried to persuade him to let us do whatever else would satisfy the situation but he wouldn't.

Then he looked at me and he said, "What's your name?"

I said, "My name is Miss Griffin." I wasn't married at the time.

And he took his little pad which he had in his hand and his pencil, and he put it down on his motorcycle and looked straight at me and he said, "Don't you know we don't 'Miss' any niggers down here!"

I didn't say anything of course. He then picked up his little pad again, and he started writing and again my friend tried to talk to him and said, "Well, Officer, what is it we have done? If we've done anything that we shouldn't have done we're willing to pay whatever is necessary."

So he wrote on; he said, "No, you're coming down on Monday to the mayor's court."

So he wrote the ticket out and gave it to us and we drove on. And of course after we left that spot my friend was saying, "It looks like we're going to have to come back down to city hall on Monday. You know how these people are about outsiders and especially, you know, if you're from the North. They're not going to be very kind to us, and maybe you'd better not use the word 'Miss' again."

So I said, "Well, I'll do the best I can."

And on Monday, sure enough, we came back down to city hall, and we had to go into the mayor's office, and he had us in this large room with this long table, and at the end of the table he and the sheriff sat. He put me at the other end of the table.

I need to back up just a little bit. When my friend came back with me on Monday he came dressed for the occasion. He had on overalls with one suspender hanging to the side, and a cap with the bill turned in the back, some old dusty shoes without strings and his sleeves rolled up, that sort of thing, collar open. He did this because he felt like doing this kind of thing would certainly make him be more lenient, which he was. He would have charged us a with whole lot more if he didn't act the way he wanted him to react, you see.

I dressed like I was on Saturday, the same way. I was well dressed, and as I talked to him I didn't change my language at all. He wasn't very pleased with me at all, but he was very pleased with my friend because of the way he reacted and the way he had come dressed and that sort of thing.

So the mayor told him to take a seat over here by the wall and he did. So the mayor was facing me down the table, and he went on to say, "Didn't you see that man standing out there with the hose on Saturday?"

I said, "Yes, I saw him."

Well, he went on to explain again that there had been a fire and all of this sort of thing, that I had run over the hose, and I explained, "Well, I didn't know that I had run over a hose. I wasn't driving fast at all, and it just felt like a ridge in the street."

"Furthermore," he said, "where were you raised?"

And I hesitated for a moment and I said, "I was reared in Georgia."

He said, "Well!" [He] put his hands on both sides of the table and he sort of sat up straight and said, looked at me, and he said, "You should have known better than to call yourself 'Miss Griffin.' " He said, "I haven't ever 'Missed' a nigger in my life and I don't ever expect to. I played with niggers. I ate with niggers. But I've never 'Missed' a nigger and

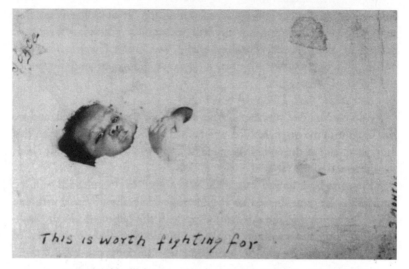

Loretta Joyce Caldwell, daughter of Leola and Grady Caldwell, a World War II
serviceman, at three months of age, 1949. (Courtesy of Leola Caldwell, Albany, Georgia)

I don't ever expect to." And of course while he was saying this, the old
sheriff was sitting there just smiling. I didn't say anything after that.

Then he turns to the sheriff and he said, "Let's see what this boy over
here's got to say for himself." So he looked over at my friend and said,
"Boy!" And the moment he said that my friend popped up and started
sort of fidgeting with his trousers and that just pleased [the mayor] to
no end.

So he said, "Boy, what's your name?" And he told him his name. He
said, "Where do you work?"

And my friend said, "Your honor, sir, I works at the primary field."
And of course the primary field meant the Tuskegee Airport. That's
where they trained the black pilots who fought in World War II. So he
told him he worked at the primary field.

He said, "What you do out there, boy?"

He said, "I's the janitor, sir." And oh, that brought a big smile when
he said he was the janitor. So the mayor looked at him, and then he
turned around to his deputy. And he said, "Now, you see, he looks like a
good boy. We're going to be real lenient on them. We're going to charge

them $17." And he had the sheriff to write the ticket out. When he wrote it out, he handed it to my friend and said, "Now you take that on around there to the office and pay them $17."

We laughed about it afterward and he wasn't angry at all. But it would have been a whole lot harder for me to have done that, though. I just couldn't have done it. But knowing my friend who did this sort of thing, he can shift from one personality to another very easily. And it wasn't very hard for him to do. Yes he really felt that he had been very deceptive.

LEON ALEXANDER

Jim Crow laws were often designed specifically to disenfranchise black citizens. County and state legislators manipulated redistricting tactics and suffrage restrictions—ranging from literacy tests and property clauses, to requiring applicants to memorize and recite selections of the U.S. Constitution—all with the goal of preventing African Americans from voting. Leon Alexander, a coal miner born in 1910, recounts how southern registrars manipulated voter registration requirements, devising ways to disqualify black Americans despite their ability to meet literacy and other arbitrary standards.

At that particular time I went up to the country courthouse to the board of registrars. I walked in and the [registrar] was in there. He started washing his hands. He washed his hands until two white people came in, and he dried his hands off and came and waited on them. Then, he went right back to washing his hands again. Finally, he came and just like this he said: "What you want, boy?" I said, "I wants to register to vote." So he got a registration form and laid it out there before me and I tried to figure it out. He came back and looked at it, balled it up, and threw it in the wastebasket. All he said was, "You disqualified, you didn't answer the question." I believe this was during the time that "Big Jim" Folsom was governor.

Well, I was a representative on a grievance committee of the United Mine Workers. I was at Edgewater Mine, so it was in the 1940s. I went

Poll tax receipt. (Courtesy of Charles Donaldson, Anderson, South Carolina)

over to the district [union] office. I had to go over there [because] we had a [grievance] case coming up. Somebody asked me where had I been. I told him I had been over the courthouse trying to register to vote. So one of them asked me: "Well, did you have any luck?" I said, "No, they didn't even read the thing. He just picked it up and balled it up and throwed it in the wastebasket and told me I didn't pass."

So Tom Crawford, who later became president of District 20, was there with a guy named Bean. Tom Crawford picked up the telephone, and he called Montgomery and he called the governor. He being a [union] representative, the governor wasn't in no hurry to talk to him, so they put him on hold, and he held for so long that he hung up. So Tom went in to the president of District 20, William Mitch. He went into his office and told him what he was up against when [he] called Montgomery, so William Mitch picked up the telephone and he called

Montgomery. And just like that he got through to the governor; so he talked with the governor, told him, "I have a man here, said he has been over to the courthouse to try to register to vote, and the registrar disqualified him without even looking at the form." [Governor] Folsom told him to tell me to go back to the courthouse again, go right back over there, but this time to take some witnesses with me.

Ed Bean and Tom Crawford volunteered to go over there with me, so we walked right back across to the courthouse. I walked in, and they were standing in the hall when I walked up there. Same guy. He saw me and his hands got dirty again, so he went to the sink to wash his hands again. So finally Tom Crawford and Ed Bean walked in, and he dried his hands off and went to wait on them, and they told him, said, "He was here before we were. Why don't you wait on him?" He said, "Well, hell, I done disqualified him." Then Tom Crawford said, "Let me see that paper that you threw in the wastebasket there." The [registrar] said, "Who is you?" He still ain't reaching at the paper so [Crawford] told him. "I'm the district representative for the United Mine Workers, and I want to see that paper. I want to see what grounds you put on there that you disqualified him on." The registrar said, "Did I have to have grounds to disqualify him?" Tom said, "No, but you better have a damn good reason for disqualifying him, and I still want to see that paper." He still wouldn't give him the paper; he stood there still trying to argue with him, and Ed Bean went around the counter and got the paper out of the wastebasket, and he smoothed it back out. And when he saw that Ed Bean had got that paper, he told him to give it to him. Bean said, "No, I'm going to give it to Governor Folsom." "What you going to give it to him for?" Bean said, "I'm just going to give it to him, [to] show him what you are doing to blacks here in Jefferson County, and if I can, I'm going to damn sure get your job." That's what Ed Bean told him. So the registrar got another form and handed it to him. I filled it out. There wasn't any difficult questions on it. At that particular time you had to have two registered voters to sign the form, [and] Ed Bean and Tom Crawford both were registered voters. So, when I filled it out, [the registrar] looked at it. He said, "Well you got to go get two white registered voters to sign it." Now that wasn't a rule that the state had, that was a rule that the board of registrars made, because there were very few qualified voters at this particular time [in Alabama].

Ed Bean and Tom Crawford both were white, so while he was telling me that, Tom Crawford asked Ed Bean: "Are you a qualified voter?" He said, "Yeah!" He said, "Are you white?" "Yes," he said, "yes, I am," and they signed it, right there in his office. [The registrar] said, "Well I'll let you know within the five days whether you passed or not."

So, Ed Bean asked him, "It didn't take five days for me to know." Said, "I didn't have no two white voters to sign to vouch for me. Nobody signed it but me. Now why you got to have five days?" The registrar said, "Well, that is the custom." Ed Bean said, "You look at that and tell me whether he answered all the questions correctly that's on there." The registrar said, "Well, this is something that is private, I don't have to tell you." He said, "Okay, don't tell me."

So we left and went on over to the district office and told President Mitch what had happened over there. Mitch picked up the telephone, and he called Montgomery again, and he relayed to the governor what he had told him. Anyway, it wasn't long before the registrar called the district office. The governor must have just called and told [the registrar] where I was because Mitch told [the governor] that I was at his office. So [the registrar] called the office and asked to speak to me. I picked up the phone and he said, "I reckon you satisfied now. You got the governor registering you to vote!" I said, "Sure enough?" He said, "Yeah. I'm not telling you because I want to tell you; I'm telling you this because the governor told me to tell you. You passed and you are a qualified voter."

The next week I received a certificate from the board of registrars notifying me that I was a qualified voter. But they didn't put me on the voting list! Now that's [when] something peculiar happened. The *Birmingham Herald* or *Post Herald* would print the entire Jefferson County voting list in the morning's paper, the morning of the election, and I had told some friends of mine that I had qualified. They had looked all the way through the voting list and ain't found my name nowhere. So I called Bill Mitch and told him, "I got the notice from the board of registrar that I had passed and was a qualified voter," I said, "but the only thing [is] my name is off of the voting list." He said, "You mean that [one in the] newspaper?" I said, "No. I mean I went to the poll, and they looked at it and told me in spite of me having a notice from the board of registrar that I had passed and was a qualified voter, that I couldn't vote."

So he called [the registrar] and asked him what happened. [The registrar said,] "Well I passed him and I sent him a notice that he had passed." [Mitch] said, "But did you put his name on the voting list?" [The registrar replied,] "Oh! That step I forgot to do!" [Mitch] said, "Well, you call the precinct where he voting and tell them." He said, "No, he have to come." [Mitch] said, "No, he ain't coming up there—you call down there and tell them to add his name to it and let him vote."

So that's how my first voting experience went because this guy had no intention of registering [me], not only no intention of registering me, he had no intention of registering any black to vote. He didn't have no intention of doing that, and the only way that we got that was by the governor threatening to fire him out of that office—the chairman of the board of registrars.

Now, when you hear me talking, it sound like I'm talking, or I'm saying that only blacks had a difficult time of registering to vote, but that is not so. It was a whole lot of white[s] had a difficult time. Whites in Walker County, white[s] in St. Clair County—especially in these mining counties. Whites had a difficult time because the coal operators didn't want them—black nor white—only those people that they controlled and wanted to vote. Those were the people, whether you white or black. If the operator wanted a black to be qualified to vote, he just send him down there and called down there and they qualified. If he didn't want to pass, whether he's white or black, he didn't pass. Now it just wasn't a black versus a white thing. This was the coal steel barons and the big coal operators in this state; [these] were the people who controlled the voting in this state.

And so I read a whole lot of times in history how they treated the black in certain instances. But it wasn't just how they treated the black in certain instances. It was how the coal operators treated men period. Whether they white or black. They played the white against the black, that was their chief weapon to keep us divided, so they could mistreat both of us. They weren't just mistreating the black; they was mistreating the white as well.

Those were the things we were fighting against. They let [select people] register when the registration is supposed to be open and free. But it wasn't open, and it definitely was not free. It was neither one of those things.

GEORGE KENNETH BUTTERFIELD JR.

North Carolina Superior Court Judge George Kenneth Butterfield Jr. remembers Wilson, North Carolina, as a city where only 40 African Americans were registered to vote in 1928. By the late 1950s, one out of every four voters was black. As Butterfield explains, the right to vote in many cases was offered as a "privilege," offered to a select few who thereby obtained access to what became an "exclusive club." This system reduced voter registration to a form of patronage, imposing a burden of indebtedness and obligation on the registrant. Combined with the ever-present fear of violent reprisals, such machinations buttressed the power of white public officials and limited the number of African American voters.

[M]y father finished dental school in '27, worked in Henderson for a year, and came to Wilson in '28. He told me when he came to Wilson that there were 40 blacks registered to vote in Wilson. Those who wanted to register found it difficult because of impediments in the registration process such as the literacy test. And it was so subjective; the registrar had to pass upon your qualifications, and it was done very arbitrarily. And of course, the majority of the black community did not want to register for fear of reprisal from the majority community. But the few blacks who did want to register were dissuaded or actually denied the right to register. And there were only 40, I'm told, in 1928 who were actually registered to vote. Many of those were Republicans, incidentally. It was a privilege. I recall my father telling me that it was considered a real accomplishment if you were permitted to register to vote. That many whites would permit blacks to register as a favor to certain blacks, to extend the privilege to them and not to others was to make the one being allowed to register feel that he had a special place in the community. It was really used as patronage or some type of device that was supposed to make you indebted to those who made it possible for you to register.

My dad came in, and he was approached by several middle-class blacks with the idea that they would try to fix it so he [could] register to vote, that if they could pull it off, he should consider it an honor and a privilege, and that it would be an exclusive club that he would belong to, and he should not rock the boat and try to change it. But they would

G. K. Butterfield's 1953 campaign postcard, Wilson, North Carolina.
(Courtesy of G. K. Butterfield, Wilson, North Carolina)

lobby certain people to get him registered. And so, he was permitted to register because he was a professional and they thought he would be a good addition to the good ole boy club. Once he became registered, he began to ask questions as to why the masses of the people could not register to vote, and that caused quite a stir in the community.

He was very active in voter registration and as time went on barriers did begin to fall. He and others would take citizens up to the courthouse. They would sit up the night before and rehearse the Constitution, because they would have to read and write the Constitution. And they would get up to the courthouse and some would pass and some would not. Even educated blacks were denied because it was just the whim of the registrar. But some were registered to vote, and as time went on, the numbers began to increase.

He and my mother's brother, who was politically involved, spearheaded the voter registration movement. So much so, that in 1953 my dad decided to run for the city council. We called it then the board of aldermen.

The city of Wilson was small at the time. It was divided into six wards—we now call them election districts—and the wards were irregular in shape. When they were first devised, they were drawn irregularly in such a fashion that the black community could never have a majority in either of these six wards. That was very purposeful in the way it was designed. Ward 3, for example, was about two blocks wide. Sort of like the twelfth congressional district now from Gastonia down to Durham—very irregular. I listen to the criticism now of the twelfth congressional district and that was the ward system in Wilson many years ago, and no one criticized it. At least from the media it was not criticized, but the ward was two blocks wide and about two miles long. And the whole purpose of it was to ensure that the black community never could reach a majority within the ward. But my dad and my uncle worked very diligently in ward 3 trying to bone up voter registration.

And sure enough, in 1953, my dad ran for the board of aldermen seat in ward 3, and there was a tie vote between him and the white candidate. And to break the tie, both names were put into a hat and a young child pulled out a name and he was victorious. So he was elected in '53 from the ward. That was unheard of.

Then in '55 he ran for reelection and won reelection. No one felt that he would win reelection. [In] 1955 they thought they could defeat him in ward 3, but what the power structure didn't know was that there was a white fellow running for mayor named John Wilson who was a long shot. The pendulum has now swung, and he's now ultra, ultra, ultra conservative. He has that problem. He was running for mayor and went to my dad and said, "Look fellow, if you can get the Negro community to support me for mayor and if I am elected, then I will appoint you as the chairman of the most powerful committee on the City Council, on the board of aldermen." So they cut a deal, a political deal. And the Negro community at that time supported John Wilson and he became the mayor.

My dad was named chairman of the finance committee. [I]t was unheard of for him to be on the board much less the chairman of the most powerful committee on the board. Back then, budgets for municipalities had to be approved by the legislature. And so it was always customary for the finance chairman to take the budget to the legislature for approval. And so when the budget was adopted that year for the city, my father had to take it to Raleigh to the legislature for approval. He presented the first million-dollar budget for this city in whatever year that was. Fifty [1950], the legislature meets in odd numbered years so that would have been '55. They didn't like him being in Raleigh in the legislature because it was a lily-white environment, and for this man to come up with a million-dollar budget from a rural eastern North Carolina tobacco town was just unheard of. The budget was approved, but then there was a determination on the part of the majority community to defeat him, and to make it impossible for any black to get elected to the board of aldermen.

So what happened, in 1957, the election was scheduled for May of '57, and in February of '57 there was a vote at one of the board of aldermen meetings to change the system from a ward system to an at-large system. It was not on the agenda. It hadn't been discussed in a working session. It came as a complete surprise to my daddy. He's sitting there on the board one night, and all of a sudden at the close of the meeting, somebody raised their hand. Yes. He said, whoever made the motion, made a motion to eliminate wards, go to at-large and not only to go to an at-large system, but to make it illegal for any voter to cast a single-shot vote. It's what they called an anti-single-shot law. You had to vote for a full slate, else your vote would be thrown out, and mathematically that is a device for suppressing minority voting strength, because even under at-large systems, if we single-shot voted, then we could enhance our vote. It could become more potent, because we weren't sharing votes with the white candidates, and single shot was a device that we used for years. So they adopted not only an at-large system, but also an anti-single-shot vote law.

Of course it had to be approved by the legislature. It was taken to the legislature by the local representative of that time, and it passed as a local bill in the legislature. And all of a sudden, we went from a district method of election to an at-large method of election, plus an anti-single-shot provision, which made it impossible, impossible. Where blacks may have been 45 or 50 percent of ward 3, when they had to run at-large, we may have been 15 or 20 percent of the registered voters of the at-large system, which made it impossible to win. And so he ran again in '57 and was defeated. Terribly defeated. And he came in last or near last. And so we went without black representation on city council from, from

Durham Committee on Negro Affairs, Durham, North Carolina, 1935.

(Durham Public Library, Durham, North Carolina)

'55, from '57 onward, up until the middle seventies. Even though blacks would run each year. Couldn't win.

In '59 our pastor, who was actively involved, decided to challenge legally the anti-single-shot provision of the law. That case went all the way to the U.S. Supreme Court, in *Watkins v. City of Wilson* (1962). And the U.S. Supreme Court upheld the lower court's decision and that was: Since the plaintiffs, the blacks, could not demonstrate that the election result would have been different had there not been the anti-single-shot provision, they had failed to prove their case, and the U.S. Supreme Court agreed. But 10 or 15 years later, the courts struck down the anti-single-shot law. We were just before our time.

STINE   GEORGE   AND   DORIS   STRONG   GEORGE

Despite Jim Crow laws, policies and practices for limiting African American participation in electoral politics and despite explicit threats and intimidation, southern blacks in some communities were able to maintain a tenuous grasp on the franchise and civic involvement. These achievements came with varying degrees of success. Stine George, born in 1931, and his wife Doris George, born in 1929, provide an illuminating commentary on black voters' troubling position as swing voters in Moultrie, Georgia, where they were both central and marginal in the town's elections.

Doris George. [White candidates] used to almost beg black folks to register to vote in Moultrie. We didn't have no problem because we were the most powerful group. We were the swinging group. The white folks [would] come over here and have some barbecue or some whiskey. If you got two white men running, they needed the black people's support to win.

Black people weren't allowed to even run. They could vote, but they had to vote for a white person. Sometimes we would use a bloc vote. We'd try to get the lesser of the two evils. Both of them was evil, and they'd come in there and say we're going to pick up your garbage. Then they would have a big fish fry for you. They'd have plenty of liquor and beer. The other one would have something else for you trying to persuade the black folks to vote for them. They still would have had a hard time running just with white people because everybody had some friends, you know.

But see, we didn't have no positions, and they didn't have to promise us very much because we didn't have nothing but dirt streets over here. They said, "We'll straighten the streets more. We'll pick up the garbage more regular," you know, stuff like that. Or either didn't say nothing, just give you [liquor and food].

Then we had some black folks would go out there and say, "We're going to support this so-and-so because he said he's going to do so-and-so and he's going to have a party for a year." At Christmastime they'd send all the people a fruitcake or a pint of whiskey. They would try and get your vote.

Stine George: That's what they'd do. All the elections in every town we had separate situations. Some of them would actually give barbecue and some of them would just give out half pints of liquor to any individual that would take it in the community. Sometimes they'd give simply

$2, go out and give all the black folks in the neighborhood. They knew who they were, the ones that registered.

DG: But anyway, both of them white, and you don't know nothing about each one, but we had some black people in [positions of leadership] because most black folks voted strictly bloc. It might be one or two, but whoever the black folks decide to support that was it. And these white folks was trying to get the black people to vote. Because see these days they try to win on the first go-round, but a lot of time you got four or five people in there. They couldn't get 51 percent of the votes without the black votes. So therefore to get black folks to come in, 400 or 500, that would help them win. But neither one promised much.

Black folks would vote, all of them vote in Moultrie. [In other communities] they'd say [that] we don't know what we're talking about; over there they don't let black folks vote, [but] they vote in Moultrie. But you still didn't get nothing. It still wasn't voting really because they didn't promise you nothing.

MAURICE LUCAS

Membership in the National Association for the Advancement of Colored People brought with it the fear of violent retaliation and loss of livelihood. Maurice Lucas of Renova, Mississippi, born to sharecropping parents in 1944, describes the discovery of his father's NAACP membership, and the action his father took to avoid being lynched. Because of this incident and others like it, the Lucas family earned the reputation of being "blacks that don't take stuff."

I can remember in 1957 Daddy joined the NAACP. Daddy's baby sister was in school [in] Nashville, Tennessee, at Tennessee State. She paid for my daddy's membership in the NAACP and the mailman that delivered it went and told the white folks that Mr. Lucas had joined the NAACP. The old mailman went and told some people, and they were going to come and then do their thing. They were bad about shooting at black people's houses [to] discourage them if they thought they were participating in any kind of civil rights activity. They came to mob us that night.

Tobacco workers' walkout, R. J. Reynolds Tobacco Company, Winston-Salem, North Carolina, 1943. (North Carolina Department of Archives and History, Raleigh, North Carolina)

But one of the white deputies was a friend of Daddy's. [He] tipped us off. Daddy and them was laying in the ditch with them rifles and started shooting, and they haven't bothered us since.

The Lucases had a history of not taking no stuff off of no white folks. My mama was like that. Mama was a little old half peckerwood. Big Mama was a great big old black woman, and she was educated. And man, she didn't take no stuff off no white folk and Papa didn't, either.

And do you know, white folks know the blacks that don't take stuff off of them and that reputation has followed us all the way to this day. It really has. We have a reputation of treating folks right, but we don't take no stuff, especially off of the white folks.

THOMAS CHRISTOPHER COLUMBUS CHATMON

Thomas Chatmon, born in Cuffee County, Georgia, in 1919, began during the 1950s what eventually became a chain of beauty supply shops throughout Florida and Georgia. Chatmon combined his entrepreneurial activities with a commitment to political activism. He helped to integrate Southern Bell Telephone Company and the local police force. Although recognizing that he and his family faced substantial risk in becoming involved with the NAACP, Chatmon founded the NAACP youth council following an incident at the Albany, Georgia, movie theater. Chatmon successfully ran for town council, but the white community refused to allow him to hold the office he had legally won.

There was a picture downtown in the old Albany Theater. Sidney Poitier was playing in this picture. A group of the Monroe High School students went down on a Sunday to see this picture. Well, we had to go upstairs, and the whites went downstairs. The picture was so popular the whites filled up downstairs, and after filling up downstairs, the whites wanted to go upstairs and sit down and asked the blacks to stand up. And this particular group of Monroe High School students told them, "No, we're not going to get up and give y'all our seats. We're up here in our place. This is our place upstairs."

So they went down and told the manager of the theater and he came up and said, "Well, y'all are going to have to get up and let these people sit down."

They said, "Well, we want our money back."

He said, "Well, come on down and I'll give you your money back." And so he did.

And that Monday morning they went to the principal, Professor Herd, and they told him what had happened. Herd told them, "Well, I'll tell you what. You go see Reverend Adams and see what Reverend Adams thinks about it." Herd sent them to Reverend Adams, who was the pastor of the Presbyterian church here because he was [also] the president of the NAACP. And they went and told Reverend Adams what had happened to them that Sunday down at the Albany Theater and he said, "Well, there's a young man in town, he hadn't been here too long, I think he's the right man for y'all to go to see."

Reverend Adams sent them to me. They came to my store that Monday morning, and I asked them may I help them and they said, "Reverend Adams sent us here to see you, Mr. Chatmon." I said, "What about?"

They said, "Well, if you've got a little time we can tell you." So I said, "Okay." So they related to me what had happened to them.

So I said, "What do y'all want to do about it?" And they said, "Well, that's why Reverend Adams sent us to you. You might have a suggestion." I said, "What we can do, we can organize an NAACP youth council." Over half of them—let's see, it was about seven or eight of them came—didn't know what I was talking about. So I explained to them the function of the NAACP youth council and I [asked], "Do you think y'all would like to do that?" They said, "Yes sir, Mr. Chatmon, we'd like to do that, anything to help us."

I immediately picked up my phone, I called Atlanta—Ruby Hurley was the overseer of this southeast area for the NAACP—and I told her who I was and what I was calling about. She said, "Mr. Chatmon, I'll send Vernon Jordan." You know Vernon Jordan I'm sure. Vernon Jordan is just like my son. He's a big man now up in Washington, Clinton's partner. But anyway, he was the field secretary for the NAACP. She said, "I'll send Vernon down, and get y'all organized." Vernon came down and we got organized. They gave us a charter, and we started having what we called Freedom Dances every Friday night out here [in] a nightclub my friend owned. He didn't charge me anything. He said, "Chat, I won't charge you a dime because I sell enough drinks and sandwiches and things to make money off of those kids."

And we had a Freedom Dance for about three months. [We were] building our treasury up. I told them, "Now we've got to have some money, y'all, to fight this battle." And that's when I really became real active in the community here. And I got so involved in it, my wife, she got a little leery. She said, "Chatmon, you know, I don't know whether you're doing the right thing or not." I said, "Well, it's needed here. Something has got to happen because things ain't going right."

So I got more and more involved, and I opened a store in Miami and the election was coming up for city commission. I was in Miami one day and my phone rang and that was Slater King on the phone telling me to come back. He wanted me to run for city commissioner. Well, I knew this was not my home. This was his home. I said, "Slater, why don't you run?" He was a very successful real estate broker at that time. I said, "You know, this is not my home." He said, "Well Chat, you know, the black people don't like the King family too well. They wouldn't support me."

The editor of a black paper, *The Florida Star*, from Jacksonville, was in Miami and I knew him, Eric Simpson. I went up [that night] to this motel where they were stopping, and I was telling him, I said, "I had a phone call today, Eric. A friend of mine in Albany wanted me to come back and run for city commission." He said, "Chat, for God's sake go. I'll fly you back up there." I said, "Why would you say that?" He said, "Man, you need to run. I want to see you do it." Well you see, I had never even considered getting in politics or anything like that. So I came back and my pastor, Reverend Benjamin Gay, I talked to him about it and he said, "Well Chatmon, I think you'd be the right one." So he and Slater carried me down; we walked around town, and I qualified. They paid my qualifying fee.

My father came all the way from Fitzgerald. He was living in Fitzgerald, Georgia, and that's about 65 miles from here. He came over and drove people to the poll all day that day to vote for his son. And he just had his fun telling people he was proud of his son. "Yes, Mr. Chatmon, we're proud of your son, too," [they would reply] because they had never had a man to run, not a black man. [My father] worked hard that day for his son.

I actually won the race. I raised a strong campaign, and the next day after the election a white guy came right there and said, "Mr. Chatmon, I merely came by to let you know you won the race. But you know, Mr. Chatmon, we couldn't let you win, but you did win it." I said, "Thank you, sir." I have never seen that man since. So that was, you know, something for me to feel proud of there. At least he was decent enough to tell the truth.

But you know, somebody had to start the ball rolling, and I opened the door for all these black boys to be elected now. Yeah, sure did. And in 1970 I ran for the U.S. Congress. I ran a strong race then. But you know it just wasn't in the books for them to let you win, not then. But I was happy that I was living at the right time at the right place, I guess to do these things.

When I ran for city commission, the Ku Klux Klan burnt a cross three blocks from my home. And, of course, the chief had been alerted that they were going to burn this cross, and I had a chance to stand on my front porch and listen to the grand dragon made this statement: "Who in the hell this nigger, Thomas Chatmon, think he is running for city commission?" There were so many black people out there around my house that night, all kind of guns and everything. And an old man by the name of Cross, he had his pistol and shotgun. He came out, he said, "Mr. Chatmon, if you tell me to go out there and blow that damn cross down, I'll go out there and blow it down." I said, "No, Mr. Cross don't do that. I ain't never seen a cross burn before. It ain't bothering me."

But the chief called me [on the telephone] in the house and said, "Thomas." "Yes sir, Mr. Petty." I called him Chief Petty. He said, "I want you to know this, Thomas, I got a man will be patrolling that block all night and you don't have to worry about a thing. Ain't nothing gonna happen." I said, "I ain't worried, Chief. I'm happy." He said, "You happy?" "Yes, sir." "Why you so happy?" I said, "All my friends out here with shotguns." He said, "Oh Lord, God, Thomas, that's what I'm trying to avoid."

[Later] I made a speech in a little town called Pelham, Georgia, one Sunday at a Baptist church. The pastor got up and asked the audience after I spoke, saying, "Now look, don't you all go back and tell these white people what Mr. Chatmon said the other day." So I told him, "Reverend, I don't mind them telling these white folks what I said because I'm telling the truth." Sure enough, some of the maids went back and did tell them. I went to Camilla [Georgia] that next weekend. My wife and I used to send cards to the beauty shops to let them know the day I was coming. They intercepted one of my cards, and they knew I was coming through there, and they laid in wait for me.

Two old *burly*, big white men, they was in a pickup truck. They drove beside me when I was fixing to leave Camilla to go to Pelham and pointed to the side and wanted me to park. Well, I didn't have nothing in mind; I didn't think nothing about it, so I just pulled on over. So one got out and came over there. I rolled my window down. He said, "What's that you got over there in the back there, boy?" I had a lot of beauty supplies in my station wagon, and I said, "Pardon?" When I said, "Pardon," that cracker slapped me so hard, boy, I seen stars. He said, "You the damn nigger from Albany, came down here and made that speech last week." Well, a white lady at that time came out of her house, it was raining just like it is now, to take in her clothes, and that's the only thing that kept that cracker from killing me. They had planned to kill me, see. Two old crackers, redneck crackers. Well, I understand one of them was a deputy sheriff. That's what I heard afterward. But I know that they had planned to kill me, and this white lady came out, and they saw her and his conscience just wouldn't let him do it.

He pointed a finger and said, "Now you be careful, boy, you be careful." Man, I was so scared, good Lord. Oh, Lord. I didn't say anything because there was nothing for me to say. I gave up because there was nothing I could do. But that's why I know God protected me all those times. I have been protected many times in dangerous spots like that. And the only somebody that could have brought me through was God himself.

[A]rriving back home early, my wife wanted to know why I come out. I told her I was feeling a little bad. I wouldn't tell her what happened because, if I had, she wouldn't want me to go back anymore. She knew where I was, and she knew what had been going on. She was always afraid something was going to happen to me. Anyway, I told her, "Don't think like that, think positive because you can't allow this fear to get to you." That's what Franklin Roosevelt told us years ago. [He said], "The only thing you had to fear was fear itself." You got to get rid of that. You can't be afraid. But I've had many experiences down here when I first came here, like I'd be riding down the highway in my new car, crackers run in the front of you and slow up, and you have to veer around and they'd duck back over, and all these kinds of things. Sometimes guys get so frustrated—and either they [whites] would kill them, or *they* [blacks] would kill them. But I wasn't thinking about anything. I came out here to make some money, and that's what I was thinking about, and that's what I kept on my mind. I know those poor crackers weren't going to buy nothing in the first place. They were nothing but devils anyway. It was bad down here. But I was already conditioned for that. I came out of it. I knew how it was. And I knew this: If I ever got financially sound that would straighten a lot of it out right there. See this thing, money is a powerful thing. Crackers respect that—your dollars and your votes, that's the same thing.

Frank Carter, Henry Hooten's father-in-law, during World War II petitioned the Escambia County School Board for the first school bus for African Amerian children in Pensacola, Florida. Until then Mr. Carter transported the children to school in his own truck, some 8–15 miles each way. Like his father-in-law, Henry Hooten tells in his narrative how he found ways to resist and overcome Jim Crow restrictions on African Americans.

(Henry and Lillian Hooten, Tuskegee, Alabama)

HENRY HOOTEN

By traveling in their own cars, black southerners restricted their exposure to potential humiliation on buses and trains. Henry Hooten and other black parents from Tuskegee, Alabama, joined together to purchase their own bus in an attempt to provide collective protection for their families. Still, while owning a bus enabled the families to avoid using segregated public transportation, it could not shield them from the potential dangers at segregated gas stations and lunch counters or from overzealous patrol officers.

We were always taught never to talk back to the white man but to tell him what he would like to hear. That's in order to save your face. You're not being Uncle Tom, but you're just being firm. Let him hear the things he would like to hear you say: "Yes sir." "No sir." "Yes ma'am." Being polite. At the same time you kept your mouth [closed].

We had a fishing club. Once a month we'd go down to Florida and fish in the Gulf of Mexico. Well, at first we would have little convoys of cars, like eight or ten or twelve cars with three or four people in a car. So one trip, we were on our way out of Alabama into Florida, which [was] mostly night driving. Well in a little town they call Laura Hill, Florida, they had a speed trap there. If you were running, say, 40 miles an hour, here on an incline, when you'd get to the bottom you'd still be doing 45 coasting, and the police would pick you up and they would fine you. So the first trip they picked us up. They picked the lead car and had everybody behind him to pull in, and each one had to pay $125 apiece, each car. So that night I made a suggestion: let's buy us a bus. If we're caught speeding we'll just have $125 rather than eight $125 [fines]. So we did, we bought a bus.

In 1949 I was a member of the recreations team at the V.A. Medical Center in Tuskegee. We were athletes just out of school, and we tried to do things for the patients. Everything we did was for the patients. We had baseball teams. We had basketball teams. We had tag and rag football teams on a modified scale and very safe. And when a patient saw you playing, if he was an athlete, [he] came out [to play]. Although he was a patient, he'd want to show you what he could do. So we played along with him. This was during the time when Larry Doby, Roy Campanella, Jackie Robinson, and Joe Black had their barnstorming baseball team. They were the few blacks that played on the big-league teams, and during the winter months they would come south and they would play us and different [teams].

Joe Black was introduced and he was on the staff of the Greyhound bus company; he was one of the vice presidents for it. So making a long story short, we bought a bus, an old Greyhound bus from the Greyhound bus company. During that time, every 10 years, Greyhound would take the old buses off and put new buses on. They would sell the old bus to the community—like church groups or organizations or whatnot, private groups.

We went up to Indianapolis, Indiana, one of the bus areas where they pulled the Greyhounds off the line at the end of 10 years. So four of us went up there and got this bus through the letter of Joe Black. Black being one of the vice presidents, they gave us a chance to view their buses. So we was able to buy this bus.

I'll never forget. We had 45 kids and mothers and dads on our way to the beach. We would leave Tuskegee at twelve o'clock at night, and we'd be in Florida at six o'clock in the morning. We had no place we could stop [like] at a motel. We had no place we could stop and eat but a segregated place. So Evergreen was the halfway point. So one night we pulled in. I was the driver of the bus. We had 45 kids or maybe 50—could have been two or three sitting in other's laps. But they had never been to the Gulf of Mexico, and we had taken them down to swim. We were taking them to Panama City, Florida. So at Evergreen, which was the halfway point as I said, we could pull in the same lanes behind the Greyhound buses and what we would do is gas up behind the Greyhound buses, and at the same time we had to stand in line to get a hot dog.

A hot dog wasn't but 25 cents at the time. But can you picture yourself feeding 45 kids [with] 25-cent hot dogs, and they're going to wait on the white man over in the other portion? They had a little cubbyhole for the Negroes to go in. So that night I had a bunch of kids, and they were scattered everywhere. And some of them went in the white side. My oldest son was one of those that went in the white side. So then we started to looking. We said, "Where is so-and-so? Where is so-and-so?" They said, "He went over next door to get him a hot dog."

Well, the white proprietor of the little restaurant there in the bus station got so excited [because] they'd never had that many blacks in there [on] both sides to get a hot dog—so they called the police. Well, the police came. The chief of police happened to own the station. So he was asking who was in charge, who was the bus driver. I was getting the bus filled up with diesel fuel. Diesel fuel was 25 cents a gallon at that time. And can you picture me filling up? One tank was 100 gallons and another tank was 50 gallons and I usually filled up both while we were there.

So the policeman asked me, "Boy, don't you know you can't go in here? This is segregated. You can't go in there and eat." I said, "Have you ever had a busload of hungry kids, no place to eat, and no place to go? Well, can you feature having a busload of 45 kids who want to eat and what are you going to do, look at them?" Then he said, "No, you can't just look at them. You know this is a segregated place. You can't come in here and eat. Well, you can't do that. I'll have to put you in jail."

I said, "Well, of course now, don't put no more gas in. We'll go. We'll leave you. I'll load them up and we're going to run out of gas down the road someplace. You wouldn't want us to run out of gas down the road when you could sell us the gas now?" [He said,] "No, no." I said, "Well, just cut my tank off. The amount that you put in there, don't put no more in it."

He said, "Well wait a minute. We can do better than this. We can do better than this."

I think what really let him feel the pinch was when I told him, "Don't put nothing else in the tank." That was a 150 gallons of diesel fuel at 25 cents a gallon and at that time that was a pretty good chunk of money. He wanted that money.

He only had about three white customers in there. He knew them, but they were laughing. [They] thought he was going to put all of us in jail. His little jail wouldn't hold all of us. So he said [to himself] I'd better feed them and sell them their gas and get them out of here.

He says, "I'll tell you [what], I'll just close my station to feed all of you." He closed the station. When he closed the station he fed everybody in both sides. He put [the white customers] to work waiting on us. He did! So evidently they were off-duty policemen. He was the chief of police and after they saw what he was going to do they helped him. They got back there and helped fix the hot dogs and everything.

See the money that he was going to get for gasoline, he wasn't going to get it because I told him, "Don't put another drop in." So he says, "All right, when are you coming back through here?" I said, "I'll be back through here tomorrow night." He says, "Well I'll tell you, I'll close soon as you get here." And we did that for most trips. We got diesel fuel and we came on home.

We got to be friends, although he was the chief of police in the little town of Evergreen, Alabama. He'd always ask me, "Henry, when are you bringing the kids down again? When you going to Florida?" I said, "Give us about two weeks. I think I'll have a load." He said, "Make it be twelve o'clock now when you get here." Twelve o'clock he'd close up the station. It would be closed when we'd get there. We'd try to make it be twelve o'clock each time to fill up with 25 cents a gallon of diesel fuel.

So that would be my halfway point to and from Florida, at Evergreen, to get service, use the restroom and then fill up with diesel fuel for 25 cents a gallon. Other than that I'd have to scuffle to find another place. But accidentally it worked. After he made that decision, that was it.

But I think we mentioned it to Joe Black, too, one time when we were making a payment on our bus that we had. "I understand that you went down to Florida and you stopped at Evergreen," [Joe Black says]. We said, "Yes. How did you know?" He says, "A policeman told me. He said y'all was very kind; you didn't create no incident and you got what you wanted."

We found that being courteous, not boastful or arrogant, you could solve the problem by talking. Just let them know.

OLIVIA CHERRY

Hampton, Virginia, native Olivia Cherry spent much of her early work life pushing against Jim Crow's barriers, first as a household worker who refused to enter employers' back doors, then as an agricultural laborer who demanded payment as promised, and finally as a clerical worker who sought employment in companies that hired blacks mainly to perform janitorial or industrial labor. In her search for a better livelihood, Cherry refused to adopt a submissive posture—whether confronting abusive public transportation drivers or refusing the belittling title of "gal" used by employers.

My name is Olivia, which I feel is a very pretty name. My mother thought that way. That's why she gave it to me. And I had trouble with my name.

I would be upstairs cleaning the bathroom. One white lady [I worked for] said, "Susie."

They loved to call me Susie. "Susie."

I didn't answer. I was a spunky kid then. I was like 13 or 14.

Finally, she come to the steps and said, "Olivia, you hear me calling you?"

I said, "Now I hear you. Now you said, 'Olivia.' That's my name."

[T]here was this white man and his girlfriend. They had a raspberry farm. They wanted us to pick the raspberries. I didn't really like [it] because it was backbreaking. So here we are picking the raspberries, and here goes my name again.

The man said, "Hey, Susie. Susie. You missed some on your row."

I knew he was calling me because this was my row, but I just kept on working.

He said, "Susie, don't you hear me talking to you?"

I said, "I told you before, my name is Olivia. Olivia. Can you say that?"

He said, "Don't be so 'd—' smart."

I went back and picked what he said I missed. It wasn't that I was working badly, I just overlooked it.

Well, another day he did the same thing.

"Susie, I want you to work down this end, and I want you to work with them." I just kept on working. He said, "Do you hear me telling you?"

I said, "Do you know my name? Can you learn my name?"

He said, "All right, whatever it is. I want you working down there."

So one day we went through this again.

He said, "Get the 'h—' off my property! I don't want you working for me at all."

I said, "Fine, because I don't want to work for you, but you have to pay me for the work I have done."

I already computed the amount. He told his girlfriend, "Pay her. Let's get rid of her."

I said, "No, this is not right. You owe me such-and-such cents."

"Pay her. Give her anything so we can get rid of her."

So she paid me, and I stepped out on the highway.

I said, "Come on, you all, you don't want to work for him. He doesn't know how to treat you."

They was standing there working and scared.

He said, "Get away from here! Get away from my property!"

I said, "Wait a minute. I'm on the highway. My mother and father paid taxes for this highway. This is not your highway." I said, "You leave me alone." And I went home and told my mother.

She said, "Oh, Lord! They're going to kill my daughter. I know they're going to kill my daughter."

[W]e were living in a place called Aberdeen Gardens that Franklin Roosevelt initiated for the low-income people, which is in Hampton near Newport News. There were 150 houses, beautiful development, where everyone had two to three bedrooms and a garage. You could use it for anything you wanted to. Everyone had a half a acre of land. Needless to say, white people were complaining, because this was a beautiful neighborhood. Out in Aberdeen we felt secure.

There were [potato] farms around us. We would go dig up the potatoes, and in the summer we children would have to put them in baskets to go to market.

[On] the potato farm, I had two close girlfriends. About seven or eight of us [were] looking for work. This man said, "Oh, yes, I'll dig the potatoes out, and you can put them in a basket."

I said, "How much?" I was always the spokesman, always the leader.

He said, "Ten cents a basket." That was 1939 or '40 so that was good money then.

So we said, "Okay."

[W]e did this, and we had to go at five o'clock in the morning because it was very hot, and we would be out in the field picking up those potatoes. One day we went and we picked the potatoes, worked diligently, and the man gave us five cents a basket.

I said, "Wait a minute. You told us 10 cents a basket."

He said, "Yes, I know what I told you," he said. "There were so many of us and we worked so fast. [H]e said, "I'm just going to give you five cents."

I said, "Okay." The girls were fussing. "Okay, that's fine." I said, "We'll see you tomorrow morning."

He looked at me.

[W]hen we left his farm, they said, "Olivia, what are you talking about?"

I said, "Don't worry, we're going back tomorrow and we're going to get even."

They said, "What we going to do?"

I said, "We're going to put the straw and stuff in the basket and put potatoes on top so you can't see it, and we get our money and leave."

[T]hey said, "Oh." "I'm scared," some said.

"Don't be scared, just be with me."

[W]e went on and that's what we did. He paid us and we come out of his farm and we got on the road just laughing and joking. [We] wouldn't even walk that way for a long time because we figured he'd be looking for us.

I was doing domestic work the next day in the area. The lady I worked for wanted you to come to the back door. I wouldn't go to the back door.

The lady said, "You must come to the back door."

I said, "No, I'm not going to the back door."

My reason was, my mother had to go to the back door to keep her job. My mother did domestic work. She didn't graduate. I wasn't better than my mother. I was avenging my mother.

I said, "I'm not going to the back door."

Two other girls and I would get off the bus, and we had a long walk. The stops were very far out there in between, and only black folks would get in the bus—sort of like it is today around here—because the white folks had their cars.

Anyway, on this particular day, it was raining so we had the umbrella. They walked me there to my house where I worked first. They said, "Come on, Olivia."

I said, "No, I go to the front door."

They led me to the front door and they went on and went to the back door. They wouldn't go to the front.

I worked for a lady one time in town that refused to let me in the front door, and I [would] go to the back and call her and come back to the front door. I refused to go to the back door.

One day I had cramps one Saturday. Mother said, "You going to work?"

I said, "Yes," because I didn't have a phone. I couldn't call her and tell her I wasn't coming. She was depending on me.

I had to walk then; it was quite a long walk, but it helped me. I knocked and rang, whatever the case was, and called her. She never did come because she was determined for me to come to the back. I went home and went to bed, and that was the end of that job.

I saw her in the grocery store a week or so after that, and her little boy come calling me and said, "Hi." She snatched him away and acted like I didn't know her.

So one day I caught the bus going to one of these ladies where I had to go through the front door, wouldn't go to the back. The bus driver, a woman, passed the stop. [This was] during the war, '42. She passed the stop and the stops were blocks and blocks away. I said, "Didn't you hear me ring the bell back there?"

She said, "What?"

I always looked younger than what I am, so she thought I was a snotty-nosed kid. She said, "What are you talking? What's wrong with you, gal?"

I said, "I rang the bell, and the stops are too far between anyway."

She said, "You better get the 'h—' off of my bus." My mother was on the bus.

The bus driver said, "Who is she? What's her name? I'm going to take all of you to your stop, then I'm going on into the [car barn]." That's where the buses park. "I have a cold. I'm sick. And then that little black gal just irritated me worse."

I wouldn't take the bus anymore because I was afraid I was going to run into her. I would walk all that way to work. But people walked then and thought nothing of it.

Then years later, after high school, going to Washington to business school, I would come back home on the bus. You get on the bus in Washington, you had to sit in the back, and it was nasty and dirty there. Anyway, they would stop in Richmond, and you go around to the back of the little [snack] stand where you're supposed to get your food, and it was just nasty, and it was slow waiting on you. It was our people waiting on us then. You could not come right to the front; you had to go to the back. I stood there one day and I said, "Oh, the heck with it. I can wait until I get home." It wasn't that far. But those were the things you had to put up with.

Then later I moved on to New York, and I integrated the accounts department in Macy's Department Store, the oldest store in the world— largest store. I never expected to get that job because, first of all, this was 1950. I went to New York to get a better job because I was a secretary, bookkeeper, and all that. You couldn't do that here in the South, in

Virginia and all. So I went there, and I went to different companies, and I was turned down for various reasons.

One lady said, "How old are you?"

I said, "Twenty-four."

She said, "Well, you look like you're about 13 or 14."

I said, "Oh, yeah?"

She said, "Don't get mad. You should be glad that someone thinks that you look younger than what you are."

I said, "Not if it's going to keep me from getting a job."

"Oh," she said.

So I went to a Dodge company to get a job in the office, and they said, "No. We don't have any jobs for you."

I said, "Why?"

They said, "We just don't have any."

I went to the phone booth and called and asked; I said, "We're taking a survey." They didn't even question who "we" were. "We're taking a survey. I'd like to know how many black people you have employed."

He said, "Oh, we have quite a few in the janitorial department."

I said, "How many do you have in the office?"

"Oh, no. We don't have any in our office."

I went to the Urban League for a job later, and they sent me to companies that would not hire me. Maybe that was what they were supposed to do so they could have a case. But when I told them they didn't hire me, then they just sent me somewhere else. So they weren't that concerned, either.

So I ended up going to one place where the man said, "No, we don't have any jobs in the office for you. Well, we don't want Negresses in here."

I said, "Why?"

He said, "We don't have any in the main office. I have some in the factory."

I said, "My mother didn't send me to school to work in a factory."

He said, "What? What did you say?"

I said, "My mother didn't send me to school to work in a factory."

He said, "Well, I don't have any work for you, so you better get out of here."

Schoolchildren after a children's protest parade, Norfolk, Virginia, June 25, 1939.
(American History Slide Collection, National Museum of American History, Smithsonian Institution)

I did.

Well, a friend of my future in-laws said to me, "Go to Macy's. I work in Macy's." She put the labels on. She was a stock girl.

Said, "Come to Macy's. You can get a job there."

I said, "You think they'll hire me? Everyone else has turned me down. Macy's? The largest store in the world? They're not going to hire a black girl."

One day I was out near there, so I said, "Well, I'm going to Macy's and see what's going on."

I went to the employment office and a girl said, "May I help you?"

I said, "Yes." I was very indignant, because I knew I wasn't going to get the job. I said, "I'm looking for a job."

She said, "Oh, yes, for what?"

I said, "Office work. I'm a secretary. I'm a bookkeeper."

She said, "Can you type pretty good?"

I said, "I can type very well."

"Oh, you can? Well, let me see what you can do." I don't remember then, but it was about 77 words a minute.

She said, "Good Lord, you sure can type."

Trying to discourage me, she called out a name of this NBC ma-chine, and it was a bookkeeping machine, but she didn't say bookkeep-ing, she said some other odd name. "Have you ever worked the so-and-so phone machine?"

I didn't even know what she was talking about. I said, "No, but I'm willing to learn."

She said, "Yeah, you're a good typist. You'll probably do well. I'll take you down to the department and give you a test on the machine."

I said, "Well, I don't know the machine."

"Well, yeah, you're right. Well, we'll give you a trial anyway. Can you come back?" She said, "Come back this afternoon and get a physical and all that." This was Friday. She said, "You can start working on Monday." And I did.

It was August. It was August the 7th or 8th, 1950, that I started working at Macy's, and I learned that I had integrated the accounts department. The girls were extremely nice to me, and I think that was because they wanted to make me feel at home. Also they were glad that they could be nice to a black girl. I think that's the way they felt. Any-way, the supervisor was a Jewish girl, and she was very nice, too. Things went well, but it got to be very monotonous, and no advancement. So after seven years, I resigned.

APPENDIX

INFORMANT BIOGRAPHICAL INFORMATION

NAME	CH	BIRTH YEAR	YEAR OF INTERVIEW	AGE AT INTERVIEW	LOCATION	OCCUPATION 1	OCCUPATION 2	OCCUPATION 3
1 Aaron, Delores Thompson	4	1924	1994	70	New Orleans, LA	Education	Government	
2 Alexander, Essie Mae	5	1927	1995	68	Greenwood, MS	Education	Household work	Agriculture
3 Alexander, Leon	5, 6	1910	1994	84	Birmingham, AL	Industry	Union	
4 Allen, Ida Bell	5	1914	1995	81	Sumter, SC	Agriculture	Household work	
5 Anderson, Dora Cordelia	2	1906	1994	88	Tallahassee, FL	Office work		
6 Artmore, Arlestus	4	1925	1993	68	New Bern, NC	Industry	Education	
7 Baldwin, Wilhelmina	3, 6	1923	1994	71	Tuskegee, AL	Office work	Education	
8 Blue, Ila Jacuth	2	1914	1995	81	Durham, NC	Agriculture	Education	
9 Blunt, Russell Evans	3	1908	1994	86	Durham, NC	Education		
10 Bodie, Mary	2	1910	1993	83	Enfield, NC	Education	Music	
11 Boyd, LeRoy	3	1925	1995	70	Memphis, TN	Industry		
12 Brown, Earl	5	1918	1994	76	Mulga, AL	Industry	Union	
13 Brown, John W.	4	1917	1995	78	Portsmouth, VA	Industry	Government	
14 Butterfield, George Kenneth Jr.	1, 3, 6	1947	1993	46	Wilson, NC	Law		
15 Campbell, Sarah	5	1922	1993	71	Vanceboro, NC	Agriculture		
16 Cavers, Walter M.	1	1910	1993	83	Charlotte, NC	Clergy		
17 Chassion, Jessie Lee	2	1926	1994	68	New Iberia, LA	Household work	Business	
18 Chatmon, Thomas	5, 6	1919	1994	75	Albany, GA	Business	Politics	
19 Cherry, Olivia	6	1926	1995	69	Norfolk, VA	Agriculture	Household work	Office work
20 Chism, Tolbert	2	1923	1995	72	Youngstown, OH	Industry	Military	
21 Coker, William J., Jr.	3, 4	1935	1995	60	Norfolk, VA	Office work	Government	
22 Cooper, John	5	1929	1995	66	Memphis, TN	Government	Government	Politics
23 Davidson, Geraldine	4	1927	1995	68	Brinkley, AR	Industry	Government	
24 Davillier, Brenda Bozant	6	1941	1994	53	New Orleans, LA	Government	Education	
25 Davis, Blanche	2	1900	1994	94	Birmingham, AL	Household work		
26 Davis, Price	App. A	1924	1993	69	Charlotte, NC	Industry		
27 Dixie, A.I.	3	1913	1994	81	Tallahassee, FL	Agriculture	Industry	Clergy
28 Dixie, Samuel	3	1919	1994	75	Tallahassee, FL	Janitorial work		
29 Donaldson, Henry	2, 5	1923	1993	70	Wilmington, NC	Industry	Military	
30 Donaldson, Laura	2	1923	1993	70	Wilmington, NC	Medicine		
31 Dulin, Maggie	3	1924	1995	71	Drakesboro, KY	Household work		
32 Federick, Booker T.	Intro.	1930	1995	65	Itta Bena, MS	Industry		
33 Fenner, Lillie	5	1907	1993	86	Halifax County, NC	Agriculture		
34 Flemming, Cora Eliza R.	2	1933	1995	62	Indianola, MS	Government		

NAME	CH	BIRTH YEAR	YEAR OF INTERVIEW	AGE AT INTERVIEW	LOCATION	OCCUPATION 1	OCCUPATION 2	OCCUPATION 3
35 Fort, Marie	6	1914	1995	81	Memphis, TN	Education	Music	Business
36 Gainey, Otto	2	1894	1998	104	Gainesville, FL	Agriculture		Business
37 George, Doris Srrong	4, 6	1929	1994	65	Moultrie, GA	Business	Education	
38 George, Stine	1, 4, 6	1931	1994	63	Moultrie, GA	Agriculture	Government	
39 Gratton, Charles	1	1932	1994	62	Birmingham, AL	Industry	Business	
40 Harrell, Willie	1, 6	1927	1995	68	Memphis, TN	Agriculture	Industry	Government
41 Hooten, Henry	1, 6	1917	1994	77	Tuskegee, AL	Medicine	Military	
42 Hunt, Edgar Allen	2, 6	1928	1995	67	Memphis, TN	Government	Industry	
43 Jackson, Ruthie Lee	2	1909	1995	86	Itta Bena, MS	Agriculture	Household work	
44 Jefferson, Harrietta Hill	2	1916	1994	78	Tallahassee, FL	Household work		
45 Jones, Charles	Intro.	1937	1993	56	Charlotte, NC	Business	Law	
46 Jones, Merlin	1, 3, 4	1922	1995	73	Memphis, TN	Military	Education	Government
47 Jones, Wilhelmina Griffin	6	1915	1994	79	Tuskegee, AL	Government	Office work	
48 Kirby, Money Alian	2	1914	1995	81	Magnolia, AR	Clergy	Business	
49 Lucas, Maurice	6	1944	1995	51	Renova, MS	Military	Business	Politics
50 Lucas, Willie Ann	1, 5	1921	1995	74	Brinkley, AR	Medicine	Education	
51 Lyons, Theresa	1	1934	1995	61	Durham, NC	Office work		
52 Matthews, David	3	1920	1995	75	Indianola, MS	Clergy	Education	
53 Mitchell, Cleaster	5	1922	1995	73	Brinkley, AR	Household work	Business	
54 Monroe, Irene	3	1912	1994	82	Bessemer, AL	Education	Business	
55 Pinkard, Otis	App. A	1916	1994	78	Tuskegee, AL	Office work	Politics	Government
56 Pointer, Ann	1, 2, 4	1927	1994	67	Tuskegee, AL	Agriculture	Hospital work	Government
57 Quigless, Milton	1	1904	1993	89	Tarboro, NC	Industry	Medicine	
58 Rann, Emery	4	1914	1993	79	Charlotte, NC	Medicine	Military	
59 Robinson, Amelia	App. A	N/A	1994	N/A	Tuskegee, AL	Education	Politics	
60 Searles, Arthur	1, 5	1915	1994	79	Albany, GA	Military	Education	Journalism
61 Shaw, Catherine	2	1909	1997	88	Durham, NC	Industry		
62 Smith, Lillian Quick	1, 2	1931	1993	62	Wilmington, NC	Education		
63 Speed, Cornelius	1	1919	1994	75	Tallahassee, FL	Agriculture	Military	Industry
64 Sullins, Della	App. A	1917	1994	77	Tuskegee, AL	Medicine	Education	
65 Sutton, Georgia	2, 3, 6	1929	1993	64	New Bern, NC	Education		
66 Thompson, Ralph	1, 5	1935	1995	60	Memphis, TN	Industry	Business	Union
67 Vaughn, Thomas Franklin	4	1920	1995	75	Pine Bluff, AR	Agriculture	Military	
68 Volter, John Harrison	2	1929	1994	65	New Iberia, LA	Janitorial work	Industry	
69 Wade, Harriet V.	3	1928	1993	65	New Bern, NC	Business		
70 Walker, Ferdie	1	1928	1994	56	Tuskegee, AL	Medicine		
71 Young, Kenneth	4	1907	1994	87	Tuskegee, AL	Education		
72 Young, Mai	4	1910	1994	84	Tuskegee, AL	Education		

SUGGESTIONS FOR
FURTHER READING

GENERAL TREATMENTS OF THE JIM CROW ERA

Cox, Oliver C., *Caste, Class, and Race: A Study in Social Dynamics* (New York, 1970).

Du Bois, W.E.B., *The Souls of Black Folk* (New York, 1903).

Franklin, John Hope, and Alfred A. Moss Jr., *From Slavery to Freedom: A History of African Americans*, 7th ed. (New York, 1994).

Fredrickson, George M., *White Supremacy: A Comparative Study in American and South African History* (New York, 1981).

Giddings, Paula, *When and Where I Enter: The Impact of Black Women on Race and Sex in America* (New York, 1996).

Hine, Darlene Clark, and Kathleen Thompson, *A Shining Thread of Hope: The History of Black Women in America* (New York, 1998).

Johnson, Charles Spurgeon, *Patterns of Negro Segregation* (New York, 1943).

——, *Statistical Atlas of Southern Counties: Listing and Analysis of Socio-Economic Indices of 1104 Southern Counties* (Chapel Hill, 1941).

Logan, Rayford W., *The Betrayal of the Negro: From Rutherford B. Hayes to Woodrow Wilson* (London, 1965).

Myrdal, Gunnar, *An American Dilemma: The Negro Problem and Modern Democracy* (New York, 1944).

Woodward, C. Vann, *The Strange Career of Jim Crow* (New York, 1955).

ONE: BITTER TRUTHS

Brundage, W. Fitzhugh, *Lynching in the New South: Georgia and Virginia, 1880–1930* (Urbana, 1993).

Carter, Dan T., *Scottsboro: A Tragedy of the American South* (New York, 1969).

Edmonds, Helen G., *The Negro and Fusion Politics in North Carolina, 1894–1901* (Chapel Hill, 1951).

Ellsworth, Scott, *Death in a Promised Land: The Tulsa Race Riot of 1921*, foreword by John Hope Franklin (Baton Rouge, 1982).

Goodwyn, Lawrence, "Populist Dreams and Negro Rights: East Texas as a Case Study," *American Historical Review* 76 (1971): 1435–56.

Lincoln, C. Eric, *The Avenue, Clayton City* (New York, 1988).

Litwack, Leon E., *Trouble in Mind: Black Southerners in the Age of Jim Crow* (New York, 1998).

McMillen, Neil R., *Dark Journey: Black Mississippians in the Age of Jim Crow* (Urbana, 1990).

Murray, Pauli, comp. and ed., *States' Laws on Race and Color and Appendices* (1951; Athens, 1997).

Williamson, Joel, *The Crucible of Race: Black-White Relations in the American South Since Emancipation* (New York, 1984).

Wright, Richard, *Native Son* (New York, 1940).

TWO: HERITAGE AND MEMORY

Berlin, Ira, Marc Favreau, and Steven F. Miller, eds., *Remembering Slavery: African Americans Talk About Their Personal Experiences of Slavery and Emancipation* (New York, 1998).

Escott, Paul D., *Slavery Remembered: A Record of Twentieth-Century Slave Narratives* (Chapel Hill, 1979).

Franklin, Buck Colbert, *My Life and an Era: The Autobiography of Buck Colbert Franklin*, ed. John Hope Franklin and John Whittington Franklin (Baton Rouge, 1997).

Franklin, John Hope, *George Washington Williams: A Biography* (Chicago, 1985).

Hurston, Zora Neale, *Dust Tracks on a Road: An Autobiography* (Philadelphia, 1942).

Johnson, James Weldon, *Along This Way: The Autobiography of James Weldon Johnson* (New York, 1933).

Murray, Pauli, *Proud Shoes: The Story of an American Family* (New York, 1956).

Painter, Nell Irvin, *The Narrative of Hosea Hudson: The Life and Times of a Black Radical* (New York, 1994).

Rosengarten, Theodore, *All God's Dangers: The Life of Nate Shaw* (New York, 1975).

Tucker, Susan, *Telling Memories Among Southern Women: Domestic Workers and Their Employers in the Segregated South* (Baton Rouge, 1988).

THREE: FAMILIES AND COMMUNITIES

Billingsley, Andrew, *Climbing Jacob's Ladder: The Enduring Legacy of African-American Families* (New York, 1992).

Frazier, E. Franklin, *Black Bourgeoisie* (New York, 1957).

Gutman, Herbert G., *The Black Family in Slavery and Freedom, 1750–1925* (New York, 1976).

Hurston, Zora Neale, *Mules and Men*, introduction by Franz Boas (Philadelphia, 1935).

Higginbotham, Evelyn Brooks, *Righteous Discontent: The Women's Movement in the Black Baptist Church, 1880–1920* (Cambridge, Mass., 1993).

Johnson, Charles S., *Shadow of the Plantation* (Chicago, 1934).

Lewis, Earl, *In Their Own Interests: Race, Class, and Power in Twentieth-Century Norfolk, Virginia* (Berkeley, Calif., 1990).

Rose, Willie Lee, ed., *A Documentary History of Slavery in North America* (New York, 1976).

Trotter, Joe, *Coal, Class, and Color: Blacks in Southern West Virginia, 1915–32* (Urbana, Ill., 1990).

FOUR: LESSONS WELL LEARNED

Anderson, James D., *The Education of Blacks in the South, 1860–1935* (Chapel Hill, 1988).

Bond, Horace Mann, *The Education of the Negro in the American Social Order* (New York, 1934).

Bullock, Henry Allen, *A History of Negro Education in the South: From 1619 to the Present* (New York, 1970).

Du Bois, W.E.B., *The Negro Common School* (Atlanta, 1901).

Hanchett, Thomas W., "The Rosenwald Schools and Black Education in North Carolina," *North Carolina Historical Review* LXV (1988): 387–444.

Higginson, Thomas W., *Army Life in a Black Regiment* (Boston, 1870).

Jones, Jacqueline, *Soldiers of Light and Love: Northern Teachers and Georgia Blacks, 1865–1873* (Chapel Hill, 1980).

Jones, Thomas H., *The Jeanes Teacher in the United States, 1908–1933* (Chapel Hill, 1937).

Kluger, Richard, *Simple Justice: The History of* Brown v. Board of Education *and Black America's Struggle for Equality* (New York, 1975).

Spivey, Donald, *Schooling for the New Slavery: Black Industrial Education, 1868–1915* (Westport, Conn., 1978).

Walker, Vanesa Siddle, *Their Highest Potential: An African American School Community in the Segregated South* (Chapel Hill, 1996).

Washington, Booker T., *Up from Slavery: An Autobiography* (1901; Urbana, Ill., 1972).

Woodson, Carter G., *The Mis-Education of the Negro* (Washington, D.C., 1933).

FIVE: WORK

Arnesen, Eric, *Waterfront Workers of New Orleans: Race, Class, and Politics* (Urbana, Ill., 1994).

Daniel, Pete, *The Shadow of Slavery: Peonage in the South, 1901–1969* (New York, 1972).

——, *Breaking the Land: The Transformation of Cotton, Tobacco, and Rice Cultures Since 1880* (Chicago, 1985).

Du Bois, W.E.B., *Black Reconstruction: An Essay Toward a History of the Part Which Black Folk Played in the Attempt to Reconstruct Democracy in America, 1860–1880* (1935; New York, 1975).

Harris, Abram L., and Sterling D. Spero, *The Black Worker: The Negro and the Labor Movement*, preface by Herbert G. Gutman (New York, 1969).

Harris, William H., *Keeping the Faith: A. Philip Randolph, Milton P. Webster, and the Brotherhood of Sleeping Car Porters, 1925–37* (Urbana, Ill., 1977).

Hine, Darlene Clark, *Black Women in White: Racial Conflict and Cooperation in the Nursing Profession, 1890–1950* (Bloomington, Ind., 1989).

Honey, Michael K., *Black Workers Remember: An Oral History of Segregation, Unionism, and the Freedom Struggle* (Berkeley, Calif., 1999).

——, *Southern Labor and Black Civil Rights: Organizing Memphis Workers* (Urbana, Ill., 1993).

Hunter, Tera W. *To 'Joy My Freedom: Southern Black Women's Lives and Labors After the Civil War* (Cambridge, Mass., 1997).

Kelley, Robin D. G., *Hammer and Hoe: Alabama Communists During the Great Depression* (Chapel Hill, 1990).

——, *Race Rebels: Culture, Politics, and the Black Working Class* (New York, 1994).

Rosenberg, Daniel, *New Orleans Dockworkers: Race, Labor, and Unionism, 1892–1923* (Albany, N.Y., 1988).

SIX: RESISTANCE AND POLITICAL STRUGGLES

Bush, Rod, *We Are Not What We Seem: Black Nationalism and Class Struggle in the American Century* (New York, 1999).

Gavins, Raymond, "The NAACP in North Carolina During the Age of Segregation," in Armstead L. Robinson and Patricia Sullivan, eds., *New Directions in Civil Rights Studies* (Charlottesville, N.C., 1991).

Korstad, Robert, and Nelson Lichtenstein, "Opportunities Found and Lost: Labor, Radicals, and the Early Civil Rights Movement," *Journal of American History* 75 (1988): 786–811.

Lewis, David Levering, *W.E.B. Du Bois: Biography of a Race, 1868–1919* (New York, 1993).

Meier, August, and Elliot Rudwick, "The Boycott Movement Against Jim Crow Streetcars in the South, 1900–1906," *Journal of American History* 55 (1969): 756–775.

Robinson, Cedric J., *Black Movements in America* (New York, 1997).

Weiss, Nancy J., *Farewell to the Party of Lincoln: Black Politics in the Age of FDR* (Princeton, 1983).

Woodruff, Nan Elizabeth, "African-American Struggles for Citizenship in the Arkansas and Mississippi Deltas in the Age of Jim Crow," *Radical History Review* 55 (1993): 33–51.

Yates, James, *Mississippi to Madrid: Memoir of a Black American in the Abraham Lincoln Brigade* (Seattle, 1989).

INDEX

Note: Page numbers in italics represent photographs and their captions.